# The Humanistic Movement
## Recovering the Person in Psychology

### Frederick J. Wertz

Editor

**Gardner Press**
*Lake Worth     London     Sydney*

copyright ©1994 by Division 32 of the American Psychological Association. Chapter 5, "Firebrand — The Experience of Being Different" ©1993 by Clark Moustakas

All rights reserved. No part of this book may be reproduced in any form, by photostat, microform, retrieval system, or any means now or later devised without prior written permission from the publisher. Printed in the United States of America.

Library of Congress Cataloging - in - Publication Data

The Humanistic movement : recovering the person in psychology / Frederick J. Wertz, editor
P. cm.
"Originally appeared . . . as a special issue of The Humanistic psychologist (vol. 20, nos. 2 & 3)"--Pref.
Includes bibliographical references and index.
ISBN 0-89876-208-1 : $24.95
1. Humanistic psychology. I. Wertz, Frederick J. (Frederick Joseph), 1951- .
BF204.H859 1993
150. 19'8--dc20     93-17204     CIP

Gardner Press, Inc.
6801 Lake Worth Road
Lake Worth, FL 33413

*To*
*each psychologist who has dedicated his or her professional life*
*to faithfully understanding and emancipating*
*the inexhaustible fullness of persons*

# CONTENTS

## I. Historical and Philosophical Foundations

1. Mainstream Psychology and the Humanistic Alternative
   *Christopher M. Aanstoos* ................ 1

2. The Institutionalization of Humanistic Psychology
   *Roy J. deCarvalho* ................ 13

3. Philosophical Foundations of Humanistic Psychology
   *Larry Davidson* ................ 24

4. Creativity, Humanistic Psychology and the American Zeitgeist
   *Mike Arons* ................ 45

5. Firebrand — The Experience of Being Different
   *Clark Moustakas* ................ 62

6. Recollections and Reflections: Snippets from an Oral History of Humanistic Psychology
   *Mike Arons and Carmi Harari* ................ 76

## II. Methodological and Conceptual Advances

7. The Idea of Human Science
   *Amedeo Giorgi* ................ 89

8. Research Methodology in Humanistic Psychology
   *Donald E. Polkinghorne* ................ 105

9. Humanistic Psychology and Personal Construct Theory
   *Franz Epting and Larry Leitner* ................ 129

10. Humanistic Values and the Future: Freedom and Activism
    *George Howard* ................ 146

11. The Three R's for Humanistic Psychology: Remembering, Reconciling and Re-uniting
    *James Bugental and Barbara G. Sapienza* ................ 159

12. Transpersonal Psychology: Its Several Virtues
    *Eugene Taylor* ................ 170

13. Brief Overview of Transpersonal Psychology
    *Edward Bruce Bynum* ................ 186

14. The Role of Transpersonal Psychology in Psychology as a Whole: A Discussion
    *Rollo May, Stanley Krippner, and Jacqueline Doyle* ................ 192

## III. Service

15. Humanizing Psychological Assessment
    *Constance Fischer* .................................... 202
16. Humanistic Contributions to the Field of Psychotherapy: Appreciating the Human and Liberating the Therapist
    *Anthony Barton* ...................................... 215
17. Secular Humanism and Rational-Emotive Therapy
    *Albert Ellis* ......................................... 233
18. Andras Angyal, Pioneer in Humanistic Psychotherapy
    *E. Mark Stern* ....................................... 243
19. Education and the Humanistic Challenge
    *Anne Richards and Arthur Combs* ...................... 256
20. The Humanistic Core of Industrial/Organizational Psychology
    *Frederick Massarik* .................................. 274
21. Humanistic Psychological Centers for Scholarship and Growth
    Humanistic Psychology Archive *David Russell* ......... 282
    Simon Silverman Phenomenology Center *Richard Rojcewicz* . 283
    Center for Studies of the Person *William Stillwell* .. 286
    Esalen and the Growth Centers *Walter Anderson* ....... 288

## IV. Impact and Future

22. The Presence of Humanistic Psychologists in the Academy
    *Scott Churchill* ..................................... 292
23. Whither Humanistic Psychology?
    *Amedeo Giorgi* ....................................... 306
24. Relational Humanism: A Psychology for a Pluralistic World
    *Maureen O'Hara* ...................................... 322
25. Celebrations and Problems of Humanistic Psychology
    *Eugene Gendlin* ...................................... 330
26. Representations of the "Third Force" in History of Psychology Textbooks
    *Frederick Wertz* ..................................... 344

About the Authors ........................................ 360
Name Index ............................................... 367
Subject Index ............................................ 375

# Preface

This volume arose as one of the contributions of the Division of Humanistic Psychology (32) to the American Psychological Association's celebration of its 100th anniversary. Having originally appeared during APA's Centennial, in 1992, as a special issue of *The Humanistic Psychologist* (Vol. *20*, Nos. 2 & 3), its central aim is to show the kind of contribution that humanistic psychology has made and can make to the field of psychology.

"Humanistic psychology" is presented in the broad and inclusive sense reflected in the membership and activities of APA's Division 32. Over its twenty year history, this division has become a home for what Maslow called "third force" psychology, that is, such humanistic approaches as those of Maslow and Rogers, such existential approaches as those of May and Bugental, such pheno-menological approaches as those of Giorgi and the Duquesne Circle, and what has sometimes been called the "forth force," Transpersonal Psychology. Including material on the history, institutions, conceptual foundations, methods, and applied areas of the humanistic approaches, the present volume displays both the diversity and coherent unity of this movement.

It is my hope that this volume will help to dispel a number of misconceptions which have arisen partly from the movement's occasional failings but more from its limited size and impact within mainstream academic psychology. For instance, humanistic psy-chology has sometimes been seen as the following: a protest without a positive disciplinary program, only or primarily concerned with psychotherapy and/or personality theory, limited to the works of such pioneers as Maslow and Rogers, anti-scientific, without a research methodology, intellectually lacking in rigor and/or self-criticism, withdrawing from the issues and achievements of mainstream psychology, individualistic and socially unconcerned (to the point of promoting narcissistic self-absorption), socially linked exclusively with the hippie counterculture of the 1960's, and a movement of the past without a present reason for being or future.

Some of the virtues of humanistic psychology that are celebrated in this volume are its long and important historical tradition; extensive philosophical foundations; intellectual rigor; methodo-logical richness; many links with surrounding scholarly trends; integrative capacity; service applications beyond therapy in the areas of assessment, education, and business; dialogue with the humanities; inclusion of spirituality and the bridging of the East-West gap; and commitment to progressive social activism.

First, the chapters address the movement's relationship to mainstream psychology (Aanstoos), its institutional founding in professional associations and journals (deCarvalho), its philosophical origins and background in the history of ideas (Davidson), its roots in the post-war *zeitgeist* (Arons), and its personal/existential meaning for an individual participant (Moustakas; Arons and Harari).

The second group of chapters focuses on methodological and conceptual issues. This part of the volume reviews humanistic psychology's critiques of the dominant, natural scientific approach (Giorgi), the development of research methodology (Polking-horne), some evolving areas of research and theory (Epting & Leitner; Howard; and Bugental & Sapienza), and issues arising in the development of Transpersonal Psychology (Taylor; Bynum; and May, Krippner, and Doyle).

The third group of chapters contain the service dimension of humanistic psychology, in particular its applications to such practical problems as those encountered in psychological assessment (Fischer), in psychotherapy (Barton; Ellis; Stern), in education (Richards and Combs), and in business (Massarik) as well as the resources provided by the leading centers for scholarship and personal growth (Russell; Rojcewicz; Stillwell; Anderson).

The final section focuses upon the impact of the humanistic movement on the field of psychology. Based on a critical assessment of its successes and failures, these chapters explore the visions, tasks, and promises of the humanistic approaches for the future of psychology in the academy (Churchill), in research and theoretical domains (Giorgi), in the pluralistic cultural world (O'Hara), in organizations and service training (Gendlin), and in the historical trajectory of the discipline (Wertz).

Above all else, I hope that every reader acquires, from this volume, a sense of the great value of the humanistic movement for the field of psychology as both enter and develop in the twenty first century.

I would like to acknowledge the encouragement, suport, criticisms, extraordinary production wizardry, and many hours of selfness effort of *The Humanistic Psychologist's* Chief Editor, Christopher Aanstoos. Also, I am very grateful for the enthusiasm and faith in this project consistently expressed by the Executive Board of APA Division 32 and for the generous financial contributions of David Elkins, Constance Fischer, Carmi Harari, Fred Massarik, Fred and Anne Richards, Maryanne Siderits, and Mark Stern, without whom this volume could never have come to pass.

Frederick J. Wertz

*New York*

# The Humanistic Movement
## Recovering the Person in Psychology

# 1

# Mainstream Psychology and the Humanistic Alternative

*Christopher M. Aanstoos*

What does it mean that a movement within contemporary psychology identifies itself as "humanistic"? Initially, even the phrase "humanistic psychology" itself seems very odd, since the modifier "humanistic" appears at first superfluously redundant when applied to the term "psychology." Isn't psychology, after all, necessarily concerned with that which is specifically "human" as its own most central focus? It is of course true that most psychologists do not in fact focus on human beings as their subject matter all, choosing instead to devote their careers to the study of certain behaviors of confined rats or pigeons, or to the development of computer models. Even most psychological research that does use human beings does so by studying them in artificial — inhuman — laboratory conditions. Despite this curious shift, it is also true that even these psychologists would affirm the central focus of the human in psychology by the very way they justify their studies. The reason given for studying rats, pigeons or computers is ultimately to augment our understanding of the human. Though they have chosen to study the human obliquely, by means of something that is not human, or in contexts that are inhuman, nevertheless, they are the first to insist that their research is uncovering something about the human as well, and for that very reason is worth supporting.

One wonders, then, if all psychologists — no matter how far removed they are from the human in their research work — affirm that their central focus is ultimately the human, why would anyone ever even conceive of the modifier "humanistic" for the discipline of psychology? Wouldn't the modifier be as superfluous as is the word "wet" in the phrase "wet water"? Nevertheless, the curious historical fact remains that, beginning in the 1960's, one branch of psychologists adopted such a label, in order to distinguish themselves from psychology as it had been traditionally established. Even more curious has been the reaction of the rest of psychology to that development. It would seem those psychologists who take an indirect approach to the study of the human risk the grave danger of missing the very phenomenon they are most centrally interested in discovering — the human. Indeed, only by somehow anchoring its findings about the nonhuman in terms of the human could such an indirect psychology have any way to tell whether its findings ever have any significance for understanding the human. At the very least, then, it would seem that this indirect psychology would be the one in need of justifying its claims to support. And it would seem that it could do so most definitively only by reference to the findings of a genuinely humanistic psychology.

This, however, has not happened. Instead, mainstream psychology for the most part remains surprisingly unaffected by that perspective at all. Psychology's establishment not only sidestepped this humanistic approach, but largely excludes humanistic psychology from its grants, its dissertations, its textbooks, its publications, its curriculum, its licensing examinations, and its accreditation standards. The establishment in psychology not only knows almost nothing about humanistic psychology, but most of what it does know are wild misunderstandings. Its introductory textbooks, for example, whose stated aim is to provide a general survey of the discipline, offer — if anything — only the most limited and caricatured versions of "humanistic psychology" (see Churchill, 1988; Henley & Faulkner, 1989, for critiques of these presentations). But that possibility is of little concern for the establishment because, for the most part, they don't want to know anything about humanistic psychology. And they don't want the next generation of psychologists (their current doctoral students) to learn about humanistic psychology either, much less do humanistic research for their dissertations.

Evidently, the modifier "humanistic" is far from superfluous. Indeed, it now appears instead to be the most divisive split in all of psychology. A split between a band of humanistic psychologists and an established order who disdain humanistic psychology. How can this be? How can the term "humanistic" be taboo to psychology, the very field that most proclaims its reason for being to discover what it can of the human?

Eschewing the term "humanistic," psychology instead continues to define itself as a positivistic science modeled after the sciences of nature. Within the confines of that identity, psychology's basic premise and goal is that psychological life — presupposed as mechanistic — be eventually subjected to prediction and control. To more fully appreciate the alternative mission of humanistic psychology (and its marginalized status) we should first reflect on its historical foundations and the relation between the humanistic approach with the natural science approach that has guided mainstream psychology.

## Historical Background

Some writers consider humanistic psychology to be rooted in the same traditions that bore natural scientific psychology, namely modernity; and hence essentially linked with the fate of mainstream psychology — "as two sides of the modern coin" (Kvale, 1990, p. 45). Certainly it is tempting to read humanistic psychology's concern for the individual self (e.g., as in self-actualization) as indicative of this modernistic lineage. However, it fails to take into account an older ancestor, namely the humanism of the Renaissance. While many analysts date the advent of modernity with the Renaissance (Jencks, 1986; McKnight, 1989), and thereby fail to distinguish these two bases, Toulmin's (1990) analysis most insightfully discriminates between them. He sees the seventeenth century's pursuit of strict rationality and its quest for certainty to be the origins of modernity, but points out that this project was a turn away from the Renaissance humanism that had immediately preceded it. The concerns of the Renaissance humanists for complexity, ambiguity, and a tolerance of diversity were set aside as the war-torn, crisis-ridden Europe of the 1600's sought to renounce ambiguity and embrace certitude, at all costs. Whereas the Renaissance humanists' were interested in the oral, the particular, the local, the timely, the modern era valued the written, the universal, the general, and the timeless. As Toulmin summarizes, "the permanent was in, the transitory was out" (1990, p. 34). Toulmin's work offers a crucial understanding by which to differentiate the humanism of the Renaissance from the rationalism of modernity, and so avoid the fallacy of depicting humanism as rooted in modernity. On the contrary, modernity over-rode humanism, and suppressed its impact on culture.

Keeping in mind this key distinction between these traditions, we can trace positivistic psychology's trajectory in terms of the development of modern natural science, and see in that route its decisive difference with humanistic psychology. For example, already in 1650 Hobbes (1650/1964) — whose formative conception of the contiguity of ideas led to associationistic psychology — was deeply influenced by the new science being promulgated by Galileo. Mandler and Mandler (1964, p. 14) report that, following a visit to Galileo, Hobbes "became fascinated with the concept of motion as a powerful explanatory principle not only of the workings of the physical world but also of the mind." Brett (1962, pp. 380-381) adds to this story the explanation that "what excited Hobbes was the possibility of deducing new consequences from the laws of inertia to spheres in which it had not yet been applied." Next, Hume, in 1739, was also much influenced by the physics — by then Newtonian — of his time. He compared the association of ideas to natural laws, declaring that "here is a kind of attraction which in the mental world will be found to have as extraordinary effects as in the natural" (Hume, 1739/1978, p. 12). Next, David Hartley, in 1749, self-consciously borrowed foundational concepts from Newtonian physics also in his refinements of the doctrine of the association of ideas. He depicted the analysis of "complex ideas... into their simple compounding parts, i.e., into the simple ideas of sensation of which they consist" as being "greatly analogous to... resolving the color of the sun's light, or natural bodies, into their primary constituent ones" (Hartley, 1749/1964, p. 83). Next, James Mill, in 1829, described cognition as a "mental mechanics" in which the contents of the mind are combined according to the laws of mechanics (Mill, 1829/1967).

By the time Wundt arrived on the scene to formally consecrate psychology as a natural science in the 1870's, using chemistry's table of elements as his model for the elements of the mind, psychology had already been very deliberately modeling itself after the emerging natural sciences for more than two centuries. Therefore, one cannot argue, as some have tried (Skinner, 1971), that psychology's own development was retarded by its lack of a scientific foundation for so long. Rather, it must be considered that these longstanding natural science foundations may be responsible for psychology's retarded development. That this obvious retardation should be due to its imitation of the natural sciences at first seems strange, since those sciences were enjoying tremendous accomplishments, most clearly manifested in their attainment of an accelerating mastery of ever greater technological power over nature, evident by the beginning of the twentieth century.

Certainly one would think that these stunning achievements would insulate the model of the natural sciences from any possible critique.

Nevertheless, Edmund Husserl, in the 1930's, intrepidly announced that Western science in general was in a state of crisis. (Husserl, 1936/1970, pp. 3-4). But the crisis of which Husserl spoke was not at the level of practical successes. Rather, it was a crisis of what science meant and could mean for human existence. Specifically, the crisis was the exclusiveness with which the worldview of modernity had let itself become totalized by the attitude of the natural sciences. As Husserl (1936/1970, pp. 6-7) noted, "merely fact-minded sciences make merely fact-minded people... Scientific objective truth is exclusively a matter of establishing what the world, the physical as well as the spiritual world, is in fact. But can the world, and human existence in it, truthfully have a meaning if the sciences recognize as true only what is objectively established in this fashion?" What would become of human presence in such an exclusionary enterprise? Merleau-Ponty (1964/1968, pp. 14-15) provides this sharply satirical sketch of its fate:

> [for science] the true is the *objective*, is what I have succeeded in determining by measurement, or more generally by the *operations* that are authorized by the variables... I have defined relative to an order of facts. Such determinations owe nothing to our *contact* with the things: they express an effort of approximation that would have no meaning with regard to the lived experience... Thus science began by excluding all the predicates that come to the things from our encounter with them. The exclusion is however only provisional: when it will have learned to invest it, science will little by little reintroduce what it first put aside as subjective; but it will integrate it as a particular case of the... objects that define the world for science. Then the world will close in over itself, and... we will have become parts or moments of the Great Object.

With that totalization questions about that which is most specifically human — all questions termed "ultimate and highest" — become "excluded questions" (Husserl, 1936/1970, p. 9). Husserl lists as excluded questions those concerned with "genuine values... ethical action... God... immortality... and freedom." Precisely because of the technological success of the natural sciences, Husserl recognized how modernity became "blinded by the prosperity they produced" (p. 6) with the consequent "indifferent turning away from the questions which are decisive for a genuine humanity," from those crucial and most burning "questions of the meaning or meaninglessness of the whole of this human existe 170 (p. 6). The consequence of totalizing this scientific exclusivity is the loss of the meaning of human existence, since science, as merely fact-centered, fails to address the question of meaning, and thereby promoted the belief in its reducibility or unreality. Along with this collapse comes the loss of

> faith in man's freedom, that is, his capacity to secure rational meaning for his individual and common human existence. If man loses this faith, it means nothing less than the loss of faith "in himself," in his own true being. This true being is not something he always already has, with the self-evidence of the "I am," but something he only has and can have in the form of the struggle for his truth, the struggle to make himself true. (Husserl, 1936/1970, p. 13)

## Contemporary Psychology: Rats and Computers

It would seem, as it did to Husserl, that psychology should be the key discipline to withstand and counterbalance this erosion of the very meaningfulness by which we are fully human. It should be psychology's task, as the science of human existence, to explicate the newly enigmatic residue of subjectivity left in the wake of this exclusivity. Rather than accepting that mission, however, psychology eagerly sought to enact its self-declared status as an empirical science of facts, a positivistic science of mechanistic determinism. Psychology, of course, has not yet developed any degree of technological mastery over its own dominion comparable to that achieved by the natural sciences. But that lacunae was self-excused by the complaint that it was much more difficult to achieve such a technology in its field. So many "variables" keep "intervening" in its experimental attempts to control human being, thereby limiting the scope of any successes to highly artificial laboratory conditions.

Despite its obvious failure to achieve the success of the natural sciences, psychology clings nevertheless to its tattered claim of membership in that club. Its justification for such continued regard is its insistence on the exclusive employment of a tightly rigorous scientific methodology. By at least *acting* just like an empirical science of facts, psychology claims to be entitled to boast of someday achieving control over human existence. Dehydrated by the hegemony of a dry as dust empiricism, psychology devoted itself throughout most of the twentieth century to an approach so inhuman that caged, starved, mutated rats became its primary subject matter. Within the past two decades a shift has occurred, wherein cognitivisim has supplanted behaviorism as psychology's dominant paradigm and, with it, rats are now out and computer models are in. Unchanged by this shift, however, is the still marginalized status of the genuinely human in psychology.

*The Psychology of the Rat*
Let us first take a look at this peculiar fascination of psychology with dominating the rat. That dream of control over the rat has been the exemplary ambition of the pre-eminent paradigm in twentieth century scientific psychology: behaviorism. In his brilliant examination of psychology's history with rats, Wertz (1986) has shown the ubiquity with which they have served as experimental subjects, pointing out that in many years more than eighty percent of psychological experiments used rats, in the process devouring over a million rats per year. Indeed, it became an almost universally required rite of passage for psychology students to achieve control over a rat's behavior in order to earn their degree. They were compelled to traverse the same trajectory as John Watson, who began his career with a dissertation on the experimental control of rats, in 1903. As psychology shifted from this early emphasis on classical conditioning to the more sophisticated principles of operant conditioning introduced by B. F. Skinner, control over this expanded behavioral repertoire also was inflicted on rats. Manipulating a rat to run through a maze or to press a bar at various times and rates in response to a variety of specific stimuli has been the basis for tens of thousands of experiments throughout this century. Indeed, those studies form the bedrock upon which psychology's scientific edifice was constructed. They constitute the very basis for justifying its recommendations for similar manipulation of human beings to ensure their submission to running "the rat race" for meager and intermittent reinforcement. Contemporaneously with the triumph of the Machine Age and the rise of the assembly line in the first decades of the twentieth century, psychology proffered its expertise as the discipline that could demonstrate how to enforce the endless repetition of rote behaviors, not to mention to achievement of docile compliance by the disturbed and incarcerated.

A steadfast project to achieve control over the rat undergirds scientific psychology. What makes the promise of such control so deeply alluring? To understand those depths, it will be necessary to go beneath the strictly scientific level, to the pre-scientific experience of the rat. For instance, the curiously pervasive presence of rats wherever there are people offers a starting point for such reflection. Alone among animal species, rats share with humans the same versatile ability to inhabit the entire range of climates on the planet. Go to the polar regions, and rats will be there. To the tropics. Rats again. Go thousands of miles over the ocean by ship. Lo and behold, rats have accompanied the journey. This shadowy parallel of the rat to the human extends to many physiological characteristics the two share, including their similar glandular and neurological make-up, their carrying many of the same diseases, and their sharing many surprising behavioral similarities. Wertz (1986, pp. 144-146) cites the following: both are omnivorous; both eat their own kind in stressful situations; both have the same gender ratio; in both males are larger and females fatter; both breed in all seasons, especially the spring; both inbreed readily and hybridize easily; in both mothers care for their young while helpless and dependent while the male does little in the rearing of the offspring; both family groups huddle together, groom each other, and the young need paternal touch to live; in both when the young attain maturity, they are evicted from the family and seek a new home of its own, sometimes in an altogether different community; if we transpose the rat lifespan onto a human scale, the rat would go through puberty at sixteen years and menopause at forty-five; both make war on their own kind, are individualistic until they need help, fight bravely when alone but only against weaker enemies, and organize to fight in hordes; neither has achieved social, commercial, or economic stability; the black rat's pitiless extermination of the brown rat has no parallel in nature except for the interracial persecutions of man; in wars of both species, the victors have been merciless.

As many of these similarities indicate, the rat is the mirror of the human; it reflects the dark side of human existence. To even call someone a "rat" is considered a gross insult. As Wertz (1986, p. 146) says:

> if rats share something in common with humans, it is the *inhumanity* of man, expressing the despicable underside in a pure and unadulterated form which trails and follows man wherever he goes... This nameless, faceless, anonymous, selfish hording element of existence so purely embodied to the rat, is the hidden side, the blind spot of man's own being.

Given these implications, it is no wonder that

> we would rather not recognize these features of ourselves. We push them to the margins, leave them in the dark as we define ourselves in terms of justice, mercy, reason, creativity and individuality... we live by traditions, obedience, and the Good, denying with all our might that vague swarming which is still ourselves, but a wild, free self outside the range we have positively allowed ourselves. (Wertz, 1986, pp. 146-147)

In the service of that suppression, scientific psychology's program of rat control assumes an unrecognized relevance. The thousands of experiments on rats show nothing if not the psychologist's ability to control every twitch and nuance of the rat's behavior. But when we now examine these experiments more carefully, we cannot help but notice a peculiar substitution. Those laboratory rats are small, docile, and white. They have been deliberately mutated and bred for generations for laboratory use. They seem most unlike the rats encountered in the real world beyond the psychologist's lab. They are nothing like those large and fearsome rats that lurk in the sewers of our civilization. Indeed, these tiny, pale white things have never even lived on their own, and would most likely merely die if turned loose. Experimentally manipulating them seems only an illusion of progress, a deceptive sham. Even here, in its most privileged realm, psychology's dream of domination and control reveals itself to be a misguided and pathetic failure, the denial of which is sustained only by psychology's self-deceptive hubris.

*The Psychology of Computers*

With this increasingly evident bankruptcy of rat psychology, mainstream thought next shifted to cognitive psychology, based on the computer model of cognition as the processing of information. The work of Newell and Simon during the 1950's, '60's and '70's was especially formative in this development (Newell, Shaw & Simon, 1958; Newell & Simon, 1961, 1972; Simon, 1969, 1979; Simon & Newell, 1964, 1971). In their approach, the human was conceived of as an information processing system, and 'its' particular processes investigated by means of that newly emergent, dazzlingly compelling information processing system *par excellence*: the computer. By such means, they were able to convincingly turn aside the behaviorist critique that mental processes were unreal and should be taboo in psychology, and a paradigm shift of historical proportions suddenly swept the field.

Unfortunately, this revolution continued mainstream psychology's sidestepping of the genuinely human. While the person was now conceptualized as mentally active, the nature of this activity was presupposed, as is evident in Simon and Newell's (1964, p. 281) revealing comment "since the thinking human being is also an information processor..." Specifically, their information processing approach prejudged the human order as a mechanistic one, asserting from the start that "the higher mental processes can be performed by mechanisms" (Newell, Shaw & Simon, 1958, p. 163). This basic conceptual foundation of the natural sciences — the assumption that its subject matter is mechanistic — was thus preserved for psychology by the computer modeling approach from the ruins of behaviorism. Old wine was poured into shiny new bottles, but the taste is as stale. The human was presupposed to be just another mechanism that could be predicted, manipulated, controlled and delivered over to whoever had the resources to pay for such a project of domination. Only now it was not merely the person's behavior, but their very mental life itself that was so promised. And just in time for the great economic shift in late-century America from the Machine Age to the Information Age. However, the computer models are proving to be as inadequate a simulation of the human order or behaviorism's mutant rats, as the critical reviews are beginning to decisively reveal (cf. Aanstoos, 1986; Dreyfus, 1979; Weizenbaum, 1976). Once again, initial hubris in the dream of controlling the human ends in disappointing actual results.

### The Humanistic Alternative

Is there an alternative? Could psychology come into possession of itself as an authentic and originary perspective on human existence? Humanistic psychology says yes, and seeks to do so by an altogether different approach. Rather than seeking domination and *control* of the human, humanistic psychology aims at *understanding*. Drawing on the *verstahen* tradition of the human sciences begun in the nineteenth century by Dilthey and the phenomenology of Husserl, such a project of understanding offers a more integrative possibility, encompassing the human more fully. Humanistic psychology does not suppress the shadowy mirror of the rat, nor seek domination over it. Wertz asks us to re-evaluate this modernist enterprise of rat control. It is time we re-examine how that psychology has projected us toward a false ideal, and led to our alienation.

> Have we of the twentieth century... in our singular attempt to annihilate our troubles — merciless nature, the bestial, the childish, the criminal, the insane, the sick, and so on — ceased to understand each other and ourselves inasmuch as all our lives, psychologists' included, contain these themes? Again and again we have met the paradox that the rat offers man no confirmation in its resolute otherness and negativity, and yet holds the mirror before humanity. In our quest to eliminate the rat we have paradoxically lost our very humanity... Only by owning our partial yet inevitable rat likeness might we approach our full humanity. (Wertz, 1986, p. 164)

In place of such a bankrupt promise of manipulation and domination, humanistic psychology offers a fundamentally different hope. It aims to respond to a alternative vision of what is needed:

We need a psychology of affirmation, not control; a psychology of witness and recognition, not test and measurement; a psychology of deep commemoration, not superficial prediction... A psychology of embrace, not engulfment... of fostering power and action instead of docility and consumption; a tolerance for ambiguity and compassion in the face of difference rather than fearful sterilization and normalization. (Wertz, 1986, p. 165).

At the same time the computer modelers were constructing images of persons as machines, Maslow proferred "the farther reaches of human nature" (1971) as the frontier for a genuinely humanistic psychology. Rather than a psychology of control, he proposed a psychology of growth, of self-realization, of peak-experiences, of transcendence, a "psychology of being" (1968). This unfettered respect and emancipation of the full range of human possibility is the vital heart of humanistic psychology. The humanistic alternative differs decisively from the conceptions of both behaviorism's passively conditioned external behaviors and cognitivism's actively processed internal cognitions. Both are derivative of a mechanistic view that presupposes a reductionism of the human to something inhuman. The humanistic alternative sets aside this reductionist prejudgment in order to comprehend the human order directly, on its own terms, *qua human*. The chapters in this volume show how this is done and exemplify the richness that can be gained thereby.

### References

Aanstoos, C. M. (1986). Phenomenology and the psychology of thinking. In P. D. Ashworth, A. Giorgi, & A. deKoning (Eds.), *Qualitative research in psychology* (pp. 79-116). Pittsburgh: Duquesne University Press.

Brett, G. (1962). *Brett's history of psychology* (rev. ed. by R. Peters). New York: Macmillan.

Bullock, A. (1985). *The humanist tradition in the west*. New York: Norton.

Cantor, N. F. (1988). *Twentieth-century culture: Modernism to deconstruction*. New York: Peter Lang.

Churchill, S. D. (1988). Humanistic psychology and introductory textbooks. *The Humanistic Psychologist, 16*, 341-357.

Dreyfus, H. L. (1979). *What computers can't do* (rev. ed.). New York: Harper & Row.

Hartley, D. (1964). *Observations on man, his frame, his duty and his expectations*. In J. Mandler & G. Mandler (Eds.), *Thinking: From association to Gestalt*. New York: Wiley. (Original work published 1749)

Henley, T. B. & Faulkner, K. A. (1989). An addendum to Churchill's review of introductory textbooks. *The Humanistic Psychologist, 17*, 329-330.

Hobbes, T. (1964). *Humaine nature.* In J. Mandler & G. Mandler (Eds.), *Thinking: From association to Gestalt.* New York: Wiley. (Original work published 1650)
Hume, D. (1978). *A treatise on human nature.* Oxford: Clarendon Press. (Original work published 1739)
Husserl, E. (1970). *The crisis of European sciences and transcendental phenomenology* (D. Carr, Trans.). Evanston: Northwestern University Press. (Original work published 1936)
Jencks, C. (1986). *What is postmodernism?* New York: St. Martin's Press.
Kvale, S. (1990). Postmodern psychology: A contradicto in adjecto? *The Humanistic Psychologist, 18,* 35-54.
Mandler, J. & Mandler, G. (1964). *Thinking: From association to Gestalt.* New York: Wiley.
Maslow, A. (1968). *Toward a psychology of being* (2nd ed.). Princeton, NJ: Nostrand.
Maslow, A. (1971). *Farther reaches of human nature.* New York: Viking.
McKnight, S. A. (1989). *Sacralizing the secular: The Renaissance origins of modernity.* Baton Rouge: Louisiana State University Press.
Merleau-Ponty, M. (1968). *The visible and the invisible* (A. Lingis, Trans.). Evanston: Northwestern University Press. (Original work published 1964)
Mill, J. (1967). *Analysis of the human mind.* New York: A. W. Kelly. (Original work published 1829)
Newell, A., Shaw, J. C. & Simon, H. A. (1958). Elements of a theory of human problem solving. *Psychological Review, 65,*, 151-166.
Newell, A. & Simon, H. A. (1961). Computer simulation of human thinking. *Science, 134,* 2011-2017.
Newell, A. & Simon, H. A. (1972). *Human problem solving.* Englewood Cliffs, NJ: Prentice-Hall.
Simon, H. A. (1969). *The sciences of the artificial.* Cambridge: MIT Press.
Simon, H. A. (1979). Information processing models of cognition. *Annual Review of Psychology, 30,* 363-396.
Simon, H. A. & Newell, A. (1964). Information processing in computers and man. *American Scientist, 52,* 281-300.
Simon, H. A. & Newell, A. (1971). Human problem solving: The state of the theory in 1970. *American Psychologist, 26,* 145-159.
Skinner, B. F. (1971). *Beyond freedom and dignity.* New York: Knopf.
Toulmin, S. (1990). *Cosmopolis: The hidden agenda of modernity.* New York: The Free Press.
Weizenbaum, J. (1976). *Computer power and human reason.* San Francisco: Freeman.
Wertz, F. J. (1986). The rat in psychological science. *The Humanistic Psychologist, 14,* 143-168.

# 2

# The Institutionalization of Humanistic Psychology

*Roy J. deCarvalho*

The founding members of the Association for Humanistic Psychology (AHP) and the American Psychological Association Division 32 included psychologists (and for AHP other interested audiences as well) sympathetic to the tradition linking the humanities and psychology, including classical phenomenology; dialogical-religious, secular, and psychological emphases of existentialism; Gestalt psychology; person-oriented neo-Freudians; the organismic psychology of Kurt Goldstein; the 20th century contributions of American personality psychologists; and psychology-oriented theologians. We also find traces of the hippie counter-culture of the 1960's, the human potential movement, and the Esalen phenomena, from which the academic humanistic psychologists sometimes sought to distance themselves. At first the only common ground shared by this eclectic group was a willingness to do something about their deep dissatisfaction with the domineering presence of behaviorism and psychoanalysis in mid-century American psychology. As humanistic psychology came to maturity, however, affirmative statements replaced mere protest. A number of humanistic psychologists stood out because of their leadership roles and because their psychological thought was sought for intellectual inspiration and legitimization. The growth hypotheses of Maslow and Rogers, the personality theory of Allport, and the existential and phenomenological psychologies of May and Bugental were some of those that came to the forefront of humanistic psychology (deCarvalho, 1991a). This group of thinkers came together in the 1960's and early 1970's under two institutions, AHP and APA's Division 32.

## The Association for Humanistic Psychology and the *Journal of Humanistic Psychology*

As Maslow distanced himself from the fields of comparative and experimental psychologies in which he earned a doctoral degree and significant academic recognition and digressed into the study of less conventional psychological subjects, he felt ostracized by the psychological community. His departmental colleagues at Brooklyn College gave him little attention; some even began avoiding him (decarvalho, 1991b).

Primarily because of the difficulties of publishing in APA journals, Maslow contacted other psychologists who shared his disappointment. In 1954, he began compiling a mailing list of about 125 names in order to provide a means of exchanging mimeographed copies of their writings. In 1961 the members of this list became the first subscribers of the *Journal of Humanistic Psychology (JHP)*. Discontented with the intellectual monopoly of behaviorism in American psychology and concerned with anomalies within the orthodox psychological paradigm related to the subjective conditions of human existence, Maslow's colleagues emerged as a distinct group within psychology seeking the construction of a separate set of theories and research (cf. Kuhn, 1970). Maslow was personally involved in the recruitment of many of these discontents. He telephoned and corresponded with them, sought to learn from their research and activities, and created networks of individuals with shared interests. Some, as was the case of Jack Gibb (1968), the 1968 president of the AHP, joined the movement "because of the contagious excitement" of a letter from Maslow.

Maslow introduced a 1961 version of this list as follows.

> This list was made up to encourage intercommunication among people in different fields who should know each other's work. I have suggested to each of them that they use it as a mailing list for exchange of reprints and mimeographed materials. Some are not known to me personally but have been suggested by others. If you know others who belong on this list, please let me know. (Archive)

Concentrating on organizations and networks rather then on individuals, Maslow included the mailing list in his *Toward a Psychology of Being* (1962) as the "Eupsychian Network."

One of the individuals on Maslow's list was Anthony Sutich (1976b; Vich, 1976). Confined to bed all his adult life with severe arthritis, Sutich was self-taught and well read in the field of psychology with interests in semantics, ethics, neo-psychoanalysis, client-centered and group psychotherapy. At their first meeting in 1949, he and Maslow shared their anger over the dominating behavioristic attitude in psychology. In the mid-1950's, Sutich felt that Maslow's mailing list was an inefficient means of communication. Their unwillingness to accept the offer to incorporate the interests of the people on the mailing list in the American *Journal of Individual Psychology* alerted many on that list to the need of establishing an independent journal (Sutich, 1976b, pp. 7-51).

In response to this pressure, Maslow wrote Sutich about how to proceed with the organization of a journal and promised to seek funding for the venture (Sutich, 1976a, pp. 52-64). They soon assembled a board of editors which included Kurt Goldstein, Rollo May, Lewis Mumford, Andras Angyal, Clark Moustakas, Joe Adams, Charlotte Buhler, Robert Hartman, Dorothy Lee, and David Riesman. The editorial statement of the journal's purpose was soon delineated and they began the search for a title. Upon pressure from Maslow, Brandeis University sponsored the venture without financial participation (Sutich, 1976a, pp. 65-88). The title *Journal of Humanistic Psychology*, was suggested by Stephen Cohen, a senior psychology student at Brandeis and Maslow's son-in-law (Greening, 1985, 1988). Although Cohen was the first to suggest "Humanistic Psychology" as a possible journal title, the first to use the term with its current meaning was Gordon Allport in 1930 (decarvalho, 1991c). With Sutich as the editor, the first issue of the *JHP* appeared in the spring of 1961. The editorial statements of the new journal and of Maslow's mailing list resembled one the other. In the case of the *JHP*, it stated the aim of publishing theoretical and applied research, original contributions, papers, articles and studies concerned with values, autonomy, being, self, love, creativity, identity, growth, psychological health, organism, self-actualization, basic need-gratification and related concepts.

The first subscribers of the *JHP* were the individuals on Maslow's mailing list. In 1968 Sutich transferred the editorship of the *JHP* to Miles Vich, who had been co-editor since 1963. Thomas Greening, the current editor, took over in 1970.

With the publication of the *JHP*, it became obvious that the journal and the increasing number of subscribers needed their own association, and so Sutich and Maslow appointed James Bugental as president pro-tem of the future association. The founding meeting of the AHP took place in Philadelphia in the summer of 1963 with about 75 participants. Maslow opened the meeting with a criticism of the exclusiveness of what he called the "low-ceiling psychology" of psychoanalysis and behaviorism. Discussions went into the night addressing methodological problems, psychological views of human nature, the significance of values in psychology and in our lives, and their feelings of professional isolation and frustration in the communication of research. "My primary impression of the Philadelphia meeting," wrote Sutich two years later, "was that of mutual discovery. Within a single day, a hundred or so like-minded individuals found that they constituted a 'belonging group.' The days of professional and intellectual isolation were over" (AHP, December 1963; November 1965; Sutich, 1976a, p. 118). The following second annual meeting in Los Angeles (AHP, September 1964) already convened twice as many members, about two hundred.

One other important event in the founding of humanistic psychology was a conference on the theoretical issues implied by the new psychology held in November of 1964 in Old Saybrook, Connecticut. Allport, Bugental, Maslow, Rogers and May and other well-known academic psychologists, such as Jacques Barzun, Charlotte Buhler, George Kelly, Clark Moustakas, Gardner Murphy and Henry Murray, were present. The *JHP* (Fall 1965) published some of the delivered papers. Two decades later, the Humanistic Psychology Institute in San Francisco changed its name to Saybrook Institute partly in homage to this founding conference.

The first meetings of the AHP were colored by protest and dissatisfaction with the status quo in psychology, primarily the exclusiveness of the behavioristic and psychoanalytical paradigms. Thus, when confronted with the need to clarify humanistic psychology, one group advocated a definition by denial, merely stating what humanistic psychology did not stand for. Another group advocated a more positive attitude by seeking to introduce human meanings and values into mainstream psychology (Bugental, 1985; Gibb, 1968, p. 1; AHP, December 1963).

The significant increase in the AHP membership during the 1960's (from seventy-five members in 1963 to five hundred in 1966) made the Association's statement of orientation, goals and policies and of the aims and methods of humanistic psychology a pressing issue. The first policy statements were vague and adopted from the essay, Humanistic Psychology: A New Breakthrough, authored by Bugental (1963), arguing that humanistic psychology seeks to incorporate the behavioristic and psychoanalytical perspectives within a broader phenomenological orientation emphasizing the existential aspects of the human condition. He also argued that people are more than the sum of isolated behaviors, that human relationships change individual character, and that people are aware, make choices, and are intentional.

All the presidents of the AHP in the 1960's gave priority to the issue of defining humanistic psychology. In 1965, Charlotte Buhler took her presidency as a challenge to clarify "the great deal of confusion regarding the objectives and methods of a humanistic psychology" (AHP, November 1965). However, There were, only small changes in the original broad statements adopted from Bugental's New Breakthrough essay of 1963. The focus of AHP's activities in the 1970's was primarily on education, networking, and the internationalization of humanistic psychology.

There was originally an additional "A" standing for American in the title of the organization (e.g., AAHP). Sutich and Maslow chose to include American at the title of the Association as a temporary device in order to avoid any suspicion of anti-patriotism due to the communism hysteria of the post-McCarthy era (Sutich, 1976a, p. 94). Because of the absence of this political threat and greater interest in humanistic psychology abroad than at home, the first "A" was dropped in 1969.

Due to the international prestige of Charlotte Buhler, AHP's president for 1965-66, member and the 1970 chair of the International Advisory Board, the international scope and membership of the AHP increased significantly. Carmi Harari of the Committee for International Organization also provided a great stimulus. He traveled extensively abroad as director of International Developments and organized local groups. In 1969 Harari, with interested British colleagues, orchestrated an international gathering of humanistic psychologists in London following the Congress of Social Psychiatry. The First International Invitational Conference on Humanistic Psychology took place in the Free University of Amsterdam, Netherlands, in 1970. The second and much larger international gathering, organized by Harari and chaired by Stanley Krippner, followed in 1971 in Wurzburg, Germany.

In the early 1970's, the AHP had chapters in several European countries including Israel, India, Iceland, and Central and South America. In 1972, for instance, the AHP sponsored conferences on humanistic psychology in London, Oslo, Stockholm, Moscow, Hong Kong, Hawaii and Tokyo. The Third International Conference in Tokyo, following the 1972 International Congress of Psychology, was heavily attended. The 1975 AHP's directory of growth centers listed fifty-two humanistic psychology-related centers in thirteen countries.

Throughout the 1970's, the AHP sought to become a network for humanistically-oriented groups, practitioners and growth centers. The first special network section of the *Newsletter*, published in 1968, had thirty-two references to growth centers in the United States. A similar listing only two years later already contained one hundred and twelve entries. In 1975, there were three hundred thirty-three references. The listings included academic and theoretical, psychotherapeutic, Gestalt, encounter, human potential, psychodrama, psychosynthesis, mystical and esoteric groups.

The 1970's was also the decade of education at the AHP. This interest was in part in response to requests from members for information on humanistically-oriented educational programs. Already in the late 1960's, the *Newsletter* began publishing lists of schools and programs in humanistic psychology. Throughout the following decade, educational topics in the form of articles, notices and information pertaining to schools and programs dominated the activities of the AHP and its *Newsletter*.

The first psychology departments with concentrations in humanistic psychology were established in Sonoma State College (SSC) in 1966, in West Georgia College in 1969, and the Humanistic Psychology Institute (HPI) in San Francisco in 1970 (AHP, July 1966; April 1969; April 1970). Hobart Thomas and Gordon Tappan were responsible for the pilot M.A. program in humanistic psychology at SSC. There were twelve full-time students enrolled in the first class. Their brochure explained that the program reflected the concerns of the founders of the AHP and the recognition that "experience itself and its meaning to the person is to be the primary phenomenon of study" (AHP, July 1966).

The HPI was created in 1970 by the AHP as an educational and research institute dedicated to Maslow's memory in order to provide an alternative university model for higher education (AHP, October 1970; December 1971). Eleanor Criswell, an AHP board member, spearheaded the HPI initiative. During this early phase, the executive board of the AHP was also the executive body of the HPI. The first graduate courses were offered through the Extension Division of SSC. The enrollment increased from thirty students in the first class to one hundred seventy the following year. In 1982, the HPI changed its name to Saybrook Institute.

Myron (Mike) Arons (1992), a student of Maslow and Paul Ricoeur, was instrumental in the establishment of the BA and MA programs of the West Georgia College at Carrollton in 1969. Convinced that a humanistic approach to teaching and learning was necessary, James Klee, Arons, and colleagues developed a curriculum centered on personal and intellectual growth as well as the development of creativity and imagination in students.

## The APA Division of Humanistic Psychology (32)

One outcome of efforts of humanistic psychologists for professional and academic acceptance was the creation of Division 32 within the APA. In 1971, 390 APA members petitioned for a humanistic psychology division with the purpose of applying "the concepts, theories and philosophy of humanistic psychology to research, education, and professional applications of scientific psychology," and of ensuring "that humanistically oriented ideas and activities operate within APA and some of its divisions" (AHP, December 1971; Summer 1972; February 1973).

The presence of humanistic psychology in the APA antedated the founding of Division 32. Abraham Maslow and Carl Rogers were presidents in 1968 and 1947 respectively. Humanistic psychologist M. Brewster Smith, presided the APA in 1978. Throughout the late 1960's, AHP scheduled its annual meetings in the same cities as the APA's annual meetings, co-sponsored joint sessions with other APA divisions, and, in co-operation with Division 32, offered the first APA hospitality suites with presentations and conversation hours. In 1969, the AHP had established an APA Liaison Committee in order to coordinate such joint meetings and disseminate information about humanistic psychology and AHP not only at APA conferences but also other regional psychological associations and various interest groups in psychology (AHP, January 1969; Summer 1970; November 1970; June 1971). More recently, Stanley Graham and Frank Farley, also a members of Division 32, were elected president of the APA. E. Mark Stern, the 1991-1992 president of Division 32, was on the 1992 ballot for the APA presidency.

Working independently from the AHP leadership, Don Gibbons, then at West Georgia College, circulated petition cards and filed a petition for the establishment of a Division of Humanistic Psychology with the APA. Upon the approval of the petition by the APA's Council of Representatives, Gibbons scheduled an organizational meeting at the APA 1971 annual meeting in Washington, DC (Harari, 1992).

Gibbons argued that such a division would benefit the AHP and what it stands for; that it would legitimize humanistic psychology in the eyes of the psychological community, thus enabling the APA to continue to act as a forum for all points of view. Humanistic psychology had as much the right to be represented in the APA as did, for example, the Skinnerian perspective. Moreover, the fact that most of the returned petition cards came from non-AHP members showed that the Division would help organize a different population in service of the humanistic cause in American psychology (AHP, April 1971; May 1971).

At first the leadership of AHP did not take these developments seriously because they knew nothing about them and had not been invited to participate. A statement prepared by John Levy, AHP's Executive Officer, and approved by the AHP Executive Board, called on AHP members to oppose the establishment of the Division because it was a divisive and inimical step to AHP's leadership role in the cause of humanistic psychology. "The basic point," wrote Levy, "is that humanistic psychology is not a specialty within psychology. It is, rather, a point of view toward the whole field of human sciences and arts. To launch a Division of Humanistic Psychology would be to create and perpetuate a false view of what the Third Force is, to encourage people to view it simply as a sub-group of the profession of psychology" (AHP, May 1971).

Believing himself to be voicing the attitude of the young people at AHP, Rollo May did not regard this move, which he described as "politicizing shenanigans," to be threatening. AHP, wrote May (1972), represents "the New Underground in psychology, and I think that it is a crucial function, as necessary for APA as for ourselves." Moreover since May perceived the movement of psychologists to be toward AHP rather than APA, he thought that he had little to fear from the establishment of such a Division. On the other hand, some AHP Executive Board members went so far as to mail personal letters to AHP members urging non-support of the proposed Division.

At the scheduled time for the Division's organizational meeting at the APA Washington convention, a large group of AHP members, including its Executive Board, assembled on the hall near the meeting room in order to get to know the organizer, who did not show up. In the absence of a leader and surprised by the large number of people awaiting the beginning of the meeting, several AHP members took over by calling the meeting to order, nominating acting officers and board members, and arranging the details for the first election. Ironically, Don Gibbons was waiting outside the entire time because he did not know that this was the meeting he had scheduled (Harari, 1992).

By the late 1950's and early 1960's, most psychotherapists at the APA were discontent with the monopoly of academic, experimental psychologists of behavioristic persuasion. In order to advance their interest, under the theoretical influence of Carl Rogers, they founded the

Psychologists Interested in the Advancement of Psychotherapy (PIAP). Later, this group began the APA Division 29 (Psychotherapy). However, at the early PIAP meetings, an attempt to make humanistic psychology an integral part of the group failed and those with a close identification with humanistic psychology sought to branch out. The time was thus ripe for the creation of a division of humanistic psychology. Not surprisingly, the petition for the creation of Division 32 and the call for an organizational meeting appealed to this group of APA members (Mahrer, 1992).

The first elected acting officers of Division 32 were Carmi Harari as President, Everett Shostrom as President-elect, Gloria Behar Gottsegen as Secretary, and Barry M. Crown as Treasurer. The same group was confirmed into these positions the following year. Other members of the Executive Board were David Bakan, Joel Fagan, Robert D. Strom, Elizabeth M. Mintz, Leonard Blank, Lawrence LeShan, James B. Klee, and Barton W. Knapp (AHP, December 1971; February 1973). Most, if not all, were also AHP members. In 1972, the growing membership earned the Division two seats in the APA Council of Representatives filled by Albert Ellis and Fred Massarik.

As the new Division became a reality, easy relationships developed with AHP. The AHP Executive Board Meetings systematically reported on Division 32 activities (AHP, December 1971; May 1972), and AHP continued to co-sponsor hospitality suites at APA conventions. At the AHP, Division 32 became regarded as a potential "anteroom" for the recruitment of new AHP members, an ensurer that humanistically oriented ideas and activities operate in APA, and a provider of status and respectability for humanistic psychology. "As an organization, we were conscious of our need to play a special role within APA in bringing a humanistic awareness and consciousness to the organization and often discussed how to do so more effectively," wrote Carmi Harari (1992) in his recollections of the early days. The presentations, invited addresses, symposia and experiential e.g., growth and encounter sessions sponsored by Division 32 introduced APA audiences to the armamentarium of humanistic psychology. (Harari, 1992)

The first issue of the *Newsletter of Division 32* appeared in 1972. Its first and second editors were Sarah Zaraleya and Al Manaster respectively. In 1985, the new editor, Christopher Aanstoos, transformed the *Newsletter* into *The Humanistic Psychologist — The Bulletin*, which ceased to be a bulletin and became an official APA divisional journal with volume 17, the Autumn 1989 issue. The *Newsletter* resumed publication in 1989 under the editorship of Fred Wertz.

## Humanistic Psychology and Transpersonal Psychology

Transpersonal and humanistic psychologies shared parallel developments in many ways. They shared the same founders, Sutich and Maslow, and the *JHP* and the *Journal of Transpersonal Psychology* (*JTP*) shared their first two editors, Sutich and Miles Vich (Harari 1992; Sutich, 1976a, 1976b; Vich, 1976). Since the early annual AHP and Division 32 meetings, we systematically find programs in transpersonal psychology, a tradition which is still true today, as well as a nurtured relationship between the two organizations and scholars. The *JHP* has published many articles on transpersonal psychology and by transpersonal psychologists.

In 1975, the Proposed Division of Transpersonal Psychology was started in the APA by Mary Jo Meadow, a leader of Division of Psychologists Interested in Religious Issues and President of Division 32 in 1989-1990. Some division 32 members, such as Arons and Harari, were involved in this attempt as secretary and treasurer of the new organization. Although sharing some common membership, the proposed and established divisions opposed merging into one single APA division in order to avoid the loss of independent identities. In the 1980's, The transpersonal organization has twice unsuccessfully sought APA divisional status and a third attempt was withdrawn in order not to be defeated. Division 32 has recently established a Transpersonal Psychology Interest Group, hospitably offering a formal organization for transpersonalists within APA.

## Conclusion

The first institutions of humanistic psychology, the *JHP* and AHP, were offsprings of the mailing list of discontented psychologists compiled by Maslow during the late 1950's, of Maslow's prestige and infectious enthusiasm, and of the administrative skills of Anthony Sutich. The organization of APA's Division of Humanistic Psychology (32) in 1971 resulted from the attempt of Don Gibbons to introduce the humanistic perspective into mainstream psychology. *The Humanistic Psychologist*, originally a Newsletter and then a Bulletin of the Division, became an APA divisional journal in 1989.

## References

Archive. Humanistic Psychology Archive. Library, University of California — Santa Barbara.

Arons, M. (1992). Suns of my student years. *Journal of Humanistic Psychology, 32,* 46-50.

AHP. (various years). *Association for Humanistic Psychology Newsletter* (renamed *AHP Perspective* since the August-September 1984 issue).

Bugental, J. F. T. (1963). Humanistic Psychology: A new Breakthrough. *American Psychologist, 18,* 563-567.

Bugental, J. F. T. (1985). Interview with the author.

deCarvalho, R. J. (1991a). *The founders of humanistic psychology.* New York: Praeger.

deCarvalho, R. J. (1991b). *The growth hypothesis in psychology: The humanistic psychology of Abraham Maslow and Carl Rogers.* San Francisco: Mellen Research University Press.

deCarvalho, R. J. (1991c). Gordon Allport and humanistic psychology. *Journal of Humanistic Psychology, 31,* 8-13.

Gibb, J. (April 1968). President's message. *AHP Newsletter,* 1-2.

Greening, T. (1985). The origins of the *Journal of Humanistic Psychology* and the Association for Humanistic Psychology, *Journal of Humanistic Psychology, 25,* 7-11.

Greening, T. (1988). Commentary. *Journal of Humanistic Psychology, 28,* 68-72.

Harari, C. (1992). Notes on the history of the Division of Humanistic Psychology in APA. The Humanistic Psychology Archive. Library, University of California — Santa Barbara.

Kuhn, T. (1970). *The structure of scientific revolutions* (2nd ed.). Chicago: University of Chicago Press.

Mahrer, A. (1992). Personal communication.

Maslow, A. H., (1962). *Toward a psychology of being.* New York: Van Nostrand Reinhold.

May, R. (1972). Rollo May writes. *AHP Newsletter,* January, 1-2.

Sutich, A. J. (1976a). The emergence of the transpersonal orientation: A personal account. *Journal of Transpersonal Psychology, 8,* 5-19.

Sutich, A. J. (1976b). *The founding of humanistic and transpersonal psychology.* Unpublished doctoral dissertation, Humanistic Psychology Institute (Saybrook Institute), San Francisco.

Vich, M. A. (1976). Anthony Sutich: An appreciation. *Journal of Transpersonal Psychology, 8,* 2-4.


*Author's Note:* I am thankful to Fred Wertz, Tom Greening, Stanley Krippner and Alvin Mahrer for their reading and comments of an early draft of this essay. I am particularly indebted to Carmi Harari's written recollections of the founding of Division 32 now at the Humanistic Psychology Archive at the University of California — Santa Barbara and extensive telephone interviews.

# 3

# Philosophical Foundations of Humanistic Psychology

*Larry Davidson*

> Man [sic] has long felt himself to be but a puppet in life — molded by economic forces, by unconscious forces, by environmental forces. He has been enslaved by persons, by institutions, by the theories of psychological science. But he is firmly setting forth a new declaration of independence. (Carl Rogers, 1978, p. 331)

Anthony Sutich (1976) has informed us that many names were originally considered for the "third force" movement inspired by the work of a variety of loosely-related thinkers; names such as orthopsychology, ontopsychology and person psychology. The committee formed to launch the new journal for this movement had decided on the phrase "Self Psychology" until Sutich received a letter from a student of Maslow at Brandeis, Stephen Cohen, who first suggested that the journal instead be entitled "The Journal of Humanistic Psychology" (Greening, 1985). While this name was officially adopted in 1961, it is unclear if this choice reflected an acknowledgement of the movement's background in the humanist tradition, or if it simply posed a less controversial choice than "self" or "orthopsychology." In his letter, Cohen referred to the relationship between this new psychology and "the whole history of humanism" (in Greening, 1985, p. 10). But had he not written this letter, or had the committee chosen to ignore it, would we still consider the third force movement to belong to the humanist tradition? And if so, what implications does this pose for the development of an alternative paradigm for psychological theory and practice?

Historically, the early roots of the humanistic psychology movement are to be found in the work of American personality theorists such as

Gordon Allport, Henry Murray and Gardner Murphy, in the interpersonal and neo-freudian schools of the psychoanalytic tradition as represented by Erich Fromm and Karen Horney, in the Gestalt psychology of Kurt Koffka, Max Wertheimer and Wolfgang Kohler, and in the thought of Kurt Goldstein. Later influences shaping the direction of this movement include the European philosophies of Existentialism and Phenomenology, and Eastern philosophical and religious traditions, all of which were imported into the United States following the Second World War (cf. DeCarvalho, 1990; Klee, 1978; Matson, 1978, 1981).

It will be my aim in the following to review the ways in which humanistic psychology has been built upon the same conceptual cornerstones that support the humanistic tradition, and to consider the strengths and weaknesses of this foundation for the development of an empirical science of psychology. I will begin with a thumbnail sketch of the history of humanism in the Western intellectual tradition to draw out the conceptual cornerstones of the humanistic perspective. While it remains a matter of debate as to what extent, humanistic psychology belongs within the humanist tradition (Giorgi, 1981; Graumann, 1981), in the second part of this paper I will argue that they share a common philosophical perspective that may be as productive in guiding psychological science as it was in fostering the art of Leonardo and Michelangelo or the political views of Rousseau and Jefferson. I will conclude, however, that humanistic psychology has not yet been able to achieve its humanistic objectives in the concrete development of psychological research and theory, and will suggest possible guidelines for future forays in this direction.

## The Humanist Tradition

In a recent series of lectures on the humanist tradition in the West, Oxford historian Alan Bullock provided a crude but useful way to differentiate between humanism and other philosophical perspectives. Using the term "man" as the pre-twentieth century designation for human being, Bullock writes:

> As a rough generalization, Western thought has treated man and the cosmos in three distinct modes. The first, the supernatural or the transcendental, has focused on God, treating man as a part of the Divine Creation. A second, the natural or the scientific, has focused on Nature and treats man as part of the natural order like other organisms. The third, the humanistic, has focused on Man, and on human experience as the starting point for man's knowledge of himself, of God and of Nature. (1985, p. 16)

The humanist perspective considers human nature to occupy a distinct ontological realm. Unlike other components of the world that can be understood as the material being of Nature or the transcendental being of the Divine, human being can only be properly understood in its own terms. Typically, aspects of human experience such as language, creativity, and self-reflection may be identified as best embodying that which is distinctively human, but it is the underlying assertion of humanism that the possession of such qualities serves to distinguish the human realm from all other spheres of reality.

From this fundamental conviction in the unique value and status of human being and experience, there follow three characteristics of the humanist tradition that Bullock identifies as its most important and constant conceptual cornerstones (1985, p. 155). The first of these characteristics may be considered an epistemological consequence of the distinctive ontological status accorded human nature. If the human constitutes a realm unto itself, irreducible to either material or spiritual being, then knowledge of the human must be similarly distinctive and non-reductive. To attempt to understand the human solely within the parameters of the physical sciences or the Judeo-Christian tradition of revealed religion is therefore to distort its nature and to lose what makes the human precisely human. This is not to suggest that materiality and the sacred will have no role to play in human life, but that they cannot be accorded a primary role in accounting for the nature of human experience. It must itself be primary, with both scientific investigation and religious belief viewed as human practices, derived, as Bullock writes, "by human minds from human experience" (1985, p. 155).

The second characteristic of humanism is the value it places on the individual and the respect for the freedom and dignity of the person that it takes to provide a foundation for all other values and rights (Bullock, 1985, p. 155). We might consider this to be the ethical and political corollary of the ontological and epistemological positions already described, in that the irreducibility and privileged status of the human is here taken to provide a guide for moral and social conduct. It is in the individual that the humanists have found those capacities that most distinguish human beings from other organisms; capacities such as the power to communicate, to reason, to reflect, and to be creative. Thus it is in the individual that they have placed the source of value for what is distinctly human — and for what, therefore, should serve as the basis for economic and political order. For individuals to exercise these powers to the fullest, two conditions have been deemed necessary: freedom and education. The state should interfere with individual freedom and expression as little as possible, and should have as one of its aims the fostering and protection of individual rights. On the other hand, potential and talent are not simply to be neglected or ignored, but are to be awakened, drawn out and cultivated by an educational process that emphasizes the growth and development of the individual's abilities. Taken together, the ultimate aim of these political and educational practices is the fullest actualization of each person's potential (Bullock, 1985, p. 156).

Bullock identifies as a third, related characteristic of humanism an emphasis on ideas, reasoning and the plurality of perspectives through which the human spirit can be expressed. Having placed more importance on processes of critical inquiry and reflection and artistic creativity than on the products of cooperative labor, the humanist tradition has been "distrustful" of abstract systems of thought and has favored the historical study of concrete human experience and symbolic expression in its social and cultural contexts (Bullock, 1985, p. 157). Viewing religion, science and art as fundamentally symbolic practices that embody the human hunger for meaning, humanists have typically accepted that there are many ways to the truth and that the way is more important than any possible destination. From this emphasis on symbolic expression there have followed interests in drama, literature, art and particularly language as embodiments of the human imagination. Culture and history have also attracted much attention, as civilizations have been viewed as constructed out of constellations of meaning rooted in the daily lives and practices of their citizens. Through studies of language, history, art and symbolic practices, empathy has come to be valued as an avenue of access to other cultures and as an important tool in understanding human experiences in their varying contexts.

These three characteristic emphases on human experience, freedom and meaning can be found interwoven in the history of the humanist tradition. Humanistic themes have been present through the history of thought. For instance, Pelagius (5th century) is known for his emphasis on human agency in contrast to the determinism that pervaded his religious community at the time. Most accounts have humanism beginning in fourteenth century Italy as a revolt against the scholasticism and authoritarianism of the medieval church. Petrarch, often considered the first humanist, suggested a reversal of the then accepted view of history which heralded the dawn of the Christian age as bringing salvation from the heathen ignorance of Roman culture and its predecessors. For

Petrarch, it was rather the cultures of ancient Greece and Rome that best illumined the human spirit, which he felt had fallen into darkness with the fall of Rome and the ascendancy of Christianity. He counselled a liberation from what then came to be called the "middle ages" by a return to, and revitalization of, the lost arts and teachings of the past; by a "renaissance" of antiquity (Bullock, 1985, pp. 13-15). The Italian humanists saw in Greek and Roman ruins and history a civilization that was focused on human beings and the difficulties encountered in everyday experiences on earth rather than on a transcendental Being and questions pertaining to an after-life. They saw in the teachings of Socrates in particular a kind of thinking that occurred on a human level and that addressed human concerns, insisting on a cultivation of the person's own life and conduct and a humility of reason in the face of realities that transcend the limits of human experience and understanding.

This turn away from the mysteries and speculations of revealed religion to experience and thought on the human scale can also be seen in the introduction of perspective into Renaissance art and in the renewed interest in civic affairs in Italian cities such as Venice and Florence. These explosions in the arts and political activity and reflection were accompanied by emphases on education (primarily a study of the classics such as Virgil, Homer, Cicero and Plato) and expression (in poetry and prose as well as architecture), reflecting the Italian humanists' belief in the unique potentiality and creativity of human beings. Not only did they attempt to ground painting and sculpture in human experience and design their buildings and cities in human proportions, but they also began to exalt the human itself as a source of value, order and reason in the world. For some, this glorification of the human came into conflict with Christian teachings of original sin and the subordination of reason to faith, bringing about significant changes in religious thought and practice. As humanism spread from Italy throughout Europe, scholars began to view the Bible as another text to be subjected to the tools and interests of historical exegesis. Others became skeptical of the necessity of a church hierarchy to mediate between God and the individual, arguing for a more direct and immediate relationship and a more personal form of religious practice. These last trends of humanist thought contributed, among other things, to the Protestant Reformation.

Humanism reappeared following the Counter Reformation and religious wars and Inquisitions in the form of the Enlightenment. If the Italian Renaissance is known primarily for its impressive contributions to art and architecture, late-seventeenth and eighteenth century humanists are known for their philosophical and political views concerning the role of the individual in the creation of knowledge and a just society. Following upon the earlier scientific advances of Galileo, Bacon and Newton, the Enlightenment saw an increased conviction in the power of human reason to discern the laws by which God, Nature and the human mind all functioned. Arguing that knowledge was derived from the activity of the mind reflecting on sensory impressions, John Locke (1690/1959) inaugurated a period in the history of philosophy that placed human experience back on center stage. Knowledge was neither innate (ala Descartes) nor revealed (as in the Judeo-Christian tradition), but was to be determined through the operation of the mental faculties on the givens of experience. This philosophical tradition, which flowed through Hume and Berkeley to Kant, led to the conclusion that knowledge was a result of the organization of sensory data through the internal structures of the human mind. We understand the world according to categories of space, time and causality, according to Kant (1787/1929), because that is how our understanding is structured. Based upon Kant's "Copernican revolution" in philosophy, human reason assumed the role of foundation for all knowledge, placing even the natural-scientific laws of Newton and the laws for moral behavior which had been the domain of religion within the framework of subjective experience.

Similar achievements were being made at this time in political theory in undermining the religious foundations of monarchy and in framing the initial arguments for democratic rule. Locke's work had equal impact in the political arena, providing intellectual justification for the 1688 English revolution and articulating for the first time the framework for a contractual view of government (Bullock, 1985, p. 52). Locke's emphasis on the rights and liberties of the individual was furthered by the thought of Rousseau, who saw government as being primarily oppressive and as corrupting the innate potential of humans to be just. Rousseau (1762/1947) argued that societies be self-determined, and ruled on the basis of a social contract through which power is delegated to government only to actualize the collective will of the people. In this view, the only valid aim of government, and the educational practices which are its main resource, is the fostering of the growth, development and actualization of its individual citizens. These emphases on individual rights, contractual government as self-determination, and the importance of education in the actualization of individual potential soon informed the thought of Thomas Jefferson and his compatriots in the Revolutionary War and founding of the democratic institutions of the United States.

One last thread of the humanist tradition will be important for our present purposes. Somewhat in contrast to the Enlightenment interest in the universal laws of Nature, but growing nonetheless out of a shared conviction in the important role of human imagination and reason in the construction of knowledge and culture, the eighteenth century saw a renewed interest in the historical sciences. Beginning with the work of Giambattista Vico (1744/1970), scholars returned to the systematic study of language, literature, and religious and cultural practices as symbolic embodiments of the human spirit. For Vico, Herder and others, each civilization and historical period represented a unique manifestation of human activity, and was therefore not to be reduced to universal laws. Human nature, like history itself, was constantly changing and there could be no truths that were applicable to all communities. As in the Renaissance, this emphasis on the historical and symbolizing nature of human being led to a pluralistic tolerance of, and interest in, various cultures and various paths to the truth. It also called for an important role for empathy, or "imaginative sympathy" (Bullock, 1985, p. 77), in affording the historical scholar insight into the lives of men and women of different times, settings and situations. In this context, there arose a renewed interest in education as the art of self-cultivation (the German concept of *Bildung*) and the origins of a Protestant theology (via Schleiermacher) which held that one way to the Divine was through the development of the individual's inner life.

These various features of the humanist tradition combined to provide a robust background for philosophical and scientific advances over the last two hundred years. From the work of Vico and Herder, for example, there developed the discipline of the *Geisteswissenschaften* or human sciences in the writings of Wilhelm Dilthey. Dilthey (1894/1977) argued that historical understanding of the inner lives and motivations of human beings provided a parallel in the human sciences to the role of physicalistic explanation in determining the laws of natural science. Kant's initial focus on the structures of human consciousness eventually led to the development of the philosophical school of Phenomenology founded by Edmund Husserl. Husserl (1913/1983) developed a method for the systematic study of subjective experience and demonstrated how the structures of subjectivity provide a basis for such human pursuits as science, logic and mathematics. Phenomenology then became influential in spawning the Existentialist philosophies of such thinkers as Martin Heidegger (1927/1962), Jean-Paul Sartre (1943/1956) and Maurice Merleau-Ponty (1942/1983). In addition, the pragmatic and pluralistic approach to political theory imported by Jefferson and others, in combination with the romanticist views (influenced by Rousseau) of American transcendentalists such as Emerson and Thoreau, contributed to the development of American philosophers William James and John Dewey. There has been a significant enough persistence of these trends into the late-nineteenth and twentieth centuries that some have been moved to refer to this period as the "new" or "third" humanism (Bullock, 1985; Mann, 1942).

## Is Humanistic Psychology "Humanistic"?

A brief survey of the history of humanistic psychology will suffice to suggest several substantive connections between the goals of this movement and those of the humanist tradition. It is widely acknowledged that humanistic psychology first arose as a protest against the images of human being (Bugental, 1963) offered by behavioristic and psychoanalytic psychologies. In their rejection of reductionistic theories that attempted to explain human conduct solely on the basis of biological or mechanistic models, the early humanistic psychologists were asserting their belief that human nature needed to be understood in its own terms. "Humanistic psychology is concerned," wrote Bugental in a characteristic statement, "with that which most distinguishes man [sic] as a unique species" (1978, p. 17). This belief in the special status of human nature and the failure of existing psychologies to capture the distinctly human represented the fundamental conviction shared by the founders of the movement. Humanistic psychology represents a recent echo of this long-standing desire for an approach to the study of human beings that begins with human experience and does not reduce the human to the non-human.

When the early humanistic psychologists were not confined to the *via negativa*, e.g., defining the human as non-mechanistic, they chose to define the human by virtue of those same capacities that the humanists had typically used to set humans apart from other forms of life. As we see in the original Articles of Association of the American Association for Humanistic Psychology, humanistic psychology was taken to be "primarily concerned with those human capacities and potentialities that have no systematic place, either in positivistic or behavioristic theory or in classical psychoanalytic theory, e.g., creativity, love, self, growth" (Sutich, 1962, p. 96). And with the earlier masters of the Renaissance and philosophers of the Enlightenment, humanistic psychology, according to its founding statement, shares "an ultimate concern with and valuing of the dignity and worth of man [sic] and an interest in the development of the potential inherent in every person" (cited in Misiak & Sexton, 1973, p. 116). From these glimpses into the mission statements inaugurating the movement, it clear that its connection to humanism is not exhausted in its ontological and epistemological convictions in the unique status of human nature and experience. It is also reflected in the emphasis which humanistic psychology places on the value, potential and dignity of the individual as capable of creativity, communication and self-actualization.

Our third cornerstone of humanism, the emphasis on the multiple expressions of the human spirit through language and culture, is also to be found in humanistic psychology in its more practical applications. Humanistic psychological theory, as it has been implemented in clinical work, has stressed the freedom and rights of individuals and the importance of empathy and allowing for self-direction in the actualization of clients' innate potential. Humanistic psychology has also shared with humanism an interest in education as the art of self-cultivation and an optimism that growth and development can be achieved by enabling the person to listen to his/her own inner voice rather than by encouraging conformity to external notions of normality. The often decried failure of humanistic psychologists to come to a consensus on the specific content and direction of their movement (cf. Berlyne, 1981; Giorgi, 1981; Rogers, 1978) may be itself only one manifestation of their pluralism and thus their traditionally "humanistic" belief in there being many valid ways to the truth (Klee, 1978).

In these and many more ways, humanistic psychology may therefore be taken fairly to represent, in the words of Floyd Matson, a "renaissance of humanism in psychology" (1978, p. 23). This link to the humanist tradition may be found most eloquently in the passage from Rogers which opened this paper, in which he compares the founding of the third force with a "new declaration of independence" from psychological theories which view human conduct as solely the product of impersonal forces (Rogers, 1978, p. 331). If one looks beyond the immediate precursors, it is not difficult to trace the historical lines which ground humanistic psychology directly in the tradition summarized above. The American personality theorists were rooted in the writings of James and Dewey as well as influenced by Gestalt psychology. Allport, for example, did postdoctoral study in Germany) (cf. DeCarvalho, 1991; Taylor, 1991). Gestalt psychology itself had an early foundation in Husserl's Phenomenology and in the Act psychology of his teachers, Franz Brentano and

Carl Stumpf (Brennan, 1982; Hergenhahn, 1986; Spiegelberg, 1972), while the interpersonalists and neo-freudians had been influenced by European sociology and anthropology in the tradition of Vico, Dilthey and Weber (cf. Fromm, 1941, 1955; Horney, 1939).

## An Appraisal of Humanism in Psychology

In order to determine whether or not the introduction of humanism into psychology has been valuable one must decide first on the intrinsic value of the contributions of the humanist perspective. If humanism is itself valued for its contributions to our appreciation of the human, then the vehicle for its introduction into academic psychology, i.e., humanistic psychology, will also be valued. Contemporary Western culture has been so permeated by the values of humanism that it is difficult for us to step back far enough even to question their validity; they have become, in the words of Jefferson, "self-evident." Particularly in the United States, we have built our very political and social order on beliefs in the dignity, worth and freedom of the individual, the right for self-exploration and expression, the need for pluralistic tolerance of multiple cultural traditions, and the hope for progress and growth into the future. It is perhaps in its resonance with these fundamental American convictions that humanistic psychology best represents a distinctly American discipline. And yet there have been criticisms of these very values as well, on political but also philosophical grounds.

The most important criticism leveled against humanism, and thus also against humanistic psychology as its derivative, has taken issue philosophically with the notion of the irreducibility of the human. It is problematic simply to insist that human nature represents an ontologically distinct form of life. While the human may in fact appear to be qualitatively distinct from other forms of life, closer examination reveals that this is only by virtue of the nature of its relation to other forms of life as well. Beginning with human experience, humanism must explore the relationships of this experience with the natural world and the spiritual world. Humanists must not take the uniqueness of their domain as a justification for overlooking the network of constitutive relationships that ground the human as a distinctive sphere. In heeding this caution, humanistic psychologists should build an explicit acknowledgement of these relationships into the methods and metaphors they employ in their scientific study of human experience.

Within humanistic psychology, there have traditionally been two ways to define the distinctiveness of the human incorporating its relations to other ontological domains. In the first case, secular humanists such as M. Brewster Smith (1982, 1986, 1990) have held that human beings are essentially biological organisms whose distinctiveness has been achieved by virtue of their position on the evolutionary scale. This position argues that human beings have become so evolutionarily advanced that they have crossed a qualitative boundary, typically represented by such achievements as the capacity for language or self-reflection, that sets them apart from other organisms. While such a view may be characterized ontologically as an "emergentist materialism" (Slavney & McHugh, 1987), it preserves a unique domain for humanistic-psychological inquiry into the nature of the 'higher' mental functions through which meaning, language and culture become possible.

In the second case, transpersonal psychologists such as Ken Wilbur (1979, 1981, 1989) have held that the human derives its distinctiveness from its spiritual connection to the sacred. This position argues that human beings are an incarnation of the Divine, created in the image of the Creator, and therefore set apart from the rest of the Creation by virtue of their potential for enlightenment. Such a position can trace its roots to the emanationist views of the Neo-Platonists, Augustine and Eastern religious traditions. In this view, a proper focus for humanistic psychology becomes the ways in which spirituality has become manifest and distorted or alienated in everyday life.

This need to study human experience in relation to other ontological domains has perhaps been best demonstrated in the works of existentialist thinkers who have influenced humanistic psychology. It has been the Existentialists, more than any other modern thinkers, who have tried to articulate the ontological distinctiveness of the human. A careful consideration of their mature positions reveals that they came to define the human primarily as an intentional relation to — and engagement in — the surrounding material, socio-political, and/or spiritual world. Sartre (1960/1963, 1960/1976), for example, turned to Marxism in order to situate human experience in its concrete relation to its political-economic context. Heidegger (1947/1977) turned in his later writings to a more theistic position in which he rejected the humanist tradition precisely for what he took to be its isolation and glorification of the human at the cost of the sacred. And Merleau-Ponty (1964/1968) consistently suggested that it was not as productive to view human experience as independent from the natural and spiritual worlds as it was to view it precisely as providing a space for their mutual "intertwining."

While these views may in fact be in line with those of the early humanists, who had a deep regard for both Nature and the Divine, it has been the perception of an isolated, independent view of the human that has served as the ground for another important criticism of the humanist tradition. From a political perspective, humanism has been criticized for being ahistorical and for promoting self-actualization as an individual pursuit above more communal concerns. As early as the Renaissance there was a debate between the virtues of the contemplative as opposed to the active life, and in the eighteenth century the humanist focus on education as self-cultivation was faulted for leading to self-absorption and a neglect of social and political problems (Bullock, 1985, pp. 27, 99). These same criticisms have been repeatedly leveled against humanistic psychology, from both within and outside of the movement itself (Campbell, 1984; Friedman, 1976; Geller, 1982; Giorgi, 1981; Graumann, 1981; Prilleltensky, 1989). While humanistic psychology may appreciate culture as an expression of the human spirit, it has been perceived as underestimating the importance of social and political context in concretely shaping people's lives. Ignoring these dimensions has led to a moralistic blurring of boundaries between psychology, politics, ethics and religion (Davidson & Cosgrove, 1991; May, 1989; O'Hara, 1989).

Despite these concerns, the goals shared by humanism and humanistic psychology seem nonetheless noteworthy, noble and worthy of pursuit. To the extent that humanistic psychology has imported these objectives into academic psychology, it should be viewed as a successful and important movement. While some within the humanistic psychology community credit the movement with "humanizing" the discipline in precisely these ways — challenging psychologists to develop less-reductive models and methods for the study of the human — they now worry that the promise of the movement may have been exhausted in this "protest" against behaviorism and psychoanalysis (Giorgi, 1987; Rogers, 1978; Tennessen, 1981). Others wonder if humanistic psychology, though successful in this protest, will now be surpassed by more scientific approaches to the human phenomena at first highlighted; cognitive developmental psychology and neuroscience being two popular examples (Smith, 1982). Still others argue that this protest battled with an overstated "straw man"; that academic psychology has in the past, and will in the future, pursue such goals without the assistance of humanistic psychology (Berlyne, 1981). Apparently, while most will agree on the goals to be achieved, there is little consensus within the discipline on the ability of humanistic psychology to provide a sea-worthy vessel for this journey.

From the above discussion, it would appear that humanistic psychology should be able to overcome any hesitations related to humanism's overstatement of the independence of the human by explicit acknowledgement and exploration of the intertwining of spirit and world, of person and culture. Humanistic psychology will only demonstrate its efficacy in this endeavor, however, by making original contributions to our understanding of human conduct and experience. The main criticism to be leveled against the movement is thus neither philosophical nor political in nature. Its major weakness is that it is perceived as having yet to produce much of lasting impact (Giorgi, 1987; Rogers, 1985). Even if we can agree that, while overstated, the goals of humanistic psychology are worthwhile, we still must wonder why, after 35 years of effort, this has been so difficult to achieve.

## Looking Toward the Future

With respect to its failure to have significant impact, humanistic psychology has certainly not reflected its humanist heritage. The art of Leonardo and Michelangelo, the political ideals of Rousseau and Jefferson, attest to the enduring quality of the contributions made by the humanist tradition to a range of human endeavors. Why is humanistic psychology perceived as having thus far failed in guiding psychology down similarly productive paths?

One possible response, suggested by Giorgi, is that it may be in the nature of humanistic psychology "never to dominate the psychological scene, but merely to bear witness that another mode of psychology is possible" (1987, p. 18). According to this view, it goes against the grain of humanistic psychologists to force their vision onto others, to manipulate their colleagues and patients in order to wrest power away from current, mainstream approaches. This understanding assumes that the movement has made substantial contributions but that these insights have met with an unappreciative reception in our alienated, dehumanized, technologically-oriented culture. Our only hope is that we will find a way to redeem our societies along with our science, making way for a more humanistic approach in our cultural and academic institutions (cf. Lerner, 1991; Levin, 1985).

Even if there is some validity to this view, it remains incumbent upon the current generation of humanistically-oriented psychologists to reflect on both the merits and limitations of the movement in order to see where progress might be made. A review of some of the more notable contributions that humanistic psychology has made (e.g., Maslow's work on self-actualization, Roger's on self-direction in therapy and education) suggests that perhaps the movement has confused its humanistic aims with the means through which to achieve them. We seem to have taken respect for the distinctively human and individual self-actualization as ends in themselves, rather than seeing them as providing points of departure for the development of ways to study and promote human growth and development. It should be with a respect for the distinctiveness of the human that we begin in developing a science of psychology, allowing that conviction to inform our methods. Such a conviction has too often appeared instead to be an end result, a "finding," of humanistic-psychological efforts. If we are to make original contributions to the understanding of psychological functioning, we cannot remain content with philosophical statements concerning various aspects of human nature. Rather, we will need to use these insights to encourage and guide our empirical investigations of various aspects of the concrete, everyday lives of people engaged in the struggle of living out their particular forms of humanity.

It will be important for us to recognize, in addition, that it is all people who are engaged in such struggles. While a real virtue of humanistic psychology has been its uncompromising insistence that all people, regardless of race, gender or IQ, have a right to pursue self-actualization, it has been difficult to remember that everyone is already engaged in this process in whatever context they happen to be living and against whatever odds they may be facing. Here too ends have been confused with means, as we have taken the achievement of human potential to be an end in itself, setting up arbitrary distinctions between those who are self-actualizing and those who are not, rather than seeing this as a process in which we are all engaged by virtue of our common nature. While Maslow's original work on self-actualization (e.g., 1968, 1970) pointed out that growth occurs indirectly through the pursuit of communal concerns that transcend the individual, some within the human potential movement have since taken self-actualization to be itself a goal for psychology. But as Friedman (1976) cogently argues, we cannot turn the process of growth into a goal without rendering it empty and meaningless. We do not grow by focusing on the self, but, as in Maslow's example of the Buddhist Bodhisattva, by venturing out from the self to an engagement with others and the world.

So how might we best use our convictions in the value and importance of human experience, freedom and meaning to guide the development of our psychology? How might we pursue a science of persons in relation to their bodily and spiritual dimensions, each other and their surrounding material, social and political worlds? I shall suggest three guidelines for future efforts in this direction.

*1) Determine the parameters that best define the nature of our subject matter and use them as a conceptual base upon which to build an empirical science.* We have seen that the human cannot be adequately defined in isolation or as independent from other ontological domains. Even if we remain convinced that the human represents a distinct and unique sphere, we need to decide how best to situate this sphere in relation to material and spiritual dimensions. Once we have mapped out the scope and nature of these relations, we will then have a basis upon which to articulate the interests, and develop the methods, for our new science. In this regard, I have found Husserl's (1952/1989) work on the various constituents of the domains of animate, psychic and spiritual reality particularly helpful in delineating the borders of the human domain as one point of intersection of Nature and Spirit. Through his concept of "regional ontology," he (1913/1983) has identified aspects of experience belonging specifically to the realm of the human, while also tracing out their connections to both higher and lower strata of sense. Of particular interest are the ways in which perceptual processes are built upon physiological sensations, to be taken up kinesthetically in the constitution of a sense of personal agency and volition (cf. Davidson, 1992). While not the only one to tackle these issues, Husserl has provided us with unusually intricate phenomenological analyses of the interweavings of Psyche, Spirit and Nature that provide an invaluable framework for a psychology of human experience. Other work of similar interest can be found in Merleau-Ponty (1942/1983, 1962), Straus (1966), Werner (1948) and contemporary neuroscience (cf. Dennett, 1991).

*2) Recognize that all people share this basic image of human being, and focus research on those groups deemed most in need of assistance.* It was an important early contribution of humanistic psychology to turn away from psychology's traditional focus on pathology to take up the more healthy aspects of human functioning. While this has broadened the scope of psychology to include such topics as love and creativity, it has also led humanistic psychologists at times to focus on esoteric phenomena that do not seem to be of pressing or wider significance. It seems to me that it would be more in line with humanistic psychology's aim of facilitating freedom and growth, and would also help in our quest to have more of an impact on the mainstream, if we focused our energies on those groups of people who are currently most in need of help from our social institutions and psychological healers. Investigating the experiences and issues of the homeless, the seriously mentally ill, survivors of sexual abuse and other trauma, those addicted to substances or struggling with chronic illness, or other wounded people will provide us with opportunities to study the range of vulnerabilities and virtues of human functioning in extreme cases. Examples of such research may be found in the work of Fischer and Wertz (1979) on experiences of being criminally victimized, Hagan (1986) on poor mothers who underuse health care, Draucker (1992) on surviving incest, Laing (1965) on the social and political context of schizophrenia, and Davidson and Strauss (1992) on recovering from severe mental disorder. Such research not only makes important contributions to areas of pressing and general concern, but also helps to restore "marginalized" individuals to the center of our image of human being. By recognizing in them the core of humanity that we all share, we will be taking an important step toward enhancing their freedom, improving their condition and justifying our own scientific approach.

*3) Develop empirical methods appropriate to the rigorous study of human experience in its complexity, richness and meaning.* Humanistic psychologists have been very divided in their attitude toward and use of "science." Some have eschewed science altogether as inappropriate for the humanistic study of experience in its meaningfulness, while others have argued for the development of new methods better-suited to this task, and still others have adopted unchanged traditional quantitative methods (cf. Giorgi, 1987). Meanwhile, it has become a truism of contemporary medical and social science that an interdisciplinary approach is required to fulfill the mandate of a "biopsychosocial model" (Engel, 1977, 1980) of human functioning. It is my impression that humanistic psychologists cannot only benefit from interdisciplinary collaborations with their colleagues in other social sciences and medicine, but that they can also make a unique contribution in terms of their understanding of the complex, rich and meaningful nature of human experience. A particularly valuable contribution would be the development of methods to be used in exploring this complexity and richness of meaning in a rigorous and empirical fashion. To take up this task, we will have to overcome what appears to have been a distaste for systematic study due to a suspicion that it will fail to do justice to distinctly human phenomena. In this respect, the field may benefit from examples set by such scientist-artists as Goethe and Coleridge who argued for a balance of Imagination with Method. While humanistic psychology has been strong on imagination, it can only benefit from a serious and sustained consideration of method. For assistance, we can consult the work of Geertz (1973, 1975), Giorgi (1970, 1985), Polkinghorne (1983, 1988), Bruner (1986), Mishler (1986) and Spence (1982) on qualitative methods and narrative research.

Perhaps it is ironic to end a review of humanistic psychology such as this with a reflection on method. Growing up in the era of behaviorism, with its rat and pigeon experiments, humanistic psychology has been wary of the application of scientific methods when this is done solely to serve the purpose of being scientific. Indeed, in such cases we have lost sight of human beings in the process of accumulating irrelevant and trivial facts. But we may not assume on this basis that all methods will equally fail us in our attempt to understand human functioning. We should strive instead to implement new methods built upon a recognition of the role of sense-making and story-telling in human experience. Methods such as those of ethnography, phenomenology and narrative research that encourage study of the lives of people as they unfold over time in their social milieu may offer us access precisely to those aspects of meaning, agency, creativity and value that most interest us. Science may liberate as much as constrict. This lesson has been taught to us as well by the masters of the Renaissance. Were we able to apply the kind of disciplined artistry in our attention to the details of human subjectivity that Michelangelo and Leonardo demonstrated in their grasp of the nuances of the human body, we would be well on our way to developing a science of psychology worthy of its humanistic heritage.

## References

Allport, G. W. (1937). *Personality: A psychological interpretation.* New York: Holt, Rinehart & Winston.

Allport, G. W. (1955). *Becoming: Basic considerations for a psychology of personality.* New Haven: Yale University Press.

Berlyne, D. E. (1981). Humanistic psychology as a protest movement. In J. Royce & L. Mos (Eds.), *Humanistic psychology: Concepts and criticisms* (pp. 261-293). New York: Plenum Press.

Bruner, J. (1986). *Actual minds, possible worlds.* Cambridge: Harvard University Press.

Bugental, J. F. T. (1963). Humanistic psychology: A new break-through. *American Psychologist, 18,* 563-567.

Bugental, J. F. T. (1978). The third force in psychology. In I. D. Welch, G. Tate & F. Richards (Eds.), *Humanistic psychology: A source book* (pp. 13-21). New York: Prometheus Books.

Bullock, A. (1985). *The humanist tradition in the West*. Great Britain: Thames and Hudson.

Campbell, E. (1984). Humanistic psychology: The end of innocence. *Journal of Humanistic Psychology, 24*, 6-29.

Davidson, L. (1992). Review of E. Husserl, *Ideas pertaining to a pure phenomenology and to a phenomenological philosophy. Second book: Studies in the phenomenology of constitution* (R. Rojcewicz & A. Schuwer, Trans.). *Journal of Phenomenological Psychology, 23*.

Davidson, L. & Cosgrove, L. (1991). Psychologism and phenomeno-logical psychology revisited, Part I: The liberation from naturalism. *Journal of Phenomenological Psychology, 22*, 87-108.

Davidson, L. & Strauss, J.S. (1992). Sense of self in recovery from severe mental illness. *British Journal of Medical Psychology*.

DeCarvalho, R.J. (1991). Gordon Allport and humanistic psychology. *Journal of Humanistic Psychology, 31*, 8-13.

Dennett, D.C. (1991). *Consciousness explained*. Boston: Little, Brown and Company.

Dilthey, W. (1977). *Descriptive psychology and historical understanding* (R. Zaner & K. Heiges, Trans.). The Hague: Nijhoff. (Original work published 1894)

Draucker, C.B. (1992). The healing process of female adult incest survivors: Constructing a personal residence. *Image, 24*, 4-8.

Engel, G. L. (1977). The need for a new medical model: A challenge for biomedicine. *Science, 196*, 129-136.

Engel, G. L. (1980). The clinical application of the biopsychosocial model. *American Journal of Psychiatry, 137*, 535-544.

Fischer, C. T. & Wertz, F. (1979). Empirical phenomenological analyses of being criminally victimized. In A. Giorgi, R. Knowles & D. Smith (Eds.), *Duquesne studies in phenomenological psychology* (Vol. 3) (pp. 141-158). Pittsburgh: Duquesne University Press.

Friedman, M. (1976). Aiming at the self: The paradox of encounter and the human potential movement. *Journal of Humanistic Psychology, 16*, 5-34.

Fromm, E. (1941). *Escape from freedom*. New York: Avon Books.

Fromm, E. (1955). *The sane society*. Greenwich, CT: Fawcett Publications.

Geertz, C. (1973). *The interpretation of cultures*. New York: Basic.

Geertz, C. (1975). On the nature of anthropological understanding. *American Scientist, 63*, 47-53.

Geller, L. (1982). The failure of self-actualization theory. *Journal of Humanistic Psychology, 22*, 56-73.

Giorgi, A. P. (1970). *Psychology as a human science: A phenomenologically based approach*. New York: Harper & Row.

Giorgi, A. P. (1981). Humanistic psychology and metapsychology. In J. R. Royce & L.P. Mos (Eds.), *Humanistic psychology: Concepts and criticisms* (pp. 19-47). New York: Plenum Press.

Giorgi, A. P. (Ed.). (1985). *Phenomenology and psychological research.* Pittsburgh: Duquesne University Press.

Giorgi, A.P. (1987). The crisis of humanistic psychology. *The Humanistic Psychologist, 15,* 5-20.

Graumann, C.F. (1981). Psychology: Humanistic or human? In J. Royce & L. Mos (Eds.), *Humanistic psychology: Concepts and criticisms* (pp.3-18). New York: Plenum Press.

Greening, T. (1985). The origins of the Journal of Humanistic Psychology and the Association for Humanistic Psychology. *Journal of Humanistic Psychology, 25,* 7-11.

Hagan, T. (1986). Interviewing the downtrodden. In P. Ashworth, A. Giorgi & A. de Koning (Eds.), *Qualitative research in psychology* (pp. 332-360). Pittsburgh: Duquesne University Press.

Heidegger, M. (1962). *Being and time* (J. Macquarrie & E. Robinson, Trans.). New York: Harper & Row. (Original work published 1927)

Heidegger, M. (1977). Letter on humanism (F. Capuzzi & J. Gray, Trans.). In D. F. Krell (Ed.), *Martin Heidegger: Basic writings* (pp. 190-242). New York: Harper & Row. (Original work published 1947)

Hergenhahn, B. R. (1986). *An introduction to the history of psychology.* Belmont, CA: Wadsworth.

Horney, K. (1939). *New ways in psychoanalysis.* New York: Norton.

Husserl, E. (1983). *Ideas pertaining to a pure phenomenology and to a phenomenological philosophy. First book: General introduction to a pure phenomenology* (F. Kersten, Trans.). The Hague: Nijhoff. (Original work published 1913)

Husserl, E. (1989). *Ideas pertaining to a pure phenomenology and to a phenomenological philosophy. Second book: Studies in the phenomenology of constitution* (R. Rojcewicz & A. Schuwer, Trans.). Boston: Kluwer Academic Publishers. (Original work published 1952)

Kant, I. (1929). *Critique of pure reason* (N. Kemp Smith, Trans.). New York: St. Martin's Press. (Original work published 1787)

Laing, R. D. (1965). *The divided self.* New York: Penguin Books.

Lerner, M. (1991). *Surplus powerlessness: The psychodynamics of everyday life and the psychology of individual and social transformation.* New Jersey: Humanities Press.

Levin, D. M. (1985). *The body's recollection of being: Phenomenological psychology and the deconstruction of nihilism.* London: Routledge & Kegan Paul.

Locke, J. (1959). *An essay concerning human understanding* (two volumes). New York: Dover. (Original work published 1690)

Mann, T. (1942). *What I believe.* New York: Knopf.

Maslow, A.H. (1968). *Toward a psychology of being* (2nd edition). New York: D. Van Nostrand.

Maslow, A.H. (1970). *Religions, values, and peak-experiences*. New York: Viking Press.

Matson, F. W. (1981). Epilogue. In J. Royce & L. Mos (Eds.), *Humanistic psychology: Concepts and criticisms* (pp. 295-304). New York: Plenum Press.

May, R. (1989). Answers to Ken Wilbur and John Rowan. *Journal of Humanistic Psychology, 29,* 244-248.

Merleau-Ponty, M. (1962). *Phenomenology of perception* (C. Smith, Trans.). New Jersey: Humanities Press.

Merleau-Ponty, M. (1968). *The visible and the invisible* (A. Lingis, Trans.). Evanston: Northwestern University Press. (Original work published 1964)

Merleau-Ponty, M. (1983). *The structure of behavior* (A. Fisher, Trans.). Pittsburgh: Duquesne University Press. (Original work published 1942)

Mishler, E. G. (1986). *Research interviewing: Context and narrative*. Cambridge: Harvard University Press.

Misiak, H. & Sexton, V. S. (1973). *Phenomenological, existential, and humanistic psychologies: A historical survey*. New York: Grune & Stratton.

O'Hara, M. (1989). When I use the term 'humanistic psychology' ... *Journal of Humanistic Psychology, 29, 263-273.*

Polkinghorne, D.E. (1983). *Methodology for the human sciences*. Albany: State University of New York Press.

Polkinghorne, D.E. (1988). *Narrative knowing and the human sciences*. Albany: State University of New York Press.

Prilleltensky, I. (1989). Psychology and the status quo. *American Psychologist, 44,* 795-802.

Rogers, C. R. (1978). Some questions and challenges facing a humanistic psychology. In I. Welch, G. Tate & F. Richards (Eds.), *Humanistic psychology: A source book* (pp. 41-45). Buffalo: Prometheus Books.

Rogers, C.R. (1985). Toward a more human science of the person. *Journal of Humanistic Psychology, 25,* 7-24.

Rousseau, J. J. (1947). *The social contract* (C. Frankel, Ed.). New York: Hafner Press. (Original work published 1762)

Sartre, J. P. (1956). *Being and nothingness* (H. Barnes, Trans.). New York: Washington Square Press. (Original work published 1943)

Sartre, J. P. (1963). *Search for a method* (H. Barnes, Trans.). New York: Knopf. (Original work published 1960)

Sartre, J. P. (1976). *Critique of dialectical reason* (A. Sheridan-Smith, Trans.). London: Verso. (Original work published 1960)

Slavney, P. & McHugh, P. (1987). *Psychiatric polarities*. Baltimore: Johns Hopkins Press.

Smith, M. B. (1982). Psychology and humanism. *Journal of Humanistic Psychology, 22*, 44-55.

Smith, M. B. (1986). Toward a secular humanistic psychology. *Journal of Humanistic Psychology, 26*, 7-26.

Smith, M. B. (1990). Humanistic psychology. *Journal of Humanistic Psychology, 30*, 6-21.

Spence, D. P. (1982). *Narrative truth and historical truth.* New York: Norton.

Spiegelberg, H. (1972). *Phenomenology in psychology and psychiatry.* Evanston: Northwestern University Press.

Straus, E. (1966). *Phenomenological psychology: Selected papers* (E. Eng, Trans.). New York: Basic Books.

Sutich, A. (1962). American Association for Humanistic Psychology: Articles of association. *Journal of Humanistic Psychology, 2*, 96-97.

Taylor, E. (1991). William James and the humanistic tradition. *Journal of Humanistic Psychology, 31*, 56-74.

Tennessen, H. (1981). The very idea of a 'humanistic psychology'. In J. R. Royce & L. Mos (Eds.), *Humanistic psychology: Concepts and criticisms* (pp. 253-260). New York: Plenum Press.

Vico, G. (1970). *The new science* (T. Bergin & M. Fisch, Trans.). Ithaca: Cornell University Press. (Original work published 1744)

Werner, H. (1948). *Comparative psychology of mental development.* New York: International Universities Press.

Wilbur, K. (1979). *No boundary.* Los Angeles: Center Publications.

Wilbur, K. (1981). *Up from Eden: A transpersonal view of human evolution.* Boulder: Shambhala.

Wilbur, K. (1989). Two humanistic psychologies? A response. *Journal of Humanistic Psychology, 29*, 230-243.

# 4

# Creativity, Humanistic Psychology and the American Zeitgeist

*Mike Arons*

This paper focuses on one "moment" of historical development in the United States, when two independent but overlapping movements emerged within the field of psychology: humanistic psychology and a surge of research interest in creativity. Both eruptions were reactions to that perceived limitations of psychology and the social climate of the times. American psychology, ostensibly and self-proclaimed to be objective, value-free and socio-culturally independent, has revealed itself as quite value-laden and bound to the paradigms of its society and times.

There has always been a spiritual quality to creativity, rooted as it is in the Judeo-Christian West, to the notion of "Original Creation": Here God did all the creating. The mode of reaching God was blind faith. This spiritual sense was again felt strongly during the European Renaissance — known for its bountiful individual creativity, but then connected with a philosophical linkage between Spirit with Nature. During the age of Enlightenment, it was science, particularly the physical sciences, which grabbed the torch of creativity and guided the Western imagination towards an understanding of the mystery of our sources, now presumed to be potentially disclosable in the regularities of nature. The mode to reaching the laws of nature was reason. Science was, Bronowski (1958) proclaimed, the greatest creative product of the Western mind and as even Maslow (1962) added: "only science could progress."

Post-war America held an almost total faith in scientific progress and its potential to reveal the ultimate meanings of our lives. Yet this faith in science increasingly contrasted with the spiritual sterility of materialistic life characteristic of that period. At this paradoxical juncture, experienced aridity in the midst of apparent progress, the creative processes themselves came to center a quest for a fuller sense of humanness. This in post-war America: rich, unscarred, unhumiliated and triumphantly naive. It is no accident that both creativity and humanistic psychology drew much original inspiration from the existential writings of post-war Europe. But much of their destiny — the directions in which these movements would evolve — included the consciousness and spiritual centered traditions of the Orient. Like the creative process itself, the movements of both creativity and humanistic psychology have been simultaneously progressive and regressive. After all, the term "originality" has two vectors, towards the new and unique and towards the origins: the source.

## Creativity *Zeitgeist*

The outbreak of interest in creativity in American psychology was ignited by J. P. Guilford (1950) in his Presidential address before the American Psychological Association. In that address he lamented the fact that for decades, practically no research interest had been shown in an area so humanly significant as creativity. He then offered four reasons why he felt such an interest had been retarded: 1) *Excessive preoccupation with I.Q. tests*, 2) *The domination of learning theory*, 3) *Prevalence of excessively rigid methodological standards*, and 4) *The inability to find agreement on criteria for researching creativity*. The first three reasons propose that the directions that much of American psychology had taken were in some ways incompatible with the study of creativity. The fourth reason suggests an inherent difficulty encountered at the problem level — an heuristic one we will consider below.

The common link between all the American psychologies at the time of Guilford's address was their lack of vitality. They did not lack activity. Indeed, as in American factories and in society generally at the time, "production rates" were high in the laboratories, in the diplomas issued, in the journals and on the therapists' couches. And, while Guilford had made only inferential reference to this point, productivity was at the time being uncritically (and soon to be demonstrated quite mistakenly) identified, both in psychology and society, with creativity. This distinction between productivity and creativity was a key one to emerge from the creativity literature.

Vitality at the theoretical and methodological levels was lacking during that period. Theoretically, both learning theory and classical psychoanalytic theory, grounded in mechanistic and Darwinian functionalistic preconceptions, held as basic a homeostatic model of the human by which "it" is "driven" toward the least amount of unpleasure, tension or anxiety. This Darwinian stress on biological adaptation — through a social Darwinism — was translated in much of psychology and the society as a whole into an almost singly valued notion of social adjustment. Norms of social adjustment were equated with psychological health. At the extreme, particularly at the applied and popular level, "social adjustment," "hence psychological norm," "hence psychological health" was frequently interpreted to be social conformity.

The applied level encompassed more than business, industry and education. It included psychology itself, as a field of work, where there came to exist inordinately narrow standards of proper behavior. Many of these were dictated by the apparent urgency for psychology to become a science, in that sense that science was interpreted by psychology. The methodological rigidity (construed as rigor) of this image of 19th century physics worked to grossly narrow the range of personalities permitted into the field or who would choose the field. It worked to preclude any interest in the individual, gender, racial or cultural issues, which were not amenable to the methodology regardless of how relevant these were to understanding of humans. The stress on the external, formal accoutrements of 19th century physics — laboratories, equipment and apparati, control and certification down to the white lab jacket — required that psychologists conform to an almost laughable stereotype. The atmosphere clearly worked against risk, exploration and speculation and towards safety, compulsive repetition and rigid exactness. One can find here, as a necessary reaction, some seeds to the study of creativity.

The value on social adjustment had been built into the testing movement almost from its inception. While such testing was developed in the name of distinguishing individual differences, a tendency away from conformity, the growth of the testing movement in America owes much to its relationship with social institutions, such as the military, business and industry, education and governmental social agencies. It is obvious that testers are employed by institutions to serve their interest. And it would have been difficult for the testing movement not to have been biased by these interests. But further, the relationship of the testing movement to the prevailing scientism of American psychology meant that no findings could be considered reliable or valid which could not pass the rigors of this methodology. Psychological tests, whatever their recognized or unrecognized limits and deficiencies, were applied to masses of people in many sectors of the society. Since these were often used in selection procedures, tests came to take on values by which critical life affecting judgments were made.

Like Ford's standardized car, the standardized I.Q. test is largely an American product. When imported from France in its early individualized form, where it had been used in a limited and selective manner, it was given a standardized form to meet both the exigencies of scientific certification and the expediency needs for mass application. Standardization removed the instrument from a context in which interpretations of test results that might have revealed originality could be evaluated in individual context. The impetus for the popularity of the standardized I.Q. test came largely from the work of Lewis Terman at Stanford University. Above all, Terman (1947) pointed out, nothing more characterized his high I.Q. subjects than *"a drive to achieve and their all around social adjustment."*

Because of what he saw as their intellectual superiority, Terman went on to call his highest scorers "genius." Thus a new link, consistent with the rationalistic-utilitarian bias of the times and the American image of "melting pot" with its dream of itself as a haven for material success, was created between genius and social adjustment. That link ran counter to traditional stereotypes which offered the image of the genius as psychologically unstable and socially non-adaptive. Some psychologists, holding to the more traditional presumptions, took strong exception to Terman's view on this matter. They pointed out, and Terman was obliged to acknowledge, that few of Terman's "geniuses" had accomplished any major creative breakthroughs, though they had indeed "succeeded" in traditional occupations such as law, military, etc. Further, according to the Lange-Eichbaum studies (1932) which Terman strongly disputed, the recognized creative geniuses of the Western world had shown a much higher proportion of emotional instability and social maladjustment than members of the population at large; in fact, the greater the genius, the greater the maladjustment.

If the more romantic image of "genius" persisted in the public mind, this utilitarian, Terman image of "genius" began to dominate in the institutions, notably in formal education. Terman's studies had shown, at least at the extremes, correlations which linked this educational mission to utilitarian productivity (vocational-professional) and psychological successes. In a mass movement not followed anywhere else in the world except in Great Britain, where the "11+" (I.Q.) exam came to determine a child's future, and feeding on the utilitarian social *Zeitgeist,* the testing craze reached the point that most American school districts required all students to be tested and often cursorily judged and academically slotted them in terms of test scores. Possible limitations and biases of the I.Q. test were first ignored, then forgotten, as the instrument gained ever wider popularity. The abuses of I.Q. testing reached such major proportions that by the 1960's, many of the major cities in the country — including Los Angeles — had banned the test. Certainly much of the rebellion in the United States, aimed at education and expressed in psychology by the creativity movement, was directed, if not exclusively at the I.Q. test, at the values which correlated so well to this test. It is no coincidence that the earliest studies on creativity after Guilford's talk focused on the limitations of I.Q. tests and showed, by implication, the extent to which these instruments were reinforcing the most conservative, devitalizing and unoriginal dimensions of the society.

J. W. Getzels and P. Q. Jackson (1962) were able to demonstrate that I.Q. tests did not measure originality and that there was no correlation between originality and intelligence as measured by the I.Q.. What's more, those scoring high *exclusively* on I.Q. tests tended to share the traditional values of their teachers and parents; they were highly goal directed and achievement orientated in terms of socio-economic goals; they lacked originality and a sense of humor; they tended to be organizationally efficient and have little time for idle inquiry and exploration; and they tended to show only minor interest in self understanding. By contrast, those scoring significantly lower on I.Q. tests but high on measures designed to tap originality, manifested considerably greater independence of judgment, considerably more awareness of their emotions and experiences; they permitted themselves to express greater emotional instability, accepted ambiguity, and tended to value self exploration and philosophical questioning over efficient and success oriented thinking.

Guilford (1950) had himself pointed out one key to this difference between the original thinkers and the high I.Q. scorers that is inherent to the I.Q. test itself. The standardized I.Q. test required, always, one correct answer. Evidently this was an answer taken from existing public knowledge, hence, by definition, unoriginal. He called the thinking leading to success on these tests "convergent" and differentiated this from original or "divergent" thinking characteristic of more creative individuals. An original answer could not have been designed into a test without diminishing the capacity for standardization of scoring.

*Expressive Role of Creativity Research*

The major scientific weakness of the research on creativity during the 1950's and 1960's can be attributed to what Guilford (1950) cited as the fourth problem leading to retardation of the study of creativity, the problem of criteria. There had never been agreement on just what creativity was. Could a child's doodles be called creative, or even potentially creative, and hence comparable to the great and recognized works of art? This is a question more centered on values than evidence. Therefore, this very scientific "soft spot" in the creativity research can serve heuristically to indicate prevailing social expression. So viewed, these studies expressed, largely by implication, the perceived problems in psychology and the society at the time. This research had a particularly American flavor. One can start with the observation that American psychologists showed a much greater, more concentrated interest in "creativity" at that juncture in history than did their colleagues in other cultures.

But the concentrated American interest in creativity shows up more clearly as a social expression when we consider the 1) type of variables researchers tended to select as relevant, 2) normative implications built into traits or variables diametrically opposed to those seen related to creativity, and finally, 3), implications of some cross-cultured studies which had a bearing on creativity research.

A number of studies, as indicated earlier, tried to differentiate creativity from other constructs which had, in psychology and the society, become confused with creativity. High scores on I.Q. correlated with "convergent," efficient, goal-directed problem solving. By contrast, creativity correlated with "divergent," open-ended cognition, old problems seen in new ways. The research on creativity — certainly in the early phase — implied value judgments. Creativity was seen as very "desirable", the "good guy", and in opposition to the "less desirable" or often the "bad guy". This reflected a strong, if indirect, form of reaction against what had been given such high value status in psychology and the society.

Examples of commonly cited traits or adjectives correlated positively with creativity were: originality, affective surprise, humor, the unpredictable, metaphorical thinking, intuition, impulse or "inner voice", formal appeal, psychological regressing in the interest of progression, risk, moods, openness to childhood perceptions and conflicts, complexity of perceptions, the ability to experience freshly, transcendence of polarities and apparent incompatibilities, seeking truth or beauty beyond expediency and needs for tension reduction, independence of judgement, whole-part integration, growth centering, preference for complexity, ambiguity, a-symmetry, mystery and playfulness with spirit and humor, incorporation of apparent polarities such as the affective with the logical sides of his/her nature, etc.

Generally, these traits or characteristics that typically correlated with creativity offered a picture or model which was alien or threatening to values dominant in psychology and the society at the time, exemplified by: stress on predictability, repetition and compulsive discharging of duties; the view of progress as linear; expediency values of socially recognized achievement, popularity, and productivity; stress on external authority, neatness, precision, and consensual validation; disdain for intellectualism, fixed social patterns and sentimental traditions; suppression of "unacceptable" emotions as well as ideas which deviate from accepted norms; and preference for finished product over process. Other characteristics which seemed to oppose creativity traits were reductionism to the unequivocal, stress on a "maturity" which fails to distinguish childishness from childlikeness, failure to distinguish the simplistic from simplicity, preference for a judgmental attitude over existential awareness (Getzels, 1962; Barron, 1963; Taylor & Barron, 1963; Taylor, 1964).

*Cross Cultural Comparisons*

Very few cross-cultural studies showed up in the literature on creativity research, but three are revealing. They suggest a need in American psychology for what was lacking in society at that period. At an early phase of the creativity focus, social psychologists such as S. E. Asch (1952) and R. S. Crutchfield (1963) had become interested in the problem of conformity. The results of these studies were surprising in that they revealed that conformity, seen as non-independence of judgement, was a dominant mode of behavior even, where it might be the least expected, at the better American universities. These results contrasted with results of like studies with students in Sweden and France where far greater independence of judgment was reported. Frank Barron (1972) and his colleagues found that second generation Italian children living in Boston did more poorly on his Barron-Welsh test than did children of the same families born and still living in Italy. Dorothy Lee (1959) related this lack of originality and conformity among Americans at the period to a variety of cultures she had studied.

These cross-cultural studies suggest that the lack of creativity, and those characteristics correlated with this, had been a serious American problem. This moves towards an understanding of why American psychologists so intently focused on this area. The creativity *Zeitgeist*, although seen as isolated at this time, was one related dimension of a much greater reaction swelling up within the American society and particularly through and against its psychology.

## The Greater Reaction

The American studies on creativity, both in their investigative and expressive aspects, paralleled and helped predispose the emergence of a humanistic psychology and a radical shift in American consciousness. Psychology has never been the same, nor has its society. The creativity *Zeitgeist* challenged a psychology defined by its ability to predict and control behavior with a vital, conscious human subject whose mark was originality which, by definition, is neither predictable nor controllable. It obliged that field to confront a greatly expanded and more complex picture of the human subject, one coinciding with the views of existential philosophers of post-war Europe. Philosophy, in the eyes of American psychologists, had already been dismissed as merely "prescientific." Frank Barron well forewarned the field of the complex and paradoxical potential of the human in his description of the creative genius:

> Thus the creative genius is at once naive and knowledgeable, being at home equally to primitive symbolism and to rigorous logic. He is both more primitive and more cultured, more destructive and more constructive, occasionally crazier and yet adamantly saner than the average person. (1968, p. 224)

The other movement, largely American and inspired by the insights of European existentialism, was Humanistic Psychology. These two reactions from within, separately and in tandem, helped in part to set the stage for major transformations which came to characterize the field and society in the 1960's and 1970's. Over those two decades, the field of psychology has expanded enormously. The definition of psychology now seen in a growing number of textbooks, reincludes the focus on experience and consciousness which is again returned to legitimacy. This, of course, is due largely to the emergence of cognitive psychology. Yet there has also been a shift from the purely academic-research to a more person-centered focus, a shift that significantly influenced the unprecedented growth of clinical and counseling oriented psychologies, which first and most fully came to recognize dimensions of the humanistic model (Zinker, 1977). Even the academic-research wing, previously monopolizing the field with its 19th century model of science, has been, albeit slowly and grudgingly, forced to open to more idiographic and qualitative approaches to research, such as phenomenology, which have from the start been linked to the humanistic movement (Arons, 1987). Yet humanistic psychology has not become the center of gravity in psychology, nor have its values and construal of the human been anything but superficially assimilated into the soul of the society. Creativity and humanistic psychology are reminders, often forgotten, of what else is possibly human. The 1960's and early 1970's were that period when that "possible human" was brought most fully to our collective consciousness. We are too close to ourselves now to know what the 1990's might bring. But at the end of this chapter we can throw a few brush strokes on the canvass of our own period in light of Rollo May's vision of history: Our Renaissance is still ahead of us (see his discussion in this volume).

*Humanistic Shift in the Focus of Creativity*

Within psychology, at the same time as the methodology was being challenged by the complexities introduced by the creativity research and the humanistic vision, the theoretical underpinnings of a behavioristic psychology were being put into serious question. Its reductionistic and deterministic model of the human was forced to confront a model of the creative dynamically inner directed human. Still, the general model of creativity was from the outset an essentially behavioristic one. The cognitive model that is now predominant is equally determined and limited by the methodology but also by traditional Western views of creativity. For creativity to be even considered present, it has been obligatory that there be some tangible creative product. It seemed self-evident to the Western mind that creativity would be product centered. Thus, preparatory to most of this creativity research, the creative individual was first identified by his or her productions and then studied in terms of how and by whom that product came into being via the focus on the antecedent processes or the predisposing personality traits.

A profound shift of emphasis occurred with the onset of humanistic psychology. Maslow (1959) for one, distinguished two major kinds of creativity: one which was obviously talent centered, the other growth centered:

> I shall confine myself to a kind of creativeness which is the universal heritage of every human being that is born and which seems to co-vary with psychological health". (Maslow, 1962, p. 127)

This second was more a creative way of life, a way as one potential realized by those whom Maslow described as self-actualizing individuals. Many of these self-actualizers, unlike the renowned creative genius, could not be recognized by tangible creative products. It was extremely difficult to identify or to study such persons with rigorous scientific methodology. And Maslow's new, broader construal of creativity might well have been ignored completely had it not been for the wedge that creativity research had placed in the doorway of general psychology. Much that had been written of the creative process and personality of recognized creative artists, scientists, etc. correlated with traits of persons whose tangible productions were absent or not apparent, or, perhaps as in the case of women (who showed up rarely in the typical creativity literature), whose characteristic products were not previously appreciated in light of this external product-centered focus on creativity. The humanists were beginning to offer a different kind of challenge to psychology, one of finding health indications, previously reserved for an elite, in the broader human potential. The aim became to understand the human subject at what Maslow would call his/her best. And that best was not necessarily indicated by the tangible-observable, but more often by internal transformations and expanded consciousness. Maslow's self actualizers were the very products of their own internally evolving creativity.

In the meantime, humanistic psychology was becoming an umbrella for a wide variety of ideas, theories, interests and approaches which shared (sometimes only this) a centering on psychological growth, or a new psychology focused on psychological health. This popularization of the "health model" was also abetted by Guilford's (1950) urging for a broadened definition of creativity, i.e., transformations from a special gift type (the Mona Lisa) to a humanly endowed creative potential (as in child's doodles). This redefinition, added to the views of Erikson (1959), Maslow (1962) and Buhler (1968, pp. 127-168), indicated the path of self actualization as a life long one. Much of the American public had little trouble identifying with this broadened model as speaking to their own personal potential, recently exploited in: "Be all that you can be... in the AAAArmy."

*Humanistic Transformations within the Society*
While Maslow was an academic psychologist, and while most of the early theoretical positions leading to a humanistic psychology came from academic psychology or philosophy, some of the first and most enduring insights into what was later to be identified under this name were developing in business, industry and social organizations. Maslow and others like Rogers and Combs, in the Dewey tradition, were reinspiring education and this abetted by considerable influence from creativity researchers like Torrance (1964). It was in the society that the problems of alienation, mechanization and inauthentic personal relationships had become the most pressing. These problems were adequately portrayed in such literature of the times as *Who's Afraid of Virginia Woolf* or *Rebel Without a Cause*. Paul Goodman (1960), among a growing band of others, was articulating the conformity and alienation so widely experienced across the nation. It was mandatory that this broadly based social pathology, articulated by the existentialists, be addressed, and this most appropriately by psychology. In light of the new personal growth model, Colin Wilson (1966) offered a new way of looking at classical neurotic symptoms, seeing these as "the rust which forms on a non-moving organism."

Maslow's (1965) writings were first taken seriously in economics and business, where success at the profit end of the enterprise had not correlated with success at the level of human relations. In fact, Maslow had theorized that profits could actually be increased if a "being" rather than "deficiency" model of motivation were adopted. The National Training Laboratories, in Bethel, Maine, had for a long time been operating an institute based on developing more authentic human relations in the business and industrial field. An array of direct experience techniques had been evolved for this purpose. It was out of this experimentation that problems of alienation, mechanization, and inauthentic personal relationships had revealed themselves as so deeply embedded in the social structure of the times. The Bethel model of "T" Groups, largely inspired by Kurt Lewin, came to support a broader model of the encounter group that burgeoned into popularity at centers around the nation, the best known being Esalen Institute. These growth centers and a wide and rapidly expanding array of approaches, theories and techniques, all centered on the "growth model", seemed to speak forcefully to people across the land as no psychology had previously done. A large disaffected segment of American society in the 1960's was more than ready for a humanistic psychology and the new vision of the creative human it fostered.

Meanwhile, in line with this new vision, the newly revitalized term "consciousness" began to take popular hold. A series of social movements sprouted up around the land, each focusing on consciousness and each speaking to the fuller actualization of individuals or groups: thus evolved the movements called "New Consciousness," "Black Consciousness," "Women's Consciousness" and "Gay Consciousness." The meaning of "consciousness" in these contexts has far more to do with the freedom, power, and holistic growth theoretically reflected in humanistic psychology than with the information processing theory which was emerging during the same period in cognitive psychology, despite the eventual dominance of the later in the discipline of psychology.

*Transformations within Psychology*

Other developments in humanistic psychology, particularly those approaches which were opening individuals to the resources within themselves, began to make the natural scientific psychology less palatable as a potential answer to human concerns. The shift in emphasis towards inner development and personal understanding predisposed a shift in emphasis from indirect (inferentially rational) to direct (spiritual) understanding and realization. If for several recent centuries it had been believed that humans could gain "salvation" only through a collective scientific understanding of natural lawfulness, which knowledge could then be reapplied through scholarship or technology, the new thrust in psychology seemed to open up the possibility of immediate, individual understanding (Arons, 1976). Personal growth and self understanding could be and were intrinsically combined and best gainable through direct experience. Increasingly, (compatible with the evolution of the writings of Maslow and other humanistic psychologists) these PERSONAL growth centers began to evolve into centers exploring dimensions of the human which purportedly extend "beyond," well "beyond," the personal...to the transpersonal.

*Transpersonal Psychology*

Maslow and the Third Force had already sketched out, in speaking of "self-actualizer," dimensions of human potential some of which were familiar to everyday personal experience and some quite unfamiliar to most people. Beyond those needs which he considered basic to survival and to which any kind of an "adjustment" or "coping" psychology might legitimately address itself, he elaborated a variety of "higher" level needs, all of which still fell within the range of human potential. Many of these higher order needs, such as appreciation for aesthetics, had long been culturally acknowledged. But Maslow (1966), remaining within a scientific ( as opposed to supernatural or theological) context, also went on to speak of experiences, or potentials, which were quite alien to that society. He spoke of "peak," transcendent, mystical and "plateau" experiences which were also, but very rarely, experienced or culturally acknowledged dimensions of that postulated human potential. Nothing could have been more alien or more antagonistic to any conventional American psychology at the time than mystical experiences.

Maslow's was not the first recent introduction of such experience in psychology. However, none of these previous intimations had really gotten off the drawing board in the positivitic climate of the times. Freud had alluded to, but shunned dealing with, the "Oceanic Experience". Bergson and Jung's influence on American psychology was slight at the time. Ironically, Fechner, "father of experimental psychophysiology" was forgotten or forgiven for his trespasses into the mystical. William James (1902/1985) was far better remembered for the first laboratory he began in psychology and soon abandoned, than for his *Varieties of Religious Experiences*. Sharing a like fate, Gardner Murphy whistled a lonely tune in this area. But reports of mystical experiences were not uncommonly reported in the research literature on creativity. Something akin to such experiences appeared with a certain regularity as part of an artist's or scientist's creative process. Of his ideas, Mozart wrote: "Whence and how they come, I know not, nor can I force them" (Ghislen, 1952).

Something as bizarre as the mystical experience had been knocking at experimental psychology's door for some time prior even to the studies on creativity. This was the all but rejected pocket of research in the area of parapsychology, directed by J.B. Rhine at Duke University and concerned with "the supernatural." There now exists a clearer distinction between parapsychology and transpersonal psychology However, even in the ancient Veda texts, these are seen as sometimes related; individuals involved in one of these spheres are often involved in the other.

There was yet another point at which experimental psychology had been introduced to what is now being called transpersonal psychology. This is the research pioneered by Leary and Alpert at Harvard on psychedelic drug experiences. Reports of drug induced experiences which bordered on, simulated, or were mystical prevalently emerged in this project. The research and drugs were so controversial at the university, in psychology and in the society, that those investigators were obliged to leave their institutions. Both Leary (1983) and Alpert left science, the former seeking direct "salvation" through the drug, the latter ultimately seeking direct "salvation" through naturally induced mystical experiences developed in the Orient.

The general stress held common to all of the above became roughly merged under the heading of transpersonal psychology. And here, perhaps as nowhere else, did a reintegration of psychology with philosophy, theology and the arts become an historical necessity (Klee, 1970). From Gudjieff and the Western esoteric to the vast spiritual literature emanating from Oriental psychology, the transcendental writers and poets of the West, the Judeo-Christian-Islamic mystical tradition, Shamanism of the Native American tradition, classical Hellenic metaphysics, all became relevant to the new kind of psychological investigation which was rapidly developing entirely outside the academic sphere. Transpersonal psychology has found no home in the American Psychological Association except with some delay and much reluctance on both sides, in the Division of Humanistic Psychology.

*Creativity and the Humanistic/Transpersonal Revolution*

Linked in their historical evolution, humanistic and transpersonal psychologies are now sometimes treated as different dimensions and destinies of the same human potential and, by some, are even seen as oppositional. Some transpersonalists, presupposing as Westerners a linear construal of the Chakra system, view the "transpersonal" as a quantum opening to the "higher" or "spiritual", while some humanists such as Rollo May (see the discussion with May in this volume), pejoratively dismiss these transpersonalists as airy fairy New Agers, or as escapists from the existential, personal and social realities of this historical age. Few, thus far, have looked at this distinction as two destinies branching from a common experience in the creative process, i.e., the tapping of the intuitive, one disposition favored in the West with its stress since the Renaissance on tangible individual creativity and the other favored in the East with its stress on internal self-development.

One juncture at which Maslow touched the line between humanistic and transpersonal psychologies was the distinction he drew between two types of creativity. The new type, not talent and product centered, and not recognized by Western researchers or Westerners in general, implies an internal, growth centered, creative process characteristic of his self actualizing subjects, but also of Eastern mystics. It may be instructive to reflect on the distinction made by Ferren (1953):

> Both artist and mystic, at the time of insight, experience a deep sense of personal fulfillment. But the mystic works gratuitously for revelation alone. The creative worker is predatory; he grabs the insight for a filled purpose; he is far less than divine, and the Promethean fire snatching symbol seems very apt.

Substitute "artist" with "Western destiny" and "mystic" with "Eastern path of salvation," and we glimpse in Ferren's description a bridge in human experience which links two apparently different outcomes at the level of "insight", in French, "prise de conscience" (the taking of consciousness). Both can be called creative paths but one taken by the Occident, the other by the Orient. Western creative individuals acknowledge the great role intuition plays in their creative success. By similar processes, e.g., suspension of ego dominance, transpersonal psychologists focus on opening to a greater collective source of all understanding, a "unitary consciousness," a universal energy, which expresses itself through everything, that is, anything which can be conceived of as separate, as *individual* and in the case of people, *personal*. This consciousness/energy is ever present for "tapping" and speaks through persons "tapping." It is sometimes referred to as "superconsciousness" and is otherwise known as intuition.

*Creativity, Humanistic Psychology and Now*

The popularized inner search crested in the late 1970's, effectively terminating at Jonesville and in narcissism, almost immediately and symmetrically replaced by Heritage U.S.A. and greed. The Age of Aquarius, by astrological birth signs, turned out to be the Reagan era. Creativity came to be explored in safe computer-simulated models where, under the control of "cognitive science" (Sternberg, 1985), it was viewed as a step by step process no different from any other "problem solving." Or it was avidly practiced as entrepreneurship, risk management and "the vision thing," now worshipped by the conservative Right, i.e., yesterday's radical Left and the former Evil Empire. Self actualization was recast in "upscaling" activity terms. We may, in the 1990's, be beyond even this. Mirror Mirror, has been discretely silent. But our current times here in America are unsettled and unsettling. Something unpleasant is oozing from the edges of "artificial time" (Rifkin, 1987), and our artificially injected bosoms of self-esteem. Now an entire society is feeling Camus' (1955 p. 4) "worm at the heart": "the undermining." The forth and back meanings of the 1960's through 1980's, which had replaced the meaningless 1950's, are dissolving, often into meanness. We reach for our deepest myths (Houston, 1991) to hold things together — or for "Virtual Reality" to put us back in charge. Our stewarted earth, in pain, bites its master. The ghost of McCluhan taunts that of Gutenberg. The ideals which served us for centuries are postmodernly melting into some transmuting species of irreal-reality which feels to many awfully foreboding and which is experienced as squiggly and chaotic. Psychedelics are back, replacing the "uppers". Our physical scientists (Bohm, 1987) now explore "Chaos Theory" and some of our humanistic-transpersonal psychologists, who yanked psychology from the old physics, are feeling right at home in this new one. Perhaps we can recognizing familiar and exhilarating messages from the creative heart, viz, chaos is pregnant with order.

## References

Arons, M. M. (1976). Transformations of science and religion. *Division of Humanistic Psychology Newsletter*, 4 (1), 1-2.

Arons, M. M. (1987). Creativity and the methodological debate: A mytho-historical reflection. In F.J. van Zuuren, F. J. Wertz, & B. Mook (Eds). *Advances in qualitative psychology* (pp.79-97). Lisse: Swets and Zeitlinger B. V. & Berwyn: Swets North America.

Arons, M. M. (1990). A new look at the enemies of parapsychology. *Theta*, 16(2&3), 24-26.

Asch, S. E. (1952). *Social psychology*. Englewood Cliffs, NJ: Prentice Hall.

Barron, F. X. (1968). *Creativity and personal freedom* (rev.ed.). Princeton, NJ: Van Nostrand.

Barron, F. X. (1972) Personal communication.

Bronowski, J. (1958). The creative process. *Scientific American, 199*, 63-64.

Buhler, C. (1968). Fulfillment and the value of life. In F. Massarick (Ed.), *The course of human life* (pp. 127-168). New York: Springer.

Crutchfield, R. S. (1963). Conformity and creative thinking. In W. Henry (Ed.), *Contemporary approaches to creative thinking*. New York: Atherton.

Erikson, E. H. (1959). *Identity and life cycle*. New York: International Universities Press.

Flanagan, J. C. (1963). Definition and measurement of ingenuity. In C. W. Taylor & F. Barron (Eds.), *Scientific creativity: Its recognition and development* (pp. 89-98). New York: Wiley.

Ferren, J. (1953). The problem of creative thinking in painting. In *The nature of creative thinking*. Industrial Relations Institute.

Getzels, J. W., & Jackson, P. W. (1962). *Creativity and intelligence.* London & New York: Wiley.
Ghislen, B. (1952). *The creative process.* Berkeley, CA: University of California Press.
Ghislen, B. (1963). Ultimate criteria for two levels of creativity. In C. W. Taylor & F. Barron (Eds.), *Scientific creativity: Its recognition and development* (pp. 30-43). New York: Wiley.
Goodman, P. (1960). *Growing up absurd.* New York: Random House Press.
Guilford, J. P. (1950). Creativity. *American psychologist, 5,* 444-453.
Houston, J. (1992). *The hero and the goddess.* New York: Ballantine Books.
James, W. (1902/1985) *The varieties of religious experience.* Cambridge, MA: Harvard University Press.
Klee, J.B. (1970). The one-dual and multiple. *Main currents in modern thought, 26,* 116-120.
Lange-Eichbaum, W. (1962). *The problem of genius* (E. Paul & C. Paul, Trans.). New York: Wiley. (Original work published 1932).
Leary, T. (1990). *Flashback: An autobiography.* Los Angeles, CA: Tarcher.
Lee, D. (1959). *Freedom and culture.* New York: Prentice Hall.
Maslow, A. H. (1959). Creativity in self-actualizing people. In H. H. Anderson (Ed.), *Creativity and its cultivation* (pp. 83-89). New York: Harper.
Maslow, A. H. (1962). *Towards a psychology of being.* Princeton, NJ: Van Nostrand.
Maslow, A.H. (1965). *Eupsychian management.* Homewood, IL: Dorsey Press.
Maslow, A. H. (1966). *I-Thou knowledge in a psychology of science.* New York: Harper & Row.
Rifkin, S. (1987). *Time wars.* New York: Holt.
Sprecher, T. B. (1964). Criteria of creativity. In Taylor & Calvin (Eds.), *Creativity: Progress and potential* (pp. 155-185). New York: McGraw Hill.
Sternberg, R. S. (1985). *Human abilities: An information processing approach.* New York: Freeman.
Terman, L. M., & Oden, M. H. (1947). The gifted child grows up. In L. M. Terman (Ed.), *Genetic studies of genius* (Vol. 55). Stanford, CA: Stanford University Press.
Torrance, E. P. (1964). Education and creativity. In Taylor and Calvin (Eds.), *Creativity: Progress and potential* (pp. 49-128). New York: McGraw Hill.
Wilson, C. (1966). *Introduction to the new existentialism* London: Hutchinson.
Zinker, J. (1977). *Creative process in Gestalt therapy.* New York. Vantage.

# 5

# Firebrand — The Experience of Being Different[1]

## Clark Moustakas

When I consider the transitions that have stood out in my development in recent years, I awaken to an acute awareness of the urgent need for freedom, autonomy, and self-direction in life and the threats to these values that surround us everywhere. Sometimes there is no other way but through direct confrontation with people who are manipulating and controlling our lives and whose aim is to deny, block and restrain us from the freedom of being and from creative self-expression. Increasingly, I am discovering the imperative of facing people openly when the truth of my world is being ignored, denied, or altered to suit their needs and purposes.

People in high professional and political positions, people of power, are daily proclaiming the necessity and justification for restrictive regulations and programs, the fine measure of their purposes and goals. All the while, the world is threatened with extinction, the environment is increasingly polluted and structures are collapsing. What "they" call growth is in reality something decaying, dying or dead. What they call 'entering a new era' is another form of darkness. In the mainstream of the everyday world, the breach between promise and actuality grows deeper and wider.

---

[1] All rights reserved. Copyright ©1993 by Clark Moustakas

## Carol: Family Firebrand

A long time ago Carol, a child I had been meeting with in play therapy, taught me how politics works in a family. She showed me how a person in authority might call something good that is actually harmful, might label something "enhancing" that is blemished, and impure. I still remember that first day when Carol paced back and forth in the playroom, a proud, defiant little girl, determined to speak out on behalf of her own truth. She had learned a critical lesson of life. In the segment that follows, drawn from a significant hour with Carol, she refers to her mother who regularly attempted to persuade her that what she offered her was in her best interests. "It's only for your own good darling," she would say, and it always turned out to be rotten for Carol.

> "I have to shine my glasses", Carol would shout over and over again, in the playroom. "*Some* glasses she gave me. I'm gonna tell her this is not good. It's not even glass."
>
> "She gave you some pretty poor glasses?"
>
> "Now listen," Carol screamed, pointing her finger, "I want some good glasses." She pretended to open the new package. "Same old glasses."
>
> "She gives you rotten ones again. You've been cheated so many times."
>
> "Yes, they always look shining but they're no good."

Ultimately Carol prevailed as a distinctive person because she dared repeatedly to bring her own light into the family darkness. No matter how often her parents tried to convince her that what they told her was for her own good she knew that something was radically wrong with the way she was being treated in her family. Carol survived because she refused to eat the apple that her parents fed her.

Carol was the trouble maker in her family because she dared to question what she was being told. She knew she did not want or need what her parents insisted was best for her. She inflamed her parents by bringing her own being into their world, by daring to be the firebrand in her family, daring to stand by her own perceptions, judgments, and preferences, and daring to decide for herself what things are and mean. She constantly agitated them, mirrored their hypocrisy, and revealed their deceptiveness and dishonesty.

## Description of the Firebrand

The firebrand is the person who recognizes what is natural, what is organic, what is alive and vital in life, the person who dares to live, to be, and to create, often in the face of interference, rejection, deceit, and betrayal. The firebrand is a burning ember, life that is in each of us and that provides the spark and energy to speak against what distorts, hides and denies our being and truth. It is that which awakens within us, when we must declare our independence or when we discover a new formula for living. It is the path that enables us to participate in the mystery of creation, uniquely and individually. The firebrand expresses herself or himself in two basic ways: As the torch that lights up the darkness, and as the carrier of the torch, throwing light into the darkness, and often disturbing complacency and brewing trouble. Being a firebrand is a way of raising temperatures and creating conflict, turbulence, and dissension.

The motive of the firebrand is not to attack or destroy others but to bring to light a basic truth, to take a stand, and to declare and own who one is, especially in the face of perceived violations of one's values and rights, and interferences with one's goals, purposes, and meanings.

In relation to one's self, the firebrand engages in reflection and self-dialogue that evokes awareness of ideas, projects and goals, insights into one's deviance from others, and particularly from mainstream people. The firebrand chooses to be different when being different represents a truth, when being different guides the fulfillment of basic human values and actualization of one's potentials.

In relation to others, the firebrand seeks to maintain what is unique and distinctive, what will enrich a relationship and keep it alive in fundamental ways. The firebrand avoids roles, categories, classifications, hierarchies, fixed routines, and practices but rather seeks to create rituals, searches for new rhythms and connections with others, keeps secrets and confidences and engages in conflicts and intimacies when these are true to experience, when these are ways of enhancing life. The firebrand is concerned with being open, honest, adventurous, and creative. If none of these processes are viable, the firebrand terminates the activity or relationship and moves on.

## Firebrand Activities

When we engage in firebrand activities, the power of our own inner light sustains us through difficult times, I share briefly a list of major firebrand events that enabled me to grow personally and professionally.

1. I was determined to do qualitative research at a university that approved only quantitative designs in doctoral programs. I committed myself to an investigation of the nature and meaning of children's learning experiences in different socio-economic settings. I believed that I could obtain this knowledge validly only through participant observations in the settings where children lived and learned. I was convinced that I could understand personality expression through communications and descriptions that came directly from the child participants. This put me at odds with my professors who were unyielding and exclusively committed to quantitative research. Their opposition opened up between us many struggles, tensions and conflicts. In spite of their threats regarding my status as a student, I persisted in what I believed to be a significant research project.

2. From the beginning of my work with children, I saw that, at times, only unconditional love and belief in the child's potentials for growth would rescue the child from a deteriorating self-image and destructive environment. This often meant affirming whatever the child expressed, the deviant and peculiar in the child, especially when others were treating the child's uniqueness as a sickness. My stand created conflict with other professionals, with colleagues and, at times, with parents and teachers. The outcome of these confrontations, observations, studies, and experiences was a series of publications on teaching and learning — *The Young Child in School* (with Minnie P. Berson), *The Teacher and The Child*, (1956), *The Authentic Teacher*, (1966), *Teaching As Learning*, (1972), *Learning to be Free* (with Cereta E. Perry), (1973), and *Who Will Listen: Children and Parents in Therapy* (1975).

3. I met all children in therapy at a school where I was employed — in opposition to the administrators of the psychological clinic. I believed that I could learn a great deal about pathology from healthy children and much about health from children labeled as emotionally disturbed, autistic, mentally retarded. This made no sense to my supervisors. I was criticized, judged, attacked, and threatened with dismissal. Accounts of my work with a wide range of children in therapy (based on observation, tape-recorded interviews, and reflective analyses) were published in a series of books, including: *Children in Play Therapy: A key to understanding normal and disturbed emotions* (1953), *Psychotherapy With Children* (1959), *Existential Child Therapy* (Editor) (1966), and *Rhythms, Rituals and Relationships* (1981).

4. I opposed institutionalization of children many, many years ago when institutionalization was virtually automatic in cases of autism,

mental retardation, and extreme withdrawal or hostility states. This put me in jeopardy with psychiatrists, social workers, psychologists, and educators, and in some instances with parents who insisted on hospitalization. Case presentations, analyses, and follow-up studies are included in the above listed titles and in the values, principles, theories, and social meanings and implications grounded in observation and experience, outlined and discussed in my publications: *Creativity and Conformity* (1967), *Individuality and Encounter* (1968), *Turning Points* (1977), and *Creative Life* (1977).

5. In my very first work in public schools, I encouraged teachers to develop relationships with children to focus on the feelings inherent in language, to be concerned with creativity, to permit freedom of choice in learning. This resulted in considerable dissension and difficulty with some principals and with the superintendent of the school district who attempted to fire me from the university which employed me. My university colleagues considered by behavior foolhardy, risky, and wasteful of time, energy, and resources.

From these first ventures in graduate education and in professional work I identified myself as a firebrand, in the sense of D. H. Lawrence (1961):

> Yea and no man dared even throw a firebrand into the darkness. For if he did he was jeered to death by the others, who cried "Fool, anti-social knave, why would you disturb us with bogeys? There *is* no darkness. We move and live and have our being within the light, and unto us is given the eternal light of knowledge. Fool and knave, how dare you belittle us with the darkness?" (pp. 437-438).

This paper is an outcome of my awakening to the significance of the firebrand in families, schools, and society. The way of the firebrand as an individual and in relationships, in dealing with problems and in pursuing issues in education is part of an extended study that I have been pursuing over the past five years and is part of a book manuscript, tentatively entitled "Being in, Being For, and Being With." During this period, a major firebrand project has been my activities with and encouragement of graduates of alternative psychology programs to revolt against violations of their constitutional rights, equal privileges and opportunities granted to all citizens under federal and state laws, conspiracies against the freedom to compete and practice one's profession, the wisdom of choosing for oneself the most effective education and training in psychology, congruent with one's own philosophy of learning, values, purposes and interests. I have taken an unwavering and persistent stand against national associations and boards of psychology who encroach on academic freedom, prescribe courses and titles, homogenize the curriculum, and in other ways tamper with the unique missions and purposes of graduate schools and programs in psychology that emphasize individuality, diversification, interdisciplinary studies, and applications that are socially relevant and that contribute directly to enhancing the lives and well-being of all people in the community and in the world. The firebrand opposes discrimination of every kind, especially that which appears under the guise of professional competency, role power, and protection of the public — too often this translates into guild interests, promotion of the in-group and rules, criteria, and doctrines that exclude and limit people who embrace different theories, values, views and beliefs and who are qualified and competent to do professional work congruent with their education, knowledge, and experience.

6. Betty, my wife, and I remained with Kerry, our daughter, throughout her open heart surgery, at a time and in a hospital where parents were excluded except during limited visiting hours. This resulted in strong and tense discussions and frequent battles with the medical staff. They wanted us out of the way but we refused to leave. I believe that our decision to remain with Kerry ultimately saved her life. Being at the hospital continuously over a period of weeks, opened my eyes to the nature of loneliness, to what happens to young children when they are abandoned by their parents and turned over to strangers who put them through frightening and painful procedures. I witnessed the shift in hospitalized children from assertiveness and protest to fear and despair, and eventually to a state of chronic depression. Like Kerry, the very life of some children was at stake. The hospital was a place that could kill as well as cure. Several children died following their open heart surgery, due to the negligence of medical staff and the absence of caretakers. From these studies of children and families in hospital settings and in therapy, I completed a series of heuristic works, including *Loneliness* (1961), *Loneliness and Love* (1972), *Portraits of Loneliness and Love* (1974), and *The Touch of Loneliness* (1975).

7. More than thirty years ago, I helped found a new psychology that would recognize the person, as a whole human being, with potentials for life and growth, that would value the internal frame of reference and self experience as fundamental and valid ways to knowledge and truth. Participation in the founding of the Association for Humanistic Psychology put me into considerable conflict with my behavioral and psycho-

analytic colleagues and resulted in my being attacked for several years at virtually every gathering of psychologists and mental health workers. With assistance from A. H. Maslow, Dorothy Lee, Carl R. Rogers, Ross L. Mooney, Gordon W. Allport, David Smillie, Frances Wilson, Sita Ram Jayaswal and others, I edited a book entitled *The Self: Explorations in Personal Growth* (1956), which helped to launch the humanistic psychology movement and made legitimate the study of loneliness, love, autonomy, individuality, qualitative studies of experience, being and becoming, creativity, the healthy personality, the person in psychology, self-actualization, and a range of topics and questions relevant to human nature, human beings, and human processes, and human behavior and experience.

The Association for Humanistic Psychology and colleagues whom I had met and worked with since its founding in 1958 encouraged me to pursue studies that had not been included or supported in conventional psychology. These included: *Personal Growth: The Struggle for Identity and Human Values* (1969), and *Finding Yourself, Finding Others* (1974), as well as many of the titles listed above.

8. I helped to establish a new graduate school, a non-conventional, residential school rooted in phenomenology, existentialism, humanistic psychology, and qualitative studies of human experience, when the voices around told me that such ventures were bound to fail and that my family and I would suffer from continual frustrations, pressures and losses. The school, the Center for Humanistic Studies in Detroit is now regionally accredited, has successfully completed its tenth year of existence with full enrollments and a substantial endowment to ensure its continuity and longevity. The outlook is optimistic and solid for this graduate school in psychology to grow and become an even more effective and resourceful center for the creative education and training of humanistic psychologists and for contributions in education and health care services. An important stream of study and activity of the Center for Humanistic Studies are the research projects based on human science inquiry and qualitative designs and methodology that have been completed by the graduates and faculty of the Center as well as applications of existential, phenomenological, and heuristic models of psychotherapy to clinical practice. Some of these research studies and applications to therapy are outlined and described in my books *Phenomenology, Science and Psychotherapy* (1988) and *Heuristic Research: Design, Methodology and Applications* (1990).

These firebrand activities have enabled me to continue to develop as an individual and to use my deviation from the norm as an opportunity for learning. The firebrand awakens in me the desire and the power to speak, to write, and to create. Virtually all of the events of my firebrand nature have at times aroused others to name-calling, abusive language, and both subtle and overt attacks. The most common charge has been that I desire to gain power and control over others. I know the difference between the power of being and knowledge, "personal-professional power," and that of role and politics. I have been warned and threatened but somehow I have persisted in holding onto my beliefs and values. I have continued to discover ways to significant growth for myself and support of others. At times only my own will, and my own strength, courage, and knowledge, affirmed me, and enabled me to continue to live in situations of intense attack aimed at bringing about my conformity or reducing me to passive silence.

One may carry a torch and awaken people without creating turmoil and disturbance. Terry Fox, the young Canadian who walked across Canada, was a firebrand. He lit up the entire country of Canada and awakened a unity among people in the fight to conquer cancer. He aroused a nation to respond affirmatively to handicapped people everywhere.

Above all else, the firebrand is true to what is alive, to what is burning within, to the callings of life and the imperative of speaking out on behalf of individual and human rights. The firebrand is a distinctive individual who responds to inner commands that will haunt the person until she or he recognizes, proclaims, and pursues them. In the words of Jung (1957):

> Hence it is not the universal and the regular that characterized the individual, but rather the unique. He is not to be understood as a recurrent unit but as something unique and singular which in the last analysis can neither be known nor compared with anything else. (pp. 17-18)

## Heuristic Meaning and Individuality

Long ago St. Bonaventure explained that there are three kinds of knowledge — "The Eye of the Flesh" that comes from direct sense experience, "The Eye of Reason", knowledge not directly observable but derived through cognitive steps, and "The Eye of Contemplation" that dwells inside one's self in spiritual meanings, and discloses to one's self absolute realities.

To these three eyes, I add the "heuristic" eye which is an eye of its own and does not belong to any category. To be heuristic means to discover through one's own internal awareness and intuition. It is this eye that we must hold onto to maintain our individuality, the eye from which we feel and know the nature and meaning of our own experience, what is true of our life. The heuristic is intuitive and personal and represents the truth of our own experience, our own becoming nature. The heuristic is the eye from which the fires of being arise. Its opposite is publicness, the passing off or sale of ourselves as familiar, the way of adjusting and adapting to others' interests and expectations; a way of becoming accessible to everyone.

Distance, averageness and leveling down are qualities of publicness, the "They" in Heidegger's (1962) terms. And *They* are always right, not because *They* are distinctive and primary, not because of their actual relation to the truth of things, but because *They* are in positions of power; they know what is right; they use their roles and status to direct and control us. *They* are insensitive to every difference, to every act of genuineness. *They* never get to the heart of the matter, caught up as *They* are in the surface of things and in rules that reflect their own fears and their need to manipulate and control others.

In such social and political systems, everyone is the other and no one is an authentic self. Full appreciation of the process of recognizing individuality focuses on awareness and understanding of oneself. To value oneself, one must value what is within, savoring it, soaking it up, coming to terms with it, rather than classifying, judging and evaluating it. The heuristic focuses on the inner truth of *being with* one's own value and meanings. In such moments, the individual is patient and permits *what is* to be, to linger and endure. Being patient means that what exists as authentic has its own time table, recognizes that growth is an unfolding process, and that new forms emerge through a readiness, a gradual opening and awakening, and through reflective consideration.

When we value individuality, we respect the right of people to direct their lives, to experience feelings in their own way, to discover their own unique pathways and meanings in life.

Bill put it this way: "I'm going to therapy because my teacher says I have a problem. I'm a hyperactive child." But what does it mean to be hyperactive? For Bill, being hyperactive meant having "wild, powerful animals inside me that are screaming to get out. I have to move. I have to move." And so move he did. He settled into ferocious rhythms, exaggerated jumps and leaps, extreme forms of being in the world — until all the wild animals were out roaming and he would sit quietly and draw or read or work in his own way. He could contain the wild creatures only so long and then they had to come out. Bill was rooted to his inner fury; he brooded with it, lingered inside of it until by its very nature he had to break out into the open, explode into wild gestures and grand movements.

Bill's experience is that of the firebrand, not different in essence from Archimedes' experience. While bathing Archimedes suddenly understandood a new principle of buoyancy. He ran nakedly through the streets shouting, "I have found it. I have found it." Bill found *it* too in permitting his wild inner animals to roam freely in grand external movements and thus discovering peacefulness, harmony, and balance in his life.

This is precisely what happens in the honoring of individuality. One discovers what one has been searching to know. In the process, there is often a sudden burst of meaning that leads to an intense, pure state, a joy in recognition, a light of knowledge or understanding that helps one to embrace one's own ideas and feelings. Thomas deHartman (1972) expresses this quality in emphasizing that the interior world contains the seed in which art awakens and takes root. The interior region of the self is the magic part of life, without which there would be no poetry, or music, or rhythm or soul.

The denial of individuality is itself the problem; it forces one to become deviant or to fight to keep alive one's uniqueness, and requires the use of vital energies to protect oneself. Or, it leads to the surrendering of oneself to the demands of others, thus the giving up of one's own source of energy and power. The turning over of one's self to someone else undermines decision making, health, and well-being.

Long ago, Otto Rank (1950) stated: "Psychologically the problem of individuality is a will problem and consciousness problem. The neurotic character represents not illness but a developmental phase of the individuality problem, a personality denying its own will, not accepting itself as an individual... the neurotic type represents the individual knowing about himself... but repressing this knowledge, not wanting to be conscious of himself." (p.221)

The individuality of behavior, should be recognized for what it is, simply behavior that is different. In encouraging the expression of individuality, we look for signs of agitation that will support people in breaking out of their prisons, in shining forth as human beings.

My therapy sessions with Tony were filled with witches, ghosts, and demons who eventually were revealed as his mother and teacher, people who attempted to manipulate and mold him and who were constantly frustrated and defeated by his peculiar ways. He found his own way with people who attempted to control him. He was skillful in using clairvoyance to cope with others' expectations and demands. With a mix of magic, recognition, and chanting, he would totally confuse the adults in his life. To them, he appeared "dumb," "slow-witted," "strange," and "dull." He kept them off balance with his wizardry. He kept them out of sync with imaginative expressions. In this way, he protected himself from rejection and attack. He was not in touch with what they called the real world. By appearing "slow" to them, he was easily dismissed as retarded. They left him alone since he had little to offer. Yet, in therapy with me he was a glorious and inventive child. I became completely fascinated and involved in "his experiments." They opened new doors for both of us. We read materials ranging from parapsychology and transpersonal reports to chemistry manuals, at the very time that he was in a slow, "preprimer" reading group in school. We created magical moments and conducted a variety of compelling experiments. Eventually Tony's teacher and mother discovered that his peculiarity, strangeness, and slow, reluctant expressions were not a form of retardation but rather expressions of a unique and individual way of being. As his therapist, I recognized this vital force in Tony, his special energy and talents. I offered him in words and actions, a life that encouraged the magic that was within him to shine forth. I found resources that would challenge and extend his learning in the areas of his interests.

To enter fully into understanding the experience of being different one must listen to oneself, to the voices within that have been silent or muted and that clamor to be heard. Daniel Levinson (1977) in his study of mid-life transitions, describes what the process is like:

> He may hear only a vague whispering, the content unclear but the tone indicating grief over lost opportunities, outrage over betrayal by others, or guilt over betrayal by himself. Or the voices may come through as a thunderous roar, the content all too clear, stating names and times and places and demanding that something be done to right the balance. He hears the voice of an identity prematurely rejected; of a love lost or not pursued; of a valued interest or relationship given up in acquiescence to parental or other authorities; of an internal figure who wants to be an athlete or nomad or artist... he must learn to listen more attentively to these voices and in the end, to decide what part he will give them in his life. (p. 108)

The renewal of contact with one's self, the declaration of one's independence, the honoring of one's individuality is what enables a return to freedom, authenticity, and a sense of power over one's own fate and destiny. The birth of individuality is a source of energy and life that can be the basis for exploring, experimenting, and knowing, a realization that the essence of selfhood is uniqueness and that ultimately one can only experience what is one's own, from one's own organism, that in each instance the verdict of meaning and relevance must come from the texture and structure of one's own experiencing and a felt bodily sense that speaks to what is actual. Acceptance of the experience of being different enables one to reach a heightened state of awareness of the important facets of one's world, the nature of feelings, the significance of people, how the constituents of one's world affect one's perceptions. Being different is a way of discovering one's self and others, a way of knowing what distinguishes wheat from chaff, what nourishes and satisfies, what uplifts and supports. Being different is not a fixed or permanent state, but is affected by the currents of everyday living, by the growing clarity of what matters, who to trust, and how to live.

Alex, at age eight, had lost the wildness of his world, the uniqueness and life of childhood. And yet, something strong lingered, something compelling drew him unto himself.

> memories would come on wings of light —
> shining bird, high pines, high pines and sun, the fire
> in a floating leaf, the autumn heat in
> weathered wood... soft lichen — on a stone —
> a light filled imminence, shimmering and
> breathing, and yet so fleeting that it left
> him breathless and in pain. (Mathiessen, 1978, p. 42)

This sense of contact with the real life within one's self is what the firebrand seeks to maintain. As a firebrand, in the determination to grow, there will be moments when the only genuine act is to toss the burning embers of one's heart and soul into the deadwood; to burn a path to creative thinking, to protest against corruption and irresponsibility, to turn on a light that exposes discrimination and injustice, to take a stand wherever people are excluding or controlling others, stifling their individuality, and threatening to destroy unique and original sources of life. Salmon Rushdie (1992) exclaims: "I have learned the hard way that when you permit anyone else's description of reality to supplant your own — and such descriptions have been raining down on me, from security advisers, governments, journalists, Archbishops, friends, enemies, mullahs — then you might as well be dead... I must cling with all my might to my own soul; must hold on to its mischievous, iconoclastic, out-of-step clown instincts, no matter how great the storm."

## Concluding Comment

Although I am emphasizing the imperative of the commitment to be alert to the violations of what it means to be an individual human being and to be politically active, I do not want to lose touch with the other side, the imperative of one's own privacy and the life of solitude. Whatever else, we must save something for ourselves, and never become just instruments for programs of others, however important they may be.

We must make sure that some part of our life is kept alive, reserved for us and that no one or nothing else substitutes for this value. Regardless of how much pulling we must do on behalf of others or of political and professional goals, we must not lose touch with the sacred spirit that is in each of us. We must keep that alive in moments of discovery, meditation, and self-dialogue. We must hold onto that which is distinctly our own, that unique and lonely center that forever seeks its own presence, recognition, and expression. In the midst of outside callings and needs, we must continue to reserve a place for ourselves, to make time and space for knowing the essence of who we are as individuals, the deep and abiding core, that is now, that is growing, that is forever.

## References

de Hartman, T. (1972) *Our life with mister Gurdjieff*. New York: Penguin.
Heidegger, M. (1962). *Being and time* (J. Macquarrie & E. Robinson, Trans.). New York: Harper & Row
Jung, C. (1957). *The undiscovered self* (R. F. C. Hull, Trans.). New York: New American Library.
Lawrence, D. J. *The rainbow*. New York: Viking Press.
Lee, D. (1959). *Freedom and culture*. Englewood Cliffs, NJ: Prentice-Hall.
Levinson, D. J. (1977). The mid-life transition. *Psychiatry, 40*, 2.
Mathiessen, P. (1978). *The snow leopard*. New York: Viking Press.
Moustakas, C. (1953). *Children in play therapy: A key to understanding normal and disturbed emotions*. New York: McGraw-Hill.
Moustakas, C. (Ed.). (1956). *The self: Explorations in personal growth*. New York: Harper & Bros.
Moustakas, C. (1956). *The teacher and the child*. New York: McGraw-Hill.
Moustakas, C. (1961). *Loneliness*. Englewood Cliffs, NJ: Prentice-Hall.
Moustakas, C. (1966). *The authentic teacher*. Cambridge, MA: Doyle.
Moustakas, C. (Ed.). (1966). *Existential child therapy*. New York: Basic.
Moustakas, C. (1967). *Creativity and conformity*. New York: Van Nostrand.
Moustakas, C. (1968). *Individuality and encounter*. Cambridge, MA: Doyle.
Moustakas, C. (1969). *Personal growth: The struggle for identity and human values*. Cambridge, MA: Howard A. Doyle.

Moustakas, C. (1972). *Loneliness and love.* Englewood Cliffs, NJ: Prentice-Hall.
Moustakas, C. (1972). *Teaching as learning.* New York: Ballantine.
Moustakas, C. (1974). *Finding yourself, finding others.* Englewood Cliffs, NJ: Prentice-Hall.
Moustakas, C. (1974). *Portraits of loneliness and love.* Englewood Cliffs, NJ: Prentice-Hall.
Moustakas, C. (1975). *The touch of loneliness.* Englewood Cliffs, NJ: Prentice-Hall.
Moustakas, C. (1977). *Creative life.* New York: D. Van Nostrand.
Moustakas, C. (1977). *Turning points.* Englewood Cliffs, NJ: Prentice-Hall.
Moustakas, C. (1981). *Rhythms, rituals and relationships.* Detroit, MI: The Center for Humanistic Studies.
Moustakas, C. (1988). *Phenomenology, science, and psycho-therapy.* Sydney, Nova Scotia: Family Life Institute.
Moustakas, C. (1990). *Heuristic research: Design, methodology and applications.* Newbury Park, CA: Sage.
Moustakas, C. & Bernson, M. P. (1956). *The young child in school.* New York: Williams Morrow.
Moustakas, C. & Perry, C. (1973). *Learning to be free.* Englewood Cliffs, NJ: Prentice-Hall.
Rank, O. (1950). *Will therapy and truth and reality* (J. Taft, Trans.). New York: Knopf.
Rushdie, S. (1992). Our lives teach us who we are. *The Chronicle of Higher Education, XXXVIII,* 18, P. B5, January 8.

# 6

# Recollections and Reflections: Snippets from an Oral History of Humanistic Psychology

## Edited by Mike Arons and Carmi Harari

To compose this article, we[1] have "snipped out" pieces of stories, recollections and reflections as samplers of what "long-timers" considered significant events and meanings for them during their association with humanistic psychology. These snippets are taken from three video sessions done from November 1991 to January 1992. Because the three sessions, one in New York and two in the Bay Area, were conversational, with one thought or story leading to or taking off from another, we have organized the chapter by looking at each group on its own. Selected excerpts from separately made interviews with Stanley Krippner and James Bugental, and one made by Krippner with Jacqueline Doyle and Rollo May were injected into one or another of the group sessions when these seemed contextually related. (Inserts of their remarks or those of other non-participants in a specific session are parenthesized.) For the sake of both economy and continuity we have taken some liberty to put all the selected comments into a quasi-narrative style, paraphrasing where an ideational context was essential; citing directly where a touch of the personal was indicated.

---

[1] The authors would like to express their appreciation to Celia Irvin, a graduate assistant at West Georgia College, for her enormous contribution to the editing of the transcripts of these dialogues.

## San Francisco (January 16, 1992)

The San Francisco group consisted of Walter Anderson, Jacqueline Doyle, Tom Greening, Rollo May, Hobart (Red) Thomas and Rachel Thomas. The session was held at the home of Sidney and Jean Lanier, Jim Bugental was interviewed the following day at his home. Mike Arons was behind the camcorder and added a few thoughts when he could not resist.

The Sonoma State Psychology Program began in 1962, Red Thomas recalled, several years before humanistic psychology got its name. The first conference held at Sonoma State that year was called "Existential," or "Third Force" psychology. The famous 1968 meeting of the American Association for Humanistic Psychology was held at the Fairmont Hotel in San Francisco. Red Thomas was Program Chairman, although he noted John Levy did much of the planning. "After that 1968 Fairmont circus," Thomas did not attend national conferences for five years, although he considered the experience "exciting." Jackie Doyle, who had participated in a month long workshop at Esalen in 1968, spoke of some of the activities which characterized the Fairmont conference, and also one she co-led at APA, where undress was being encouraged as a group growth vehicle. More generally, for many, the 1968 AAHP meeting was their first exposure to Will Schutz and an array of Esalen encounter techniques consisting of "T" groups, Sensitivity training, Gestalt, Psychodrama, Sensory Awareness, Fantasy Workshops, Role Playing, Body Work and Symbolic Realization. (As Harari added, all of these would soon become identified with humanistic psychology: "Here in all of this was introduced the concept of the 'small group process,' the group was a self-contained learning experience.") (Bugental noted many of these had their roots at National Training Labs and owed much to Kurt Levin's work at Iowa).

It was recalled that the late 1960's was also the time Paul Bindrim was doing his nude marathon groups. The subject of nudity in AAHP turned the attention of several minds to the 1969 Silver Springs Maryland Conference, which is the first Jackie fully recalls. A downstairs kitchen in the Maryland hotel was being reconstructed and this came to serve as "headquarters" for what became an extremely long, partially nude, and in all ways very primitive snake dance (or Conga line) which wound its way from the kitchen to and through the hotel lobby. The rhythm and beat was provided by a creative conversion into instruments of pots and pans and other available utensils.

Recalling Fritz Perls' therapy demonstration at this meeting, Jackie Doyle said that he was "brilliant in analysis of gesture but cold and didn't have a heart. In AHP we treasured a gentle caring approach to one another." After an encounter with Perls at Esalen, Rollo quit AAHP for the first time. (Maslow also was "disgracefully humiliated by Fritz at Esalen," recalled Bugental). But "four or five years later, Fritz seemed to change. He was completely different. He knew he was going to die." Tom Greening and Walt Anderson recalled of his style: His approach was to "Pull off your mask," he was a "showman, fascist in character structure — Fritz imposed a standard of 'real' vs. 'false' language." (Jim Bugental saw Fritz as "tremendously creative, with astounding insight, when he was 'on' with himself, but when he was 'off' he was blind and humiliated people.")

His was the approach of breaking "old forms." That was and still is an approach which some strongly identify with humanistic psychology. At the same time as humanists were trying to tear down, they saw themselves as loving and caring, noted Anderson. We were all breaking sterile forms, rules, values of obedience, etc., noted Doyle. On the subject of AHP's role in world affairs, Jackie Doyle said she heard that in the Begin-Sadat talks with Carter at Camp David, AHP type books and writings were influential resource materials. Two suitcases of books by humanistic authors were sent to Raisa Gorbachev. These were said to have played a very significant part in Soviet policy development. As evidence, "phrases from these books," according to Greening, "appeared in Gorbachev's speeches." But concern was expressed even in regards to this international achievement. "I fear naive acceptance on the part of the Russians as AHP representatives aid them to break old forms with no new ones to replace them... could be misleading as well as opening and creatively constructive."

Walt Anderson remarked: "There was an extreme belief among humanistic psychologists that free flowing expression could solve problems. All this comes from a romantic view that we have hidden our real self which needs revealing from below the socially conditioned self. This romantic idea of a hidden self needing simply to be released is very much part of the Rogerian tradition. While Rogers could open things up, he couldn't always deal with the negative after-effects. "The problem with Carl," Rollo added, was that "He felt no negativity or anger should be expressed or solicited... Rogers was confronted with his inability to deal with the negative during a VA experiment" in which he had participated and had, himself, written up. The external judges, including Rollo May, determined he couldn't deal with negativity and anger. Red Thomas took issue with this characterization: "Carl would see what it is without denying it." (Stan Krippner recalled that when he told Rogers "I can understand the value of person-centered counseling if you have a long time, but what is the value of an extremely disturbed person coming in for one hour?" Rogers replied that "being with the person for one hour is the most valuable gift you can give him.")

Walt Anderson returned to the thesis of negativity. Rollo concurred: being non-judgmental is part of a romantic philosophy, as though there is a 'true self' waiting to be discovered. This denial of negativity was characteristic of much of the humanistic movement. Questioned about the shadow side of the "touch freely" wing of humanistic psychology, Anderson responded, "There is a repressing pretense of 'no anger' among some of our 'heart' types. This refusal of the negative has always been the shadow side of much of our movement. In fact, there has never been one movement, one humanistic psychology... There have been three aspects of humanistic psychology: first as philosophy and orientation, second, AHP as organization and, third, the meetings. These three were often disassociated aspects of an apparently same movement. This represents the unintegrated aspects of humanistic psychology."

At prompting from Mike, Rollo reiterated his larger historical vision. "We have yet to come to the Renaissance that we need to look forward to. Most human beings haven't been viewed as human and to arrive at a point where we can become human and be human and live through this famine is our great idea and great aim. Our present is in a great period of war and uncertainty. The danger is escaping from the reality of conflict. This is the great myth and error of the transpersonal view. People seek ultimate truth in Buddhism, etc. which is fine in its own right. But there is the problem of leaping to resolution without facing struggle or conflict. It is necessary to have the courage to hold on to our partial sense of reality. I once met the Dalai Lama and asked him if he thought everybody should become Buddhist. His answer was 'Buddhism can help Christians become better Christians; Christianity can help Buddhists become better Buddhists.'" (Questioned by Krippner, May made it clear his argument was not with transpersonal psychology per se but with any truth, such as "psychology of adjustment" which, when held as overriding truth, blocks out problems and negativity.)

Nearly all participants present were turned on to Abe Maslow by his book *Towards a Psychology of Being*. Rollo said: "He was a hell of a good human being and we should be more open to his memory. He was not a great intellect (in the critical-analytical sense), but was wide-eyed and had this sense of 'opening up life.'" (Jim Bugental noted: "Abe was a fountain, he gushed ideas and interesting new slants. He felt that if 10% of his ideas bore fruit, he was well pleased"). Jackie recalled that at a talk at the University of New Mexico in 1958, Abe spoke of Eleanor Roosevelt who overcame her pathological shyness to become a great stateswoman. Abe picked her out as a self-actualizing person. He stressed that humans can and do grow and develop throughout life. Maslow spoke to people. He was the pioneer. "He pointed towards the goal, identified the path that others have pursued. He was the source of that sense of joy and discovery that so many share as a result of the movement." Mike noted: "Abe inspired in his writings, which brought students to Brandeis. Jim Klee, who Abe recommended, was for many the more inspiring teacher." (Krippner had few contacts with Abe other than at conferences. He recalls one Council Grove Conference in Kansas when Maslow had to leave early. "He woke up too weak to carry his own suitcase. I was alarmed at (his) loss of strength. A few months later he was gone. Towards the end, Maslow spoke more frequently of the plateau experience which was different from the peak experience in that it is not so intense but can last longer. It is an experience more common in the final stage of life: to live life in the Tao or as an 'observing self': as being fully lucid").

### New York City, November 15, 1991

The New York group met at the home of Carmi Harari where, the following day, the Board of Division 32 was to meet. Present were Glen Boles, Erick Craig, Carmi Harari, Ruth Heber, Steve Hendlin, Steve Rosen, E. Mark Stern, and Sarah Zaraleya-Harari. Mike Arons doubled in this session as both cameraman and participant.

Carmi was the original Director of International Development of AAHP and Sarah Zaraleya recalled that when she first met him he was talking about taking a group around the world. "It's curious how history is written," Carmi observed. "We had just returned from our 1972 trip around the world, some seven weeks which took us to Paris, Iran, Soviet Union, India, Nepal, Thailand, Hong King and Japan, then to Hawaii for APA-AHP and on to Squaw Valley for stateside AHP. I found a whole set of correspondences, backdated, from the Academy of Science and the Soviet psychology organizations to the effect that our proposals for a meeting on scientific parapsychology were unacceptable and that under no circumstances would we be given permission to come to the USSR.

Orwellian, given that we came to the USSR with a full set of enabling correspondence and documents referring to arrangements for our visit and our meetings: which all came off extremely well."

The AAHP international conference was held in 1970 at the Free University in Amsterdam. Carmi recalls his correspondence with Charlotte Buhler. "The debate was over whether the registration fee should be $15 or $10 dollars." Charlotte was selected by the then new humanistic program at West Georgia to be a special speaker at the APA meeting held in New Orleans. "My, could she be difficult" recalls Mike Arons. "Then in her seventies, she was formal, stiff and demanding. She came to the meeting in a wheel chair and insisted that everybody cater to her. Despite everybody responding to her every request she never ceased complaining. On the podium she was a beautiful, dignified lecturer in the best Germanic professorial style. The evening after our session we wheeled her to the French quarter and into Preservation Hall. She began to catch the beat. Within a 'hurricane' or two, she was out of her wheelchair and formal air, mixing with the crowd. Then, she wildly sang and danced the rest of the night away with us on Bourbon street. This was still another side of Charlotte." (Jim Bugental recalls how Charlotte who, with Karl Buhler, used to hold "parties" in her home. These were not cocktail parties but salon-like gatherings with intellectuals like Victor Frankl invited to come and talk about their ideas.)

Andras Angyal as person and therapist introduced Mark Stern to humanistic psychology. He felt you could radically change the past but not the future. Angyal was very friendly with Maslow. He died before the first issue of *JHP* came out. Glen Boles related his early experiences with humanistic activities. "Mark Stern and I met at Columbia University's Teachers' College. I was going through Janov's primal therapy. At the same time, around 1970, there was the GROW Institute in New York and a man named Smith running it. Harold Streitfeld, who was program chair for the 1970 AAHP Silver Springs meeting, was running Aureon Institute and Alexander Lowen was doing his Bioenergetics workshops with Piarrakos, who was moving in a more transpersonal, spiritual direction." Carmi Harari said, "I was introduced to humanistic psychology ideas at CCNY by Gardner Murphy around 1939-1942. He introduced me to many who were instrumental in the early stages of the movement, including Gordon Allport and Moreno's psychodrama." (Stanley Krippner had said that Gardner Murphy had been the teacher with the greatest influence on him. He was his graduate assistant at the University of Hawaii in 1961. "Murphy pulled together a number of ideas and gave them form. There was no Murphian tradition. He allowed no labels. His was a bio-social construction of personality.") Steven Hendlin reported that he got his start in AHP at Berkeley in 1969 and 1970 when he was introduced to drugs, radical politics, Fritz Perls and Jim Simpkin at Esalen and began reading Jourard, May and the humanistic literature. "We felt like elders to those at Wisconsin or Columbia." That was a place, time and period of "antiwar teachers taking a stand against the Vietnam War; (a time of) Black power; Black Panthers, Norman Brown, Herbert Marcuse in San Diego, and Encounter groups. Encounter groups went beyond connecting. They were a way of being honest with self and others. I loved coming of age as a Berkeley radical." Steve Rosen objected to Hendlin's Berkeleycentrism. "A lot of things were happening at Brooklyn College at that time." "We lived in a naive time," Hendlin noted, 'You're with us or you're not with us.' It was the time of the counter culture and the Human Potential Movement. I saw in the 1977 AHP Program announcement the theme was Common Ground. It was a life changing experience for me. Al Huang led a large group dance. I saw a woman surrounded by men and walked right up to her and said, 'You are beautiful. Are you Jewish? I'm going to marry you... I handed her my resume...She phoned her parents and told them 'I met the man I am going to marry.' We just celebrated fourteen years together." "In Florida," Erik Craig reflected, "we felt in those times that we were going to have a big impact and we'll make people love one another enough to transform war and the world. That was the *zeitgeist.*"

One of the more remarkable events in the history of humanistic psychology, Carmi recalls, was how Division 32 got established. "It came into being as a result of an unsuccessful abortion." Mike Arons interjected that Don Gibbons of West Georgia College, who would not be endorsed by every one of his colleagues as a model of a humanistic psychologist, initiated the idea of a humanistic division of APA and sent around petitions for approval of this new division. "I tried to talk him out of it because most of us wanted to be outside APA. We were anti-establishment." "By the way," Mike added, "Gibbons was the person who also had the idea for the Association of Humanistic Education which subsequently came into being at West Georgia. I supported that one." Carmi continued: "Those of us on the AHP Board feared the establishment of humanistic division of APA would be competitive and harmful to AHP. We sent a letter around to the petitioners urging them *not* to support the new division, but it was a *fait accompli*. The petition went before the Council of Representatives and was accepted. The organizing meeting was scheduled at APA in Washington and a group of us (anti-Division 32ers) took over the dais. The organizer, Don Gibbons, did not show up at the meeting. It turns out, however, that he was just outside the door in a conversation with Dorothy Morgan" (a colleague from West Georgia College, Mike added), "apparently unaware that the meeting had started. So we went on to establish the Division and the Acting Executive Board, with Carmi as President, Everett Shostrom as President-Elect and Albert Ellis as Representative to APA Council."

AHP made a point at that period, Carmi noted, to attract minorities, Blacks and Hispanics, poor people, etc. This has always been a problem for AHP given that it attracts people who are privileged, like college teachers and students, in a world of suffering. "It's still a problem for AHP," Mike said, "For instance, this year's AHP conference will be held at the Saint Francis hotel in San Francisco, instead of on a college campus which many more could afford. It is the hotel-oriented crowd being catered to because AHP membership is mostly white middle class and concentrated in the Bay Area. But next year's meeting may be in Albuquerque, partly because this location may attract more Hispanics and Native Americans." The Native American culture is now having its influence not only on AHP and transpersonal psychology but on a growing number of young people whose values seem to take much from the 1960's, when the push was for a radical individualism, that is, a self-contained self. "But, I wonder if we are seeing new ways of relating emerge, to each other and to the earth. My daughter," Mike said, "invited me to join her at a Rainbow Gathering in Cherokee National Forest. Many of the activities, rituals and dress were similar to what I have seen at AHP or transpersonal meetings. But there were significant differences. Everybody brings some natural raw food contribution, such as beans, rice or barley which are all placed by a group of volunteer chefs in a huge cauldron. The better part of the day was used to prepare this food creation. The cauldron is then placed in the middle of the huge circle of participants who then speak from their hearts about why they came, how they feel, and their concerns about the earth. Then something different happens, really anti-utilitarian. Rather than, as one might expect, each participant bringing his or her bowl to the huge stationary cauldron in the center, the heavy cauldron itself is carried by a number of people to each individual who is served from it. I see in this ritual, perhaps, a new value system, new notions of intimacy emerging which combine the best of collectivism but with a very deep respect for each individual and the earth." Steve Rosen suggested that this was the process of individuation, which Jung wrote about: individuation and coming together again, the interconnection of individual, group and source.

### Alverno Center, South Bay area, (January 19, 1992)

The second California group met at Alverno Center, south of San Francisco, where the mid-winter meeting of the AHP Board was being held. Participants were Liz (Elizabeth) Campbell, Eleanor Criswell, Jim Fadiman, Maureen O'Hara and Arthur Warmoth. Mike Arons was behind the camcorder. Some themes which emerged were: how the participants were brought into humanistic psychology, Michael Polanyi, the 1968 conference in San Francisco, AHP and politics; Rogers and politics; Maslow and his East-West connections.

Jim Fadiman came to humanistic psychology after the organization and journal had already been established, "I was a grad student at Stanford and my education there was terrible. Of course I really didn't give it much of a chance. I had taken psilocybin with Timothy Leary and Richard Alpert in Paris and that put me in touch with a very different world, like culture shock, but more like universe shock. So I was reading what was assigned by day and *The Tibetan Book of the Dead* at night... when I ran into Tony Sutich and volunteered to help him. He was a remarkable being, more disabled than anyone I had ever met and as basically in a better mood than anyone I had ever met. It was wonderful to notice how he made his living as a therapist and people came to him and said their lives weren't working and they had a look at him and he just looked at them and said 'My life is working.'"

Art Warmoth came to Brandeis because one of his instructors had suggested that he check out Maslow who was doing some interesting things there. "A course called Will, Choice and Ego was taught by Jim Klee. Jim was at least as important a figure in my education as Maslow was." After Maslow resigned as chairman, the department became completely traditional. Klee left for West Georgia with Mike. The new chairman at Brandeis was the least imaginative member of the faculty. Based on this experience, Maslow, when he came to the west coast told people, "Don't try to have a well rounded program. Hire only those with some humanistic inclinations." Mike noted that he received and acted on the same advice from Abe when he developed the West Georgia Program. "There is a strange understanding in the academic world," Fadiman observed, "that each faculty member has his own niche, so that if a program is correctly designed no one has any interest in what the others teach. This leads to personal and intellectual isolation. Whereas in some areas such as existential, humanistic or transpersonal psychology, if someone suggests that we co-teach, that would be fun. According to humanistic values, being lonely is not a good deal."

Liz Campbell came into humanistic psychology via the growth center route. "I was just one of the people that happened on the movement. I came to Esalen after trying to live like Zorba by taking my daughter to Greece. That didn't work. At Esalen I worked with people like Fritz, Will Schutz and Stanley Kellerman. Later I went to Kairos. I made the rounds of the centers, a circuit rider."

Maureen O'Hara was a biochemist when she came from England in 1969, studying green slime in swimming pools. "I couldn't even spell psychology... I was teaching at Oberlin College and two women biology students, who had been to Esalen the year before, brought NTL encounter groups to Oberlin. They got everybody involved, faculty, their wives, everybody. These students had figured out that this is what education was all about. Then I went to NTL, the most exciting experience of my entire life. Seventeen year olds were teaching about life to sixty-five year olds and they were letting them do it. It was so synergistic... Those same two students asked me to sponsor a course on human sexuality. Not to teach where babies come from, Oberlin students knew that, but to teach women how to tell their prospective lovers to wait a minute while they get their diaphragm out of the drawer. These were interpersonal issues. We went from that one course to a whole department centered on interpersonal relations... then I began to explore myself. In England, with the class system, people don't talk about the self the way Americans do. So this voyage of self-exploration has been quite a revelation for me."

Eleanor Criswell was an education major at University of Kentucky. As a student in the program, however, she hated education as it was being taught. Earlier as an undergraduate "I had been interested in people like Dewey, Moustakas, Maslow and Combs and in my exploration of these theorists, I finally came to see education as the intentional development of human beings. My entire life since has been spent as an educator, a college teacher... Once I got into humanistic psychology, after studying with Art Combs and Sidney Jourard at Florida, and coming to the west coast, I would sit around trying to figure out ways of expanding it. I would write to publishers asking them to send me a list of their books on humanistic psychology, knowing that they had none. Now, of course there are many."

Addressing Eleanor, Jim noted, "You came up in a supportive environment. By contrast, it was my job at Stanford not to be found out.

It was clear in my heavy mystical states that I would not be a credit to my country. While all this was going on, studying at Stanford, working one day a week with Tony Sutich, I was working on psychedelic research with two groups, one with federal support, the other investigating it. I dressed in costumes, as people did in the 1960's, only mine was coat and tie. So they wouldn't know what I was thinking. Humanistic psychology was one of those places I could talk about what I really thinking."

Maureen recalled that she had been put in touch with postmodern thinking while still a student in England. Her science teacher, also an artist, acquainted her with an approach to science (which later became recognized in creativity literature as "detached-engagement"). This involved Michael Polanyi's notion of "indwelling," where one personally entered into the subject and established an internal relationship with it and then "stepped back" psychologically for a distant perspective on it. Such a relationship had been alien to her instruction in science and seemed alien to many scientists. Art Warmoth noted how Maslow had embraced the works of Polanyi which seemed to him to have given so much support to his own thinking. Mike Arons recalled how Maslow had written his own book on the *Psychology of Science* and then, having read Polanyi's *Personal Knowledge,* recommended this to his Brandeis students as by far the better treatise on the subject.

The topic turned to the famous 1968 AAHP conference at the San Francisco Fairmont hotel. Jim remembered, "we got thrown out of the place. Fritz started a workshop before hundreds of people with a long nonsensical sound like a child playing with its tongue: 'blabblablalablalb'...that was the level we were at. This was our determination to demonstrate that whatever the structure was, it was wrong. The Fairmont didn't appreciate that point of view. Particularly since we weren't taking over (occupying) the whole hotel. In retrospect, I think they probably gave us the right decision in allowing us to move to places where we did dominate the whole place. If we were going to destroy anything it was ourselves. It wasn't much fun when there wasn't anybody to offend." Liz, having looked over the historical list of conference themes pointed out that the one in 1968, was called: "Human-istic Psychologist as the Disciplined Romantic." Mike recalled that concept came from Colin Wilson. Art asked, "Wasn't there some kind of protest by the Street People, something about integrating the hotel?" In 1968, Fadiman indicated, "that was the year which on the racial front in San Francisco, the issue was just to get Blacks to work in hotels. That is how far we have come. So our parading around the lobby, singing and dancing, we were not looked upon as a politically astute organization."

This raised the issue of AHP and politics: Eleanor responded, "There were times when the organization was not politically astute. There were times when it shaped itself quickly as soon as it got the point on it. I remember sitting around the Board debating if we should come out against the war in Viet Nam." Liz asked, "What was the result?" Eleanor said "We voted to be against it." Maureen asked "How public did you make that?" Eleanor answered "As public as AHP was." Mike Arons added that it took a very long time for AAHP to take a political stand. "I remember this debate was very heated at Board Meetings in Honolulu in 1972 especially as this centered around the question of opposition to the Viet Nam War. John Levy (and Sidney Jourard as Krippner recalls) was against politicizing the organization, he felt it should remain psychological." Eleanor reflected that "I always felt it was political by its very nature. It didn't have to be political to be political. We talked about personal freedom, human rights, actualization of human rights and so on. That is political." "We were always deeply political," added Jim Fadiman, "the question was would we also be shallowly political?" Inherently, we were not only against the Viet Nam war, we were against war. So to name the war we were against was becoming topical... The questions is, should we take a position for or against what is in season?"

"I remember a lot of times with Carl (Rogers)," Maureen recounted, "the relationship between the personal and the political was the ongoing conversation. Alan Nelson, about 1974, really screamed in Carl's face when Carl would insist 'I am not a political person.' 'How can you say that?' Alan asked. 'How can you say the teacher and the pupil are in an equal power relationship; the therapist and client, management and worker? You who seek that equality, how can you say you are not political?' At that moment Carl got it. He got it. He saw there was no place to hide from making political change rather than to deny it. Later he began doing encounter groups in Northern Ireland and South Africa."

"Carl felt out of place at Esalen," Jim Fadiman recalled, he was American Gothic. "Remember, he came from a background in which dancing was looked at with moral suspicion." Whereas, Art noted, Maslow felt at home at Esalen. He loved the place and the people. He was very much appreciated by the people at Esalen but he was not sure if they really understood him. He was bothered that what he said there was accepted uncritically. At Brandeis, by contrast, he had a truly brilliant faculty all of whom like Ulric Neisser, Dick Held and Richard Jones, knew his ideas well. There, his views were well understood but not especially appreciated. They thought some of these were a bit off the edge. Maslow had a real problem getting the two parts of the country together for himself. Fadiman added "Maslow's complaint about Esalen: 'Where's the library?'"

## Editor's Perspective (Frederick J. Wertz)

The intention of the oral history project was to let "longtimers" recount their memories of humanistic psychology. It was neither to sell nor to denigrate the movement. Some of the negativity which emerged in these sessions, often about prominent figures in the movement, has been viewed as one-sided or unfair by some who have read drafts of this chapter. Some pointed out that much in the early group activities actually started with —even centered on — the negative side of relationships, in ourselves, as well as values, conventions, rules and structures in the establishment.

Ideally, and perhaps that is a next step in this project, these differences can be dialogued. In historical retrospect, we are all coming to grips with the negative — with negativity — which as indicated in the San Francisco session, by the use of Jung's term "Shadow," is a necessary and ultimately positive direction.

Perhaps the positive in the early years was so outstanding that many of us didn't quite hear this critical side as well as we do now. And perhaps a less judgmental attitude was creatively apt for that period and stage. Most of us, to lean on Bugental's characterization of Maslow, were then "gushing out" or trying out new ideas and possibilities. And, in our estimation, over the past thirty years, considerably more than ten percent of this "fountain" of humanistic insights has been formally or informally incorporated into psychology, other fields and world consciousness.

# 7

# The Idea of Human Science

*Amedeo Giorgi*

I've been asked to clarify the idea of human science, particularly because I have been arguing that psychology should be a human science since the mid-1960's (Giorgi, 1970). When I appealed to the idea of human science at that time, it was because I believed in the institution of science for the purposes of gaining rigorous knowledge about the phenomena of the world. However, my commitment to science was not a blind one. If there were compelling reasons why psychology should leave the institution of science, I would have been willing to conduct my psychological labors within another context. In other words, the issue was not so much one of being pro or con science, the former for reasons of prestige, etc., and the latter because it dehumanized persons, perhaps, etc. but precisely a question of seeking the intrinsic appropriate context for the adequate acquisition of psychological knowledge about humans. When I was a graduate student, I read about the *Geisteswissenschaft* tradition in Germany, and I often wondered why it was not explored more in North America. At the first opportunity, I explored the writings of Dilthey (1944), Brentano (1874/1973), Spranger (1928) etc. and I found that the context was indeed feasible even though a lot still had to be worked out.

About a quarter of a century later, I still think that the human science context is appropriate for a psychology that is primarily interested in persons and I shall try to indicate why. I shall describe the necessity for a human scientific context for psychology, and its meaning, from a theoretical psychological perspective. That is, I shall not go into the historical development of the human sciences (see Gusdorf, 1960 for such an account), nor shall I give a theoretical analysis of the possibility of the human sciences as such (see Giorgi, 1990, for an outline of such a possibility). Rather, I shall try to demonstrate the logic behind the argument for conceiving of psychology as a human science.

There is no escaping the fact that the fundamental tension in the development of scientific psychology is between the meaning of science and the meaning of being human. There exists factually a highly successful theory and practice of science, as a cultural institution, that developed primarily in dialogue with nature. From an historical perspective it is understandable that the same context that worked with nature should also be applied to humans. However, a critical reflection upon such an extrapolation shows that such a move is not necessarily so obvious and reasonable. Thus, the argument of this article is to show, briefly, that within the history of psychology, objections to such an extrapolation without modification have been made even if not heeded, and secondly, to show that a meaning of science that would be intrinsically applicable to humans is conceivable. However, a human science would require critical modifications from the articulations of science as a natural science. This paper obviously cannot be exhaustive regarding the latter point, but a sufficient number of examples to demonstrate the possibility will be given.

## Tensions Between Psychological Subject Matter and Science in the History of Psychology

It can be fairly easily established that a scientific viewpoint is a derived viewpoint, chronologically speaking. All human beings first find themselves in the everyday world following the many activities offered there. In the course of time, and especially through education, one discovers that certain types of problems cannot be resolved immediately and call for sustained study and a different attitude. Thus, a scientific attitude became established and cultivated. In the modern sense of science, this attitude was elaborated and refined to a great degree with respect to the problems of the physical world. When the concern shifted to social and human problems, especially during the mid to late 19th Century, the viewpoint of the natural sciences was not only sophisticated and refined, but also its successes brought it a well-earned prestige. Thus, the first attempts of the men and women who desired psychology to be a science, rather than a philosophy, was to try to apply the methods and rules of science — that is, the sciences of nature — to the phenomena of psychology. At a metatheoretical level, the history of twentieth century psychology is the history of the many attempts to implement this project, through various conceptualizations, and the objections to those attempts. Sometimes the objections were to the forms of the attempts (e.g. Behaviorism, etc.) and at other times to the very attempt to imitate the natural sciences as such. The objections are obviously in the minority, but they do span the 20th Century even if they were rarely heeded. Here I shall only present a sampling of the objections since the meaning of these objections is the basis for seeking psychology as a human science rather than a natural science. Essentially, all of the objections revolve around the inability of the natural scientific perspective to take up and formulate psychological problems in a way that is faithful or relevant to the way the problems are lived in everyday life. In other words, certain psychologists experienced a tension between the dictates of science and the essential characteristics of the psychological phenomena as lived.

In one of his talks introducing Gestalt psychology in the 1920's Wertheimer (1925/1967, p. 1) wrote:

> We go from the world of everyday events to that of science, and not unnaturally assume that in making this transition we shall gain a deeper and more precise understanding of essentials. The transition *should* mark an advance. And yet, though one may have learned a great deal, one is poorer than before. It is the same in psychology. Here too we find science intent upon a systematic collection of data yet often excluding through that very activity precisely *that* which is most vivid and real in the living phenomena it studies. Somehow the thing that matters has eluded us... Psychology is replete with terms of great potentiality — personality, essence, intuition, and the rest. But when one seeks to grasp their concrete content, such terms fail. (Italics in original)

Wertheimer, of course, goes on to show how he believed that Gestalt theory could meet the essentials of the phenomenon and still be scientific. But in offering his view, it is clear that it was the idea of science that had to be modified. Wertheimer (1925/1967, p. 2) argues:

> Is "*science*" really the kind of thing we have implied? The word science has often suggested a certain outlook, certain fundamental assumptions, certain procedures and attitudes — but do these imply that this is the only possibility of scientific method? Perhaps science already embodies methods leading in an entirely different direction, methods which have been continually stifled by the seemingly necessary, dominant ones. It is conceivable, for instance, that a host of facts and problems have been concealed rather than illuminated by the prevailing scientific tradition... Perhaps something in the very nature of the traditional outlook

may have led its exponents at times to ignore precisely that which is truly essential (Italics in original).

Wertheimer is thus seeking the essential aspects of phenomena and finds that the received repertoire of methods or procedures might not be sufficient. He wants to remain within a scientific perspective, but clearly wants to do different kinds of things to grasp the essential aspects of the phenomena in which he is interested.

In 1932 Bartlett (1932/1967) published a book on remembering. Bartlett was aware of Ebbinghaus's classic study, and even though he did not want to leave the experimental tradition, he did not carry out studies the way Ebbinghaus did, using nonsense syllables and a memory drum. Rather he used stories, pictures and symbols. The reasons Bartlett followed another path are as follows. He (Bartlett, 1932/1967, p.2) writes:

> It was inevitable that, once the experimental method was introduced, it should sooner or later extend its application into all fields of psychological study... Ebbinghaus was trying to find a way to apply Fechner's exact methods to a study of the "higher mental processes," and particularly to memory... His ideals were the simplification of stimuli and the isolation of response. He secured the first by using nonsense syllables as his memory material, and the second, he curiously thought, followed immediately.

Bartlett (1932/1967, p. 3) goes on to explain that:

> In reality, the experiments are much less easy than was assumed by Ebbinghaus. Any psychologist who has used them in the laboratory knows perfectly well that lists of nonsense syllables set up a mass of associations which may be very much more odd, and may vary from person to person, than those aroused by common language with its conventional meaning.

In commenting on justifications for the use of nonsense syllables, Bartlett (1932/1967, p. 3) laments, "Once more the remedy is at least as bad as the disease." Bartlett's (1932/1967, p. 12) arguments for choosing the type of material he did are that:

> The psychologist whether he uses experimental methods or not, is dealing, not simply with reactions, but with human beings. Consequently the experimenter must consider the everyday behavior of the ordinary individual, as well as render an account of the responses of his subjects within a laboratory... I have employed as nearly as possible the sort of material most closely resembling that commonly dealt with in real life. I have not

hesitated to vary this from person to person, or from time to time, and to adapt the conditions of its presentation, if it appeared to me that by doing so I could best get comparable conditions on the subjective side.

Consequently, because of how he perceived human beings in the everyday world Bartlett found that he could not follow the Ebbinghaus model. Nevertheless, he conducted psychological research, and his respect for human behavior as it was lived in everyday life forced him to be primarily descriptive and qualitative in his approach.

Humanistic psychology set out to study "those human capacities and potentialities that have no systematic place either in positivistic or behavioristic theory or in classical psychoanalytic theory" and to "greatly speed up the emergence of a more adequate — a more scientific — picture of the full possibilities inherent in the nature of man" (Sutich, 1961, pp. viii-ix). Once again, the established psychological perspectives seemed not to capture the human person as psychologists knew him or her at work, at home, in the consulting room and elsewhere in everyday life. To access such a person, humanistic psychology was calling for the study of different phenomena and different modes of access.

Another challenge came in 1972 with a slightly different emphasis by Chein (1972) when he confronted one part of the psychological world with another. In his book, Chein (1972, p. 8) asked:

> The opening sentence of "Ethical Standards of Psychologists" is "The psychologist is committed to a belief in the dignity and worth of the individual human being." But what kind of dignity can we attribute to a robot? What is there in an impotent reactor that is of such intrinsic value as to require an unemotional commitment by psychologists to a belief in its worth?

It is indeed interesting to wonder why there should be such a conflict between the image of the person as contained in the ethical statements of the APA and the image of the person emerging from the scientific practices of psychologists. The former image, of course, is based upon real world contexts, the latter upon artificially constructed situations. Chein (1972, p. 9) states, "if there is any antinomy here, it is not as Koch would have it between psychological science and the humanities, but between our professed concerns as psychologists and our dedication to scientific method." Once again, the idea of science adopted by psychology seems to constrain the attributes that one can assign to a human being.

Finally, Faulconer and Williams (1985), in 1985, argued against the use of objectivistic concepts for the sciences because they blocked access to intelligibility for phenomena. They (Faulconer & Williams, 1985, p. 1182) write:

> The objectification of history and culture — and indeed of all human behavior — that historicism effects, arises from a commitment to a concept of cause inherited from the physical sciences. The more fundamental question addresses this concept itself: Is human being intelligible through this concept of causality? Is it possible for an account of human being to be both coherent and intelligible on the one hand, and on the other, not to use the modernist concept of causality? We shall argue that intelligibility is possible only when this notion of causality is rejected.

Thus a major explanatory principle of the natural sciences, causality, is being rejected as a principle of intelligibility for human phenomena based upon how temporality unfolds for human awareness. If the principle of causality is rejected, must science itself be rejected, or can one imagine a different way for science to be science?

This quick survey of the tensions between being human and being scientific shows that psychologists in their concrete work, if not always in their theorizing, have been sensitive to the tensions between the demands of science and the essential characteristics of being human. However, in the history of psychology, the perception of this tension has lacked either an adequate articulation of how to overcome the tension or an adequate community of sufficient numbers to institutionalize an alternatively articulated theory of science. The reasons for lack of development cannot be gone into here and more properly belong to the field of the sociology of knowledge. In any case, it would be one role I would envision for humanistic psychology. It should be able to provide a theoretical basis for approaching human phenomena rigorously and nonreductionistically in both helping and research practices. As such, it would be numbered among the human sciences. I shall now turn to one way of visualizing such a possibility.

## The Meaning of Human Science

The first thing to be clarified is that the meaning of human science is not limited to having humans as a subject matter. That is obviously a necessary condition, but not a sufficient one. What is also required is that the human being is treated *as human*, whatever that might entail for each human science. Thus, the problem of the human sciences is that some fundamental comprehension of the meaning of being human is required and, in such a way, that the specific interests of each of the several human sciences can be specified without reducing the properly human dimension. Implicitly, maintaining a genuinely human level of presence throughout the research process is done in many ways, but it is not always optimized, thorough or consistent. For example, when one thematizes or uses reflective consciousness, language, culture, symbols, the ability to make tools, and so on, an essentially human level of discourse is maintained. The question is whether methods, concepts and procedures borrowed from the natural sciences can allow for the manifestation of the *human as human*. Usually one ends up with an ambiguous mixture, a hodge-podge as a result of the clash between human presence and reductionistic procedures. Rather, the challenge is to develop methods with sufficient largesse, so that the essential humanness of human beings can manifest itself in each research situation without being reduced and without blurring qualitative distinctions, and at the same time, allow rigorous analysis of whatever data are obtained.

Now, from the side of science, the important thing to remember is that in order for a science to be distinct from other sciences, it would require a different, complex phenomenon that would motivate systematic study. Psychologists close to the beginning of psychology's independence were aware of this, and so Ladd (1892, p. 24), for example, wrote, that to establish psychology as an independent science, one would have to clarify the "nature, scope, problems and legitimate methods of Psychology and the relations which it sustains to other forms of science and to metaphysics." Thus, one would have to show how the human as human could consistently manifest itself as one defined the nature, scope, problems and method of the several human sciences. The persistent problems that have prevented a facile answer to this question have been essentially two: a) the difficulty of articulating the essential aspects of "human as human" and b) the fact that a strong definition of science already exists and that the existing definition of science developed in dialogue with nature rather than humans, and so it never had to grapple with the meaning of "human as "human." So, if natural science methods were to be applied uncritically to human phenomena, one would get the "human as natural," which is indeed what one often gets in mainstream psychology, but not human as human.

It was precisely this reductionistic definition that motivated the founders of humanistic psychology to attempt to redefine psychology. Thus, if one accepts uncritically certain *achievements* of the natural scientific approach as the defining characteristics of "science as such," (e.g. universal laws, measurement procedures, etc.), one is taking an outcome that is contextually dependent, abstracting it from its context, and then abstractly positing it as a criterion for the human sciences. But if the issue of the human as human was never considered, then the uncritical positing of the criterion (e.g., universal laws) becomes unsupportable. Rather, one should not look at the achievements of the natural sciences as criteria, but at the entire context from which the achievements emerged. From that perspective one can see more clearly whether or not the same criteria are transferable to the human sciences or whether they have to be modified or dropped altogether. That is the strategy that will be used in this article in order to show that an idea of science that is oriented toward the essentially human is possible. The scientific goal or "telos" is respected throughout; the process and achievement looks different because the phenomena being studied are human phenomena, and they are not reducible to "phenomena of nature."

Since the goal of this article is to show how the idea of science can be maintained in the face of human phenomena, I shall not dwell upon the problems concerning the meaning of human extensively, as large and as important as they are. In another article in this collection (Giorgi, 1992) I have spoken to this issue at more length, so here I will merely utilize Merleau-Ponty's (1942/1963) notion that one can define humanness in terms of acts of transcendence. To be able to transcend a situation means that humans always have the possibility to alter the meanings of situations in which they find themselves, even to the extent of construing a new reality. They do not always actualize this ability, but to speak of humans as transcending means that such a possibility always exists. Obviously, this description is hardly exhaustive of humanness; it's only meant to point to a dimension that motivates a different conceptualization of science.

### Relativization of the Achievements of Natural Science and the Implications For Human Science

By relativization of the achievements of the natural science I mean that such achievements were once correlated with contexts and that to understand the achievements better, the awakening of the original contexts would be helpful. Once the original context is reawakened, the manner in which one ought to proceed to implement a human science perspective will also become transparent. This analysis will be done briefly, and strictly theoretically, rather than historically, because of space and time limitations. It is only intended to show that the *very possibility* of a human science exists and to give an indication of the direction and type of analysis to be followed rather than being a demonstrative and conclusive account of such a possibility.

## A) The Laboratory

For a very long time in psychology, the laboratory was seen to be the ideal place to perform psychological research, and it is still regarded as such by many. When psychologists depart from the laboratory, it is usually reluctantly and apologetically, and only because they are forced to do so by reality. There is a tradition of research in "naturalistic settings" as well, but it, too, receives less emphasis. But, we no longer ask today, what is a lab? Why was it invented? We take for granted that it is the privileged setting for doing psychological research. After all, wasn't it the criterion used to mark the beginning of modern psychology?

We have to remind ourselves that a lab, after all, is a creation of human beings. It belongs to the culture of science and it is the incarnation of a specific idea, or even better, ideal. It is the place where all factors can be controlled; most are to be held constant, one is to be systematically varied, and then another factor is to be left free to indicate its dependence upon the variable that is systematically varied (the independent variable). The "telos" of a lab is *control*. The assumption here is that the researcher must know everything that is going on, and the extent to which he can know the variables in an a priori way, to that extent is he or she better prepared.

But what assumptions does such a structure have for the phenomenon being studied? It assumes that the phenomenon being studied is simply a product of the forces acting on it. It assumes that the causal relation, or its probabilistic version, is the best way of understanding the phenomenon. But what if a human, with the possibility of acts of transcending the lab situation in terms of meanings, is at the center of the phenomenon being studied? Suddenly, the very assumptions for the construction of the lab are violated. The human person brings with him or her a center of initiative, a way of interpreting labs and research tasks that have little to do with the way they are constructed. What would be a setting in which a phenomenon that expresses initiative or meanings can be studied? What characteristics would such a setting have? It becomes complicated, indeed, so that perhaps not one setting will do for all research. Or better still, perhaps one would have to go into the everyday world to find settings for research that are "comparable" to the situations where the phenomena are initially manifested in the everyday world. In fact, this is the principle that would guide phenomenologically inspired research: psychology at the human level would not so much require lab settings as settings that are analogues of the everyday world where the original phenomena take place. Control in phenomenologically inspired research does not mean so much control of physical variables or uniformity of setting as having a situation where the meanings expressed by the participants of the research, whether behaviorally or experientially, can be meaningfully discriminated and interrelated so that the phenomenon can become comprehensible. In other words, a different idea of "research setting" emerges because the phenomenon to be studied displays qualitatively different characteristics. What is common, therefore, is that some idea of a research setting is required for both natural and human sciences, but the concretization of the idea differs because of certain essential differences between natural and human phenomena.

Now, of course, one could place a human person physically in a lab and still do human science research, but then, the fact that it is a lab is somewhat indifferent. Similarly, one could approach a "natural setting" and do natural science type of research, as Bruce and Read (1988) did, by studying aspects of the phenomenon that are not directly revelatory of the human as human. Consequently, the issue is not laboratory vs. natural setting, or "everyday, ecologically" based research vs. labs as Banaji and Crowder (1989) contrast it, but the spontaneous lifeworld manifestation of a phenomenon as opposed to the analogue setting, whether it be a lab or a natural setting. The criterion for evaluating the research is the degree of fidelity vis-a-vis the everyday, spontaneous manifestation of the phenomenon and the analogue research setting. The criterion is more structural and thoughtful (conceptual), following the essential human contours of the phenomenon than physical, or based upon apparent similarity. Thus, the way to preserve science for humans is not by a direct imitation of what natural science did, but by rethinking the meaning of the research setting in relation to the subject matter of the phenomena being studied.

## B) *The Causal Relationship*

During the above discussion the idea of the causal relation was mentioned because it was one of the implicit assumptions surrounding the construction of the lab. Moreover, in our historical presentation we already saw that Faulconer and Williams (1985) had argued against the notion of causality in human phenomena because it did not faithfully capture human temporality well. Here, another reason will be advanced for not using the notion of cause.

But, first of all, why did the natural sciences themselves employ causality as a principal means of understanding natural events? Primarily because it is the fundamental way of understanding dependency relationships between things, processes or conditions and events. "If A, then B" is the classic formulation. But the causal relation depends upon genuine independence between the two events whose relationship one is trying to understand. Or, to say the same thing, causality applies where external relationships dominate and a grasp of the causal relation renders an event explainable.

Now is such a way of understanding relationships between events useful for human phenomena? Not really, because human phenomena are intrinsically conscious and where consciousness exists the intentional relationship as articulated within phenomenology is important, and that implies the primacy of meaning and the analysis of meaning over causality. Where intrinsic relationships exist, causality recedes as an explanatory principle because true independence between events and phenomena does not exist as is required by causality.

Merleau-Ponty (1942/1963, p. 226) has argued forcefully that psychology can advance in its analysis of behavioral relations "only if causal or mechanical thinking were abandoned for dialectical thinking." And dialectical thinking is required whenever action on one aspect or pole of a situation is manifested in another pole or aspect. Dialectical thinking is required whenever one believes that one is influencing an aspect of a phenomenon only to find that other aspects, or the whole, express consequences simultaneously. Human phenomena display such relationships constantly: perception and action, subject and world, body and mind, self and other, perception and emotion, etc, are all interdependent in such a way. For example, it requires activity on the part of the body to perceive anything whatsoever, so perception is not a linear effect of energy from the thing in the environment, even if energy is required, but it is arbitrary to start with the energy emitted from the thing rather than the activity that makes the body receptive to energy.

At best, an idea of "circular causality" would have to be used, but that concept fails as well as soon as one has to allow for the role that meanings play in human affairs. Once meaning is admitted as a relevant factor for intelligibility, causality is transcended, even if, from a more narrow perspective a role for causality is admitted, because the cause is taken up and placed in the midst of a network of meanings. For example, I may twist my ankle on a stone — and so the hurt ankle was "caused" by the stone — but the implications of the hurt ankle may vary widely. If it is a week-end, for example I may just lie down and put my foot up, so that it may heal quickly. But if it happened during a working day, I may not have that option. Or, if the injury happened to an athlete with a big event coming up, it may be disastrous for him or her. Thus, the human significance of the event is not between the foot and the stone, but how it is taken up in the meaningful world of the person. At that level, "linear causality" loses all meaning. Rather one has to use "dialectical analyses" or, more strongly, analyses of meaning based on the notion of intentionality. The criterion here is: Rendering dependency relationships intelligible; causality works for external relationships, but meaning is required for internal ones.

*C) Measurement*

There is probably no activity that causes more misunderstanding than that of measurement. Indeed, because of the development of statistics and probability theory, today it is almost axiomatic to believe that measurement and science are one and the same thing. However, as in the last two instances, it all depends. Measurement is not automatically the only scientific mode of elaborating and determining dimensions of phenomena. It too is contextualized and not absolute.

In order to relativize measurement, the same question will be asked of it as we asked before: What function does measurement serve? Why have natural scientists taken up measurement? Basically because by means of it one can establish an exact essential identity of a dimension of a thing, e.g. its shape (geometry) or its magnitude (mathematics). More generically, however, it is a way of being rigorous, but not the only way of being rigorous. Many thinkers in the humanistic tradition have expressed this point, but Heidegger (1967/1977, p. 96) did it well and succinctly when he wrote:

> The scientific fields are quite diverse. The ways they treat their objects of inquiry differ fundamentally... Precisely from the point of view of the sciences or disciplines no field takes precedence over another, neither nature over history nor vice versa. No particular way of treating objects of inquiry dominates the others. Mathematical knowledge is no more rigorous than philological-historical knowledge. It merely has the character of "exactness,"

which does not coincide with rigor. To demand exactness in the study of history is to violate the idea of the specific rigor of the humanities.

Thus, to seek rigor via measurement is not automatic. Mathematical measurement is a means of achieving rigor when the phenomena studied can fall under what Husserl calls "exact forms." Sciences that have "forms" as their objects imply that only the forms of the objects are thematically considered and not their contents (e.g. triangles, regardless of what triangular object, an ashtray or a gem, may have motivated the study of the pure form). Exact objects, in addition, have forms whose variations can be known and determined with precision. Inexact disciplines based upon vague objects do not have such precise variations; they are much more fluid. Husserl, insists moreover, that the essences representing the types of sciences (exact sciences vs. inexact or descriptive sciences) not be confused because they differ substantially: He (Husserl, 1913/1983, pp. 166-167) writes:

> Geometric concepts are *"ideal"* concepts, expressing something which cannot be "seen"; their "origin" and therefore their content are essentially other than those of *descriptive concepts*; as concepts they express, not "ideals," but essences drawn immediately from intuition simpliciter. Exact concepts have as their correlates essences which have the characteristic of *"ideas" in the Kantian sense...* The *firmness and the pure distinguishability of generic concepts*, or generic essences, which have their extension in the realm of fluidity, must not be confused with the *exactness of ideal concepts* and of genera which include only the ideal in their extension. It can then be seen, furthermore, that *exact sciences and purely descriptive sciences* do indeed combine but that they cannot take the place of the other, that no exact science, i.e. no science operating with ideal substructions, no matter how highly developed, can perform the original and legitimate tasks of pure description. (All italics in original)

The relevance of these statements for our point about measurement being only one form of rigor should be obvious. If the phenomena we are dealing with do not have exact variations, but only inexact and fluid ones, then it does not foster rigor to use mathematical or geometric concepts on such phenomena no matter how exact the concepts may be in themselves (e.g. to use scales to measure personality). On the other hand, rigor will be fostered if inexact concepts are used with inexact phenomena, because what matters is the relationship between concepts and phenomena and not the use of exact concepts "as such" without any awareness of the phenomena to which they are being applied. To state it starkly, the use of exact concepts with vague phenomena is only the illusion of rigor since the exact concepts matched against richer phenomena leave a residue that cannot be theoretically ignored.

One clear implication of this line of reasoning is that psychology as a human science might be far better off trying to invent new descriptive methods than in adapting statistical procedures because human phenomena rarely manifest the "exact forms" required in order to be essentially determined by mathematical procedures.

Space will only permit three such examples, but also, multiplying examples, which would be easy to do, would, hopefully, be redundant. In each case the strategy is the same. I take a value of the natural scientific perspective and awaken its original theoretical context so that the function it serves can be seen more clearly. Once the function is clearly seen, the value of the issue can be relativized. Thus, an overall sense of being scientific is still preserved, but the particular way in which the awakened function — a setting that will permit the intelligibility of the phenomenon to be seen as clearly as possible, a concept that will help make orderliness comprehensible, and a procedure for determining rigor — is maintained, is quite different from the way that sedimented practices in the natural sciences have maintained the same function. In other words, one is not to maintain the practice as such, but the meaning of the practice.

## Human Phenomena And Science

So, we return to the primary question: What can a human science possibly mean? It means that the relationship between the methods and procedures of obtaining the best possible knowledge and the essential qualities of the phenomena about which we wish to obtain such knowledge must essentially match.

What is the minimum that can be said about human phenomena? Firstly, that they are not thing-like and that, because of consciousness, intentional relations and meanings become guiding concepts for comprehending them. It also means that human phenomena are not primarily substantial, but relational. The phenomenon does not end at the skin, but in the world, as far as the meanings being bestowed by a person can stretch according to interests, goals, modalities and possibilities. Thus, when daydreaming, the boundary of the phenomenon may be the heavens; when remembering it could be the beginning of the twentieth century; when anticipating, it could be the end of the world; when depressed, it could be even within the skin of a heavy body; when caring, it could be with unfortunate sufferers, and so on. The philosophers have already expressed this notion: humans are becoming embodied selves in the world with others. A human is always being meaningfully in a situation.

What is the minimum that can be said about science? It is primarily a knowledge producing enterprise. But it seeks the best possible type of knowledge that humans can produce. Thus science seeks knowledge that is: systematic, methodical, general and critical. To be systematic implies that different aspects of knowledge can be related to each other; to be methodical means that a set of procedures that is intersubjective is available for all qualified persons; to be general means that the knowledge obtained has a power of application beyond the situation in which it was obtained, and finally, to be critical means that the knowledge gained must be subjected to relevant challenges.

Logically, there is no reason why the type of knowledge described in the last paragraph cannot be applied to a type of creature that relates to the world and others in situations with the characteristics of awareness and meanings. Thus, the grounds for a human science are logically there. The creativity and courage to implement the appropriate practices are really all that is required for a viable psychology as a human science. Fortunately for us, even that task has been initiated since the 19th Century. True, its history is sporadic, haphazard, often apologetic, but nevertheless, there are some shoulders to stand on.

## References

Bartlett, F. C. (1967). *Remembering: A study in experimental and social psychology.* Cambridge, Eng.: Cambridge U. Press. (Original work published 1932)

Brentano, F. (1973). *Psychology from an empirical standpoint.* London: Routledge & Kegan Paul. (Original work published 1874)

Banaji, M.R. & Crowder, R. G. (1989). The bankruptcy of everyday memory. *American Psychologist, 44,* 1185-1193.

Bruce, D. & Read, J. D. (1988). The how and why of memory for frequency. In M. M. Gruneberg, P. E. Morris, & R. N. Sykes (Eds.) *Practical aspects of memory: Current research and issues* (Vol. 1, 317-322) New York: Wiley.

Chein, I. (1972). *The science of behavior and the image of man.* New York: Basic Books.

Dilthey, W. (1944). Selected passages from Dilthey in Hodges, H.A. (Ed.), *Wilhelm Dilthey: An introduction.* London, Routledge.

Faulconer, J. E., & Williams, R. N. (1985). Temporality in human action. An alternative to positivism and historicism. *American Psychologist, 40,* 1179-1188.

Giorgi, A. (1970). *Psychology as a human science.* New York: Harper & Row.

Giorgi, A. (1990). Towards an integrated approach to the study of human problems: The parameters of a human science. *Saybrook Review, 8,* 111-126.

Giorgi, A. (1992). Wither the humanistic psychology? *The Humanistic Psychologist, 20,* in press.

Gusdorf, G. (1960). *Introduction aux sciences humaines: Essai critique sur leurs origines et leur developpement.* Paris: Les Belles Lettres.

Heidegger, M. (1977) What is metaphysics in Krell, D. F. (Ed. and Translator). *Martin Heidegger: Basic writings.* New York: Harper & Row. (Original work published 1967)

Husserl, E. (1983) *Ideas pertaining to a pure phenomenology and to a phenomenological philosophy.* (F. Kersten, Trans.) The Hague: Nijhoff.(Original work published 1913)

Ladd, G. T. (1892). Psychology as so called natural science. *Philosophical Review, 1,* 24-53

Merleau-Ponty, M. (1963) *The structure of behavior.* (A. Fisher, Trans.). Boston: Beacon Press. (Original work published 1942)

Spranger, E. (1928). *Types of men.* (P. Pigors, Trans.). Halle: Niemeyer.

Sutich, A. (1961). Introduction. *Journal of Humanistic Psychology. 1,* vii-ix.

Wertheimer, M. (1967/1925). Gestalt Theory. In G.W. Ellis (Ed.), *A sourcebook of Gestalt psychology.* New York: Humanities Press, pp. 1-11.

# 8

# Research Methodology in Humanistic Psychology

*Donald E. Polkinghorne*

In this paper I use the term "humanistic" to refer to the position that human existence includes unique characteristics, such as self-reflection, purposefulness, language, and culture (Kinget, 1975), that differentiate it from the existence of other life forms and from physical objects. I make a distinction between the terms methodology and method. Methodology addresses the epistemological theory that informs the use of particular research methods. The humanistic methodology is the epistemological contention that the research methods employed to study human existence must have the capacity "to be rigorously faithful to the full richness of human existence" (Aanstoos, 1985). The natural science methodology claims that the only way to produce objective and certain knowledge is by use of the research methods developed to study physical reality. Human science methodology encourages the use of a wide range of methods — those using natural language data as well as those using numeric data.

Since the beginnings of American psychology, there have been individual psychologists who have advocated the discipline assume a humanistic position. For example, the father of American psychology, William James, espoused a humanistic model of the person (Child, 1973). In the 1930's and 1940's personality theorists such as Allport (1937), Murphy (1947), and Henry Murray (1938) embraced a humanistic position. Before the late 1950's and early 1960's, however, humanist advocates had not been organized as a movement.

The general humanistic movement became intertwined with the counterculture movement of the 1960's and early 1970's (Smith, 1990). It was hesitant to dissociate itself from any dictum, no matter how immoderate, whose authors claimed allegiance to humanistic principles. One of the extreme dictums was an anti-intellectual call to reject all attempts to generate knowledge through critical inquiry. Inclusion of these extremes under the humanistic rubric served to encapsulate the humanistic movement within psychology and functioned to suppress a response by academic psychology to its call for a methodological dialogue (Giorgi, 1981; Smith, 1990).

I am limiting my investigation of humanistic psychology and research methodology to those positions that have contained proposals to confront seriously the challenge of exploring human phenomena by means that are methodical, critical, and systematic (Giorgi, 1987). These proposals maintain that the characteristics of the subject matter of psychology — the person — have priority over and are determinate of which research procedures are appropriate for the discipline. They also maintain that in order to display the complex and problematic dimensions of human existence it is necessary to develop new ways of inquiry to supplement the present array.

## The Historical and Intellectual Context

*Humanism, Existentialism, and Humanistic Psychology*

Humanistic psychology is part of a late twentieth century expression of the periodic humanist impulse to reclaim and celebrate the virtues of the human spirit (Kendler, 1987). The twentieth century humanism shares the values of previous humanist expressions such as Classical Greece and the Italian Renaissance. Its awakening was displayed in the existentialist motif of Continental literati and philosophers. These writers proclaimed that human existence is more than mere physical existence and is to be respected and honored. They decried the dehumanization of people by bureaucratic mazes and technological indifference. One of their basic themes was the rejection of mechanics as the source metaphor for understanding human existence. They held that the theme of mechanistic determinism should be replaced with the themes of freedom, choice, and responsibility (Friedman, 1964). In the 1950's and 1960's humanistic psychologists "Americanized" the motifs of the Continental existentialists. They edited translations (May, Angel, & Ellenberger, 1958) and provided interpretations applicable to American readers—for example, (Maslow, 1968; May, 1960).

*Study of the Human Realm*

Throughout most of Western history, inquiry about human beings was held to require different methods of investigation than inquiry about other existents. Humans differed from natural objects because they possessed a soul. Descartes held that matter (body) and spirit (soul) were two substances. Matter could be studied with the new scientific procedures described by Bacon. These procedures could uncover the laws that could explain and predict the movements of matter. Mind, however, could not be studied with the new science because mind was pure thought and did not occupy space (Barrett, 1987).

The discoveries of the scientific study of matter provided humankind with power to control nature. During the 18th and 19th centuries the studies of the physical realm were so successful that Europe was able to create enough energy to transform itself from a rural to an industrial society. All the while, the study of human existence remained outside the province of science; it was the responsibility of theology and philosophy. During the mid-19th century, however, a summons was given to investigate human beings with the same scientific methods that had been so successful in the study of matter. Comte, the sponsor of positivism, was one of the essayists who proposed that the study of human phenomena be brought into conformity with the study of matter. He argued that all "fictitious" or "negative" philosophical speculation about the human realm should be given up and, in its place, the "positive" or scientific study of human beings should be undertaken. In response to the summons, during the two decades between 1859 and 1879, the basic contemporary academic disciplines for the scientific study of the human realm were originated (Giorgi, 1986b).

The move to use natural science methods to study human phenomena was met by resistance from various fronts. For example, Dilthey argued that the study of the human realm required hermeneutic or interpretative methods in order to disclose or understand (*verstehen*) the meaning of and reasons for human expressions and actions. He maintained that because the human realm consisted of meanings, inquiry into it required procedures that could interpret its expressions, that is, a *Geisteswissenshaften* (a science of expressions of the human spirit). Dilthey distinguished this kind of inquiry from that which investigated the physical realm (*Naturwissenschaften*). Neo-Kantian philosophers also maintained that there was a dichotomy between the kinds of methods appropriate to investigate the physical realm and the kinds appropriate to the human realm. Windelband contrasted the "nomothetic" study of governing laws of the physical sciences with the "idiographic" study of individual human phenomena (Polkinghorne, 1983). Allport, who studied in Germany and was a forerunner of the organized humanistic psychology movement, proposed that American psychology acknowledge Windelband's notion of two kinds of science (Misiak & Sexton, 1973).

In spite of these resistances, the new disciplines formed to study the human realm adopted, in the main, the natural science methodology. They embraced the notion of a unified science; that is, there is only one approach to develop sure knowledge and that approach is the same for all subjects of scientific inquiry. The unified approach produced knowledge statements that explained and predicted occurrences by demonstrating that they are the result of covering laws. Only the methods of natural science (thereby excluding Dilthey's *verstehen* and Windelband's idiographic methods) could generate valid covering law statements (Hempel, 1965). Human phenomena that could not be studied by natural science methods were held to be inaccessible to critical investigation.

The requirements of natural science methodology meant that certain aspects of the human realm were excluded from the purview scientific investigation. This was misinterpreted by some to mean that the human realm consisted of only those aspects that can be studied by methods that conform to the natural science methodology. For example, it was held that human movement can be predicted in the same manner that any other physical movement could. The understanding of human behaviors did not require acknowledging unique human characteristics. Thus, one could study how rats or pigeons learn and respond to their environments and be able to predict how humans learn and respond. Concepts such as purpose, reasons, and aspiration nor the idea of teleological explanation were thought necessary to account for human actions.

Among the new scientific disciplines, psychology was a leader in the adaptation of natural science methods to the study of human beings. American psychology, in particular, took the initiative to purify its research methods. In order to conform to the tenets of a true science as it came to be reconstructed by the Vienna Circle, some American psychologists moved to exclude conscious experience as a subject to be studied by the discipline (Watson, 1913). It was held that allowing references to internal conditions (such as motives or traits) could hinder psychology's progress as a pure natural science. Data that were not publicly observable were not to be admitted; this meant that any use of introspection and self-report was suspect. The psyche was to be studied, if at all, only through its behavioral manifestations (Child, 1973). This meant psychology had to restrict its subject matter to very narrow limits.

## The Humanistic Response

It was against this situation in American psychology that the humanistic psychology movement rebelled. More psychologists were moving outside the academy to provide therapeutic services. The restricted methodology of the discipline produced only a caricature of the people practicing psychologists were seeking to understand and aid. Many of the leaders of the humanistic psychology movement were practicing clinicians and they called for the reform of their discipline so that it would: (a) offer an appreciation and guidance for therapeutic interventions that can draw on the potential that humans have for creative actions and caring responses, (b) advance a personality theory that acknowledges the unique and special characteristics of the human realm, and (c) adopt a research methodology that is responsive to the complexity and openness of human phenomena.

The topic of this paper is the last of these areas of reform called for by humanistic psychologists. The basic methodological position of the humanistic psychology movement is that the study of the person requires the use of research procedures that can address the "questions raised by considering people as agents who can act in a purposeful and meaningful manner" (Polkinghorne, 1982, p. 47). Their message took two forms — a protest and a promise (Misiak & Sexton, 1973). They *protested* against the exclusive use by psychology of methods designed to inquire about the regularities of the natural realm rather than those of the human realm. They *promised* to advance "new and creative research strategies that would study uniquely human phenomena in rigorous but more adequate ways than traditional psychology did" (Giorgi, 1987, p. 9). The purpose of this paper is to delve into and spell out the ways humanistic psychologists have exhibited these two expressions.

## As a Protest Movement

*Humanism versus Behaviorism*

In its early years humanistic psychology appeared to focus most of its attention on protesting against the defects in the methodological commitments of American psychology (Berlyne, 1981). Psychology had prized itself on taking its place in the American universities as a science among sciences. Its disciplinary goal was acceptance as a true science using the same methods as the esteemed physical sciences (Danziger, 1979b). The supposed essential features of a true science had been reconstructed from an examination of the practice of natural scientists by the logical positivists. These features included translating research variables into objective measurements, testing of hypotheses deduced from a theoretical network, and employing covering law explanations (Hanfling, 1981). Psychology, however, has not been very successful in developing a corpus of knowledge statements linked together in a single theoretical network. Instead of discovering a system of laws that governed human behavior, psychology has only developed a series of independent empirical generalizations (MacIntyre, 1981). Its lack of success as a natural science has been attributed to its youthfulness as a discipline and its lack of a Newton, that is, a person who will discover the basic law that will tie together the empirical generalizations into a theoretical network (Toulmin, 1972).

The original members and associates of the humanistic psychology movement were disturbed that their discipline had surrendered to a restrictive and radical logical positivist view of science (See Bakan, 1967; Braginsky & Braginsky, 1974; Chein, 1972; Giorgi, 1970; Kelman, 1968; Koch, 1959; Koch, 1961; Koch, 1964; Rosenthal, 1971; Sanford, 1965). They accused their behaviorist colleagues of being more interested in methodological correctness than in understanding human beings. The discipline of psychology appeared to be defined by its adherence to a particular methodology instead of by its subject matter (Koch, 1959).

Humanistic psychologists criticized the discipline's covenant with logical positivism and the exclusive commitment to publicly observable stimuli and behavioral responses. Commitment to the natural science methodology required psychology to neglect the more human aspects of the discipline's subject matter and to ban inquiries about mind, consciousness, and experience. The experiences of choice and freedom were said to be illusionary (Skinner, 1956; 1971). This position implied that human behavior was fully predictable and, thus, controllable by manipulation and management of environmental variables.

Humanistic psychologists also remonstrated, perhaps unfairly, that the behaviorist psychologists' pledge to the natural science methodology was an indication that they, in fact, believed that human beings were simply complex mechanical objects. Humanistic psychologists complained that the received research methodology did not provide for the investigation of those unique attributes and possibilities of the human subject — for example, creativity, freedom, love, purposeful action — that were of greatest interest to therapists and the public.

## Changes in the Discipline of Psychology

The psychology that was the subject of the early humanistic attack no longer exists. The behaviorist program to exclude mental phenomena from psychology's subject matter was eroded by the development of cognitive psychology. Cognitive psychology and humanistic psychology are historically parallel and both were interested in including mental processes in the domain of psychology's researchable questions. Nevertheless, there seems not to have been significant dialogue between members of the two movements. Cognitive psychologists, although they explored mental operations, retained the essential features of logical positivism and the natural science methodology. They used the information-processing operations of the electronic computation machine as the prototype of human mental activity (Neisser, 1966). Their early efforts produced mechanical-like explanations of mental processes that were similar in form to the previous explanations of behavior. In recent years cognitive psychology has begun to investigate complex processes—such as artistic creation—and has found the computer model insufficient to explain these more complex mental processes (Gardner, 1985). Another significant movement that helped loosen psychology's bond to a radical logical positivism was the emergence of qualitative methods in developmental psychology. For example, Piaget's conclusions about the development of thinking processes in children (Piaget, 1952) were derived from his observation of and interaction with his own children.

Besides the effects of the growing cognitive and developmental emphases in psychology, the behavioral program's own lack of success also contributed to the significant alterations the discipline has passed through in the last thirty years. The research program failed to discover general covering laws to explain human behavior (MacIntyre, 1981) and failed to provide a utilizable knowledge base that served the needs of psychotherapists (Morrow-Bradley & Elliott, 1986) or to solve America's educational, crime, and addictive problems (Sarason, 1981).

It is apparent that psychology is no longer committed to the radical research methodology that produced behaviorism. Dramatic changes have occurred in the philosophy of science that have served to undercut the philosophic base on which psychology had based its methodology (Hesse, 1980). Psychology's attachment to positivism and to an absolutely pure natural science methodology has been loosened. It is difficult to assess the importance of humanistic psychology's protest in producing this alteration.

## The Promise to Develop New Research Methods

To accomplish its promise to reform the research methodology of psychology, Humanistic psychology had to complete two tasks: (a) finding or creating responsible investigative tools that can display the full range of features that make up human existence, and (b) stimulating American psychology to adopt these procedures as featured methods of its research program. Rogers (1986), in his address at the 1985 Quarter Century conference of the Association for Humanistic Psychology (Arons, 1985; Smith, 1985), gave his assessment of humanistic psychology's progress toward accomplishing the two tasks.

He noted the perception that humanistic psychology has not made a significant contribution to mainstream, academic psychology stands in stark contrast to the impact of humanistic psychology on American culture. Rogers assessed the lack of interest by academic psychologists stems from the rejection of the logical-positivist approach by humanistic psychologists. He saw challenges to this operationalist methodology as having begun in the 1950's and listed a series of important books that have addressed this issue (Bleicher, 1980; Miles, 1984; Polkinghorne, 1983; Patton, 1980; Reason, 1981). These works hold that certain knowledge is impossible, no single methodology is appropriate to all studies and research should be based on empathetic "indwelling" rather than separation of researcher and participant (Rogers, 1986, p. 7). Rogers also mentioned that he had been unable to find any APA approved doctoral programs in psychology that are "humanistically oriented"; that is, that encourage dissertations based on a humanistic methodology. I believe this situation has not changed since Rogers' presentation.

Since the 1950's and 1960's, American academic psychology has expanded the areas of human experience that are considered appropriate for study (for example, consciousness). It continues, however, to adhere in the main to the use of research procedures that were adopted by the discipline during its logical positivist and behaviorist period. Psychology has been the most resistant of the disciplines that study humans to expand its methodological procedures. It has yet to adequately come to grips with the methodological implications of the changes in the philosophy of science that have taken place in the last half of the twentieth century (Polkinghorne, 1991a). The reasons for academic psychology lagging behind the methodological developments of other human disciplines may lie in areas other than considerations of methodological integrity (Polkinghorne, 1991b).

Humanistic psychology has been successful in its first promissory task of identifying and creating research approaches that meet the requirements of the humanistic methodology; it has not, however, been successful in its second task of convincing academic psychology to alter its general methodological commitment. During its thirty year history humanistic psychology has made considerable progress toward identifying and describing research procedures appropriate for the humanistic methodology. Members and associates have engaged in various scholarly strategies in achieving this progress. They have: (a) searched through the traditions for epistemological and theoretical advancements in understanding the special characteristics of human existence, (b) explored alternate research efforts developed in other human disciplines, and (c) invented original research procedures.

*Epistemological Traditions*

The message of the Enlightenment tradition was that by applying the proper scientific principles humankind's knowledge would continuously progress. When the accumulation of knowledge reached a threshold level, the vision of the heavenly kingdom would become an earthly reality. All that was required was the faithful application of the natural science methodology. Countering this call was a second tradition. The second tradition warned that progress in human affairs required more than mere amassing of technical information. Essential to betterment of the human condition was a deeper understanding of human beings. This understanding would require inquiry systems that differed from the natural science system. It would require systems tailored to reveal the complex meaningfulness of the human realm.

The first strategy of Humanistic psychologists has been to look to this second tradition as a philosophical and methodological support for their position. The second tradition can be traced back to Vico, an Italian thinker, who wrote at the beginning of the eighteenth century. Vico advised that the study of human actions (history) required a method that is distinct from the study of nature. Human beings differ from inanimate objects in that humans are observers of nature and creators of society, art, and self. Similar ideas were posed by Herder at the end of the eighteenth century. Herder's ideas were highly influential in Germany and laid the intellectual framework for romanticism and for the later development of Wundt's second psychology, his folk-psychology (Leahey, 1980). Wundt believed that social phenomena such as language, myths, and customs could not be understood in terms of more primitive psychological processes. Investigation of the higher mental processes required analytic tools that can work with whole mental configurations. Wundt suggested that inquiry about these uniquely human phenomena employ careful genetic and comparative descriptions as well as critical analysis (Danziger, 1979a; Leary, 1979).

During the twentieth century, the voices of the second tradition, which were primarily European, grew louder and more profuse. They called attention to the possible nefarious consequences of limiting the understanding of human beings to that which shows itself when a rigid logical positivist lens is used. They have shifted the epistemological discussions from attempts to establish a sure knowledge foundation to full and careful descriptions of human experiencing (Polkinghorne, 1990b). The second tradition has been a rich reservoir for humanistic psychologists as they have expanded and deepened their own articulation of and apologia for a humanistic methodology. Four of the postulates humanistic psychologists have appropriated from the second tradition are constructivism, systemic organization, existential-phenomenology, and pragmatism.

*1. Constructivism.* It was apparent by the 1950's that logical positivism had failed in its attempt to reconstruct science into a formally united system of theoretical statements grounded in the certainty of sense experience. Wittgenstein, in his later works (Wittgenstein, 1968), noted a linguistic and conceptual opaqueness to knowledge statements. Production of knowledge is a human activity. We have no methods that can free us of the human condition so that we might know people and things as they "really are," that is, we cannot escape our pre-judgments and conceptual contexts so that we might view through the purity of God's eyes (Gadamer, 1975). Human knowledge is a construction built out of publicly languaged ideas, not a transparent reflection of an independent reality (Rorty, 1979). Kuhn, a student of Wittgenstein, further undermined logical positivism with his description of the history of science as revolutionary passages through various research paradigms (Kuhn, 1970). Another source of critical reflection on the limits of the conventional or received view of science was provided by feminist thought (Gergen, 1988). By 1974, Suppe (1977) could report that "the vast majority of working philosophers of science seem to fall on that portion of the spectrum which holds The Received View fundamentally inadequate and untenable" (p. 116).

One of the responses to the loss of certain knowledge foundation was a skepticism accompanied by a radical relativism regarding knowledge claims. This theme, which appeared in some postmodern philosophers, harps back to the notion of an encapsulated mind with no method by which it can escape its subjectivity. Humanistic psychologists have had to be critical of the parts of the second tradition that undercut the very notion of worthy knowledge distinctions (Polkinghorne, 1990a). Other parts of the second tradition have provided more viable ideas for a humanistic methodology. The phenomenological position furnished a more viable description of the human intentional openness to other people (Schultz, 1973) and objects (Husserl, 1931). This connectedness to others and things allows communities to make consensual judgments among knowledge claims without appeal to a sure foundation (Habermas, 1979).

*2. Systemic organization.* Systems thought provided humanistic psychologists with a theory to account for the appearance of unique characteristics in human beings without having to introduce the notion of new substances, such as a "life force" or "soul." The characteristics of a realm are the result of its structure or organization as well as the inherent properties of its matter (Laszlo, 1973). As the complexity of organization passes through a threshold, novel and innovative capacities emerge (Miller, 1978). The unique characteristics of the human realm — self-awareness, language, culture, et cetera — are expressions of the complex configured interaction that produces human being. The properties of the level of organization that is human existence are autonomous — that is, they are not susceptible to explanation on the basis of theories and laws that explain phenomena of less complex realms (Jacob, 1974).

Systems thinking holds that understanding complex wholes, such as human beings, requires a focus on the total system rather than on its separate parts. The analytic strategy of traditional methodology called for breaking apart an event into its constituent variables and focusing research on the relations among these separated parts. The systems' strategy calls for understanding the event directly by perceiving wholes rather than parts (Gray, Fidler, & Battista, 1982). When we perceive a person as a whole, the person's actions take on meaning and become understandable in relation to the goals and purposes of the whole person. Systems research aims at discovering how the components of a system are organized and at producing descriptions of the integrating patterns and structures that reflect the unity of the whole (Buckley, 1968).

Systems theory has emphasized the importance of the Gestalt or part-whole structure in human understanding. Lakoff (1987) holds that Gestalt structures serve as the sources of the metaphorizing work of cognition. Narrative plots, which function as temporal Gestalts, serve to give meaning to life events by describing their contribution to a configured episode (Polkinghorne, 1988; Sarbin, 1986).

*3. Phenomenological-existentialism.* Phenomenological existentialism has provided humanistic psychology with its major philosophical support. Of great importance for the humanistic methodology is the phenomenological idea that the source of knowledge is human experience, not a system of formal relationships among linguistic concepts. In addition, humanistic psychology has appropriated: (a) Husserl's invention of a method for the study of experiential phenomena (Husserl, 1931), (b) Heidegger's recognition that human understanding is grounded in action in the service of practical ends and that the science of formal assertions is derivative from and dependent upon this more basic practical understanding (Heidegger, 1962); (c) Merleau-Ponty's demonstrations of the centrality of embodiment in human knowledge and the stratified organization of consciousness (Merleau-Ponty, 1962; 1963); (d) Gadamer's analysis of the constituents and circular process of human understanding (Gadamer, 1975); and (e) Ricoeur's explorations of the function of metaphor and narrative in the creation of meaning (Ricoeur, 1977; 1984-1989).

*4. Pragmatism.* Aspects of American pragmatism were used to support the humanistic methodology. For example, Peirce's (1955) exploration of the creative process of abduction in which researchers decided;what factors they would examine and his incorporation of human action into epistemology, and Dewey's attack on the sensorimotor model of the brain and its accompaniment—stimulus-response psychology (Dewey, 1896). James' (1950) explorations of consciousness and beliefs provided humanistic psychology a patron endorser of the importance of the realm of consciousness for psychology. In recent years a new pragmatism has been proposed (Margolis, 1986) to serve as a test for deciding among knowledge claims. The pragmatic test of a knowledge claim is whether it functions successfully in guiding human action so that it fulfills its intended purpose.

*Other Human Disciplines*

A second strategy used by humanistic psychologists to fulfill their promise of methodological reform has been to examine research designs developed in their sister human disciplines. Although psychology has continued to resist an expansion in methodological approaches, most of the other human disciplines have incorporated active research programs specifically informed by a methodology designed to inquire about the meaningfulness of human action. These designs make use of linguistic data and qualitative analysis and are generally referred to as "qualitative research."

Employment of these designs have allowed the sister disciplines to experiment with and refine the data gathering techniques and analytical procedures employed in these investigations. Historically, these designs have been identified most closely with anthropology and its ethnographic field studies of "foreign" cultures (Stocking, 1983). Malinowski's 1922 study of the Trobriand Islanders is often recognized as the beginning of the systematic use of these procedures in human disciplines other than history (Easthope, 1974). Another early use of such techniques was by sociologists of the symbolic interactionist school at the University of Chicago in the 1920's and 1930's (Meltzer, Petras, & Reynolds, 1975). These sociologists were influence by Mead's (1934) understanding of the self as an active creator of meaning. A more recent example of qualitative research design in sociology is Glasser and Strauss's grounded theory procedures (Glasser & Strauss, 1967).

In spite of efforts to "cleanse" the human disciplines of research programs that were inconsistent with the natural science methodology (Hempel, 1942), most of the human disciplines continue to accept qualitative research as part of their stock of research designs. "Qualitative research has emerged as a serious approach to inquiry in education, its status has evolved... to a respected member of the research community" (LeCompte, Millroy, & Preissle, 1992, p. xvi). In the last decade there has been an upsurge in publications addressing the technical and theoretical issues of qualitative research designs based on the humanistic methodology (Polkinghorne, 1991a). Examples of this burgeoning literature are the 17 monographs in Sage Publications' series, *Qualitative Research Methods* and the six titles in its *Applied Research Series*.

Humanistic psychologists have borrowed from the designs developed in its sister disciplines for use in their own research. Two examples of this borrowing are van Zuuren's (1986) adaptation of Glasser and Strauss's grounded theory method for her study of "the experience of breaking the rules," and Gergen's (1989) dialogic adaptation of the participant-observation method.

*Humanistic Research Programs*

The strategies of exploration of the second research tradition and the investigation of research programs from other disciplines have served humanistic psychology in the development of a viable supporting philosophical position and in the provision of a store of serviceable research examples. The third strategy called for the production of original humanistic research programs specifically designed to study psychological phenomena. In carrying out the third strategy humanistic psychologists have taken a variety of approaches.

Humanistic psychology developed a number of original research programs specifically designed for the humanistic methodology. Humanistic psychologists proposed various terms to distinguish their research approach from that traditionally employed by American psychologists. For example, human science as opposed to natural science (Giorgi, 1970; Polkinghorne, 1983), Taoist versus controlling science (Maslow, 1966), and soft versus and hard sciences (Child, 1973). Other distinctions include: practical versus theoretical knowledge (Hoshmand & Polkinghorne, 1992), professional versus academic knowledge (Polkinghorne, 1992), inquiry into human action versus inquiry into behavior (Howard, 1988), and the study of understanding versus causation. Other useful distinctions include the focus on community or on agency (Bakan, 1966), and on the masculine or the feminine (Hubbard, 1988).

Within the array of research programs developed by humanistic psychologists are included those that emphasize the use of numeric data and statistical analysis and those that emphasize the use of linguistic data and qualitative analysis. Some humanistic researchers have held that designs which employ numeric data and statistical analysis are superior to the those that employ linguistic procedures (Barker, 1971/1972; Coward & Royce, 1981). These humanists remain nearest to academic psychology's natural science methodology. Although they advocate retaining the numeric form of data and statistical analysis, they use them to investigate humanistic variables. Rychlak pointed out that the numeric research procedures of the natural science methodology are theory-independent and humanistic constructs can be translated into operational definitions and investigated using the tradition methods of psychology (Rychlak, 1977). For example, Rogers examined the humanistic constructs of empathy, warmth, and genuineness using numeric procedures (Patterson, 1984).

Others have held that linguistic procedures are superior for studying human phenomena. Their position is farthest removed from the received tradition of academic psychology. They opposed any use of quantification and computational analysis in the study of the human realm. They sought to replace psychology's traditional research procedures with ones that employ linguistic data and analysis. The rationale for this position is that the character of the human realm is meaning and that meaning manifests itself in language. Numeric procedures so distort the human realm as to misunderstand it. It is analogous to believing that counting the letters in a poem is related to understanding it (Reason & Rowan, 1981).

The most well known of the humanistic programs using qualitative procedures was developed by Giorgi (1975) at Duquesne University in the early 1970's. He designed procedures for the investigation of psychological phenomena which were informed by Husserl's phenomenological method for the study of experience. Foundational issues of the phenomenological program, such as its descriptive procedures, validity, reliability, and verification were addressed in a special issue of the *Journal of Phenomenological Psychology* (Giorgi, 1986a). Wertz (1983) showed that there were common analytic procedures across the variety of phenomenological psychology research undertakings. An exemplar study of the phenomenological psychology research program is Fischer and Wertz's (Fischer & Wertz, 1979; Wertz, 1985) study of the experience of being criminally victimized. Other original programs developed by humanistic psychologists include Moustakas' heuristic research at the Merrill-Palmer Institute in Detroit (Moustakas, 1990) and Barrell's (1986) experiential research program at West Georgia University. Aanstoos' 1986 survey of humanistic research programs (Aanstoos, 1987) identifies five principal humanistic programs (phenomenology, experiential, phenomenography, hermeneutic, and imaginal) and seven auxiliary programs (perceptual, genealogical, dialectical, Kierkegaardian, critical, descriptive-I, and descriptive-II). He says that these twelve do not exhaust the entire range of humanistic programs, and that there are more under development (for example, ethnomethodological, feminine, and dialogal research).

Humanistic methodology supports the development of these diverse research programs. There is no single method that is privileged in the production of knowledge about human existence. Each method, including those that employ numeric procedures and those that employ qualitative procedures, is a lens that can bring into focus particular aspects of human being. But while raising some aspects to figural view, each method hides other aspects in the ground (see Gelso's, 1979, "bubble hypothesis"). The lens's created by methodological procedures are not transparent. Each adds its own configurative synthesis in order to construct its results. Thus, methods lead to knowledge claims that represent human constructions, not reflections, of the known (Polkinghorne, 1991a). Reliable knowledge, thus, is not the consequence of using the correct method. Instead, humanistic methodology calls for a repertoire of research procedures. Choice of method for a particular project depends on which is most useful for addressing the research question.

## Appraisal and Future Directions

Humanistic psychologists have supplied a strong philosophical ground for the humanistic methodology. They have also provided a large array of research procedures appropriate for the investigation of the human realm. These procedures range from tightly controlled experiments to hermeneutic interpretations. The humanistic methodology holds that the special characteristics of the human realm does not allow for investigations to produce indubitable knowledge about it. The realm is a "living integrity" (Zaner, 1981, p. 68) that is complex, systemic, and contextual. It consists of strata of patterned regularities with varying degrees of consistency. Its regularities are unstable compared to the regularities of the physical realm. Because of the human realm's fluidity, knowledge of it cannot remain static. The body of humanistic knowledge is not a progressive accumulation of law-like relationships, rather it is a collection of sense-making assertions that provide for a deepened understanding of human existence. The acceptability of research findings in the humanistic methodology is modeled on the judicial process. It is the cogency of evidenced argument that convinces informed critics that makes the findings worthy of inclusion in the body of knowledge. There have been exemplary research productions based on the humanistic methodology. For instance, *Women's Ways of Knowing* (Belenky, Clinchy, Goldberger, & Tarule, 1986), *Research on Adulthood and Aging: A Human Science Approach* (Thomas, 1989), and *Habits of the Heart* (Bellah, Madsen, Sullivan, & Tipton, 1985).

The present state of the development of research programs based on the humanistic methodology presents several tasks:

*1. To advance exemplars, criteria, and ideals that embody the highest achievements of humanistic research.* These ideals will provide researchers and critics a position from which to note which research projects exhibit a solid, cogent, and trustworthy course of knowledge generation. Strauss and Corbin (1990) provide a list of seven criteria for making judgments about qualitative research projects. Criteria developed in the humanities (for example, Browne & Keeley, 1990) and in history are closely aligned to humanistic methodology and can be adapted as standards for identifying which humanistic research projects exhibit excellence and are to be held up as exemplars.

*2. To understand more clearly the relationship, if any, between theoretical knowledge generated by systematic research procedures and practical knowledge generated by professional experience and reflection.* In the traditional approach, it was the academic researchers who were the developers of reliable and trustworthy knowledge. Professionals were expected to apply this knowledge in their practice. In fact, professionals have developed their own second body of knowledge and do not often utilize the knowledge developed in the academy. I propose that there are two different types of knowledge generation providing two kinds of knowledge (Maslow, 1966). Practitioner knowledge is heuristic, attuned to individual differences, and displays itself as human wisdom; academic knowledge is public, attuned to general understanding, and displays itself as knowledge statements (Hoshmand & Polkinghorne, 1992). The recognition of these two types of knowledge can redefine the relationship between the academy and the practice of psychology.

*3. To re-engage psychoanalytic method as a possible source of humanistic research procedures.* Humanistic theory was identified as the third force in psychology, being differentiated from behaviorism, the first force, and psychoanalysis, the second force. Humanistic theory criticized psychoanalysis for its hydraulic base metaphor and its emphasis on the satisfaction of primitive drives as the motivation for human behavior. Humanistic methodologists dismissed psychoanalysis research as reductive attempt to understand human existence as merely another part of the physical realm. Hillman (1983) has depicted Freud as a figure oscillating between two traditions, science and the humanities. Freud developed the psychological case history as a method for configuring a patient's inner events (the soul) and outer events (the case) into a unified and meaningful narrative (Polkinghorne, 1988). Kvale (1986) has examined psychoanalytic therapy as a research approach and found that its characteristics are similar to those advocated by humanistic methodology and Wertz (1986; 1987) found common analytic elements and metapsychological underpinnings within psychoanalytic and phenomenological research procedures. Psychoanalytic research shares with humanistic methodology a grounding in the human interactions between clients and therapists.

4. *To produce methods of judgment adequate for decision making in a situation of uncertainty.* The notion that the employment of the correct method assures the production of certain truth has been discredited. The radical skeptical response to the lack of certain knowledge was to propose that all knowledge claims are equal; that is, they proposed to replace absolute certainty with absolute relativism. Neither of these positions are acceptable; scholars and professionals are required to decide among alternatives and to choose actions that affect peoples' lives. We need to learn how to make judgments without being able to depend on the surety of our knowledge. We need to develop pragmatic procedures for developing knowledge claims and providing psychological services "in-between" certainty and relativism.

Humanistic psychology has, perhaps, had its most direct influence on the practice of psychotherapy. It proclaimed that people have an untapped potential to become self-determining, self-actualizing, and healthy individuals and groups. This message has served to support new therapeutic approaches aimed at personal and communal growth. It has been carried from its American sources to countries around the world. Humanistic psychology's promise to develop a science of the person (Coulson & Rogers, 1968) has been folded into the efforts of a larger, world-wide network of philosophers, historians, and scholars from the human disciplines and the humanities. Within this network, the particular task of humanistic psychology, because it is part of the organization of American psychologists, is to bring methodological changes within the discipline. These changes would support and encourage the use of research procedures that are designed to display the full range of human phenomena (Polkinghorne, 1984).

## References

Aanstoos, C. M. (1985). Definition of humanistic psychology. *The Humanistic Psychologist, 13* (2), Inside Cover.

Aanstoos, C. M. (1987). A comparative survey of human science psychologies. *Methods, 1* (2), 1-36.

Allport, G. W. (1937). *Personality: A psychological interpretation.* New York: Holt.

Arons, M. (1985). A quarter century of humanistic psychologies. *The Humanistic Psychologist, 13* (2), 55-60.

Bakan, D. (1966). *The duality of human existence.* Boston: Beacon.

Bakan, D. (1967). *On method: Toward a reconstruction of psychological investigation.* San Francisco: Jossey-Bass.

Barker, E. N. (1971/1972). Humanistic psychology and scientific method. *Interpersonal Development, 2*, 137-172.
Barrell, J. J. (1986). *A science of human experience.* Acton, MA: Copley.
Barrett, W. E. (1987). *Death of the soul: From Descartes to the computers.* New York: Doubleday.
Belenky, M. F., Clinchy, B. M., Goldberger, N. R., & Tarule, J. M. (1986). *Women's ways of knowing: The development of self, voice, and mind.* New York: Basic Books.
Bellah, R. N., Madsen, R., Sullivan, W. M., & Tipton, S. M. (1985). *Habits of the Heart.* Berkeley: University of California Press.
Berlyne, D. E. (1981). Humanistic psychology as a protest movement. In R. R. Royce & L. P. Mos (Eds.), *Humanistic psychology: Concepts and criticisms* (pp. 261-293). New York: Plenum.
Bleicher, J. (1980). *Contemporary hermeneutics: Hermeneutics as method, philosophy, and critique.* London: Kegan Paul.
Braginsky, B. M., & Bragnisky, D. D. (1974). *Mainstream psychology: A critique.* New York: Holt, Rinehart, & Winston.
Browne, M. N., & Keeley, S. M. (1990). *Asking the right questions: A guide to critical thinking* (3rd ed.). Englewood Cliffs, NJ: Prentice Hall.
Buckley, W. (Ed.). (1968). *Modern systems research for the behavioral scientist.* Chicago: Aldine.
Chein, I. (1972). *The science of behavior and the image of man.* New York: Basic Books.
Child, I. L. (1973). *Humanistic psychology and the research tradition: Their several virtues.* New York: John Wiley & Sons.
Coulson, W. R., & Rogers, C. R. (Ed.). (1968). *Man and the science of man.* Columbus, OH: Charles E. Merrill.
Coward, H. G., & Royce, J. R. (1981). Toward an epistemological basis for humanistic psychology. In J. R. Royce & L. P. Mos (Eds.), *Humanistic psychology: Concepts and criticisms* (pp. 109-134). New York: Plenum.
Danziger, K. (1979a). The positivist repudiation of Wundt. *Journal of the History of the Behavioral Sciences, 15*, 205-230.
Danziger, K. (1979b). The social origins of modern psychology. In A. R. Buss (Eds.), *Psychology in social context* (pp. 27-45). Chicago: University of Chicago Press.
Dewey, J. (1896). The reflex arc concept in psychology. *Psychological Review, 3*, 357-370.
Easthope, G. (1974). *A history of social research methods.* London: Longman.
Fischer, C. T., & Wertz, F. J. (1979). Empirical phenomenological analysis of being criminally victimized. In A. Giorgi, R. Knowles, & D. L. Smith (Eds.), *Duquesne studies in phenomenological psychology* (pp. 135-158). Pittsburgh: Duquesne University Press.
Friedman, M. (Ed.). (1964). *The worlds of existentialism: A critical reader.* New York: Random House.

Gadamer, H.-G. (1975). *Truth and method* (Barden, Garrett Cumming, John, Trans.). New York: Seabury Press. (Original work published 1960)

Gardner, H. (1985). *The mind's new science.* New York: Basic Books.

Gelso, C. J. (1979). Research in counseling: Methodological and professional issues. *The Counseling Psychologist, 8,* 7-35.

Gergen, M. (1989). Talking about menopause: A dialogic analysis. In L. E. Thomas (Eds.), *Adulthood and aging* (pp. 65-88). Albany: State University of New York Press.

Gergen, M. M. (Ed.). (1988). *Feminist thought and the structure of knowledge.* New York: New York University Press.

Giorgi, A. (1970). *Psychology as a human science.* New York: Harper & Row.

Giorgi, A. (1975). An application of phenomenological method in psychology. In A. Giorgi, C. T. Fischer, & E. L. Murray (Eds.), *Duquesne studies in phenomenological psychology* (pp. 82-103). Pittsburgh: Duquesne University Press.

Giorgi, A. (1981). Humanistic psychology and metapsychology. In J. R. Royce & L. P. Mos (Eds.), *Humanistic psychology: Concepts and criticisms.* New York: Plenum.

Giorgi, A. (1986a). Phenomenological views of science, validity, and reliability [Special issue]. *Journal of Phenomenological Psychology, 17* (2).

Giorgi, A. (1986b). Status of qualitative research in the human sciences: A limited inter-disciplinary and international perspective. *Methods, 1,* 29-62.

Giorgi, A. (1987). The crisis of humanistic psychology. *The Humanistic Psychologist, 15(1),* 5-20.

Glasser, B. G., & Strauss, A. L. (1967). *The discovery of grounded theory: Strategies for qualitative research.* Chicago: Aldine.

Gray, W., Fidler, J. W., & Battista, J. R. (Ed.). (1982). *General systems theory and the psychological sciences.* Seaside, CA: Intersystems.

Habermas, J. (1979). *Communication and the evolution of society* (McCarthy, T., Trans.). Boston: Beacon Press. (Original work published 1976)

Hanfling, O. (1981). *Logical positivism.* New York: Columbia University Press.

Heidegger, M. (1962). *Being and time* (John Macquarrie Edward Robinson, Trans.). New York: Harper & Row. (Original work published 1927)

Hempel, C. G. (1942). The function of general laws in history. *Journal of Philosophy, 39,* 35-48.

Hempel, C. G. (1965). *Aspects of scientific explanation and other essays in the philosophy of science.* New York: Free Press.

Hesse, M. (1980). *Revolutions and reconstructions in the philosophy of science.* Bloomington: Indiana University Press.

Hillman, J. (1983). *Healing fiction*. Barrytown, NY: Station Hill.
Hoshmand, L. T., & Polkinghorne, D. E. (1992). Redefining the science-practice relationship and professional training. *American Psychologist, 47*, 55-66.
Howard, G. S. (1988). Science, values and teleological explanations of human action. *Counseling and values, 32* (2).
Hubbard, R. (1988). Some thoughts about the masculinity of the natural sciences. In M. M. Gergen (Eds.), *Feminist thought and the structure of knowledge* (pp. 1-15). New York: New York University Press.
Husserl, E. (1931). *Ideas: General introduction to pure phenomenology* (Gibson, W. R. Boyce, Trans.). New York: Macmillan. (Original work published 1913)
Jacob, F. (1974). *The logic of living systems*. London: Allen Lane.
James, W. (1950). *Principles of psychology*. New York: Dover.
Kelman, H. C. (1968). *A time to speak: One human values and social research*. San Francisco: Jossey-Bass.
Kendler, H. H. (1987). *Historical foundations of modern psychology*. Philadelphia: Temple University Press.
Kinget, G. M. (1975). *On being human: A systematic view*. New York: Harcourt Brace.
Koch, S. (1959). Epilogue. In S. Koch (Eds.), *Psychology, a study of a science*. New York: McGraw-Hill.
Koch, S. (1961). Psychological science versus the science-human antinomy: Intimations of a significant science of man. *American Psychologist, 16*, 629-639.
Koch, S. (1964). Psychology and emerging conceptions of knowledge as unitary. In T. W. Wann (Eds.), *Behaviorism and phenomenology*. Chicago: University of Chicago Press.
Kuhn, T. S. (1970). *The structure of scientific revolutions* (2nd ed.). Chicago: University of Chicago Press.
Kvale, S. (1986). Psychoanalytic therapy as qualitative research. In P. D. Ashworth, A. Giorgi, & A. J. J. de Koning (Eds.), *Qualitative research in psychology* (pp. 155-184). Pittsburgh: Duquesne University Press.
Lakoff, G. (1987). *Women, fire, and dangerous things: What categor-ies reveal about the mind*. Chicago: University of Chicago Press.
Laszlo, E. (1973). *Introduction to systems philosophy: Toward a new paradigm of contemporary thought*. New York: Harper & Row.
Leahey, T. H. (1980). *A history of psychology: Main currents in psychological thought*. Englewood Cliffs, NJ: Prentice-Hall.
Leary, D. L. (1979). Wundt and after: Psychology's shifting relations with the natural science, social sciences, and philosophy. *Journal of the History of the Behavioral Sciences, 15*, 231-241.
LeCompte, M. D., Millroy, W. L., & Preissle, J. (Ed.). (1992). *The handbook of qualitative research in education*. San Diego: Academic.

MacIntyre, A. (1981). *After virtue.* Notre Dame, IN: University of Notre Dame Press.
Margolis, J. (1986). *Pragmaticism without foundations: Reconciling realism and relativism.* New York: Basil Blackwell.
Maslow, A. H. (1966). *The psychology of science: A reconnaissance.* Chicago: Henry Regnery.
Maslow, A. H. (1968). *Toward a psychology of being* (2nd ed.). New York: Van Nostrand Reinhold.
May, R. (Ed.). (1960). *Existential psychology.* New York: Random House.
May, R., Angel, E., & Ellenberger, H. (Ed.). (1958). *Existence: A new dimension in psychiatry and psychology.* New York: Basic.
Mead, G. H. (1934). *Mind, self, and society.* Chicago: University of Chicago Press.
Meltzer, B. N., Petras, J. W., & Reynolds, L. T. (1975). *Symbolic interactionism: Genesis, varieties, and criticism.* London: Routledge & Kegan Paul.
Merleau-Ponty, M. (1962). *Phenomenology of perception* (C. Smith, Trans.). New York: Humanities. (Original work published 1945)
Merleau-Ponty, M. (1963). *The structure of behavior* (Alden L. Fisher, Trans.). Boston: Beacon Press. (Original work published 1942)
Miles, M. B., & Huberman, A. M. (1984). *Qualitative data analysis.* Beverly Hills: Sage.
Miller, J. G. (1978). *Living systems.* New York: McGraw-Hill.
Misiak, H., & Sexton, V. S. (1973). *Phenomenological, existential, and humanistic psychologies: A historical survey.* New York: Grune & Stratton.
Morrow-Bradley, C., & Elliott, R. (1986). Utilization of psychotherapy research by practicing psychotherapists. *American Psychologist, 41,* 188-206.
Moustakas, C. (1990). *Heuristic research.* Newbury Park, CA: Sage.
Murphy, G. (1947). *Personality: A biosocial approach to origins and structure.* New York: Harper.
Murray, H. A., & al, e. (1938). *Explorations in personality: A clinical and experimental study of fifty men of college age.* New York: Oxford University Press.
Neisser, U. (1966). *Cognitive psychology.* New York: Appleton-Century-Crofts.
Patton, M. Q. (1980). *Qualitative evaluation methods.* Beverly Hills: Sage.
Patterson, C. H. (1984). Empathy, warmth and genuineness in psychotherapy. *Psychotherapy: Theory, Research, Practice, Training, 21,* 431-438.
Peirce, C. S. (Ed.). (1955). *Philosophical writings of Peirce.* New York: Dover.
Piaget, J. (1952). *The origins of intelligence in children.* New York: International Universities Press.

Polkinghorne, D. E. (1982). What makes research humanistic? *Journal of Humanistic Psychology, 22*, 47-54.

Polkinghorne, D. E. (1983). *Methodology for the human sciences: Systems of inquiry.* Albany: State University of New York Press. EDCO 502

Polkinghorne, D. E. (1984). Further extensions of methodological diversity for counseling psychology. *Journal of Counseling Psychology, 31*, 416-429.

Polkinghorne, D. E. (1988). *Narrative knowing and the human sciences.* Albany: State University of New York Press.

Polkinghorne, D. E. (1990a). Language and qualitative research. *Theoretical and Philosophical Psychology, 10*, 3-24.

Polkinghorne, D. E. (1990b). Psychology after philosophy. In R. N. Williams & J. E. Faulconer (Eds.), *Reconsidering psychology: Perspectives from Continental philosophy* (pp. 92-115). Pitts-burgh: Duquesne University Press.

Polkinghorne, D. E. (1991a). Qualitative procedures for counseling research. In C. E. Watkins & L. J. Schneider (Eds.), *Research in counseling* (pp. 163-207). Hillsdale, NJ: Lawrence Erlbaum.

Polkinghorne, D. E. (1991b). Two conflicting calls for methodological reform. *The Counseling Psychologist, 19*, 103-114.

Polkinghorne, D. E. (1992). A postmodern epistemology of practice. In S. Kvale (Eds.), *Psychology and postmodernism* (pp. 146-165). London: Sage.

Reason, P., & Rowan, J. (Eds.). (1981). *Human inquiry: A sourcebook of new paradigm research.* New York: John Wiley & Sons.

Ricoeur, P. (1977). *The rule of metaphor: Multidisciplinary studies of the creation of meaning in language* (R. Czerny, Trans.). Toronto: University of Toronto Press. (Original work published 1975)

Ricoeur, P. (1984-1989). *Time and narrative* (K. McLaughlin & D. Pellauer, Trans.). Chicago: University of Chicago Press.

Rogers, C. (1986). Toward a more human science of the person. *Methods, 1*, 7-27.

Rorty, R. (1979). *Philosophy and the mirror of nature.* Princeton, NJ:: Princeton University Press.

Rosenthal, B. G. (1971). *The images of man.* New York: Basic Books.

Rychlak, J. F. (1977). *The psychology of rigorous humanism.* New York: Wiley.

Sanford, N. (1965). Will psychologists study human problems? *American Psychologist, 20*, 192-202.

Sarason, S. B. (1981). *Psychology misdirected.* New York: Free Press.

Sarbin, T. R. (Ed.). (1986). *Narrative psychology: The storied nature of human conduct.* New York: Praeger.

Schultz, A. (1973). *Collected papers* (M. Natanson, Ed.). The Hague: Martinus Nijhoff.

Skinner, B. F. (1956). *Science and human behavior*. New York: Macmillan.
Skinner, B. F. (1971). *Beyond freedom and dignity*. New York: Knopf.
Smith, M. B. (1985). Thoughts stimulated by the quarter century conference. *The Humanistic Psychologist, 13* (2), 5-7.
Smith, M. B. (1990). Humanistic psychology. *Journal of Humanistic Psychology, 30*, 6-21.
Stocking, G. W. (Ed.). (1983). *Observers observed: Essays on ethnographic fieldwork*. Madison: University of Wisconsin Press.
Strauss, A., & Corbin, J. (1990). *Basics of qualitative research: Grounded theory procedures and techniques*. Newbury Park, CA: Sage.
Suppe, F. (1977). The search for philosophic understanding of scientific theories. In F. Suppe (Eds.), *The structure of scientific theories*. Urbana: University of Illinois Press.
Thomas, L. E. (Ed.). (1989). *Research on adulthood and aging: A human science approach*. Albany: SUNY Press.
Toulmin, S. (1972). *Human understanding: The collective use of concepts*. Princeton, NJ: Princeton University Press.
van Zuuren, F. J. (1986). The experience of breaking the rules. In P. D. Ashworth, A. Giorgi, & A. J. J. de Koning (Eds.), *Qualitative research in psychology* (pp. 304-331). Pittsburgh: Duquesne University Press.
Watson, J. B. (1913). Psychology as a behaviorist views it. *Psychological Review, 20*, 158-177.
Wertz, F. J. (1983). Some components of descriptive psychological reflection. *Human Studies, 6*, 35-51.
Wertz, F. J. (1985). Methods and findings in an empirical analysis of being criminally victimized'. In A. Giorgi (Eds.), *Phenomenology and psychological research* (pp. 155-216). Pittsburgh: Duquesne University Press.
Wertz, F. J. (1986). Meaning and research methodology: Psychoanalysis as a human science. *Methods, 1*, 91-135.
Wertz, F. J. (1987). Common methodological fundaments of the analytic procedures in phenomenological and psychoanalytic research. *Psychoanalysis and Contemporary Thought, 9*, 563-603.
Wittgenstein, L. (1968). *Philosophical investigations* (G. Anscombe, Trans.). (3rd ed.). New York: Macmillan. (Original work published 1953)
Zaner, R. M. (1981). *The context of self: A Phenomenological inquiry using medicine as a clue*. Athens: Ohio University Press.

# 9

# Humanistic Psychology and Personal Construct Theory

*Franz R. Epting and Larry M. Leitner*

George Kelly was one of the invited participants at the Old Saybrook Conference. Therefore, from the beginning of Humanistic Psychology, as a recognized term in the literature in psychology, there was a close bond between Personal Construct Psychology and the field of Humanistic Psychology. We will attempt, in this paper, to examine the nature of this relationship. We will do this first by introducing the reader to the humanistic themes within Personal Construct Psychology. Next, we will discuss some of the impact of Personal Construct Psychology on humanistic thought. The article will conclude with an overview of humanistic elaborations of the theory.

Because Kelly chose to represent his theory in a very formal way (a fundamental postulate and eleven corollaries) and because he chose an assessment system (the role construct repertory test) requiring abstract cognitive descriptions which were analyzed using factor analysis, some scholars have been all too ready to place the theory outside the humanistic camp. In some textbooks on personality psychology, Personal Construct Psychology is placed in the section on cognitive-behavioral approaches. In fact there have been few papers which have explicitly taken on the task of highlighting the humanistic themes in Personal Construct Psychology which are, in our view, the very essence of the theory (Epting, 1984; Epting & Amerikaner, 1980; Epting, Probert, & Pittman, in press; Holland, 1970; Rigdon & Epting, 1985). It seems very clear to us that Personal Construct Psychology is first and foremost a humanistic theory.

## Humanistic Themes in Personal Construct Psychology

*Constructive alternativism* is the term Kelly used to describe the philosophical stand he took in order to develop the theory. Constructive alternativism places the person in the position of having a great deal of freedom in deciding what the world is like. In Kelly's words, "the assumption is that whatever nature may be, or howsoever the quest for truth will turn out in the end, the events we face today are subject to as great a variety of constructions as our wits will enable us to contrive" (1955 p. 1). This places the person in the position of creating the meaning that life will have. It also places the person in the position of having choices in the kind of life she or he will live. But more than choices, it puts forth a type of challenge to keep discovering what different things life might hold if we only could allow ourselves the opportunity to create new meaning. With this it holds out hope and excitement about the possibilities and opportunities that life might have in store for us all if we but had the courage to step from the security of our present world into the unknown with its implied dangers.

The leading message here is that one can always begin again. Life does not have to be confined to any one pattern. Again in Kelly's own words, "Events do not tell us what to do, nor do they carry their meanings engraved on their backs for us to discover. For better or worse we ourselves create the only meaning they will ever have during our lifetime. The facts of life may even be brutal but they are nevertheless innocent of any evil intent" (1970 p. 3). The person in Personal Construct Psychology is one who is in the position of making meaning; constructing the world out of personal experiences rather than having the world dictate the meaning of one's existence. Constructive alternativism places us all in a position of toleration for the life styles of others. Since there is no fixed meaning for things, then there might be any number of effective ways to live. Using constructive alternativism challenges one to substitute opportunity for certainty. It invites the person not to be caught up in the immediacy of things but to adopt the largest perspective possible in order to interpret events.

Personal change is the central concern of this theory; the place to start is with the person's own view of the world. Taking what Kelly labeled the *credulous approach,* the therapist is urged to understand as fully as possible the client's view of things and accept this view as a legitimate place to begin the therapy. The client is treated with the dignity of one who holds a valuable view of what things are all about. It is the therapist's job to understand the point of view of the client and come to have what Kelly termed a *role relationship* with the client. The therapist's interactions with the client are based on the therapist's understanding of what the world of the client is all about. It would be no surprise then that the client's *complaint* is the starting point for the therapy.

It is from this stance of credulity and basic acceptance that the therapist attempts to engage the client in a cooperative venture in order to see how some of the complaints might be alleviated. In this adventure there is an interesting combination of the enterprises of invention and discovery. The discovery concerns helping the client find out what and how things are presently experienced and structured, whereas the invention involves opening up new experiences and possibilities for the future. In what Kelly termed the *invitational mood*, the client is invited to entertain new possibilities and try out new world views. Fixed role therapy is one of the most dramatic examples of implementation of these principles (Epting & Nazario, 1987; Kelly, 1973). In this procedure the person is actually invited to take on a new identity including a new name for a brief period of time. In the less dramatic and usual course of events, the therapy involves understanding the way the person's system of constructions of experience operate.

There are many different concerns with characteristics of the system (e.g., looseness or tightness, dilation or constriction, permeability or impermeability, etc.). In addition there is an assessment of emotional forces of anxiety, hostility, aggression, threat, etc. This all goes into a detailed four step procedure (formulating the problem, understanding the client's construction of the problem, evaluation of the client's construction system, and management and treatment) that Kelly termed *transitive diagnosis*. Transitive diagnosis is concerned with the transitions (personal changes) in life, and is contrasted with the usual categorical procedure involved in conventional diagnosis. "(W)e are looking for bridges between the client's present and his future. Moreover, we expect to take an active part in helping the client select or build the bridges to be used in helping him cross them safely. The client does not ordinarily sit cooped up in a nosological pigeonhole; he proceeds along his way" (Kelly, 1955 p. 775). Recently Raskin and Epting (in press) have developed the thesis that Szasz and Kelly have much in common in their opposition to conventional diagnosis and to the conception of disorder as a mental illness.

## Contributions of Personal Construct Psychology to Humanistic Psychology

Given the humanistic underpinnings of Personal Construct Psychology discussed above, it should come as no surprise that a number of humanistic psychologists refer directly to the impact of Kellian thought on their theoretical development. We will focus on existential-humanistic therapy (e.g., Bugental, 1987; 1990; Yalom, 1980), experiential therapy (e.g., Mahrer, 1978; 1983; 1986; 1989a; 1989b), as well as philosophy of science and personality work (e.g., Rychlak, 1968; 1977; 1979). In our opinion, it is no coincidence that these three famous humanistic psychologists (Bugental, Mahrer, and Rychlak) were students at Ohio State while Kelly taught there and have elaborated so many of Kelly's ideas. Their stature in the field clearly shows the impact Kelly had on the development of humanistic psychology.

*Existential-humanistic Therapy*

Bugental's (e.g., 1987; 1990) approach to existential-humanistic psychotherapy can be seen both as compatible with and drawing on aspects of Kelly's work. Bugental argues that life changing psychotherapy must deal with the client's *subjectivity*. In his discussion of this critical concept, Bugental states, "We are subjects rather than objects, actors not the acted upon, and this sovereignty is the essence of our subjectivity... It is the autonomy which escapes the cages of objective determinism" (p. 7). He elaborates this by stating that, "in their deepest nature, human beings are causes; not simply caused" (p. 8). Such views obviously have much in common with Kelly's ideas of an active, inquiring person whose behavior is the test of his or her creations (i.e., constructs) instead of the inevitable outcome of conditioning, biology, or instinctual drives.

Bugental elaborates his approach to therapy by focusing on the primacy of process over content. This is consistent with Kelly's emphasis on the person as a mysterious process (Leitner, 1985; Mair, 1977a). He then discusses the utility of thinking in terms of *levels of consciousness*, a concept quite similar to Kelly's notion of levels of awareness. Further, Bugental views emotions as valuable clues yet not central, in and of themselves, to the therapeutic work; this is very similar to Kelly's description of emotion being to the psychotherapist what blood is to the surgeon. Bugental then focuses more on the future, as manifested by intentionality, than the past as the primary determinant of human action. Once again, this is strikingly similar to the Kellian notion of *anticipation* as the hallmark of human experience. Finally, the goal of therapy is seen as increasing the person's experience of choice in life; symptom reduction may or may not occur in such a therapy. This goal is very consistent with Kelly's (e.g., 1980) own emphasis on adventuresome, risky choosing as a hallmark of healthy personality functioning.

Given these consistencies, it should come as no surprise that Kelly clearly is an intellectual reference point in Bugental's work. For example, a major part of Bugental's discussion of working on resistances (which he views as the central task of life changing psychotherapy) involves dealing with the "self and world construct system" (1987, p. 178). He concludes this discussion by saying:

> This self and world construct system is, of course, much broader than the resistive functions; it includes as well the constructive, functional structures which make the client's life possible and provide the fulfillments which that life yields. We see, therefore, that it is *the embracing framework* within which the resistance patterns are set (1987, p. 179, emphasis added).

This statement clearly shows the impact of Kelly's thoughts on Bugental's evolving work in humanistic existential psychotherapy. It would be most interesting to see how Bugental's work would change, should he more deliberately incorporate other classic Personal Construct Psychology ideas (e.g., the essential nature of the dialectic as exemplified in the use of contrast, constructive alternativism, etc.).

*Experiential Psychotherapy*

Mahrer (1978, 1983, 1986, 1989a, 1989b) has developed an approach to psychotherapy heavily influenced by humanistic and existential theories which he has termed *experiential psychotherapy*. Not surprisingly, there are many areas where Kelly's ideas can be seen in Mahrer's work. For example, according to Mahrer, the first criterion of a good theory of psychotherapy is that it should tell the therapist what to do (1983, p. 6). This is very similar to Kelly's view on a theory of therapy. Kelly felt that his fundamental postulate would lead to a theory of personality "which permits psychotherapy to appear both lawful and plausible" (1955, p. 50). Kelly elaborated this position in his views on *transitive diagnosis* (diagnosis leading to treatment implications) and on the process of assessment (Leitner, in press).

Secondly, Mahrer believes that a good theory of psychotherapy should be "growing, practical, heuristic, not a static vocabulary" (1983, p. 9). In other words, therapy involves dealing with people as processes, not as static entities. Thus, a theory of therapy should be a theory of process. In this regard, Kelly's emphasis on process permeated his writings (Leitner, 1985; 1988).

Mahrer also argues that a good theory of therapy "tells what falls within and without its domain" (1983, p. 12). In other words, a theory should tell the clinician what events the theory can address as well as what events it cannot. Once again, Kelly's thoughts on *range of convenience* (range of application) seem appropriate here. Kelly argued that every theory has a set of events that it can best explain (the *focus of convenience*). However, there will be some events that fall outside the explanatory capacity of the theory.

Finally, Mahrer argues that a good theory of therapy is not only linked to clinical practice; it also is "linked to its parent theory of human beings" (1983, p. 13). Such a view is quite consistent with Kelly, who developed a complete approach to psychotherapy based upon his theory of human beings. Epting (1984) details how this entire approach is logically derived from the parent theory.

In summary, Mahrer's views on a good therapeutic theory closely parallel Kelly's. Since Kelly was one of Mahrer's professors, his impact on Mahrer's work is not surprising. A challenge for the experiential therapists would be to elaborate on specific connections between their practice and Personal Construct Psychology to determine areas of agreement as well as disagreement.

*Philosophy of Science*

Kellian thought has had an enormous impact on the field of philosophy of science. For example, Rychlak (1968) has detailed an entire approach to philosophy of science within personality theories. Rychlak argues for a more "Kantian" as opposed to "Lockian" approach to personality. Such an approach rejects the blank slate of behaviorism by focusing on the inner, meaning making capabilities of the person. Further, it assumes that the person is actively involved in creating the world; reality is more invented by the person than discovered. Both of these assumptions are consistent with Kelly's assertion that it is how the events are construed, not the events themselves, that determine their meaning. Rychlak emphasizes the inherent power of the dialectic in creating meaning. The concept of the dialect is central to Kellian thought. It can be seen in the bipolar nature of personal constructs as well as in Kelly's views on how change occurs in psychotherapy. Kelly argues that *contrast reconstruction* (shifting the definition of the self from one pole to the contrast pole) often is the first step to a more substantive reconstruction of the world.

Rychlak later (1977, 1979) introduced the concept of teleology as central to a psychology of rigorous humanism. Such a concept is consistent with Kelly's emphasis on the future beckoning, more than the past determining, what the person does. Finally, one can see Kelly's influences in Rychlak's approaches to defining terms. For example, when wrestling with how to define *mind*, Rychlak (1977, p. 294) states, "We face a theoretical issue here, and, theoretical formulations can always be changed if they prove uninstructive." This is very similar to Kelly's arguments that theories always change as they proved less useful.

Clearly then, Kelly's influence can be seen in the evolution of Rychlak's thoughts. Rychlak has perhaps more systematically incorporated Kelly's ideas into his work than any other non-Personal Construct Psychology humanistic psychologist. An interesting challenge would be to elaborate some therapeutic implications of Rychlak's work to ascertain their compatibility with Personal Construct Psychology psychotherapy.

## Humanistic Elaboration of Personal Construct Psychology

Given the humanistic foundations of Personal Construct Psychology as well as its influence on several prominent humanistic psychologists, it is understandable that it has been elaborated in humanistic directions. This section of the paper will focus on some of these elaborations by briefly providing the reader with an overview of some of the exciting work in the theory performed since Kelly. We cannot provide an exhaustive overview of this work; rather we hope to clearly explain some of the more intriguing elaborations. We will focus on Rowe's (1989) work on depression, Fransella's (1977) treatment of stuttering, Ravenette's (1977, 1988) assessment of children, Epting and Neimeyer's (Epting & Neimeyer, 1984; Neimeyer & Epting, in press) work on understanding personal constructions of death, Mair's (1977a, 1977b, 1979, 1980, 1985, 1989) views on self, psychology, and narrative, Bannister's (1960, 1962) approach to schizophrenia, and Leitner's (1985, 1987, 1988; Leitner & Dill-Standiford, in press) views on terror and interpersonal connection.

### Depression

Dorothy Rowe (1983, 1987, 1988, 1989, 1990) has made a substantial contribution to understanding and treatment of depression by carefully exploring the construct systems that people use in order to develop and keep themselves trapped in this dreadful state. In the most comprehensive presentation of her work in *The Depression Handbook* (Rowe, 1991) she outlines the building blocks that go into constructing the prison of depression. This is an analysis of six beliefs which if held as core constructions (fundamental convictions) will assure depression. They are as follows, "1. No matter how good I appear to be, I am bad, evil, unacceptable to myself and to other people. 2. Other people are such that I fear, hate and envy them. 3. Life is terrible and death is worse. 4. Only bad things have happened to me in the past and only bad things will happen to me in the future. 5. Anger is evil. 6. Never forgive, and never expect to be forgiven" (Rowe, 1991 p. 89). She discusses how these beliefs are interrelated and form the world view of depression.

After dealing with some of the factors which contribute to blocking the person from escaping the prison of depression, she goes into great detail in describing the journey out of this prison. This covers a range of topics which include: 1) preparing for the journey, 2) dealing directly with suicide as no solution at all, 3) a number of new meanings which need to be explored along the way such as forgiveness, changing relationships with others and ways to validate the self, 4) finding the courage to leave loneliness behind, 5) helping others and trying out new things. In contrast to traditional cognitive views of depression, this work is a detailed exploration of the content of depressive constructions representing *both* the affective and cognitive aspects of this experience.

*Stuttering*

Using both the role construct repertory grid procedure and self characterization techniques, Fransella (1970, 1972, 1982) produced a construct procedure for exploring the experiences of persons who stutter. In her work she found that persons who stutter had very elaborate constructions about stuttering and what it means on emotional, cognitive, and behavioral levels but had very impoverished construction about verbal fluency. Her work concentrated on helping people explore their understanding of the experience of fluency. As a result of this work, she was able to show that the stuttering behavior started to change as people came to understand and experience themselves in a different way. "Stutterers improve and remain improved if they are able to take advantage of instances of fluency by actively construing them. Others have this same fluent episodes but do not *experience* fluency" (Bannister & Fransella, 1971, p. 138).

*Children*

In the area of developmental psychology the work of Tom Ravenette (1977, 1988 in press) serves as an excellent example of the inventiveness of an investigator who has chosen to explore the personal world of children. Working as an educational psychologist consulting with teachers and school principals about problematic children, Ravenette comes armed with a testing kit containing blank pieces of paper. He invites the children to draw a picture or to turn a few simple lines he has drawn on the page into a picture. After some initial exploration of the picture he often asks them to draw the opposite picture to the one they had just produced. In this way the child is invited into a most interesting dialogue about the total school situation and the teacher is brought into the picture, so to speak, by inviting the teacher to appreciate the child's world view. The child is presented as a person with a set of concerns, feelings, understandings, and beliefs which make the problem more understandable both to the child and the teacher. The child is not seen as a problem which needs to be fixed but as a person who has a construction of the world which makes his or her "problematic" behavior the only reasonable things that could be done at the moment. Ravenette has found a set of questions which are most helpful in aiding in this process. One of these is to invite the child to "say what he considers from his own point of view the trouble with different people might be." In reply he might get, "the trouble with most fathers is they favor the girls more than the boys" (Ravenette, 1977, p. 270-271). Ravenette also frequently asks children not to describe themselves but to say what they think others would say about them. For example a child might be asked, "John, what would your father say if someone asked him to describe you. Can you tell me what your father might say if someone asked him that question?" Ravenette finds that his reflected description is much easier for the child and leads to more interesting responses than asking the child to talk about herself or himself directly. This is just a sample of Ravenette's techniques and procedures but hopefully provides a fair sampling of his work. Also in the developmental area but on a more global level, Philida Salmon (1985) has provided an experiential approach to life span development. She is particularly concerned with the social construction of lives and the role of personal and social power in such a conception of persons.

*Death Threat*

For the past twenty years there has been a sustained effort to explore the personal concerns about death (Epting & Neimeyer, 1984; Neimeyer

& Epting, in press). This work began with Kelly's conception of threat and his mentioning that death is an event which is threatening to many people. From this conceptual base, Krieger, Epting, and Leitner (1974) created the Death Threat Index which is an instrument designed to investigate the extent to which a person has integrated death into his or her construct system. Produced both as a structured interview and as a brief questionnaire, participants are asked to consider a number of bipolar construct dimensions (e.g., open vs. closed) and to consider where they would place their self, ideal self, and death on these dimensions. The extent to which they place death on the opposite pole to both self and ideal self indexes the level of death threat. There have been a number of research studies carried out, and by all accounts, the Threat Index is among the most extensively developed instruments in the field. For example, high death threat physicians were found to use more denial strategies when confronting a patient's death (Neimeyer, Behnke, & Reiss, 1984). Hospice patients were found to be dramatically lower in death threat compared to other groups of patients (Hendon & Epting, 1989). Older adults with low death scores made more explicit body disposal arrangements (Rainey & Epting, 1977).

Recent factor analytic work has yielded three subscores (threat to well-being, uncertainty, fatalism) as well as still allowing for a global threat score (Neimeyer, Moore, & Bagley, 1988). In addition, a recent development in the basic scoring procedure has offered not only the standard *death-threat profile* but has provided the opportunity to attain profiles for *death acceptance, depression*, and *death-attraction*. This instrument can also be used easily in interviews and in workshop settings (Prichard & Epting, in press). Participants are asked to carefully examine the construct dimensions on which they placed death on the opposite pole to where they placed their self and ideal self. Participants are then asked to pick out a set of five or six dimensions that truly seem to matter to them; ones they really thought it important that death be placed on the opposite side of the construct from self and ideal self. It has been found that this type of procedure leads to most interesting conversations about death and personal concerns about living.

*Schizophrenia*

Bannister (1960, 1962, 1963, 1965; Bannister, Adams-Webber, Penn & Radley, 1975; Bannister & Fransella, 1966; Bannister, Fransella, & Agnew, 1971; Bannister & Salmon, 1966) has elaborated a Personal Construct Psychology approach to schizophrenia that presents a serious challenge to traditional, reductionistic, medical models of this disorder. Basically, his theory holds that the schizophrenic's constructions of the future are *serially invalidated* by the person's interpersonal world. Invalidation is experienced when one's personal meanings are inconsistent with the events of the world. Serial invalidation leads to a progressive loosening of the construct system as, when constructs are too vague, they cannot be tested concretely in the world; without such concrete tests, the schizophrenic protects the self against further invalidation.

Bannister has provided an impressive amount of data in support of his hypothesis. For example, he has shown that thought disordered schizophrenics do show a greater looseness in the linkages between their constructs. Further, when serially invalidated, most persons begin to loosen such that the linkages between their constructs become more similar to thought disordered schizophrenics. Bannister, Adams-Webber, Penn, & Radley (1975) systematically *validated* the construing of thought disordered schizophrenics and reported greater tightening of the linkages between constructs. Finally, Bannister & Salmon (1966; see also Salmon, Bramley, & Presly, 1967) reported that the difference between schizophrenics and "normals" on Personal Construct Psychology measures of conceptual disorganization are greatest when interpersonal construing is measured; it is much less noticeable when the schizophrenic construes the non-interpersonal world. Thus, in contrast to traditional assumptions about schizophrenia, Bannister's work would suggest that thought disorder might be reversible by psychological treatments and that "theories of 'schizococcus' would perhaps have to postulate an unlikely bug that bites 'person thinking' rather than 'object thinking' brain cells" (Bannister & Fransella, 1982, p. 167).

*Mair's notions of self and psychology*
Mair (1977a, 1977b, 1979, 1980, 1985, 1989) has been responsible for many humanistic elaborations of Personal Construct Psychology. First, his notion of *community of self*, in which many different selves are available for relating to and understanding the world has important implications for psychotherapy. The idea that one has multiple selves may enable clients to risk experimenting with aspects of themselves that otherwise might appear too threatening in a more monolithic system. In other words, if this is just one of many selves, the client does not have to construe certain experiences as leading to massive conclusions about the nature of reality. Such a notion encourages risk, action, and freedom.

Second, Mair (e.g., 1977b) has been a leading figure in separating the person within Personal Construct Psychology from the constructs the person creates to understand the world. For Mair, the person always is a mystery lying behind the constructs themselves. This is a critical distinction in that it clearly separates Personal Construct Psychology from traditional cognitive behavioral theories that are antagonistic to its humanistic emphasis.

Finally, Mair (1989) has become a forceful advocate of non-traditional methodologies for exploring the experience of the person. He argues strongly for the use of narrative research methodologies as well as poetry in understanding central aspects of human experience. In so doing, he not only elaborates construct research paradigms in more humanistic ways; he also is a part of a growing movement utilizing non-traditional research methodologies within personality psychology.

*Terror and interpersonal connection*

Leitner (1985, 1987, 1988; Leitner & Dill-Standiford, in press) has been working on understanding the nature of deeply intimate relationships (*ROLE relationships*) from a Personal Construct Psychology perspective. In so doing, he has attempted to elaborate the relational, interconnected aspects of Personal Construct Psychology. Elaborating Kelly's sociality corollary, Leitner (1985) has argued that, in ROLE relationships, one person is construing the most central meaning making aspects of another. However, since most others will not expose their most central meanings to a total stranger, each person must be willing to allow the other to see his or her most central processes. Exposing my central meanings to you can be enormously enriching, particularly if you validate me. However, should you reject, either blatantly or subtly, my most fundamental definers of who I am, I will experience overwhelming invalidation.

Thus, persons are confronted with a dilemma between opening one's most central meanings to others and risk overwhelming invalidation (terror) versus closing one's core from others and settling for a safe yet empty existence. Since ROLE relationships can be so terrifying, it is not surprising that people have found numerous ways to retreat from the genuine ROLE experience of human to human engagement. *Experiential personal construct psychotherapy* (Leitner, 1988), the term used to describe the clinical approach, attempts to engage the person on these issues. In so doing, experiential personal construct psychotherapy confronts the person with the challenge of struggling with the therapist over ways of engaging versus retreating from ROLE relationships. This places the interpersonal struggle into the living relationship of the therapy room. This lived immediacy challenges both participants to grow as each encounters the other (see Leitner, 1987, for a case description).

Obviously, these elaborations have much in common with the increasing emphasis on relationships both within humanistic psychology as well as in personality psychology more broadly. Further, it clearly elaborates on the existential roots of Personal Construct Psychology in that the concept of ROLE relationships is very similar to Buber's (1970) notion of "I—Thou" relationships. Finally, the issues of meaning and meaninglessness, so central in Leitner's work, clearly have existential implications (see Yalom, 1980).

## Conclusion

In conclusion, we hope this article has shown that Personal Construct Psychology has had an impact on the field of humanistic psychology. Kelly's radically liberating ideas continue to influence many thinkers within the field. Further, this impact is far greater than most humanistic psychologists recognize. The more recent humanistic elaborations of Personal Construct Psychology only underscore the continued potential contribution of the theory to the broader field. In this regard, a theory which gives dignity to the person while maintaining theoretical respectability has the potential to revolutionize psychology in both its academic and applied contexts.

## References

Bannister, D. (1960). Conceptual structure in thought disordered schizophrenics. *Journal of Mental Science, 106*, 1230-1249.

Bannister, D. (1962). The nature and measurement of schizophrenic thought disorder. *Journal of Mental Science, 108*, 825-842.

Bannister, D. (1963). The genesis of schizophrenic thought disorder: A serial invalidation hypothesis.*British Journal of Psychiatry, 109*, 680-686.

Bannister, D. (1965). The genesis of schizophrenic thought disorder: Re-test of the serial invalidation hypothesis. *British Journal of Psychiatry, 111*, 377-382.

Bannister, D., Adams-Webber, J. R., Penn, W. I., & Radley, A. R. (1975). Reversing the process of thought disorder: A serial validation experiment. *British Journal of Social and Clinical Psychology, 14*, 169-180.

Bannister, D. & Fransella, F. (1966). A grid test of schizophrenic thought disorder. *British Journal of Social and Clinical Psychology, 5*, 95-102.

Bannister, D. & Fransella, F. (1982). *Inquiring man: The psychology of personal constructs. Malabar, FL: Krieger.*

Bannister, D., Fransella, F. & Agnew, J. (1971). Characteristics and validity of the grid test of thought disorder. *British Journal of Social and Clinical Psychology, 10,* 144-151.

Bannister, D. & Salmon, P. (1966). Schizophrenic thought disorder: Specific or diffuse? *British Journal of Medical Psychology, 39,* 215-219.

Buber, M. (1970). *I and thou.* New York: Charles Scribner.

Bugental, J. F. T. (1987).*The art of the psychotherapist.* New York: Norton.

Bugental, J. F. T. (1990). *Intimate journeys.* San Francisco: Jossey Bass.

Epting, F. R. (1984). *Personal construct counseling and psychotherapy.* New York: Wiley.

Epting, F., & Amerikaner, M. (1980). Optimal functioning: A personal construct approach. In A. W. Landfield & L. M. Leitner (Eds.), *Personal construct psychology: Psychotherapy and personality (pp. 55-73).* New York: John Wiley & Sons.

Epting, F. R., Nazario, Jr., A. (1987). Designing a fixed role therapy: Issues, techniques, and modifications. In R. A. Neimeyer & G. J. Neimeyer (Eds.), *Personal construct therapy casebook* (277-289). New York: Springer.

Epting, F. R., & Neimeyer, R. A. (1984)(Eds.). *Personal meanings of death.* New York: Hemisphere.

Epting, F. R., Probert, J. S., & Pittman, S. D. (in press). Alternative strategies for construct elicitation: Opportunities for adventure. *International Journal of Personal Construct Psychology.*

Fransella, F. (1970). Stuttering: Not a symptom but a way of life. *British Journal of Disordered Communication, 5,* 22-29.

Fransella, F. (1972). *Personal change and reconstruction: Research on a treatment of stuttering.* London: Academic Press.

Fransella, F. (1982). Stuttering to fluency via reconstruing. In R. A. Neimeyer & G. J. Neimeyer (Eds.), *Personal construct therapy casebook.* New York: Springer.

Hendon, M. K., & Epting, F. R. (1989). A comparison of hospice patients with recovering and ill patients. *Death Studies, 13,* 567-578.

Holland, R. (1970). George Kelly: Constructive innocent and reluctant existentialist. In D. Bannister (Ed.), *Perspectives in personal construct theory.* London: Academic Press.

Kelly, G. A. (1955). *The psychology of personal constructs* (2 vols.). New York: Norton.

Kelly, G. A. (1970). A brief introduction to personal construct theory. In D. Bannister (Ed.), *Perspectives in personal construct theory.* New York: Academic Press.

Kelly, G. A. (1973). Fixed role therapy. In R. M. Jerjevich (Ed.), *Direct Psychotherapy: 28 American originals* (pp. 394-422). Coral Gables, FL: University of Miami Press.

Kelly, G. A. (1980). A psychology of the optimal man. In A. W. Landfield & L. M. Leitner (Eds.),*Personal construct psychology: Psychotherapy and personality*. New York: Wiley Interscience.

Krieger, S. R., Epting, F. R., & Leitner, L. M. (1974). Personal constructs, threat, and attitudes toward death. *Omega, 20,* 87-95.

Leitner, L. M. (1985). The terrors of cognition: On the experiential validity of personal construct theory. In D. Bannister (Ed.), *Issues and approaches in personal construct theory* (pp. 83-103). London: Academic.

Leitner, L. M. (1987). Crisis of the self: The terror of personal evolution. In G. Neimeyer & R. Neimeyer (Eds.), *Personal construct therapy case book* (pp. 39-56). New York: Springer.

Leitner, L. M. (1988). Terror, risk, and reverence: Experiential personal construct psychotherapy. *International Journal of Personal Construct Psychology, 1,* 261-272.

Leitner, L. M. (in press). Dispositional assessment techniques in experiential personal construct psychotherapy. *International Journal of Personal Construct Psychology.*

Leitner, L. M. & Dill-Standiford, T. (in press). Resistance in experiential personal construct psychotherapy: Theoretical and technical struggles. In L. M. Leitner & N. G. M. Dunnett (Eds.), *Critical issues in personal construct psychotherapy.* Malabar, FL: Krieger.

Mahrer, A. R. (1978). *Experiencing: A humanistic theory of psychology and psychiatry.* New York: Bruner Mazel.

Mahrer, A. R. (1983). *Experiential psychotherapy: Basic practices.* New York: Bruner Mazel.

Mahrer, A. R. (1986). *Therapeutic experiencing: The process of change.* New York: Norton.

Mahrer, A. R. (1989a). *Dreamwork in psychotherapy and self change.* New York: Norton.

Mahrer, A. R. (1989b). *How to do experiential psychotherapy: A manual for practitioners.* Ottawa: University of Ottawa Press.

Mair, J. M. M. (1977a). Metaphors for living. In A. W. Landfield & J. K. Cole (Eds.), *Nebraska symposium on motivation* (vol. 24). Lincoln: University of Nebraska Press, pp. 243-290.

Mair, J. M. M. (1977b). The community of self. In D. Bannister (Ed.), *New perspectives in personal construct theory.* London: Academic.

Mair, J. M. M. (1979). The personal venture. In P. Stringer & D. Bannister (Eds.), *Constructs of sociality and individuality.* London: Academic.

Mair, J. M. M. (1980). Feeling and knowing. In P. Salmon (Ed.), *Coming to know.* London: Routledge.

Mair, J. M. M. (1985). The long quest to know. In F. R. Epting & A. W. Landfield (Eds.), *Anticipating personal construct psychology.* Lincoln: University of Nebraska Press.

Mair, J. M. M. (1989). *Between psychology and psychotherapy: A poetics of experience*. London: Routledge.

Neimeyer, G. J., Behnke, M., & Reiss, J. (1984). Constructs and coping: Physicians' responses to patient death. In F. R. Epting & R. A. Neimeyer, (Eds.), *Personal meanings of death* (pp. 159-180). New York: Hemisphere.

Neimeyer, R. A., & Epting, F. R. (in press). Measuring personal meanings of death: 20 years of research using the Threat Index. In G. J. Neimeyer, & R. A. Neimeyer (Eds.), *Advances in Personal Construct Psychology* (vol. 2). Greenwich, CT: JAI.

Neimeyer, R. A., Moore, M. K., & Bagley, K. (1988). A preliminary factor structure for the Threat Index. *Death Studies, 12*, 217-225.

Prichard, S., & Epting, F. R. (in press). Diversity from simplicity: A review of the Threat Index. *Omega*.

Rainey, L. C., & Epting, F. R. (1977). Death threat constructions in the student and the prudent. *Omega, 8*, 19-28.

Raskin, J., & Epting, F. R. (in press). Personal construct theory and the argument against mental illness. *International Journal of Personal Construct Psychology*.

Ravenette, A. T. (1977). Personal construct theory: An approach to the psychological investigation of children and young people. In D. Bannister (Ed.), *New perspectives in personal construct theory*. London: Academic Press.

Ravenette, A. T. (1988). Personal construct psychology in the practice of an educational psychologist. In G. Dunnett (Ed.), *Working with people* (pp. 101-121). London: Routledge.

Ravenette, A. T. (in press). Transcending the obvious and illuminating the ordinary: Personal construct psychology and consultation in the practice of educational psychology. In L. M. Leitner & N. G. M. Dunnett (Eds.), *Critical issues in personal construct psychotherapy*. Malabar, FL: Krieger.

Rigdon, M. A., & Epting, F. R. (1985). Reduction in death threat as a basis for optimal functioning. *Death Studies, 9*, 427-450.

Rowe, D. (1983). *Depression: The way out of your prison*. London: Routledge.

Rowe, D. (1987). *Beyond fear*. London: Fontana/Collins.

Rowe, D. (1988). *Choosing not losing: The experience of depression*. London: Fontana/Collins.

Rowe, D. (1989). *The construction of life and death: Discovering meaning in a world of uncertainty*. London: Fontana/Collins.

Rowe, D. (1991). *The depression handbook*. London: Fontana/Collins.

Rychlak, J. F. (1968). *A philosophy of science for personality theory*. Boston: Houghton Mifflin.

Rychlak, J. F. (1977). *The psychology of rigorous humanism*. New York: Wiley Interscience.

Rychlak, J. F. (1979). *Discovering free will and personal responsibility*. New York: Oxford University Press.
Salmon, P. (1985). *Living in time: A new look at personal development*. London: J. M. Dent & Sons.
Salmon, P., Bramley, J., & Presly, A. S. (1967). The "word in context test" as a measure of conceptualization in schizophrenics with and without thought disorder. *British Journal of Medical Psychology, 40*, 253-259.
Yalom, I. (1980). *Existential psychotherapy*. New York: Basic.

# 10

# Humanistic Values and the Future: Freedom and Social Activism

*George S. Howard*

### Self-Determination as a Humanistic Dream

Clearly, there are several central tenets of humanistic approaches to the study of the person. Depending upon the theorist one reads, constructs like consciousness, self-actualization, creativity, spirituality, self-determination, free will, growth and development, experience, phenomenological field, and the like receive varying degrees of emphasis in humanistic theorizing. Tageson (1982) sees seven themes in humanistic psychology: (1) the approach tends to be phenomenological; (2) holistic rather than reductionistic themes tend to prevail; (3) a place for an actualizing tendency is common; (4) self-determination is important: (5) authenticity is a central theme; (6) humans are seen as self-transcendent; and (7) approaches tend to be person-centered rather than method-centered. The definition of humanistic psychology that comes closest to my own theoretical and experimental interests highlights the importance of Tageson's (1982) point #4, and comes from Polkinghorne (1982), "What seems to define us as humanistic psychologists is not our commitment to particular methods of research but to our understanding that human beings exist within an experience of meaning and retain the possibility of acting with self-determined purpose" (pp. 47-48). From this perspective, any methodology that sheds light upon the nature of humans as self-determining active agents, involved in the creation of meaning, plans, purposes, goals, intentions, and so forth, can be considered humanistic.

While humanists highlight the role of human freedom, creativity, spontaneity, will, and intentionality in the genesis of human action, this ambition clashes with the goal of many mechanistic approaches to psychology which strive to explain as much of human action as possible through nonagentic, causal mechanisms (whether the causes be environmental, genetic, physiological, social, psychodynamic, etc.). The tension between these humanistic and mechanistic scientific ambitions is highlighted nicely by Berger (1963):

> Freedom is not empirically available. More precisely, while freedom may be experienced by us as a certainty along with other empirical certainties, it is not open to demonstration by any scientific methods... Every object of scientific scrutiny is presumed to have an anterior cause. An object, or an event, that is its own cause lies outside the scientific universe of discourse. Yet freedom has precisely this character... The individual who is conscious of his own freedom does not stand outside the world of causality, but rather perceives his own volition as a very special category of cause, different from the other causes that he must reckon with. This difference, however, is not subject to scientific demonstration... There is no way of perceiving freedom, either in oneself or in another being, except through a subjective inner certainty that dissolves as soon as it is attacked with the tools of scientific analysis. (pp. 122-124)

While Berger's claims were originally factually correct, recent methodological refinements now make possible demonstrations of precisely what Berger claimed to be impossible. That is, we are now able to provide scientific evidence of self-determination or behavioral freedom in human actions.

As many humanistic theorists (e.g., Howard, 1992; May, 1981; Rychlak, 1979) have asserted, one would be ill-advised to deny that nonagentic causes exist and influence human actions in important ways. What the humanistic theorist denies is that a thorough understanding of the nonagentic causes on humans will lead to perfect understanding of human behavior. That is because the causal influence of self-determination (or freedom of the will) has not yet been included in the analysis. Given all the mechanistic influences at work in a person at any point in time, there is still some freedom of action (sometimes very small, sometimes enormous) available to the person. Thus, a task of humanistic psychology is to come to understand how persons express their freedom in the formation of human action, as these people make their way through a world populated with nonagentic, causal influences.

## Research on Self-Determination

A recent line of research has demonstrated that humans can self-determine their actions to a large extent in a broad array of domains (Howard & Conway, 1986; Howard, DiGangi, & Johnson, 1988; Howard & Myers, 1990; Howard, Youngs, & Siatczynski, 1989). The crucial aspect of the new methodology for investigating volitional behavior is that it requires the active cooperation of the research subject. If, for whatever reason, the subject chooses not to cooperate fully with the experimenter, a serious underestimate of that subject's degree of volitional control will be obtained.

One of the first procedures developed involves the experimenter dividing the total time for the experiment into a large number of equal-length time blocks. The experimenter then randomly assigns each of the time blocks to either "try to ___" or "try not to ___" conditions. For example, if one considered subjects' ability to control between-meals snacks, as a part of their ability to lose weight, the instructions for each subject on half the studies' days would be to "eat as many snacks as you wish" whereas on the other half of the days, subjects would be instructed to "try not to eat any snacks." Differences in mean number of snacks consumed on "eat" versus "not eat" days is a reflection of the subject's ability to volitionally control snacking behavior. Studies of self-determination in alcohol consumption, exercise adherence, procrastination, binge eating and purging have also been conducted.

The methodology used in these studies enables removal of the effects of all possible nonagentic (e.g., environmental, physiological, etc.) causal influences save one from these estimates of subjects capacities to self-determine their actions. The uncontrolled factor is the possibility that subjects must conform to the experimenter's demands (or that the subject must be obedient to an experimenter's authority, cf. Milgram, 1974). The plausibility of this rival interpretation, in which conformity is a factor, was specifically tested in several studies (Howard & Conway, 1986, Study 2; Howard, Myers, & Curtin, 1991, Studies 1 & 2; Howard et al., 1989, Study 2). In every case, conformity was found to contribute real but minuscule amounts to the effects of self-determination. For example, in one study (Howard et al., 1991 Study 2) subjects were given three separate commands to obey each day by an experimenter (e.g., try to eat celery; try not to read any psychology; try to strike your children). Commands were made in three different domains, ethically neutral, ethically moderately important, ethically very important. Subjects were completely capable of separating "try to — " from "try not to — " days in the ethically neutral domain. They were modestly successful in the moderately important ethical domain, and showed no evidence of separating groups of "try to — " from "try not to — " days in the ethically important domain. The evidence of previous studies on self-determination show subjects chose to "go along" with the experimental instructions, but were not compelled to do so (i.e., the evidence suggests that subjects might have done otherwise, "disobeyed" had they so desired).

Research in this domain has only begun. Researchers need to specify exactly how human self-determination achieves its effects in a world of nonagentic, coercive mechanisms. Scientists always strive for a deeper, richer understanding of powers (or capacities, or generative mechanisms) that underlie observed experimental relationships. Polkinghorne's (1982) definition of humanistic research gives a clue as to one of the wellsprings of self-determination. He ties this capacity for freedom of the will to the fact that "human beings exist within an experience of meaning." Subsequent studies (Howard, Curtin, & Johnson, 1991) probed the way in which an action's meaning for the person (and changes in its meaning) is related to that individual's ability to self-determine his or her actions (and to changes in his or her ability to self-determine) in that domain. Thus, the common expression that someone will move an issue to a front burner implies that the meaningfulness (importance) of that issue is being enhanced in order to secure greater ability to self-direct actions more precisely in that domain. How is meaning created in human lives?

All human thought might be considered forms of storytelling (Howard, 1989; 1991). This link between meaning and storytelling is one of the rich interfaces between humanistic psychology and the humanities and arts. Polkinghorne (1988) claims that "we make our existence into a whole by understanding it as an expression of *a single and developing story*" (p. 150). McAdams (1985) agrees, and highlights the role of storytelling in the development of identity:

> My central proposition is that identity is a life story which individuals begin constructing, consciously or unconsciously, in late adolescence. As such, identities may be understood in terms directly relevant to stories. Like stories, identities may assume a "good" form — a narrative coherence and consistency — or they may be ill-formed... The life-story model of identity suggests how the personologist, or anyone else seeking to understand the whole person, may apprehend identity in narrative terms. Further, the model suggests hypotheses about identity which can be

tested in research, and less rigorously, in personal experience. (pp. 57-58)

Finally, research methodologies have been developed and validated (Howard & Fisher, 1990; Howard, Maerlender, Myers, & Curtin, 1992) that extract the core of a person's life-theme from his or her autobiographical materials. All these recent developments in research methodology are humanistic in that they do not seek to make human nature conform to the demands of preexisting scientific methodologies. Rather, like other humanistic research methods (e.g., phenomenological methods), the techniques were developed to fit with important capacities of human nature (e.g., subjectivity, self-determination, meaningfulness, life-themes, etc.) that were not explored (nor found to exist) in the physical sciences. In the process we are moving toward a satisfactory, affirmative answer to Rogers' (1973) challenging question "Dare we develop a human science?"

### From the Individual to the Group: Constraints on Freedom

If each of us weaves the facts of our lives into a meaningful story. Where do those story-lines (or life-themes) that characterize our lives come from? Surely, each of us does not create our own storied identify *ex nihilo*. Mair (1988) highlights the role of dominant cultural worldviews (what he colorfully refers to as the great stories of our race, place, and time) as templates that structure the form of our individual stories.

> Stories are habitations. We live in and through stories. They conjure worlds. We do not know the world other than as story world. Stories inform life. They hold us together and keep us apart. We inhabit the great stories of our culture. We live through stories. We are *lived* by the stories of our race and place. It is this enveloping and constituting function of stories that is especially important to sense more fully. We are, each of us, locations where the stories of our place and time become partially tellable. (p. 127)

So, while the story of George Howard (for example) is unlike any other life-story ever told, it borrows heavily from several great stories of my race, place, and time. That is, my life and beliefs (my very identity, in McAdams' [1985] terms) borrow heavily from the stories of the march of Western civilization, Roman Catholicism, the Protestant ethic, liberal democracy, science, liberal education, and psychology.

There is a reciprocal relationship between my story and these great stories. First, I tell myself into existence by writing myself into these great narratives. I actually become who I am by becoming a member of the relevant community of the faithful — a citizen of the United States, a member of the Christian community, a scientist, a psychologist, and so forth. But then I begin to exert a small but important role in the emerging future of each of those relevant communities. For example, for about twenty years (roughly from college through tenure) I was being formed into a psychologist and a scientist by psychology and science (as understood by my race, in my place, and at that time). But, during that time I had no influence upon the path of those communities. But, the program of research on self-determination outlined above will exert a small influence upon psychology and (because psychology is partly a science) might eventually also achieve some minuscule impact on the course of science. We are, each of us, brick-by-brick building the future of humanistic psychology, liberal democracy, science, Roman Catholicism, and other great stories of our times, places, and races. And while membership in a community offers an individual the freedom to shape the future of that community, it also extracts its own price for the opportunity. Sin, taxes, and editorial review are but three of many freedom-inhibiting devices with which we must come to grips. Once again we find our personal freedom wrapped within the embrace of various constraints — we are not completely free to do anything we please. Human life involves telling our unique story within the flow of the great stories in which we partake. And while we now have compelling evidence for the existence of human freedom (at the level of the individual), such findings do not guarantee that humans are free to alter societal (group level phenomena) trends.

*Imagine!*
I sometimes think of myself as if I were a fish! (I'd like to picture myself as a twenty-five-inch rainbow trout, but an eight-inch sucker might be closer to the truth.) So here I am in this stream of life, and I think, "I could burrow into the mud today" or "Maybe I'll lie under that log for awhile" or "Perhaps I'll swim upstream and see what's happening." Well, one might say I'm self-determining — right? But we know that events — like whether or not a worm gets washed downstream or a fly lands on the surface of the stream — are really important considerations in what a fish will eventually do. Whether or not those potential dinners are imbedded with hooks could be of more than minor import upon our finny friends' life course. And we fish don't even like to think about the possibility of apocalyptic events like droughts, acid rain, floods, hydroelectric plants, chemical spills, and the like. So you can see why it

is problematic — even for our self-determining fish — to predict his or her life course.

While fish-metaphors can sometimes be helpful, it is important to know exactly where they fail. While humans are like six-inch suckers in some ways, they are very different in other ways. For example, humans possess the capacity for "foresight and understanding" (Toulmin, 1961) in ways that fish never will. Humans can project themselves into possible futures in ways that suckers probably never will. By empathically experiencing how life would feel in such a hypothetical future, humans can evaluate whether creating such a future would represent a desired ambition or an apocalyptic nightmare. Based upon his or her evaluation, the self-determining agent might then act in such a way as to make the possible future more (or less) likely to occur. But, of course, there are some events (such as humans polluting a fish's streams) over which our self-determining finny-friends have no control. So perhaps there is a greater wisdom behind the fact that six-inch suckers are extremely limited in their powers of foresight and understanding.

## Projecting Humanistic Values into the Future

### In Stories We Trust

Why do futurists spin their tales of the future? Why did George Orwell write the futuristic novel *1984* (Orwell, 1949)? Orwell painted a worst-case scenario in extrapolating several trends that he saw in society at that time. Why does one tell a horrific tale of the future? Undoubtedly, it is done to jolt readers into the realization that unless determined action is taken in the present, the future could be nightmarish. Not only is this an important fictional style, the genre is growing in importance as a strategy for scientists concerned about the future of our planet (e.g., *State of the World: 1991* by Lester R. Brown, 1991). Such studies extrapolate present trends in an array of issues of global ecology (e.g., pollution, population growth, ozone depletion, non-renewable energy use, food production, deforestation, desertification) and demonstrate precisely when (at current rates) the planet will become uninhabitable due to each of (and a combination of) these problems. Such objective, dispassionate predictions of apocalyptic consequences represent (in my opinion) a related rhetorical style to the *1984*-type futuristic, fictional, horror tale. But these *State of the World* projections (Brown, 1991) are not fictional — they dramatize the reality that we are not now a sustainable global society. As these trends become more compelling with each passing year, the chances grow slimmer that humanity will exert the sorts of herculean efforts necessary to reverse the trends, in order to avert catastrophe. Obviously, we will all watch in horror as each of these particular dramas play themselves out over the next three or four decades. Recalling the 1960's slogan, "If you are not part of the solution, then you are part of the problem," one might wonder what positive role (if any) humanistic psychology is playing in this worldwide, ecological drama.

Telling horror stories of the future represents a strategy that first seeks to identify a value with which we can all agree — such as a habitable world where there is still a place for human dignity. The futurists then point to current trends which, if sustained, seriously endanger that value. Therein lies the horror — a future devoid of a current "good" (such as living space, sufficient nourishment, clean air, human freedom, etc.).

Many of us, in our work as therapists, consultants, educators, and the like, are involved in various aspects of the humanist ambition of facilitating the growth and development of the hopes and dreams of humans. Rogers (1951) was especially insightful in demonstrating how helpers, by entering the experiential world of others, can facilitate the articulation of the others' ambitions and hopes. But, alas, there are numerous biological, political, social, and economic forces at play that profoundly impact the lives and possible futures of all humans. The remainder of this article considers the spectre of a demographic trend that has the potential for ravaging the futures of many billions of human beings.

*The Ticking Population Bomb*

Our world is perilously close to being overpopulated with human beings. Population is the crucial key to all the pressing environmental issues we face — it represents a common cause of many problems:

> The size of the human population affects virtually every environmental condition facing our planet. As our population grows, demands for resources increase, leading to pollution and waste. More energy is used, escalating the problems of global warming, acid rain, oil spills and nuclear waste. More land is needed for agriculture, contributing to deforestation and soil erosion. More homes, factories and roads must be built, occupying habitat lost by other species that share the planet, often leading to their extinction. Simply put, the more people inhabiting our finite planet, the greater the stress on its resources. (Weber, 1991)

What is the current status of this common cause of many of lifeboat earth's maladies? Is world population increasing, remaining constant, or declining? It was not until 1810 that the earth's population reached one billion. It reached two billion in 1927, three billion in 1960, four billion in 1974, five billion in 1987, and is projected to reach six billion by 1998 (data according to the Population Reference Bureau, 1989). The data are so clear that it is impossible to argue with Malthus' (1798/1964) seminal insight that while population increases geometrically, food production increases only arithmetically. But in the face of such inexorable natural processes, some predictions can be made with great confidence.

The population of any species cannot increase indefinitely on our planet. Continued population increases coupled with relatively steady death rates (the current circumstance for the world) represents an inherently unstable situation. Either the world's birth rate must decline or the death rate will (of necessity) increase.

> In summary, the world's population will continue to grow as long as the birth rate exceeds the death rate; it's as simple as that. When it [the worlds population] stops growing or starts to shrink, it will mean that either the birth rate has gone down or the death rate has gone up or a combination of the two. Basically, then, there are only two kinds of solution to the population problem. One is a "birth rate solution," in which we find ways to lower the birth rate. The other is a "death rate solution," in which ways to raise the death rate — war, famine, pestilence — *find us*. The problem could have been avoided by population control, in which mankind consciously adjusted the birth rate so that the "death rate solution" did not have to occur. (Ehrlich, 1968, pp. 34-35.)

Our inability to curb our birth rate demands increases in the death rate. The outline of how mortality will increase in the future is already taking shape. The World Health Organization (W.H.O.) now estimates that 40,000 children (i.e., less than 5 years old) needlessly die each day — that is, 14,600,000 such children die every year.

> The children will die of disease, hunger and neglect. Most could have been saved with medicine, food, money, and attention if only they had been provided. To allow people of any age to die when they could have been saved is moral slaughter, a reality almost too obvious to pronounce... Of course, as the W.H.O. tables show, adults, too, die of preventable or curable disease and malnutrition. But of the yearly total of 50 million victims, one-third have not lived to their fifth birthday. The chance of living beyond the fifth birthday in one of these countries where children have big bellies and lolling heads is *one in eight*. Two-thirds of the dead children did not achieve their first birthday. (Rosenthal, 1991, p. A15)

I am sad to say that these tragic deaths are already factored into the figures (and projections) of population growth. If we managed to save a substantial number of these unfortunate children, the population growth would be even more alarming! When pondering such depressing world trends, one might be struck by the similarity between populations of lemmings and humans. But the death of children is far from the only effect of overcrowding. Homelessness (Jones, Levine, & Rosenberg, 1991), environmental degradation (Young, 1991), the traumatization of children (Melton, 1991; Garbarino, Kostelny, & Durow, 1991), crime and violence (Siegel, 1983), migration and refugee problems (Vernez, 1991; Williams & Berry, 1991) — and their psychological consequences too numerous to catalogue — are also produced by overcrowding.

## The Humanists' Dilemma:
## Too Many People — Too Much of a Good Thing

A core humanistic belief is that people possess an innate value. Each person represents a valued end in and of himself or herself. But human beings are quickly becoming their own worst enemy. Overpopulation is rapidly becoming the single, greatest threat to the growth and happiness of all individual humans. It requires a basic rethinking of our notions of rationality to understand how too many "goods" constitute an intolerably "bad" circumstance. And, as ecologists have recently acknowledged, there is no technological cure in the offing for this problem. What is required is a basic rethinking of our reproductive attitudes and behaviors — what is required is a sweeping revision of the psychology of reproduction. Humanists might take the lead in championing the cause that the future welfare of all humans rests upon the species' ability to control its rate of reproduction.

The task facing psychologists in population control is daunting challenge. One could argue that in fighting overpopulation, we are pitted against the effects of a million years of evolution — as the cardinal goals of evolution appear to be adaptation and reproductive efficiency. While there is ample evidence that individuals are able to change and self-determine their actions to varying degrees, it is much less clear that we as a species can voluntarily alter enduring population trends. We must never lose sight of the fact that if we (as a species) are unable to effect a birth rate solution, our world will inflict a death rate solution upon us.

What can humanistic psychologists (indeed, any psychologists) do to fight the population threat? Howard (1993) lists four fronts along which psychologists can work: 1) helping society to move from economic to ecological worldviews; 2) consciousness raising and changing reproductive behaviors; 3) changing societal institutions to favor reproductive responsibility; and 4) conducting research on the behavioral mechanisms related to the exacerbation and amelioration of ecological problems.

As humanistic psychologists gaze imaginatively into the future, there are many crises that arrest our attention. By applying traditional humanistic principles to these quandaries, I believe we will come to see how we must work to alter these possible futures. But fear that we will not be able to reverse current apocalyptic trends in world population should not dissuade us from acting for the best. William James (arguably the first American, humanistic psychologist) showed why action is an important response — even when the ultimate success of that action remains in doubt. Acting in the service of a virtuous cause — regardless of the action's ultimate success — constitutes the best possible use of the time that remains to us as we prepare to greet death.

> We stand on a mountain pass in the midst of whirling snow and blinding mist, through which we get glimpses now and then of paths which may be deceptive. If we stand still, we shall be frozen to death. If we take the wrong road, we shall be dashed to pieces. We do not certainly know whether there is any right one. What must we do? Be strong and of a good courage. Act for the best, hope for the best, and take what comes... If death ends all, we cannot meet death better. (James, 1956, pp. 30-31)

## References

Berger, P. L. (1963). *Invitation to sociology: A humanistic perspective.* Garden City, NY: Doubleday.

Brown, L. R. (Ed.) (1991). *State of the world.* New York: Norton.

Ehrlich, P. R. (1968). *The population bomb.* New York: Ballantine Books.

Garbarino, J., Kostelny, K., & Durow, N. (1991). What children can tell us about living in danger. *American Psychologist, 46,* 376-383.

Howard, G. S. (1989). *A tale of two stories: Excursions into a narrative approach to psychology.* Notre Dame, IN: Academic Publications.

Howard, G. S. (1991). Culture tales: A narrative approach to thinking, cross-cultural psychology, and psychotherapy. *American Psychologist, 46,* 188-197.

Howard, G. S. (1992). Steps toward a science of free will. *Counseling and Values* (in press).

Howard, G. S. (1993). On a certain blindness in human beings: Psychology and world overpopulation. Manuscript (under review.)

Howard, G. S., & Conway, C. G. (1986). Can there be an empirical science of volitional action? *American Psychologist, 41,* 1241-1251.

Howard, G. S., Curtin, T. D., & Johnson, A. J. (1991). Point estimation techniques in psychological research: The role of meaning in self-determined action. *Journal of Counseling Psychology, 38,* 219-226.

Howard, G. S., DiGangi, M. L., & Johnson, A. (1988). Life, science, and the role of therapy in the pursuit of happiness. *Professional Psychology: Research and Practice, 19,* 191-198.

Howard, G. S., & Fischer, T. (1990). The validity of life-themes. *Methods, 5,* 1-17.

Howard, G. S., Maerlender, A. C., Myers, P. R., & Curtin, T. D. (1992). In stories we trust: Studies of the validity of autobiographies. *Journal of Counseling Psychology., 39,*

Howard, G. S., & Myers, P. R. (1990). Predicting human behavior: Comparing idiographic, nomothetic, and agentic methodologies. *Journal of Counseling Psychology, 37,* 227-233.

Howard, G. S., Myers, P. R., & Curtin, T. D. (1991). Can science furnish evidence of human freedom?: Self-determination versus conformity in human action. *International Journal of Personal Construct Psychology, 4,* 371-395.

Howard, G. S., Youngs, W. H., & Siatczynski, A. M. (1989). A research strategy for studying telic human behavior. *Journal of Mind and Behavior, 10,* 393-412.

James, W. (1956). *The will to believe.* New York: Dover Publications. (Original work published in 1897).

Jones, J. M., Levine, I. S., & Rosenberg, A. A. (Eds.) (1991). Special Issue: Homelessness. *American Psychologist, 46,* 1108-1252.

Mair, M. (1988). Psychology as storytelling. *International Journal of Personal Construct Psychology, 1,* 125-138.

Malthus, T. (1964). An essay on the principle of population. In G. Harding (Ed.), *Population, evolution and birth control: A collage of controversial readings.* San Francisco: Freeman. (Original work published 1798)

May, R. (1981). *Freedom and destiny.* New York: Norton.

McAdams, D. (1985). *Power, intimacy, and the life story.* Homewood, IL: Dorsey Press.

Melton, G. B. (1991). Socialization in the global community: Respect for the dignity of children. *American Psychologist, 46,* 66-71.

Milgram, S. (1974). *Obedience to authority.* New York: Harper & Row.

Orwell, G. (1949). *Nineteen eighty four: A novel.* London: Secker & Warburg.

Polkinghorne, D. P. (1982). What makes research humanistic? *Journal of Humanistic Psychology, 22,* 47-54.

Polkinghorne, D. P. (1988). *Narrative knowing and the human sciences.* Albany, NY: SUNY Press.

Rogers, C. R. (1951). *Client-centered therapy: Its current practice, theory and implication.* Boston: Houghton-Mifflin.

Rogers, C. R. (1973). Some new challenges. *American Psychologist, 28*, 379-387.
Rosenthal, A. M. (1991). Is this still news? *The New York Times*, July 2, 1991, p. A15.
Rychlak, J. F. (1979). *Discovering free will and personal responsibility.* Oxford, England: Oxford University Press.
Siegel, M. (1983). Crime and violence in America: The victims. *American Psychologist, 38*, 1267-1273.
Tageson, C. W. (1982). *Humanistic psychology: A synthesis.* Homewood, IL: Dorsey.
Toulmin, S. (1961). *Foresight and understanding.* New York: McGraw-Hill.
Vernez, G. (1991). Current global refugee situation and international public policy. *American Psychologist, 46*, 627-631.
Weber, S. (1991). *Population growth.* Fact sheet distributed by Zero Population Growth (11400 16th St. N.W. #320; Washington, D.C. 20036).
Williams, C. L., & Berry, J. W. (1991). Primary prevention of acculturative stress among refugees: Application of psychological theory and practice. *American Psychologist, 46*, 632-641.
Young, J. E. (1991). Reducing waste, saving materials. In L. R. Brown (Ed.), *State of the world: 1991.* New York: Norton.

# 11

# The Three R's for Humanistic Psychology: Remembering, Reconciling, Reuniting

*James F. T. Bugental and Barbara G. Sapienza*

> We shall not cease from exploration
> And the end of all our exploring
> Will be to arrive where we started
> And know the place for the first time.
> — T. S. Eliot, *Four Quartets*, Little Gidding, V.

Psychology has explored for a hundred years, has created systems, methodologies, generalizations, and a tidal wave of publications. This remarkable productivity has been largely devoted to the study of organisms and such studies carefully maintain an objective stance — whether the objects studied are rats, pigeons, or college sophomores.

As ingenious, varied, and devoted as these efforts have been, the human species, which they supposedly serve, finds itself today without an adequate base from which to respond to the immense challenges and mounting threats to its continued existence.

This unrelenting emphasis on the objective perspective has left us ill-equipped to deal with the great issues our world now faces — poisoning the atmosphere, pollution, homelessness, exhaustion of natural resources, the growing gulf between the haves and the have-nots, and other world macroproblems.

What is too seldom squarely faced is that all such problems are, at root, problems of human subjectivity — of will, of values, of relationship, of selfhood, of perceived threat and emotionally mobilized response. With only few exceptions, we already have the objective science and technology for responding to these threats. What we do not have is the psychological know-how to mobilize ourselves and our resources. Teaching pigeons to poke ping pong balls or rats to press levers ends up being futile (if not downright frivolous) in the face of these world-wide, life-essential, genuine psychological problems. And the same may be said of motivational studies employing simplistic explicit questionnaires or purely objective observational schedules.

One may even question the pertinence of counseling efforts forced to identify limited and objective goals and constricted to procedures and time limits set in advance of any encounter with the subjective of the experiencing person whose needs are the identified goal to be served.

So it is that the humanistic orientation in psychology calls us to recognize (for the first time?) that we have arrived where we started — with the immediacy of lived experience.

## Humanistic Perspective

It is our task to see the lived human experience with fresh eyes, to know the place in which we dwell as though for the first time. We must confront the immense inner world of our subjectivity — of thinking, feeling, intending, memory and anticipation, relating with others and maintaining our own separateness, dreaming and planning, triumphing and failing. When we turn in this direction and look for investigations that probe beneath the surface of observable actions and explicit reports, we may be shocked. There are, of course, some creative and path opening exceptions, but much of the psychology of human subjective experience has developed only a short distance from where it was when William James wrote his Principles just over 100 years ago.

The split between treating human beings as objects to be studied and founding our study on the reality of our being subjects as well pervades all thinking about our own nature — whether as scientists, as practicing professionals, or as individual persons.

So long as being totally objective was regarded as the sine qua non of being scientific, this partial view of human nature prevailed. Thus it is striking that it took the ultimate in scientific objectivity, physics, to acknowledge how fundamental is the limit of such a stance. Niels Bohr, dean of atomic physicists:

There is set a fundamental limit to the analysis of the phenomena of life in terms of physical concepts, since the interference necessitated by an observation which would be as complete as possible from the point of view of atomic theory would cause the death of the organism. In other words: The strict application of those concepts which are adapted to our description of inanimate nature might stand in a relationship of exclusion to the consideration of the laws of the phenomena of life. (1934, p. 22, emphasis in the original.)

Recognizing that the life of an object of study would be ended by physical analysis, Bohr wisely demonstrates that the purely objective approach is incompatible with life. Human life, in particular, is thus beyond the reach of such approaches.

From another angle, a further testimony is presented to the futility of strict and exclusive objectivity even in the physical sciences. Fundamental to the objective view is the notion of object constancy, the belief that who the observer is makes no difference if only he or she is truly "objective", that is describing without distortion that which is observed. Much of psychological science and clearly the exponents of psychotherapy treatment manuals and arbitrary peer review procedures base their work and teachings on object constancy. It is time that our learnings from physical science were brought up to date: "every intervention to make a measurement, to study what is going on in the atomic world, creates, despite all the universal order of this world a new, unique, not fully predictable situation" (Oppenheimer, 1954, p. 62).

## Subjectivity and Objectivity

For far too long the objective and the subjective orientations in psychology have been regarded as adversaries or, at least, alternatives. It is past time to recognize that they are neither. Any thorough going exploration of human phenomena must take account of both that which is overt and explicit and that which is implicit and inward. Indeed, the theoretical physicists are contending with a similar recognition: "contemporary physics compels the physicist to look upon himself as a subject" (Weizsaecker, 1952, p. 62).

Of course, what is true for psychology as a science is so with even greater emphasis for psychotherapy as a healing discipline. Finally and primarily, it is similarly handicapping within the living experience of each individual.

And so again we come back to the place from which we started and hope truly to see it for the first time yet again. To do so we must open ourselves and our perspective to the vital subjective disciplines of remembering, reconciling, and reuniting. These "three R's" are a convenient mnemonic around which to organize our postulations.

## Remembering

We begin by remembering that human beings are both objects and subjects, not one or the other. Remembering so, we recognize that neither aspect can substitute for the other and that they are in constant interaction, each affecting the other in evident and in more subtle ways.

Remembering includes the recognition that this relatedness and interdependence is characteristic, not alone of our intertwined inner and outer aspects, but of our individual living and our community being as well. Further, this same interdependence-duality is intrinsic in the connection between the human and the natural (other-than-human) worlds.

Just as our overt expression of our being is intimately related to our inner experience in interaction with the outer, so too is the object to be studied related to the person who studies. One does not exist without the other; the persons in these roles nourish and sustain each other. From one perspective — that of their role identities — it is evident that each creates the other.

When we, as therapists, see the person consulting us only as an object — attending chiefly or exclusively to that which is overt and explicit — we are, ourselves, subtly drawn into becoming robot-like and sterile; in a word, objects. Then we may well project onto the client that which is unrecognized within ourselves, whether hate or love, fear or hope, dread of the work or investment in it.

If we are unaware of our subjective experiencing when in a therapeutic relation, we become little more than automatons, carrying out preprogrammed procedures, responding by reflex more than reflection, and looking only to "cure" or "success" for any meaning to what we do.

Therapists who cherish awareness of their own subjectivity in the midst of the engagement with the client have the added resource of a rich inner flow of cues, intuitions, observations, and relationship information. Thus such therapists' work is informed by intention, choicefulness, creativity, adaptability, and values, and it is productive, aesthetic, and more lastingly satisfying to both partners in the enterprise.

Yet there is a resistance to giving the subjective its equal and rightful place as an aspect of the whole. Much as many clients presenting neurotic symptom patterns hold off the very changes that are needed in their lives, fearing to venture from the known-objective into their inner mysteries, just so do many in psychology need to deny the whole subjective realm.

Change can be threatening, can call into question much that we have believed and valued, much that we have invested with our identities. Change that involves taking into account the subjectivity of therapists soon discloses how partial has been our prior understanding, soon confronts us with surprises for which we have no well prepared responses, sooner or later evokes emotions of awe and humility. It is no small matter to open oneself to ambiguity, uncertainty, incompleteness, and the relinquishment of seemingly certain and clear-cut patterns.

### Reconciling

When we undertake to incorporate the reality of subjective-objective wholeness, we discover, in time, that they are parts of a continuum, a whole. Reconciling is forwarded by this kind of reflecting, for it leads us to realizing how partial is either aspect when it is deprived of the other. Once this recognition is firm, we find our interest enlivened and our vision widened. No longer can we be content with a half-blind conception of human life and possibilities.

The tendency to view matters in terms of polarities persists, of course, but gradually that habit yields to the appreciation of continuity. Thus each morning we are reminded by the sunrise of the fact of darkness, and there follows the promise of light. Thus each human is individual; yet all are deeply related. So, it gradually become conscious, all dichotomies very likely overlay deeper unity: body-mind, life-death, spirit-thought, and even we-they, I and Thou.

Manifestly, what is involved here is a healing of the split within ourselves. We have learned to devalue and even suppress a vital part of our own nature. As a consequence we have been ill prepared to confront the increasingly complex problems that we face as individuals, as societies, as a species. This healing is essential if we are to save much of what we cherish in life — our posterity, the beauty of our planet, the richness of possibilities, and the depth of the human experience.

Implicit in what has just been said is a point of such importance that it needs to be made explicit: Accepting the simultaneity of the objective and the subjective is not simply an additive matter. It is the deeper recognition of a basic unity in what we study, in the people with whom we work, within ourselves. That unity becomes the more important mode of grasping what we experience, and the aspects — objective and subjective, explicit and implicit, ailing and healing, perceptual and experiential — are recognized as usual facets, but are not mistaken for the whole.

Tension. Dichotomies create tension. To see wholes requires a readiness to hold the tension within ourselves. At first that may seem too exhausting, but with time we discover that we not only can hold the tension but that it enriches us. It is no simple play on words to recognize the relation of tension to intention. As the Gestalt psychologists taught, an incompleted act evokes tension within us (pragnanz) which pulls toward completion, i.e., the experience of intention. Thus incorporating the dichotomy facilitates the thrust toward action. The pathology of intention is evident in those who "dwell only in their heads" — in other words, live only subjectively — as well as in those who compulsively "act out" with little awareness other than that of the external, objective realm. In both there is a flatness of being which bespeaks the absence of productive tension.

Roy deCarvalho (1988), a major collator of the views of the "founding fathers" of humanistic psychology observes how they expressed similar theses. He notes that Rollo May sees the human predicament of dwelling in dichotomies as propelling us into the search for ourselves, for the meaning of our living (p. 133). In a similar way, the Jungian analyst, Marion Woodman (1991), urges us to hold the tensions of both parts of a struggle. Doing so and being patient with the tension, even celebrating it, makes it possible for the new to be born. Like May, she has learned that through tension — and even, at times, suffering — come freedom and birth, a theme found in the teachings of many spiritual teachers as well.

## Reunion

A frequent theme in humanistic psychology is the need for wholeness, the reduction of partialness, and the coming together of apparent opposites. We have just been speaking of reconciliation in this vein and recognized there that an additive appreciation of the meaning of wholeness was insufficient. Thus now it is time to expand our reflections about unity in being. We begin by coming at the matter from a different angle.

The concept of self-actualization was forwarded by Abraham Maslow and has become an established way of speaking of the healthful side of human life. Here's how he speaks about the nature of self-actualization (1962, p.109):

A development of personality which frees the person from the deficiency problems of youth, and from the neurotic (or infantile or fantasy or unnecessary or "unreal") problems of life, so that [the person] is able to face, endure and grapple with the "real" problems of life (the intrinsic and ultimately human problems, the unavoidable, the "existential" problems to which there is no perfect solution).

In the same vein, DeCarvalho (p. 147) cites Rollo May speaking of the inborn human power to create oneself and Carl Rogers recognizing what he terms "the organismic tendency toward fulfillment."

Just what is the common implication of these several views? To be whole is, in our view, not so much a condition to be attained and then held throughout one's life span as it is a direction in which to move, a perspective and value system to guide one's choices. It is not a catalog of desiderata to be filled like a shopping list. Indeed, it is dubious that anyone ever is completely whole — whatever that might mean.

The importance of the concept of wholeness rests on the recognition that each person has far more potential latent within than that person can ever fully live out. One cannot reach the limit of any significant capacity. Artists of all kinds have long recognized this infinite potential within which their efforts are set. Philosophers, theorists, and writers continually discover further possibilities opening up in whatever work they undertake. Athletes, poets, and many others similarly confront the endlessly receding horizon of their capacities.

It is important to recognize that this inexorable rediscovery of the limitlessness of any endeavor's possibilities occurs as inner potentials (vision, inspiration, imagination, creativity, aesthetic promptings) begin to find expression in external forms (paintings, essays and books, musical compositions, etc.). Once again the unity of the subjective and the objective is demonstrated.

It is this approach to the infinity of subjective potential that is central to the work of the existential-humanistic psychotherapy of which we write (Bugental, 1976, 1987). There it is referred to as "searching." It is a way of tapping into the endless flow of inner awareness in its many dimensions, and it aids clients in discovering new possibilities in life situations in which they previously had felt hopelessly trapped.

Reunion of one's external capabilities with the internal promptings may lead to an inspirited and inspiring production in almost any field. These desirable qualities are apt to be lacking in the person who performs solely because of external demands (epitomized in the slave) or the person who dwells only in inner imaginings (perhaps most extremely represented in schizophrenia).

The path toward wholeness is through inner subjective experiencing and into objective expression of some kind. For Rogers experience is the highest authority; "the touchstone of validity is my own experience" (1961, p. 23). When we, as individuals, are committed to continuing identification with our inner subjective experience and its external facets, then we are best able to work effectively with other persons in genuine relationship. This is the "I-Thou" relation of Buber (1958).

In the psychotherapy situation, we do well to begin our work with the here-and-now experience of the moment in therapy when two human beings face each other for the first time. Knowing that this moment is life, we can be at once physically (objectively) present and subjectively accessible and expressive in and to the immediate engagement. Thus we are attuned to recognize the ways in which the new client resists full involvement. In this moment are the seeds of all other moments between these two people and in themselves, past, present, and future.

Therapist attention to client resistance to full presence is, in fact, attention to ways in which clients diminish themselves and lose wholeness. As we help our clients become aware of how they are thus making themselves partial in the moment, we are not only aiding their being more present and aware in the therapeutic effort, but we are pointing the direction in which resides their freedom to move toward being whole.

As psychotherapists, our necessity and our goal are the same: ourselves to be as truly and fully present, to utilize the lived moment as completely, to be as genuinely committed to the work and the relation as possible. Thus we express our own seeking toward unity of being and implicitly invite and demonstrate to the client the lively actuality of this commitment.

As psychotherapists we have the privilege and responsibility of being with other human beings who may be in pain or who may yearn for a more fulfilling experience of being alive. They come to us because their inner experience is poorly according with their outer living, because, in other words, there is too much disunity in their being. By our listening, our guiding, our instructing, and our requiring we help them discover more fully how it is that they see themselves and their worlds, how they limit both, and how they may open possibilities not previously evident.

To carry this effort into effect, therapists and clients must form alliances, which is to say they must realize (i.e., recognize and make real) a reunion with each other as well as retaining their separateness. It is in the setting of this alliance — with the understanding, empathy, and privacy it offers — that clients can risk bringing their innerness to outer expression.

## Reflections

In our time and our western world we have come to a way of perceiving ourselves which is in marked contrast to that of other cultures and other epochs. We see each person as individual, separate, and alone in confronting the contingencies of life. We are apt to be skeptical about relationships, community, and trust generally. Essentially, living is deemed a lonely and hazardous task.

To be sure we value love, loyalty, and constancy, but we view these as episodic, as chance-derived, and as having uncertain futures. Divorce rates climb. Families scatter. Organizations serve for a time and then close. Many relations with friends, colleagues, or vocational associates are dependent on external circumstances — employment, residence location, activity needs (e.g., participants in a sport or hobby) and so when the external situation changes, the relation falls away.

Human beings are only truly human when in relation with other human beings. Feral children soon pass a point of no-return. If they are not restored to the human community in time, they remain essentially subhuman at the level of their animal foster parents. Yet for our time generally the quality of human relationships is likely declining as their inception and continuance more and more depend on external or objective variables.

It is an anxious recognition that is suggested: We are in the process of becoming less human and more object-like. Another way of understanding this situation is to see it as requiring a reunion with each other at a subjective level.

The current times have been described as the "Me-Epoch." Cultural and ethical critics cite multiple evidences of what they see as selfishness, ruthless competition, and irresponsible accumulations of wealth and power at the expense of others. These conditions and characterizations doubtlessly are accurate, but simply accusing the offenders stops short of being sufficient.

What is needed is a conscious and effective campaign to reassert our essential commonality with others. This means helping us overcome the I-we dichotomy. This means recognizing at a deep subjective level that I is always a part of we. This means recognizing feelingfully that I without we is less than I truly has the potential of being.

The Emersonian image of the lone hero standing out against the world has much to commend it as it portrays the courage needed to deal with opposition. Yet it is an insufficient model in its implicit isolation of the hero from the human community which is equally part of his or her nature. Every therapist — indeed, almost every person — has known one or more individuals who were stoutly convinced that the world was wrong and only that one person had the truth. Sometimes that one person is a psychotic whose vision could be vastly destructive; sometimes that one person is a genius whose contribution is much needed by the world.

Human beings must not and cannot be relieved of the responsiblities of deciding which critic to support and which to ignore or lock up. This cannot be simply a we decision to be settled by poll, nor is it solely an I choice. The dichotomy must be overcome; we must as individuals and as members of the community grapple with these matters. Authorities may aid the struggle; they cannot be the sole arbiters.

It is from this paradox of choicefulness that many are impelled to retreat to the me first orientation. It seems to offer a relief from obligation, a perspective that is less diffuse, and a practical advantage. These benefits are illusory. One who takes refuge in me first actually diminishes his or her power in the world and sets up the high probability of becoming increasingly isolated and unfulfilled.

## Conclusion

Each human being, by her or his very nature, is at once apart from all others and a part of all others. To try to deny either facet of this paradox is to reduce one's range and potency of being. To attempt this destructive course is another instance of our blind allegiance to objectification of our being. That pattern bids fair to being the black plague of our time. Nor is this an exaggerated appraisal of its significance. Paul Tillich wrote, the human "resists objectification, and if [the human's] resistance to it is broken, the human itself is broken" (1951, p. 98).

And so at the end of all our exploring we arrive back at the place from which we started, and we hope to see it repeatedly with the freshness of first sight.

## References

Bohr, N. (1934). *Atomic theory and the description of nature.* New York: AMS Press.

Buber, M. (1970). *I—thou.* New York: Scribner's.

Bugental, J. F. T. (1965). *The search for authenticity: An existential-analytic approach to psychotherapy.* New York: Holt, Rinehart & Winston.

Bugental, J. F. T. (1975/1976). Toward a subjective psychology: Tribute to Charlotte Buhler. *Interpersonal Development, 6,* 48-61.

Bugental, J. F. T. (1976). *Psychotherapy and process.* Reading, MA: Addison-Wesley. [Now published by McGraw-Hill]

Bugental, J. F. T. (1987). *The art of the psychotherapist.* New York: Norton.

DeCarvalho, R. (1988). *A history of humanistic psychology.* Unpublished doctoral dissertation. University of Wisconsin.

Fromm, E. (1941). *Escape from freedom.* New York: Rinehart.

Kelly, G. A. (1955). *The psychology of personal constructs.* New York: Norton.

Mahrer, A. R. (1986). *Therapeutic experiencing: The process of change.* New York: Norton.

Maslow, A. H. (1962). *Toward a psychology of being.* Princeton, NJ: Van Nostrand.

May, R. (1969). *Love and will.* New York: Norton.

May, R. (1977). *The meaning of anxiety* (rev. ed.). New York: Norton.

Oppenheimer, J. R. (1954). *Science and the common understanding.* New York: Simon & Schuster.

Rogers, C. R. (1961). *On becoming a person. Boston: Houghton-Mifflin.*

Tillich, P. (1951). *Systematic theology* (Vol. 1). Chicago: University of Chicago Press.

Weizsaecker, V. V. (1952). *The world view of physics.* Translated by Marjorie Greene. Chicago, IL: University of Chicago Press.

Woodman, M. (1991, March). *Unpublished interview with J. Marler.* KPFA, Berkeley, CA.

# 12

# Transpersonal Psychology: Its Several Virtues

*Eugene Taylor*

Transpersonal psychology, if known to mainstream psychologists at all, is most often associated with New Age crystal gazers, astrologers, believers in witchcraft, drug users, meditators, occultists, spiritual healers, martial artists, and other purveyors of pop psychology, in short; everything that a truly legitimate scientific and academic psychology is *not*. The stereotype is, of course, inaccurate. For, like the fabled philosopher's stone, its seemingly weird exterior masks a more important philosophical challenge, the full articulation and subsequent flowering of which may yet prove to be the undoing of the reductionistic mainstream. The problem is that no survey of its history and meaning up to the present publication has been able to tease out which half of the Transpersonal movement is the chaff and which the wheat. Herein is one attempt at the riddle.

## Historical Roots

In order to get the flavor of what Transpersonal psychology is and to assess what its potential contributions to the future of psychology might be, it is absolutely essential to understand its history, which is at once quite recent and very old. It is very old in the sense that the Transpersonal orientation toward inner experience can be identified as a major component of indigenous psychologies, particularly from the classical traditions of Asia. The Transpersonal attitude also has affinities with the mystical traditions of Judeo-Christianity, and has drawn some of its inspiration, as well, from sources as diverse as the shamanism of primitive, non-technological cultures to the Sufi rituals and poetry of Islam. It is Emersonian and transcendentalist in many respects. Even William James used the term on one occasion in 1890 (Vich, 1988); in fact, James's interests in psychical research, mystical religious experience, and phenomenology definitely presaged what was later to come (Taylor, 1978, 1991).

The history of Transpersonal as a movement in psychology is quite new, however, and is closely allied with the origins of humanistic psychology in the early 1950's. (Vich, 1988).

Just after World War Two, significant changes were taking place in both psychology and psychiatry. Not the least of these was that psychoanalysis gained new credibility as a result of the growth of psychiatric services in the military. Once psychoanalysis was introduced into the mental health care network of the Veterans Administration, it soon gained a foothold in general hospital departments of psychiatry throughout the United States. As a result, psychoanalysis came to control almost all clinical teaching in psychology and psychiatry where certification was mandatory, roughly from the late 1940's up until the advent of the community psychiatry movement in the early 1960's.

Meanwhile, within academic psychology a major era of scientific laboratory work with rats that attempted to legitimize the so-called hypothetico-deductive method came to an end, as it became widely recognized that behaviorism and stimulus-response theory had failed as a major organizing paradigm of experimental research. Grand theory construction gave way to tentative model building. Psychology remained behavioral and was not yet able to become fully cognitive in its general orientation.

Within this slightly more pluralistic atmosphere, a concatenation of voices from a variety of different disciplines coalesced around the first threads of more liberal theorizing about personality. The earliest focus came through the work of Carl Rogers, whose client centered therapy had become the first uniquely American challenge to the hegemony of psychoanalytic technique in clinical practice (Rogers, 1942). In a radical departure from focussing on the neurotic and psychotic, Rogers proposed a non-directive approach aimed at discovering meaning and value in the normal personality.

While a natural lightening rod for dissent, Rogers had not held the field alone. Theoretically, during psychology's darkest conceptual period of the 1930's and 1940's, the most successful dissenters to the reductionistic paradigm of the S-R psychologists had been personality theorists such as Gordon Allport, Gardner Murphy, and Henry A. Murray. But the academic voice of the new era to emerge by the late 1950's, in addition to the clinical voice of Rogers, was Abraham Maslow, who pioneered in the description of the self-actualizing personality (Maslow, 1954). Maslow believed that psychology might yet reorient itself away from pathology and statistical definitions of normality by studying the healthiest examples of modern culture.

The new orientation away from rats and sick patients and toward the fully functioning human being became known as humanistic psychology, which emerged out of the academic fields of personality and motivational psychology and the clinical practice of psychotherapy (deCarvalho, 1990). To this banner numerous distinguished personalties were attracted. These included existential psychologists and psychiatrists such as Victor Frankl, Rollo May, and Medard Boss, phenomenological psychologists like Amadeo Giorgi, Adrian van Kaam, and Wilson van Deusen; anthropologists like Ashley Montegue and Margaret Mead, and a host of others like Gregory Bateson, James Bugental, Charlotte Buhler, and more (May, 1958, 1964; Sutich, 1976).

Perhaps the earliest formal organization to herald the new psychology was the California Institute for Asian Studies, founded by Alan Watts in 1956. Watts, a Unitarian minister, had drawn wide attention to classical eastern psychology through promotion of his own books, such as the enormously popular *Psychotherapy East and West* (1961) and through his support of the writings of D. T. Suzuki, foremost interpreter of Zen in America. Watt's Institute boldly broke with tradition and, unaffiliated with any formal academic institution, began offering graduate study in eastern religion, philosophy, and psychology.

Maslow, meanwhile, had met Anthony Sutich through Ernest Hilgard. Sutich, an aspiring California psychotherapist who had already made important contributions to ethics and psychology, shared Maslow's interest in a growth-oriented model of personality. A growth-experience, Sutich would later write, was the direct achievement of a significantly improved level of integration in interpersonal behavior, accompanied by increased emotional liberation and continuous emotional development. These changes, Sutich thought, could lead to a permanent reorientation of the self (Sutich, 1967).

Maslow and Sutich eventually collaborated together in launching the *Journal of Humanistic Psychology* (1961) and they worked to found the Association for Humanistic Psychology (1963). Interdisciplinary from the very start, the original editorial board of the *Journal* included, among others, Abe Maslow, Andreas Angyl, Charlotte Buhler, Kurt Goldstein, Rollo May, Clark Moustakas, Lewis Mumford, and David Reisman (although not Eric Fromm, as some historians have thought).

The self-conscious focus of the humanistic movement, or the so-called Third Force, became, in addition to the problem of values in science, emotional development within the individual, interpersonal relationships, sensitivity training, encounter techniques, existential studies, and ways to enhance the self-actualizing personality.

By the early 1960's, humanistic psychology had become solidified as an academic movement. One of the best estimates of its support came from The Saybrook Conference, held in upstate Connecticut in 1964, where the major aims of the movement were discussed and plans made for expansion. In attendance were such lights as Carl Rogers, Rollo May, and George Kelly. Gordon Allport and Henry Murray came from Harvard, Gardner Murphy from the Menninger Foundation, and Jacques Barzun from Columbia. The conference has since been considered important for two reasons: first, because it was devoted solely to theoretical issues and second, because the founding of humanistic psychology is often dated from that meeting (deCarvalho, 1990).

In parallel with this event, however, was the proliferation of the American counter-culture movement, brought about by widespread experimentation with psychedelic drugs and strong public sentiment among the young against the Vietnam War. Maslow's call for a eupsychian network was realized with the proliferation of Gestalt therapy groups, growth centers specializing in sensitivity training, and the widespread availability of counter-culture psychotherapies made possible through such groups as the Unitarian Religious Education Programs throughout the country. Soon humanistic psychology as a purely academic endeavor was absorbed into these widespread counterculture activities in what came to be known as the Human Potential Movement. American folk-consciousness soon became indistinguishable from humanistic psychology, as growth centers and alternative psychotherapies proliferated everywhere.

As the membership in the Association for Humanistic Psychology began to grow and the Human Potential Movement was drawing much national attention, the humanistic movement became invigorated by the founding of the Humanistic Psychology Institute in 1970, located in San Francisco and initially sponsored by the Association for Humanistic Psychology. While masters level degrees were given in programs at Sonoma State and West Georgia College between 1966 and 1969, HPI became the first doctoral program formally representing the new psychology in the United States. It attracted a sizeable number of students intent upon pursuing alternative Ph.D. degrees in subjects previously forbidden by establishment institutions. The goal of many of these students was to expand the human potential network through local, regional, and national conferences and to derive an income from psychotherapeutic practice after graduation.

Forcasting changes that were already in the wind, the Menninger Foundation, in cooperation with the Association for Humanistic Psychology, launched the first of several annual meetings on the voluntary control of internal states, called The First Council Grove Conference in 1969 (Fadiman, 1969, 1970). Biofeedback, psychedelic-assisted psychotherapy, meditation, yoga, cortical stimulation, and East-West exchange of ideas were discussed. The cross-pollination among attendees launched what came to be called the science of altered states of consciousness, catalyzed in no small measure by publication of Charles Tart's edited collection of papers under the same title (Tart, 1969).

Meanwhile, humanistic psychology was becoming more institutionalized. Maslow and Sutich rapidly sensed that as the humanistic movement had become solidified around ego-development, psychotherapy for personal growth, and encounter group work, that issues about consciousness, altered states, transcendence, and spiritual disciplines were being entirely neglected. Actually, ideas about spirituality and inner experience had been perking between the two of them since about 1966 (Sutich, 1969). Eight years after founding the *Journal of Humanistic Psychology*, they bolted from the fold, turned over their operations to a younger group of colleagues, and founded the *Journal of Transpersonal Psychology* and its own separate supporting association. The first issue of the new journal appeared in 1969, dedicated to the study of ultimate human capacities, unitive consciousness, peak experiences, ecstasy, mystical experiences, and self-transcendence. Its board included James Fadiman, Stanislav Grof, Abe Maslow, Victor Frankl, Michael Murphy, Miles Vich, Sidney Jourard, and others.

Conceptually, the early Transpersonal psychologists argued that consciousness does exist as a phenomenon that can be studied by science. Moreover, conceptual analysis of the world's religious literature, combined with extensive clinical observations in psychotherapy, and a host of insights from personal experience, usually derived from the practice of deep meditation, allegedly indicate that interior consciousness is marked by a number of discrete levels arranged in an hierarchical fashion.

Finally, they somewhat audaciously claimed that these levels incorporate the physical, mental, celestial, and infinite dimensions of personality (Smith, 1976; Wilber, 1984).

After the death of first Maslow and then Sutich, a younger generation emerged, for better or for worse, as the new leaders. The activities of both the journal and the association coalesced around such figures as Charles Tart, Professor of Psychology at the University of California, Davis; Huston Smith, professor of Religion at Syracuse; Ken Wilber, popular interpreter of unitive consciousness; Stan Grof, physician and psychedelic researcher; Francis Vaughan, California psychotherapist in private practice; Roger Walsh, physician and social activist; John Welwood, psychotherapist and member of the editorial board of the *Journal of Transpersonal Psychology*; Robert Frager, aikido instructor; Richard Alpert, the popular guru, also known as Baba Ram Das; Dan Goleman, a science writer for the *New York Times*; and Elmer and Alyce Green of the Menninger Foundation.

As well, several important organizations within the Transpersonal movement emerged during this time. One was the Institute of Noetic Sciences, founded by the Apollo astronaut, Edgar Mitchell, in 1973. The Noetic group currently runs projects on spontaneous remission, creative altruism, meditation, and death and dying. The extent of its viability can be gauged by the fact that it maintains contact with some 25,000 members (INS, 1990).

Second was The International Transpersonal Psychology Association, founded by Stan Grof, which held its first conference in Iceland in 1973. (Vaughan, 1982). Additional conferences have been held in Finland, Brazil, the United States, Australia, and India.

Third was Naropa Institute, the Buddhist college in Boulder, Colorado founded by a former Tibetan monk, the late Chogyam Trungpa. Patterned after Nalanda University, the great Buddhist center of learning in India, Naropa began offering its first courses in Buddhist philosophy, Tai Chi, Tangka painting, tea ceremony, Tibetan and Sanskrit, anthropology, physics, and cybernetics in the summer of 1974. Two hundred were expected and two thousand came (Fields, 1981, 317).

Fourth was the California Institute of Transpersonal Psychology, founded by Robert Frager in 1976. Accredited by the state of California, the Institute grants doctorates in psychology to students who have gone through four years of training and therapy in the transpersonal orientation (Frager, 1974).

While these milestones represent the de facto institutional core of transpersonal psychology in its early days, much has transpired since then to reinforce its staying power in modern culture. Within mainstream psychology, for instance, the humanistic practitioners were finally able to gain recognition within the American Psychological Association when they gathered enough signatures in the mid-1970's to qualify as one of the APA divisions. Within Division 32, as it was called, a special interest group then sprang up urging for the formation of a separate APA Transpersonal Division. The Transpersonal Interest Group started its own *PDTP newsletter* (Proposed Division of Transpersonal Psychology).

The true power base of the Transpersonal movement, however, is the economic appeal of its New Age ideas to the New York publishing industry. Through this line of influence transpersonal writers and practitioners circumvent mainstream academic and professional organizations, ride in on the coattails of such best sellers as Bernie Segal's *Mind, Medicine, and Miracles*, and are able to maintain direct contact with the American public. Their principal channels are through the older established avenues of public lectures, and weekend conferences, now adding a well-developed network of alternative health care clinics, advertising in alternative life-style publications, and the widespread sale of mass market books.

Why this appeal? Humanistic psychology as a popular phenomenon was originally known for its emphasis on human potential. Individual experimentation was the theme. Transpersonal psychology refined this interest in a significant segment of the 1960's counter-culture population because of its emphasis on meditation as a means of controlling states of consciousness. Commitment to some form of personal discipline was now introduced. Today, the transpersonal orientation finds public support within numerous special interest groups because of its appeal to an ethic of higher consciousness and its differentiation into a variety of fields that address value-oriented issues, particularly in psychotherapy, business, ecology, human rights, religion, and medicine. Meanwhile, its votaries continue to apply meditation techniques in psychotherapy and to theorize on the cartography of inner experience.

## Some Limits

Toward these aims the scientific laboratory psychologist revolts. Science and religion are indiscriminately mixed in the same sentence. The neutrality of science is violated by a teleological agenda. Personal opinion is made over into fact. Conjecture is elevated to the status of theory.

The truth in these caveats is that Transpersonal psychology has some serious drawbacks. First of all, it appears philosophically naive. Its metaphysical base, described as the perennial philosophy (Huxley, 1949), is built upon an unquestioned monism. Unitive experience is considered the goal of the developing personality. All experiences of higher consciousness are considered "the same." To the logical positivists, these are not even intelligible sentences, because they are not verifiable in physical terms. To the deconstructionists, they are metaphors of language, referring to what? To the comparative linguists the claim of unity must be reconciled with the radical differences in experience posited by differing traditions.

Second, both humanistic and transpersonal psychology falter on the question of economics. Their schools and professional organizations are not well endowed. There are few grants available for research, and the amounts are either small or go largely to the same people. There are hardly any scholarship funds for students, and there are even fewer jobs open to graduates, except as entrepreneurial psychotherapists. One might say that they are a community of interpretation which as a cultural institution has not yet become economically viable in terms of attracting new capitol investment or talented young leaders. Consequently, they remain marginalized as a loose-knit collection of the same individuals.

Third, because of a strong emphasis on experience and practice, both humanistic and transpersonal psychologists have been associated with an anti-intellectual outlook. True, they write books and articles that contain footnotes and bibliography, but they are just as liable to mix popular and scholarly works together in the same text, treating different kinds of literature equally, or they appropriate, sometimes uncritically, technical works from the humanities and the sciences that, only when taken out of their disciplinary context, corroborate the unitive hypothesis. As well, the style of publication is often standard APA format; that is, scientific reference citations are superimposed onto a narrative text more literary in form.

Fourth, both humanistic and transpersonal psychologists tend to be unrealistic about the extent of their influence. There may be many books on the market about physics and consciousness, but this interpretation has virtually no influence on the way mainstream physics is conducted within the scientific community. Humanistic and transpersonal techniques have no impact on curriculum development throughout the United

States, except at a handful of smaller schools. Nor are they directly involved in the implementation of public government policies toward health and education. Even a journal such as *The Humanistic Psychologist* cannot be said to have a wide effect when its circulation is only twelve hundred.

## Some Virtues

The virtues of the transpersonal movement, however, may in the end outweigh their liabilities. I will name only three of the largest classes that represent important contributions to psychology.

### Qualitative Research

The great fault of modern psychology is that it is entirely too quantitative. Psychologists are in danger of becoming mere methodologists when the only thing that counts is the design of the experiment. This, unfortunately is the core vision of most graduate programs in the discipline. But the fetish for numbers, which justifies psychology as a science, necessarily diminishes the importance of the individual subject who is at the heart of the experiment and upon whom all the numbers rest. Individual differences are factored out when averages are taken on large scale samples. At the same time, a good theory, grounded in evolutionary biology, should also produce comparable results across species. Ideally, then, it does not matter if the subject is a rat or a person. What counts is the data generated by the anonymous organism.

Transpersonal psychology, on the other hand, shifts the focus to the idiosyncratic variance of the individual. The goal is not objective knowledge of the species, but self-reflective knowledge of one's own inner states of consciousness,—the examination of one's own motives and needs for purposes of character development. The goal is not the manipulation, prediction, and control of others, but the growth of inward understanding and self-knowledge.

In this regard, we have the reinstatement of the person at the center of a psychology that presumes the human mind to be an essence extractor far superior to any machine or method heretofore devised by man (or woman). Transpersonal psychology thus represents a useful model for the development of a person-centered science. Science becomes, not science for the sake of simply generating more science, but rather, one important tool by which we corroborate various aspects of human experience where we can. Human beings instead of science become the central focus of psychology.

The caveat is added, however, that such a person-centered science should not be seen as a mere compliment to the academic psychology of manipulation and control. One would not simply just add a transpersonal psychologist to the staff of a department that was cognitive and behavioral in orientation. Rather, the reductionistic attitude in the discipline in all likelihood will not prevail, while Transpersonal psychology, at least according to its votaries, in this regard, represents at present the most cogent example *of its probable successor.*

## *The Phenomenology of the Science-Making Process*

Another important contribution of the transpersonal orientation is understanding the psychology of the science-making process itself. The rhetoric of the reductionistic mentality has long been that science produces the only real knowledge about the world. Science is able to do this because it has been shorn of all religious cant and abstract philosophy. Superstition and metaphysics have been replaced with theoretical skepticism about all ultimate truth claims until what is put forward as the truth can be backed up by concrete evidence.

This orientation has worked admirably well in gaining control over the physical, material world and over large parts of biology. But when we come to the life of the mind, to beliefs, values, and choices, the mechanical analogy breaks down. Scientific principles based on the philosophy of reductionistic materialism cannot account for either the creation of science as a phenomena of western culture or the urge manifested by specific individuals toward science-making, itself.

Transpersonal psychologists have opened up this problem along two different lines of discussion (Maslow, 1966; Giorgi; 1970; Harman, In preparation): The first seeks to re-examine the implicit philosophical assumptions of science, while the second attempts to address various dynamics of the scientific personalities who hold these beliefs.

The general conclusion of the Transpersonalists is that successful science is based on a metaphysics of physicalism. Science-making is built upon an attitude about how reality shall be defined that is consensually shared by a group of adherents, and which, if agreed and acted upon, leads to approximately consistent results regarding its manipulation, prediction, and control. The first principles of this group presume that there is a physical world separate from our observation of it; that information from this world, known to us wholly through the senses, can be rationally and logically analyzed; and that the laws governing causal interactions between material objects, by which we come to control them, can be identified. Other corollaries then follow; for instance, in order for a phenomenon to be studied, it must be measured in some way, and so on.

At the same time, the issue that this specific philosophy of science raises for Transpersonal psychology is, 'what kind of a world gets constructed if one believes in a completely different definition of reality?' Here, we may enter the life-world of the shaman and find an iconography of healing with important consequences unavailable to the western medical mind-set. We may enter the frame of reference of the Buddhist meditator and discover a vast realm in which there is control of consciousness, instead of our domination of the physical world. Similarly, if we return to the adoption of the scientific world view, we should predictably loose these other realms of knowledge. How then do we acknowledge and gain access to the potential resources of these multiple realities?

In conjunction with this inquiry is an investigation into the kind of personality who holds the beliefs of the scientific world view. In general, according to the Transpersonalists, the primary characteristic of the scientific personality is a denial of the transcendent. Such denial takes the form of proclamations: Personal consciousness cannot heal the physical body. Consciousness cannot become "awakened" beyond normal alertness. There is no evidence for the existence of an unconscious. All of the basic forms of energy in the universe, nuclear, magnetic, and electrical, have already been discovered by physics. No higher powers other than human reason exist, and if there were, scientists would have discovered them a long time ago, and so on.

According to the Transpersonal orientation, a completely different kind of personality will have to evolve in the future than one who holds these views, and in some way, the iconography of the transcendent will figure prominently in the belief system of this new person. The subjective-objective dichotomy will change. Complementarity will have a more central role in physics. Within psychology the experience of transcendence will be a primary consideration in psychotherapy. Theories of learning will incorporate at once biochemical, cognitive, and intuitive ways of knowing. The scientist to evolve will have methods at hand to alter personal consciousness in the same way that materials in the physical world can now be manipulated. Personal mythologies and narrative imagery may yet stand as equals to statistical and mathematical formulas in the different domains that they govern.

*Interdisciplinary Communication*

Academic psychology has willingly sacrificed an important dialogue with history, with the humanities, and with religion in its quest for identity among the natural and social sciences. Courses in the psychological novel, the psychology of art, the psychology of religion, are taught outside psychology departments, or may be found within the departments as occasional electives, the persistence of which over time is ephemeral at best. Virtually no instruction appears in most academic psychology departments in consciousness raising, self-knowledge, or personal development.

Consequently, there is virtually no connection made between the transformation of individual consciousness and our most pressing social problems. Such problems academics seem either to ignore or to approach as detached intellectual exercises. Transpersonal psychologists, on the other hand, despite their meager economic resources, lack of institutional affiliation, and small political clout, idealistically attack a number of these problems head on.

One is preventative medicine. The dialogue between psychology and medicine, alive and well in the Transpersonal movement, is grounded, the transpersonal adherents believe, in the inherent ability of consciousness to influence the physical body. If scientific research into the voluntary control of internal states has shown us anything, they say, it is that, with proper training, individuals can develop a larger measure of control over their own health and well-being. Diet, exercise, and concentrated personal disciplines that harness our capacities for visualization, relaxation, and breath control in the context of one's spiritual belief system are the means of approach.

Immunologists cringe, for instance, at the mere mention of the word psychoneuroimmunology. The new revolution in the neurosciences at least acknowledges that the center of gravity for much modern research is now occurring at the interface between molecular genetics, biochemistry, neurology, immunology, endocrinology, and psychiatry. Advocates of holistic health have taken their cue from these endeavors and made the claim that there is legitimate scientific evidence for the ability of personal consciousness to willfully strengthen the body's immune response. Hence, advances in neuroendocrinimmunology by the methods of straight forward bench scientists have been transmuted by

Transpersonal psychologists into the new field of *psycho*-neuroimmunology. While the scientists are studying nuclear medicine and making great strides in molecular pharmacology and neuroimaging techniques, the Transpersonal psychologists are attracting physicians, anthropologists, doctors and physicists to the study of energy medicine, based on the perceived phenomenological effect of such forces as *chi* and *prana*, drawn from the world's indigenous healing traditions.

In addition to medicine, an entirely new era of communication may also open between psychology and the arts. Here, we find that Saul Bellow practices anthroposophy, meditates, and does yoga for his arthritis. There, we discover that Erik Hawkins, the famed dancer and one-time husband of Martha Graham, improved his dance technique with aikido. Such examples suggest that painters, sculptors, actors and actresses, filmmakers, musicians, and composers have much more to tell us then merely the objective steps in the creative process. They are the stewards of intelligent worlds that may far transcend the merely rational, without which the human personality may sicken and die.

Another potential area of exchange may occur between psychology and religion. The Transpersonal psychologists, for instance, have long promoted the dialogue between Eastern and Western thought. Zen has been presented to the west as a formal psychology (Akishige,1977). Transpersonal psychologists have been conducting numerous seminars with His Holiness The Dalai Lama on Tibetan and Western views of the mind-body problem. The noted philosopher, Robert McDermott, Rudolf Steiner scholar and student of Auribindo, has recently become head of Alan Watt's old group, The California Institute for Integral Studies. Esalen Institute has recently updated its extensive bibliography on meditation, referencing over 1,200 experimental studies. As well, Fadiman & Frager (1976) have produced the first psychology text to incorporate non-western systems in a discussion of personality theory. Such materials may suggest a radical revision in the way we define cross-cultural psychology. We may have to take greater cognizance of unique indigenous expressions of personality and consciousness, rather than blithely assume that cross-cultural means simply the use of western scientific methods on subjects from different cultures.

## The Forecast

How, then, are we to regard the Transpersonal movement in psychology? I believe that it should be correctly placed, not within the German experimental laboratory tradition, or the lineage of English mental tests, or even against the backdrop of the European depth-psychologies like psychoanalysis. Rather, I see it as falling within the context of the nineteenth and twentieth century Anglo-Saxon psychologies of personality transformation. In this vein, it has closer links to the philosophical outlook of William James, whose *Varieties of Religious Experience* fueled the American self-help movement; or Carl Jung, whose Analytic Psychology is the widespread basis for contemporary dream-workshops, or Aldus Huxley, who wrote about the perennial philosophy.

These historical links suggest that the experiential orientation has always been a part of psychology, albeit a peripheral one in the modern scientific era. It may yet have a more central focus, showing that Transpersonal psychologists were pioneers before their time. But in the end, the presently unanswerable question may turn out to be 'how can there possibly be a dialogue between psychologists who hold to a metaphysics of experience with those who cleave to a metaphysics of physicalism?' The answer may require an epistemological leap beyond the mere accumulation of more objective data, or the present attempt to justify a subjective science of the spirit simply in empirical terms.

This means that, while the iconography of the transcendent may yet enter into psychology, through a science of consciousness, for instance, such a psychology of the future may not have any of the names in the present-day Transpersonal orientation associated with it. The function of the transpersonal movement will then be associated mainly with the ideological struggles in psychology during the second half of the twentieth century that we now endure. Let me say emphatically that this is not an insignificant role to have played in the history of the discipline.

## References

Akishige, Y. (Ed). (1978). *Psychological studies on Zen* (2 vols.). Tokyo: Komazawa University.

deCarvalho, R. J.(1990). A history of the "Third Force" in psychology, *Journal of Humanistic Psychology, 30,* 22-44.

Fadiman, J. (1969). The Council Grove Conference on altered states of consciousness, *Journal of Humanistic Psychology, 9,* 135-137.

Fadiman, J. (1970). The Second Council Grove Conference on altered states of consciousness, *Journal of Transpersonal Psychology 9,* 169-174.

Fadiman, J. & Frager, R.(1976). *Personality and personal growth.* New York: Harper & Row.

Fields, R. (1981). *How the swans came to the lake: A narrative history of Buddhism in America.* Boulder, Shambhala.

Frager, R. (1974). A proposed model for a graduate program in Transpersonal psychology, *Journal of Transpersonal Psychology, 6,* 163-166.

Giorgi, A. (1970). *Psychology as a human science: A phenomenologically based approach.* New York: Harper & Row.

Greening, T. (1976). Commentary, *Journal of Humanistic Psychology, 16,* 1-3.

Harman, W. (Ed.) (In preparation). *The metaphysical foundations of modern science: A reassessment.* Palo Alto, Calif.: Institute of Noetic Sciences.

INS (1990). *Annual Report of the Institute of Noetic Sciences,* Sausalito, California.

Maslow, A. H.(1966). *The psychology of science: A reconnaissance.* Chicago: Regnary.

Maslow, A. H.(1958). *Motivation and personality.* New York: Harper & Row.

May, R., (1958). The origins and significance of the existential movement in psychology. In R. May, E. Angel, & H. F. Ellenberger (Eds.), *Existence: A new dimension in psychiatry and psychology.* New York: Basic Books.

May R., (ed) (1964). *Existential psychology.* New York: Random House.

JTP. (1988). Cumulative Index, 1969-1988, *Journal of Transpersonal Psychology, 20,* 185-208.

Rogers, C. R. (1942). *Counseling and psychotherapy: Newer concepts in practice.* Boston: Houghton: Mifflin.

Smith, H. (1976). *Forgotten truth.* New York: Harper & Row. @ref = Sutich, A. J.(1967). The growth-experience and the growth-centered attitude, *Journal of Humanistic Psychology, 7,* 155-162.

Sutich, A. J. (1969). Some considerations regarding transpersonal psychology, *Journal of Transpersonal Psychology, 1,* 11-20.

Sutich, A. J. (1975). Process character of definitions in transpersonal psychology, *Journal of Humanistic Psychology, 15,* 39-40.

Sutich, A. J.(1976). *The founding of humanistic and transpersonal psychology: A personal account.* Unpublished doctoral dissertation, Humanistic Psychology Institute, San Francisco.

Tart, C. (Ed.). (1969). *Altered states of consciousness.* New York, John Wiley & Sons.

Taylor, E. I. (1978). Psychology of religion and asian studies: The William James legacy. *Journal of Transpersonal Psychology, 10,* 1.

Taylor, E. I. (1991). William James and the humanistic tradition. *Journal of Humanistic Psychology, 31,* 1.

Vaughn, F. E. (1982). The transpersonal perspective: A personal view, *Journal of Transpersonal Psychology, 14,* 37-45.

Vich, M. A.(1976a). Anthony Sutich: An appreciation, *Journal of Transpersonal Psychology, 8,* 2-18.

Vich, M. A.(1976b). Anthony J. Sutich, 1907-1976, *Journal of Humanistic Psychology, 16,* 3.

Vich, M. A. (1988). Some historical sources of the term "Transpersonal," *Journal of Transpersonal Psychology, 20,* 107-110.
Vich, M. A.(1990). The origins and growth of Transpersonal psychology. *Journal of Humanistic Psychology, 30,* 47-50.
Watts, A. (1961) *Psychotherapy, East and West.* New York: Pantheon.
Wilber, K.(1984). The developmental spectrum and psychopathology: Part I, stages and types of pathology, *Journal of Transpersonal Psychology, 16,* 75-118.


Author's Note: Acknowledgments are gratefully extended to Miles Vich, Rollo May, James Fadiman, Karen Furgeson, Stanley Krippner, Carmi Harari, and Madeline Nold for comments on various drafts of this manuscript.

# 13

# A Brief Overview of Transpersonal Psychology

*Edward Bruce Bynum*

> I am one of those spirit-souls who dwell in the light-god. I have made my form in his form, when he cometh to [the city of] Tetu. I am a Spirit-body among his Spirit-bodies.
> *(Egyptian Book of the Dead)*

## A Working Definition

Transpersonal psychology is both an evolving clinical and scientific tradition within psychology and also an ancient psychospiritual lineage. Transpersonal psychology can be understood to be the study of non-ordinary states of consciousness not traditionally covered by the discipline of ego psychology. This includes states of consciousness such as meditation, religious ecstasy, trance and "unitative conscious experiences" often described in the esoteric and spiritual literature of humankind. This would also incorporate the study of the psychophysiological techniques and introspective disciplines associated with these states of consciousness. Finally the field includes both metaphysical and philosophical paradigms often encountered in the contemporary fields of theoretical physics, neuroscience and cognitive psychology. The transpersonally oriented clinician's perspective is often inclusive of anomalous experiences and does not reflexively *reduce* noetic or spiritual experiences to organic, psychopathological or even unconscious causes and dynamics, nor *elevate* disturbed psychological states to the sublime. Also the range or spectrum of consciousness is not necessarily localized to one mind or set of body-mind boundary conditions, or for that matter to one life-time.

## Transpersonal Psychology and the History of Ideas

Archaeological and anthropological data suggest that human civilization first took root in ancient EgyptoNubian soil not far from the place where Homo Sapiens first arose from the mysteries of Africa (Diop, 1974; Jackson, 1970; Fairservis, 1962). In this region of east Africa, perhaps 8 to 10,000 B.C., a sustained culture began to work out the first great ideas about death and rebirth, consciousness itself, transcendence and the dynamics of the soul. Neanderthal Man buried his dead, perhaps reflecting some intuition of the noetic, but he was an evolutionary dead end and he did not write about it. Africa wrote about it.

In the *Egyptian Book of the Dead*, also known as the papyrus of ANI, or as the ancient Kemetic Egyptians themselves referred to it, the *Book of the Comming Forth By Day and The Going Forth By Night* from 4000 B.C., can be found all the major ideas in template form that have exercised a profound influence on the history of spiritual thought (Budge,1960). Here is found seminal ideas on the dynamics of death and resurrection, divine judgement and retribution, encountering the luminous spirit, the dynamic transformations of personal consciousness into the divine consciousness, the holy trinity and even the story of the Kristos. It also contains detailed descriptions of the netherworld which are strikingly similar to certain descriptions of the Bardo states in the *Tibetan Book of the Dead* or the *Bardo Thodol* (Evans-Wentz, 1960). We should not forget that ancient Egypt, Ethiopia and Kundalini Yoga-rich Dravidian India were connected by sea faring trade routes and cross-fertilized each other in many ways, including religious ideas and psychospiritual disciplines.

These psychospiritual ideas and disciplines evolved at the same time as did a sophisticated mathematics, astronomy and, due to the art of mummification and battle field traumas, a fairly well developed medical knowledge. Some areas of psychophysical knowledge were not surpassed until the middle of the 19th century in Europe (Finch, 1990). Of the thousands of medical papyri of that time only a few have reached our day, the most famous being the Edwin Smith and Ebers papyri which described the diagnostic applications of pulse-taking, over 200 anatomical terms, the meninges of the brain, cerebrospinal fluid and an early form of successful neurosurgery termed trephination, all 35 centuries before the Alexandrian Greek Hemophilus of the 4th century B.C. This sophisticated medicine and science was intimately associated with the symbols and practice of the Uraeus, also known as the Kundalini serpent

(Finch, 1990). The psychological knowledge of these peoples included the awareness of the dynamic unconscious. They employed it both in medical and religious-psychospiritual contexts and referred to it as the Amenta (King, 1990) and the primeval waters of NUN (Hornung, 1986). It was a transpersonal perspective on the unconscious.

The places where these psychospiritual disciples were practiced were called the "Houses of Life" which served both as temple and library in the mystery school system. The most famous were Abu-Simbel, Luxor, Abydos, Karnak and others in the Nile valley. Many of the Greek luminaries studied in these "Houses of Life" including Pythagoras, Thales, Democritus and numerous others who aided in the Greek transmissions of Egyptian philosophy to Europe (James, 1989; Bernal, 1987; Diop, 1991). The Greeks emphasized the rational dimension of this philosophy and played down the transpersonal and spiritual dimensions (Schwaller de Lubicz, 1982). When the Assyrians, then the Greeks under Alexander (333 B.C.) and finally the Romans under Caesar finally conquered the Egyptians, the mystery schools were suppressed and eventually repressed by the edicts of the Roman emperors Theodosius and Justinian in the 4th and 6th century A.D. and the Christian Church was made the state religion. With the Arab Jihads of the 7th century, the mystery schools were actively persecuted and many of the practices were dispersed by secret societies to West Africa and Europe where they re-emerged in the "secret sects" such as the Rosicusians and Free Masons in Europe and the religious systems of West Africa (Asante, 1984). The transpersonal and psychospiritual disciplines of the Kemets became merely Al-Kemet or "Alchemy." In Europe the members of these societies would over time have a profound influence on the Renaissance and the enlightenment (such as on Bacon, Franklin, Jefferson, John Adams, 51 signers of the American Declaration of Independence).

By the late 19th century, transpersonal ideas had been officially purged from rational science but re-emerged in the sciences of the mind. Freud rediscovered the dynamic unconscious, an intrapsychic process, but had to acknowledge a trans-personal consciousness he termed, the "racial memory." Jung splashed into the collective unconscious, a transpersonal memory or store-house consciousness phenomena similar to the Yogic Akashic Records or Mahayana Buddhist Alayauijnana. William James scientifically studied mystical and transpersonal episodes in his *Varieties of Religious Experience* (1902/1961). With the influx of Yogic teachers from India such as Vivekananda and analytic western psychology in the late 19th and early 20th century, the stage was set for the formal re-emergence of transpersonal psychology.

## Transpersonal Psychology Today

Currently transpersonal psychology has two areas in one body, one of theory and the other of practice. Theoretically there are many voices, but two stand out, Ken Wilber and Michael Washburn, neither of whom is a clinician or a formally trained psychologist. Wilber's *Atman Project* (1980) is a vast, intricate, integration of individual human development from birth to death from a transpersonal perspective and it brilliantly illuminates the "spectrum of consciousness." It is complemented by his *Up From Eden* (1981), a transpersonal vision of our collective evolutionary drama. The two have become a scheme for many in the field because of the exhaustive range that they cover. Washburn's (1988) *The Ego and the Dynamic Ground* is also a transpersonal vision of human development and the two authors complement each other. Wilber's more cognitive approach frames a *hierarchical structure* of consciousness while Washburn's more affective approach unveils a *process* view of transpersonal development. Both are "pure" presentations of transpersonal development and need a clinical practice base. This is where Stanislav Grof's (1985) *Beyond the Brain: Birth, Death and Transcendence in Psychotherapy* fleshes out the picture. It offers both a clinical and theoretical "map" of the realms of transpersonal experience and a set of clinical procedures. The "messiness" of clinical reality is present. Further in this direction is Walsh and Vaughan's (1980) *Beyond Ego: Transpersonal Dimensions in Psychology*. There are many others in this expanding field and much of the future lies in the direction of integrating theory and practice. To this end many excellent journals have arisen (*Journal of Transpersonal Psychology, Revision, Meditate, East/West*).

## A Vision of the Future

The integration of theory and practice is crucial. The "spiritual supermarket" also offers the opportunity to observe many different transpersonal disciplines. Given the skills of western psychology and eastern introspective paths, a discipline will arise that clinically studies the pitfalls of different paths in order to help the student on his or her way much as successful psychotherapy does with neurosis. Each lineage already does this; now we can work with each. This kind of cross-fertilization often leads to genius. The study of dream states for the purpose of conscious evolution will also emerge stronger in the future, including transpersonal dimensions of dreaming and lucid dreaming (Bynum, 1993a, 1993b; Krippner, 1990; LaBerge, 1985; Saraswati, 1984). Also the future will see the field transcend its almost exclusive preoccupation with "Eastern and Western" methods and will open to the Personalism dimension inherent in many forms of ancient African mysticism and the African unconscious (Bynum, in process; King, 1990). This will greatly expand our view of human development. Finally I believe that the field will turn its attention to a primal root phenomenon of transpersonal experience, one as old as the Kemetic seers, and the Vodic Rishis of India and yet as modern as next year's headlines. It is a psychic, somatic and thoroughly transformative phenomenon and discipline, open to experimentation, verification and one that may usher in a new paradigm for the field and perhaps our species. I refer to the luminous and transcendental serpent, the mysterious Kundalini.

## References

Asanta, M. K. (1984). The African-American mode of transcendence *Journal of Transpersonal Psychology, 16*, (2), 167-178.

Bernal, M. (1987). *Black Athena: The Afroasiatic roots of classical civilization. Vol. 1: The fabrication of ancient Greece 1785-1985.* New Brunswick, NJ: Rutgers University Press.

Budge, E. A. W. (1960). *The book of the dead: The hieroglyphic transcript of the papyrus of ANI.* Secaucus, NJ.: University Books.

Bynum, E. B. (1993a). *Families and the interpretation of Dreams*, Ithaca, NY: The Haworth Press.@ref = Diop, C. A. (1974). *The African origin of civilization.* Westport: Lawrence Hill.

Bynum, E. B. (1993b). *Transcending psychoneurotic disturbances: New approaches in psychospirituality and personality development.* Ithaca, NY: The Haworth Press.

Bynum, E. B. (in process). *Oldawan: The African unconscious.*

Diop, C. A. (1991). *Civilization or barbarism: An authentic anthropology.* Brooklyn, NY: Lawrence Hill Books.

Evans-Wentz, W. Y. (1960). *The Tibetan book of the dead.* London: Oxford University Press.

Fairservis, W. A. (1962). *The ancient kingdoms of the Nile and the doomed monuments of Nubia.* NY: Crowell.

Finch, C. S. (1990). *The African background to medical science.* London: Karnak House.

Grof, S. (1985). *Beyond the brain: Birth, death and transcendence in psychotherapy.* Albany, NY: SUNY Press.

Hornung, E. (1986). The discovery of the unconscious in ancient Egypt. *Spring: An Annual of Archetypal Psychology and Jungian Thought*, pp. 16-28.
Jackson, J. G. (1970). *Introduction to African civilizations*. Secaucus, NJ: Citadel Press.
James . G. G. M. (1989). *Stolen legacy*. Newport News, VA: United Brothers Communications Systems.
James, W. (1961). *Varieties of religious experience*. New York: Collier Books. (Original work published 1902)
King, R. D. (1990). *African origin of biological psychiatry*. Germantown, TN: Seymour Smith.
Krippner, S. (Ed.). (1990). *Dreamtime and dreamwork: Decoding the language of the night*. Los Angeles: Tarcher.
LaBerge, S. (1985). *Lucid dreaming: The power of being awake and aware in your dreams*. Los Angeles: Tarcher.
Saraswati, S. S. (1984). *Yoga nidre*. Munger India: Bihar School of Yoga.
Schwaller de Lubicz, R. A. (1982). *Sacred science: The king of pharaonic theocracy*. Rochester, VT: Inner Traditions.
Walsh, R. N. & Vaughan, F. (1980). *Beyond ego: Transpersonal dimensions in psychology*. Los Angeles: Tarcher.
Wilber, K. (1980). *The atman project*. Wheaton, IL: Quest Books.
Wilber, K. (1981). *Up from eden*. Garden City, NY: Anchor Press/Doubleday.

# 14

## The Role of Transpersonal Psychology in Psychology as a Whole: A Discussion

*Rollo May, Stanley Krippner, and Jacqueline Larcombe Doyle*

**Editor's Introduction (Frederick J. Wertz)**

The unusual circumstances of this piece deserve an opening comment. Rollo May was committed to making a contribution to this volume from its inception. Originally, his chapter, entitled "The Human Dimension of Humanistic Psychology," was to be Rollo's reflection on the most significant developments in the movement. One evening last summer, I received a call from Rollo, who with considerable intensity expressed his desire to address the matter of transpersonal psychology. Rollo said that his reading of William James (1985) had reaffirmed his conviction about the importance of spiritual life, and that he wanted to correct the misunderstanding of his previous criticisms of transpersonal psychology. It is of the utmost importance at this time, Rollo conveyed, that transpersonal psychology be viewed in the proper perspective, within the context of the whole of psychology.

A few weeks after our conversation, Rollo suffered a stroke. I felt sure that Rollo would not be able to complete this project, and so I was surprised by the vigor and determination with which he communicated his desire to do so during his period of recovery. Since writing was out of the question, we decided that a good form for the work would be a dialog with Stanley Krippner, who generously agreed to participate. In the ensuing time, however, Rollo's health entered an even more serious crisis; he underwent brain surgery, spent months in the hospital which he later characterized as "unconscious," and emerged without much of his speech faculty. His recovery from that operation has been little short of miraculous, and he has summoned amazing strength to continue with this project, which has remained an important concern throughout this trying period of his life.

Rollo arranged to meet with Stanley Krippner and Jacqueline Doyle, who kindly agreed to participate, sharing her ideas and supporting Rollo in the expression of his ideas on transpersonal psychology. She also agreed to appear in his place at the APA Centennial Convention in Washington, DC. After a lengthy planning conversation between Jacqueline and Rollo, they met with Stanley over lunch, on June 9th, 1992 in Tiburon CA, with a tape recorder running. What follows is an edited transcription of their conversation, which was prepared by the staff of Saybrook Institute thanks to the cooperation of the new President Bruce Francis. To me this is a moving testimony not only to Rollo's resoluteness and strength in pursuing what is of great importance to humanity but also to the respect and affection of those who, like Stanley and Jacqueline, have rallied to facilitate Rollo's continuing presence in the field of psychology.

The remarks of the participants in this discussion — Rollo May, Stanley Krippner, and Jacqueline Doyle — are prefaced by their initials M, K and D, respectively.

K: For me Transpersonal Psychology is a psychological perspective or frame work which assigns primary importance to experiential reports of concern or contact with entities, beliefs or realms greater than oneself using them as a basis for conducting and interpreting psychological theories, intervention and research. When I say theory I mean development theory, motivational theory, personality theory. When I say interventions I mean psychotherapy, counseling, and education.

D: I appreciate your definition of Transpersonal Psychology because it doesn't delineate Transpersonal Psychology as a total psychology but one which is additive to other forms of psychology such as Ego Psychology. It explores a realm beyond what is presumably covered within ego psychology. And I think the difficulty arises when it's implicitly viewed as supplanting or being hierarchically arranged with other psychological concepts. In other words of greater value or of a merit above and beyond. Then a contest is set up. Preparatory to today's luncheon I had dinner with Rollo last night and our discussion referred back to the letter he had written in the *APA Monitor* years ago (May, 1986), and some of the responses that came back to him, and his feelings about them. Rollo said he never intended to attack Transpersonal Psychology itself. He was surprised his letter was construed as an attack on Transpersonal Psychology (e.g., in the responses published in the July, 1986 *APA Monitor*). Instead he was attacking the use, which sometimes occurs, of transpersonal themes and transpersonal psychology as a way to avoid tangling with the real issues of psychology and our day, problems of value such as peace and war and so forth. He said at times these themes are being thrown aside in what becomes an escape into the higher realms. He has always objected to the use of psychology, not just transpersonal psychology as in this case, as a method of avoiding the problems of being human and of living in the world.

K: Sure, I've seen the same thing with psychoanalysis.

D: That's right. I asked, "are you referring to the old days when psychology was criticized for being used in the service of teaching adaptation of the personality to a status quo which may not have been humane or therapeutic" and he said, "Exactly." That was exactly the kind of thing he'd always objected to. So he views teaching conformity, to certain social values or adaptation to untenable life situations, as taking a way out that was not for the good of the human. In the case of transpersonal psychology, he added that he felt sometimes it involved taking too easy a way out for the personality, to go high on the topic and avoid tangling with their own ego level issues as they might, for instance, include the dark side. Presumably through transpersonal methods, one can achieve a beautiful experience, like a Zen-like experience. Flying off into beauty and escaping the paradox of being human is what he objects to. Rollo is deeply concerned with the spiritual aspects of the human being and of psychology, and has always been, he says. Issues of death, of the breakdown of love and so forth. Then we talked about how, within transpersonal psychology, the achievement of a state called "peace" is heralded as an important achievement. He said "when you achieve peace, you are no longer a psychologist." You have left the reality behind you. The reality is made up of the paradox of being human, which contains within it the struggle with the evil or the darkness within one's soul, with the beauty, the spirituality and the other very positive creative aspects. But once you've achieved peace you're no longer in the struggle; you've risen to a realm which is beyond human in his estimation.

K: Here he is!
D: Oh, good.
K: I think that the three of us agree that some of the extreme fringes of transpersonal psychology seem to recommend divorcing the person from the social matrix, taking the individual out of the social context, out of the struggle to be human, out of the encounter with important human issues and put him or her on some elevated plane that really robs that person of one's humanity.
M: Oh, now that's marvelous. I was very surprised, and very hurt by the responses to my letter published in the *Monitor* several years ago. It was completely misunderstood. You know that I am very interested in the primitive and the spiritual.
K: Yes.
M: And I will continue to be. Now I wonder what motivated the attack. I was very surprised and shocked at what was written in response.
K: My feeling is that it was a political reaction. They were so eager to get their division. That superseded clear thinking, clear reading, articulate presentation. It was what I would call a knee-jerk reaction.
D: When your letter was published, I had some brief conversations with Francis Vaughan and I know that they felt there was a need to respond and defend the position and intellectual development that they had been spawning and nourishing through this budding field of transpersonal psychology, in which they had great investment.
M: So tell me again, though, why would they need to defend it?
D: Well, they felt that it was a critique of the field.
M: It was a criticism.
D: ...of the field.
M: That it was an attack?
D: I don't know that they saw it as a critique of individuals, but of the field or of the mode of thought that was developing. So they naturally felt that it was important to put out the positive side of it.
M: Ken Wilbur (1983) says we were all growing toward Eden. We will be happier and happier. We will be freed from our problems. This is impossible and undesirable. We would cease to be human. This is what I fight against.
D: Uh huh...
M: Did you know him very well?
K: No, not well but I had a couple of talks with him over the years.

M: The idea was that we were growing towards increasing perfection. So all a person had to do was sit tight, and these good things will automatically come about. Well I don't believe it at all!

D: Rollo, you're saying "I don't think we can just sit tight and wait for that to happen." How do you see a personality evolving toward less painful states?

M: It would happen by virtue of our devotion or hard work, our... You see what I am against is the belief that this comes automatically. Higher states are not achieved automatically. And the way that America is effecting the world seems to me to be tremendously significant. For instance, in ten, twenty years, the Amazon will have been gutted. Now I see that as a threat to all of us. The taking of this view, that psychological evolution is going to occur if we simply sit tight, concerns me. The Amazon's being destroyed very quickly. Progress is not automatic; we do not become better every day without effort.

K: Some estimates give the Amazon twenty more years at this rate. But the destruction of the Amazon has not been stopped, it's just slowed down, so it's still going on and of course what needs to be done is to stop it, and that's, pretty far away I'm afraid.

D: You are indicating that this kind of world problem is clear evidence of evil afoot in the world in terms of destruction. That example is very clear. If you were to move this to the individual psychological level, to development of the individual's psyche, how could you compare it? Transcendent development is accomplished through the individual struggling with the forces internal to personality rather than waiting on the sidelines for transcendence to fall upon them.

M: Very good. Now, Ken was over to my house one evening, and Don Michael and Walt Anderson were also present, and others. I asserted my view that progress is not automatic. Ken stopped the discussion, and he said that you're working on the wrong premises. He later withdrew from the dialogue. He wouldn't listen, implying that his ideas had reached some state of perfection and he shouldn't be questioned. All of us are always questioning and attacking each other's ideas to sharpen them. In the wake of his intolerant behavior, I may have been angry when I wrote that letter to the APA.

K: Was the altercation with Wilber before you wrote the letter or after you wrote the letter?

M: This event with Wilber came before the letter to the APA.

D: So you were a little hot under the collar when you wrote that letter.

M: Yah, yah, I sure was.
K: Well we all know that you're a person of great passion, Rollo, and your passion will spill off into the printed page from time to time.
M: Well, I'm afraid so.
D: Rollo, it seems that you're implying that there is a certain aspect of true believership within transpersonal psychology that is dangerous because it is separate from the scientific dialogue which has taken place within psychology, not that it has ever been totally value-free or should be.
K: If I understand you, Rollo, what you're saying is, number one, the letter might have been a little angrier than the way you would write it now and number two, you have no problem with the subject matter of transpersonal psychologists, because you've certainly been interested in spiritual and existential concerns all of your adult life, but it's some of the uses that they put this to and some of the practices that they put this to that disturbs you.
M: Mostly. Very well put.
D: Well, it's very interesting, the presumption that we as individuals and as a species are evolving toward higher and higher states is quite separate from the fact that the Amazon is being devoured as we sit here and have our lunch, and that the planet may not survive with some of the destructive forces at play.
K: Yes, the world might not be fit for human habitation in another twenty or thirty years.
D: So there may be another scenario that needs to be considered as equally plausible: that destructive forces could grow and overtake us if we're not conscious of them and don't keep our eye on them and manage them very well. So I think that there are important concomitants to these different possibilities.
M: Yes.
D: Last night, Rollo, you said a great deal about your readings of William James, and of how much you're in agreement with him.
M: William James was always open to new truths. I spent part of the summer reading his book on the varieties of religious experience... (K: Um Hmmm)... a marvelous book! And he doesn't at any point hold that all we have to do is sit tight and everything will be hotsy totsy.
D: Rollo, last night you said: "when a person achieves peace he is no longer a psychologist. He has left the reality behind. Reality is made up of the paradox."

K: I think it's a very good point because in some ways Carl Jung said the same thing. He said, "you are never completely finished with your individuation. This is a lifelong struggle." And I think that there is a conflict between this point of view of the individual always growing, always encountering, always dealing with paradox, and never really coming to an end as long as one is fully human. There's a difference between this and the people who think they've achieved enlightenment or bliss consciousness, and they can sail on that for the rest of their life without effort!

D: Or even peace, which is a simpler statement, but one that puzzles me. Rollo, your book on anxiety (May, 1973), for instance, points to the fact that there is an optimal level of anxiety to be maintained in life, that the goal is not peace but the balance of stress and creativity.

K: Hans Selye (1974) said that there's an optimal level of stress. He did not want to be misinterpreted that stress was always negative. He said there can be positive stress, and there is an optimal level of stress that keeps us functioning.

D: Right. Peacefulness is an unclear goal to me, and not one that attracts me. [she laughs] Because somehow the turmoil, the yeastiness of life is made up of what happens in conflicts within the individual and between people as they try to sort out the meaning of life for themselves, and that's not necessarily a peaceful process.

K: I think that I'd agree with that and in my work on personal mythology, I and other people point out that the individual is always engaging in dialectic; one myth is the thesis, and then the person outgrows that myth, goes into an antithesis, then they see that maybe the antithesis has to be moderated a little bit, and then they come to a synthesis with the best of both myths. But they don't stay there, they don't stay there because another four or five years, that synthesis becomes the new thesis, and they might go on from there. As you keep growing, you're always dealing with a dialectic, an exploration of your cutting edge.

D: That's right. That's beautifully stated, Stan.

K: Thank you.

M: What do you think will be the general point of view of the people at the APA Centennial?

K: I think people will be very open to this point of view, as you've just put it. I think there will be two extremes. There will be some very extreme transpersonalists who will be very upset by what you say, but then there will be some very extreme psychologists of the old school who think that any concession to transpersonal or transcendental concerns is harmful. You know, that this is all superstition, hogwash and we should just eliminate these topics from psychology all together. You know we're still wondering if it's possible for you to be at the Centennial meeting of APA...

D: Implicit in what we have been talking about is the creation of a hierarchy of psychological states: the valuing in psychological discussion of certain emotions as superior to others. The spiritual, beneficent, peaceful states, happy states that make us into smiling buddhas, so to speak, are the aim of development. My question about transpersonal psychology is whether there is a group of psychological states that are pointed toward as the goal or outcome of maturation, in distinction to other psychological theories including humanistic psychology? My suspicion is, at times, that other emotions such as anger, sadness and frustration are not viewed, valued as highly in transpersonal theory.

K: Definitely not.

M: A very important point that is often covered over by transpersonal psychology that anger, for example, can be a very constructive emotion.

D: To the extent that that's the case, it is a problem to me because, as a psychologist and therapist, I want to value the emotions that my clients have, seeing, in each, creative potential for clarifying and shaping the individual's goals, choices and development.

M: Yes. An example is a case of mine in *Power and Innocence* that shows the constructive use of anger: "Mercedes" (see May, 1972, p.81).

K: I think that anger can serve very important purposes, both personal and social purposes, if it is directed and used wisely. There are many people in Rio de Janeiro who are very angry about the destruction of the rain forest, and they are taking that anger and channelling it in very worthwhile social directions.

D: Exactly.

K: Without the anger, they might be sitting at home and saying "well, this is just the karma of the planet." Or "this is just fate" or "this was meant to be".

D: And certainly the anger of the Jewish population and of other people concerned with social justice has come out of the humiliation of the Jews and the degradation of them in the Second World War. Negative states often breed more enlightened states to follow them. But I sense that anger is viewed as suspect in the transpersonal world, and I'd like greater clarification from the transpersonalists for my own edification. Last night you said that you understand the impulse toward the transpersonal theory, because people are always trying to escape the narrowness of human life. You went on to say that the spiritual impetus is always there, but it is effective only when people have covered, beforehand, the steps of developing the ego and the personality so that there's a good base for embracing the spiritual, for pursuing the spiritual impetus. Then it's no longer an escape from the problems of the daily life or of the personality. I'm quoting Rollo May. (Laugh)

M: Yeah, I know this. [laughter] It's so good there's nothing I can add.

K: Fine! It's a good thing you took notes, Jackie!

D: And you also said that a person doesn't get rid of anger or selfishness in the personality, that negative forces are always there to be fought with. And when anger in the personality is denied or repressed, one gets into trouble. Then the shadow emerges and is out of control.

M: I feel they these negative forces are not adequately handled by transpersonal psychology. I feel this is a very important point.

K: My definition of Transpersonal Psychology (above) is a very common sense definition that really covers the waterfront. A lot of humanistic psychologists will say "Yes, these concerns are *part* of psychology, but we shouldn't put them at the center of psychology; they are one of many human potentials, one of many human experiences." Transpersonalists would say, "no, we take these experiences of something greater than oneself and put them at the center of what we're all about." So for me, the main difference between the transpersonal and humanistic is one of emphasis. I think that the humanistic psychologists, that I know at least, are certainly interested in transcendental experience, and in the use of mediation, guided imagery and other transpersonal psychotherapy techniques. They're interested in near death experience, in people who claim they're born again, and in people who have had a mystical, religious or transcendental episode in their lives. I think that transpersonalists would say "well, yes, but this is what we're all about, and this has to be the center of what we're doing." Some humanistic psychologists think that way too, so they could be both humanistic and transpersonal. I don't see any big dividing line between the two; for me it's one of emphasis.

D: I have some more quotes from my discussion with Rollo last night that I want to enter into the record of the tape. You feel there is, in transpersonal psychology, a denial that aggression is a part of the wholeness of the personality. You want to see the development of better psychologists who see into the significance of human life. If aggression is not taken into account, or not held as acceptable in theory, it appears as a breakthrough or as a shadow, out of control. In talking about Ken Wilber, and his *Up from Eden* (1983), you felt he was hypothesizing that we will all ultimately outgrow and be beyond our evil. Your deep reading of William James' work last year reemphasized that problems cannot be left behind in life. Rollo said: "Peace as the object of life is a dictatorship. Because what Peace is for me is not necessarily what Peace is for you." You summarized by saying that you're not against the fourth dimension of psychology, transpersonal. You only feel opposed to it if it provides an escape from the painful aspects of life.

K: Very well put.
M: Yes.
D: And you went on to say, one can't leap over the present experience. For instance, a therapist has to be where the client is, with his or her present life experience. One can't leap over the present complexity and jump to spirituality because development includes and proceeds hand in hand with the all experiences clients wrestle with in real life.
K: That sounds pretty good to me.
M: Incidentally I want, always been a pity I'm not a youngster that I could come to you for therapy. [K: Ahhh... (laughter). D: Oh, Sweetheart! (laughter...)] She has a marvelous point of view, doesn't she?!
K: Yes she does! Well you were our first choice for this luncheon, you know.
D: Great!

## References

James, W. (1902/1985) The varieties of religious experience. Cambridge, MA: Harvard University Press.
May, R. (1986). Letter to the editor. *APA Monitor, 17*(2), p.2.
May, R. (1950/1970) The meaning of anxiety. New York: Norton.
May, R. (1972). *Power and Innocence.* New York: Dell.
Selye, H. (1974) Stress without distress. Philadelphia: Lippincott.
Wilber, K. (1983) Up from Eden: a transpersonal view of human evolution. New York: Random House.

# 15

# Humanizing Psychological Assessment

*Constance T. Fischer*

As is often the case in the evolution of the social sciences, the early figures in psychological assessment were intrigued by the whole individual coping with a complex world. Henry Murray's (1938) personality theory and use of his Thematic Apperception Test portrayed the person as being pushed forward in unchosen ways from the past, as well as purposefully projecting self into an environment that both accommodated and pressed back. Gordon Allport (1937, 1961) encouraged a case study method of engaged involvement with the subject. He distinguished such "ideographic" efforts to describe and understand a particular event or individual from "nomothetic" efforts to gather data from many people in order to develop general laws or patterns. George Kelly (1955) proposed that the purpose of testing should be to "survey the pathways along which the subject is free to move." That subject could explore, reflect on, and revise his or her ways of construing the world. Bruno Klopfer (e.g., 1954) characterized his approach to the Rorschach as phenomenological, and his students celebrated this projective technique for being a means of going beyond sterile aptitude testing, toward assessing the whole, dynamic individual — the perceiving/thinking/feeling/defending/acting person. Molly Harrower (1956) promoted projective counseling, wherein the client and counselor discussed the former's inkblot responses, allowing the client to gain insight while helping the assessor to refine his or her psychodynamic exploration. Harrower's writings are filled with the excitement of clients' liberating self-discoveries via the Rorschach testing process.

Alas, much of this inspiration was lost as followers developed procedural refinements, norms, experimental studies — the building blocks of natural science. The challenge and exhilaration of demonstrable "prediction and control," along with the reward of becoming accepted among other sciences, readily captivated psychology. Concomitant allegiance to "objectivity" turned the study of personality into a technical gathering of "responses," "productions," "reaction times." The subject's task was to emit recordable, scorable behaviors and verbalizations. When not in the service of psychometric interpretation, these productions served reductive psychoanalytic interpretation. Psychometric studies have nearly extinguished the latter abuses, such as concluding that "the response of 'spider' on Card I demonstrates the mother's frigidity." But quantitative, laboratory-style correctives and advances also have carried researchers and assessors ever further from conceptions and practices that could take into account that humans are more than objects. It is extremely difficult to move from T-scores, bar graphs, and check marks on a profile sheet to an actual person's life and circumstances. Conclusions are unilateral (from tester to subject), deductive, abstract, and are typically limited to categories, causes, deficits, and probabilities. The field known as "individual differences" is not ideographic, but nomothetic; a particular person is described as marks on bell-shaped curves.

## Humanistic Critiques and Calls

This natural science dominance in assessment gave rise to numerous calls for reform, primarily in the 1960's and 1970's. George Rosenwald (1963, 1965a, 1965b, 1968) was the first of many psychologists to point out that testing should be a means rather than an end in itself. He urged colleagues not to banish their empathic sensitivities and creativity from the testing situation, and to desist from automatically applying old tests and categories to all testees. Alan Towbin (1964) said that psychologists had come to see themselves as "super technicians" providing personality x-rays. He proposed that rather than regarding clients as passive respondents to stimuli, we could regard them as purposive beings whose test behavior is not fundamentally different from their other behavior. We could actually talk directly to them about their responses. Theodore Leventhal and his colleagues (Leventhal, *et al*, 1962) argued that tests should be only part of the diagnostic process, and that patients should be invited to present their views of the issues during testing as well as in the interview. Idiosyncratic transference variables could be explored, and the patient would be introduced to a therapeutic relationship. Gertrude

Baker (1964) invited the patient's therapist to be present while she discussed the testing with the patient. In a similar vein, Joseph Richman (1967) suggested that "patients and their families can tolerate a great deal more information and hard facts than is generally recognized." Elsa Strauss (1967) urged colleagues to have the courage to report their personal impressions (as such) rather than rely only on technical data.

Today we do not regard these critiques as radical. But I know from my efforts to publish a call for assessment reports to be written so clients could read and commentary them (Fischer, 1970), that the majority of reviewers and editors regarded these practices as "too controversial," "irresponsible," "unethical," "unprofessional" and "nonscientific." In the early 1970's half of the respondents to a survey of psychologists said that even upon direct request they would not provide even a verbal account of their testing report to the client (Vane, 1972). Eighty-eight percent said that they rarely or never allowed clients access to reports. Rationales reported there and elsewhere were that clients were incapable of understanding the technical nature of the reports; writing for lay persons would dilute the scientific/professional status of the psychologist; there are no ways of reporting psychopathology and dynamics in non-technical language; clients are too fragile or too defensive to read the truth about themselves; discussion requires too much time; and that clients might argue with the professional.

During the 1970's, other psychologists suggested concrete ways of conducting assessments that would encourage active participation of the client and that would respect the integrity of the client's life. Among these authors were: Jose Arcaya (1973), Ray Craddick (1972), Charles Dailey (1971), Constance Fischer (1972), Fischer and Stanley Brodsky (1978), Richard Dana and Shirely Leech (1974), Phillip Erdberg (1979), Timothy Leary (1970), Louise Riscalla (1972). See Fischer (1985) for other similarly minded contributors.

### The Current Scene

Today I find that many experienced assessors discuss their findings with their clients/patients. This shift is occurring in part because some of the above authors have trained a generation of graduate students, and in part because some practitioners were receptive to the humanistic critiques of the 1960's and 1970's. Over time, for diverse reasons, consumers have come to expect more forthrightness: many participated in the 1960's counter-establishment movement; the Buckley Amendment granted access to school records; media psychologists talk in everyday language; managers have been provided feedback on their Meyers-Briggs patterns; postmodernist citizens know that truth is perspectival; and feminists are suspicious of categorical and deductive procedures. Cognitive-behavioral psychologists are accustomed to assessing behaviors, thoughts, and emotions directly with clients. In their efforts to be atheoretical and cross-disciplinary, the new DSMs are patient-friendly; criteria can be read to patients to determine differential diagnoses. Many self- and object-relations psychologists are interested in patients' views of their formulations. Paul Lerner (1991), for example, advocates such discussions of Rorschach findings. Finally, by now academic psychologists are far outnumbered by the practitioners they have graduated. Working directly with clients, as psychotherapists and assessors, has required greater flexibility, interaction, and cooperation than laboratory-based and theory-oriented psychologists have found necessary.

Nevertheless, the dominant picture remains one in which university training in assessment is exclusively training in testing and in unilateral clinical inference. For the most part, graduates evolve their own ways of attending to the client as a person. Professional literature on report-writing continues to protest that reports are test-oriented instead of client-oriented, and that they are too technical to be useful to most service providers. It seems to me that to attend more consistently to that "whole person coping with a complex world," we require a rigorous humanistic approach and systematic practices.

## Principles and Practices of Individualized Assessment

I have had the fortune of teaching in the Psychology Department of Duquesne University for the past twenty-five years. Colleagues and graduate students pursue an empirical existential-phenomenological psychology, which we also characterize as a human-science psychology. Within that context I have been developing and teaching a human-science approach to assessment, most of which has been published in my textbook, *Individualizing Psychological Assessment* (Fischer, 1985). Hundreds of students and practitioners have found the following principles and practices viable, and have contributed their own variations.

Everyday events, as witnessed in an assessment session, and as reported by or about the client, are the data. The life-world is our point of departure into test materials, norms, research, clinical lore, diagnostic schemes, and other resources derived from immediate life. Characterizations and suggestions developed through use of these tools are in terms of the person's actual life. For example, Mark Jones was referred by his therapist for evaluation of possible Axis II personality structure. The issue turned out to be whether therapy ought to be planned as long term, or whether Mark's outbursts at home and his having quit several jobs could be understood as circumstantial. When I asked Mark for an example of a work problem that his teachers way back in grade school would recognize, Mark mentioned that his last employer said he was "cocky, and helter-skelter" with customers. In light of elevations on both MMPI scale 9 (hypomania) and the Rorschach egocentricity index, I asked Mark about the possibility that what his manager saw might be Mark energetically keeping himself oblivious to whether he was "doing okay." After discussion, we were in agreement, and we went on to explore how Mark could modulate his interactions in ways that would maintain "confident Mark" (his words) while also letting employers and customers know that Mark is paying attention to them. We role-played one alternative, and developed several other concrete suggestions that wound up in the assessment report. The report affirmed Cluster B (Axis II) patterns, but also illustrated that Mark could be helped to find ways to be himself and yet not upset other people.

Thus, with ongoing life as the point of departure and of return, assessment based on human-science psychology is descriptive, contextual, collaborative, interventional, and structural.

*Descriptive*

The client's actions and discussion while with the assessor are described as examples of whatever abstract characteristics were suggested by test patterns. In discussion and reports, constructs are grounded in examples. The assessor mentions his or her own reactions as part of the picture, and refers to him or herself in first-person. An excerpt from a report:

> After I read the Bender instructions to Ms. Seale, she sat still, shoulders drooped forward, pencil held listlessly. She looked at the floor, and after a while mumbled that she wasn't good at drawing. Later we agreed that this was a good example of what she meant by "having low self-esteem." I mentioned that I had felt a bit impatient with her, and wasn't pleased with myself about that. She had sensed my reaction, and felt all the more uncomfortable and hesitant to start.

Compare this description with a too common kind of formulation: "The patient's passive-dependent orientation and lack of self-confidence resulted in long reaction times." This formulation's advantage is its brevity. But it covers over more than it reveals about the person, and it seems to imply that Ms Seale's conduct is determined by traits. The longer, descriptive version also illustrates how Ms Seale both shapes and is shaped by her particular world.

*Contextual*

The assessor, being interested in actual people and their situations, first asks the referring party for the background of the request for an assessment. In Ms Seale's case, a therapist had asked for an assessment of suicidality. The context of the issue turned out to be that Ms Seale was very quiet in sessions, seemed despondent, and would not answer the therapist's questions about whether she was feeling "self-destructive." The assessor then clarifies background with the client. When I asked Ms Seale about her therapist's concern, she explained that she hadn't understood that "self-destructive" referred to suicide. She did sometimes think that she couldn't wait much longer for life to get better, but had not thought of killing herself.

Client and assessor then "contextualize" the problematic behavior. In this instance we found that Ms Seale has waited for others to take initiative when she has felt that they are "supposed to in charge," like a therapist and an assessor. She had also been slow to act when in unfamiliar circumstances, in which she might be criticized. We went on to identify times when she had not held back (what I have termed the "when nots" of the problematic approach). Ms Seale reported that she "rough houses" with her little nephews, argues with her younger sister, and has initiated new arrangements of the candy bars in the movie theater where she clerks. By looking at specific contexts, we discovered how Ms Seale surpasses the characterization of being passive dependent, and we discovered starting points through which she and her therapist could work toward greater freedom.

*Collaborative*

As already indicated, client and assessor *labor together* to reach useful understandings. This is not merely feedback by one person at the end of an evaluation. Instead, both parties work together throughout the assessment to revise their evolving impressions. Excerpt:

> *Client:* No that's not it. I don't think I 'avoid complex or emotional situations' [low Afr, Zd = -4]. I have the courage to hang in. I just choose some one thing to hold on to 'til I get through the situation.
>
> *Assessor:* Like you pressed so hard on your pencil but didn't check against the card [Bender Gestalt]? (Client nods.) So what

we called 'being determined' is also a way of keeping things simple, of getting through?

*Client:* (laughing) Like a horse with blinders plodding straight ahead!

Such evolving descriptions and analogies allow assessor, client, and readers to work together from shared referents. Indeed, clients can read these individualized reports and notate in a Comments section at the end of the report any reflections since the last session, along with any disagreements or clarifications in regard to the written report.

*Interventional*

In order to collaborate, the assessor interrupts usual procedures at natural breaks. The assessor also may interrupt the client's movement, to explore alternatives. In other words, the goal is not just to describe or classify the person's present state, but to identify personally viable options to problematic behavior. For example, after recording several of Mr. Jordan's dysphoric, futureless TAT stories, I handed him a card showing a male looking out a window (#14); but just as he sighed and just before he spoke, I interjected: (with exaggerated lugubrious tone) "Well, it's just a man standing there. You can't tell what's happened. He'll just have to wait. He couldn't possibly be thinking about taking initiative on his own." After a startled pause, Mr. Jordan grinned in recognition of his pattern. As we discussed stories others have made up, he became more acutely aware of how his stance had been shaping his life. On the next two cards he tentatively told stories in which the person planned ahead despite the absence of guarantees. Thus we assessed Mr. Jordan's readiness to move on, rather than merely documenting his depression.

Interventions also can help the client to recognize points at which a change in course may be advisable. Ms Connely's Rorschach showed a repetitive sequence of "big" animals, damaged objects, and then explosions. This led to a discussion of her having habitually anticipated being hurt by people in authority, and then carrying out "preemptive attacks" (my term, which she smilingly affirmed). The assessment reported on her new understanding, and on her agreement to test out whether she indeed was in danger before letting loose her "blow ups." We identified her experiencing someone in authority as like a 'big animal' as the sign for such reflection.

*Structural*

Human-science assessment is structural in several senses. Explanation *is* description of how the client comports him- or herself when perceiving certain situations in particular ways. There is no sought-for cause or explanatory trait. When the assessor's narrative descriptions provoke interpersonal understanding for the reader, the account is adequate; it is more than adequate when that understanding carries practical implications, such as the suggestion developed with Ms Connely. Copying Bender designs, coping with the ambiguous inkblots, and so on, each evokes structurally similar earlier experiences, which are thus available for collaborative exploration.

In the interest of providing continuity with the other contributions to this volume, I would like to highlight the following themes of humanistic psychology that are among those that are evident in the above systematic practical applications of individualized assessment. The themes include: the perspetival nature of truth; nontotalizing approach; openness to disagreement; recognition of the client's self-reflectivity; emphasis on the experiential world of the client; use of everyday and narrative language; respect for interpersonal transparency and openness; the client as an active participant rather than as passive object; the psychologist as engaged collaborator rather than as disinterested scientist; respect for privacy; assumption of freedom and potential; celebration and use of humor; use of metaphor.

## Teaching Individualized Assessment

The following introduction to human-science psychological assessment is provided to Master's students in Duquesne University's Psychology Department. During the same year the students take courses in existential-phenomenological foundations, qualitative research, human-science courses in human development, social psychology, group process, psychotherapy, and related electives.

*Standard material*

Students first become familiar with traditional tests and standardized administration. They are examined on testing concepts (standard error of measurement, drift, false positive, etc.). They observe demonstrations of the Wechslers, TAT, Bender, and DAP. They administer several batteries and then each student is videotaped while testing a classmate and being observed by a doctoral teaching assistant. Through this process, students learn standardized procedure before they then learn how they may deviate for specific purposes. They become aware of their personal impact on testees and of the uniqueness of each *inter*action even with standardized procedures. Moreover, they learn as testees what it is like to be involved in each subtest and instrument, and later can address those situations with clients.

*Person-in-process*

Several assignments and class exercises develop sensitivity to "person in process" — to the dynamic person encountering obstacles, invitations, dangers, options. In a demonstration with the Bender cards, I role-play drawing tiny, light figures, and ask the class, "what's possible from here?" — I show how a loud voice is not available from that posture, but can become possible through transitions. I also demonstrate drawing bold, large, rushed figures, and indicate that careful listening is not yet possible from that stance. At home, the students try out other variations, and learn that terms like "passive dependent" and "expansive" can point to a range of circumstances, and that although they capture repetitive stances, they may not pertain pan-situationally.

I demonstrate collaborative and interventional use of the Bender with a student volunteer. The class is surprised to recognize the person they know from study groups, socializing, and so on, as he or she goes about the drawing task and discusses the experience with me. As I ask the volunteer for other instances of whatever happened on the Bender (e.g., false starts, rushing to get done), the students see how tests provide a common ground for discussion of evoked life experiences. They also see that there are no single or absolute meanings of test productions.

Each student draws from an envelope the name of a classmate, and later presents him or her with a two-page series of glimpses of that classmate. Re-presentation of the glimpsed moments is intended to *represent* the classmate. The receiver is deeply moved as he or she recognizes self and personal history at levels unknown to the describer. Both parties gain respect for the power of their simple assessment descriptions, and in turn for the utility of Husserl's oft-quoted dictum to "return to things themselves."

We experiment in class to open ourselves to the life world possibilities of construct-laden sentences that have shown up in that week's assignments. For example, in place of "Ann lacks self-confidence," we suggested: (a) "Ann said she is unsure that she could tell her boss that she disagreed"; (b) "Ann has been afraid that she would be fired if she disagreed with the boss"; and (c) "When Ann has slunk back in her chair rather than join in discussion, her boss has given someone else the chance to formulate policy proposals." We also have explored potential dynamic meanings by playfully varying original evocative wording. For example, "Long, seemingly untamed hair and a strand of pearls softened April's image and yet bespoke a tension, an incongruity," were creatively rendered as (a) "Untamed April imagines that pearls bespeak softness"; (b) "April softens seemingly untamed tension, speaking pearls"; and (c) "Long stranded, April speaks a tension, softening an incongruity."

*Truth as interpersonal*
In another classroom exercise, I ask for two volunteers to read to us from a children's book, *The Phantom Tollbooth* (Juster, 1961). The rest of us jot down moments that are coming to represent the two students' relation to one another, to the task, and to us. The exercise heightens our awareness that, for example, what we described variously as Jack's reading softly and tentatively was located in our leaning forward to hear as well as in his low volume and frequent pauses. As we share our jottings, we discover a clear consensus *and* that several students have worded their observations in ways that furthered our insight. In a similar exercise, Richard Dana (1982) asks students to share separately written reports based on the same observed interview and test data. We learn that despite variation in perspective, personal interests, and creativity, we reach documentable, useful agreements. I present slides of Andrew Wyeth's paintings, and we rediscover that the truth of subject matter is among the viewed object, the painter or author, and ourselves.

Assessments of undergraduate students and of clients in clinical settings are read by the assessee, who writes comments and further suggestions both on the margins and at the end of the report. This practice encourages students to word their reports in ways that are true to both assessor's and client's perspectives. New understandings for both parties evolve during this step as well during earlier collaboration.

*Writing to Individualize*
Throughout the course the teaching assistants and I emphasize that descriptions must be written in terms of everyday life. If the student doesn't return to the life world from test scores and categories, that student literally doesn't yet know "what in the world" he or she is talking about. Prior to crafting three formal reports, students try out writing about observed action and context, and about collaborative discussion, by describing a classmate administering tests and a stranger in action (restaurant and laundromat scenes prevail!), as well as the glimpses of a

classmate. Just as we do with assessees, the assistants and I provide suggestions into the student's project and style, not just generalizations about report-writing. We point out that use of first person emphasizes the interpersonal context of the assessment. Use of past tense emphasizes that actions are not the product of a set personality, and that one may act differently in the future. For example: "John said that he has often yelled at his wife" vs. "John yells at his wife."

## Toward the Future

Historically, humanistically oriented psychologists have eschewed professional involvement in assessment, seeing it as demeaning and objectifying. Those who have practiced in the above sorts of ways, however, have found the work especially rewarding, both in regard to helping clients to explore their understandings and possibilities, and in showing colleagues the utility of a rigorous approach to the particular, whole, situated, complex, evolving person. Nevertheless, this work can be more demanding than psychotherapy, and does hold the psychologist more immediately accountable. Individualized assessment certainly affords a unique opportunity to demonstrate the utility and validity of humanistic approaches. Psychology is poised to be more open-minded in regard to theory, and is ready to consider ways to integrate natural-science traditions with ways of thinking that can encompass our rising social consciousness.

I am hopeful that descriptive, narrative research and assessment will lend themselves increasingly to interdisciplinary and interprofessional dialogue, with the life world as the common referent. Perhaps we are ready to return to the spirit of Henry Murray's (1938) diagnostic council, in which psychiatrists, psychologists, anthropologists, sociologists, and others shared observations and understandings of the same person. I am less hopeful, but equally eager, for humanistic personality theory, research, and assessment to become thoroughly structural, in particular for it to integrate the neurophysiological order of existence into our formulations.

My own newer efforts at "humanizing psychological assessment" include three thrusts. One is to sensitize doctoral students to the social/political/economic context of lives by arranging for them to conduct assessments of clinically referred clients in the latters' homes. There they can tailor suggestions into the client's particular setting. Moreover, there they experience the power of family, neighborhood, cultural differences, history, poverty, and racism, and they encounter their own biases. They see that to help individuals we also have to change society, with a starting point being our reports (Fischer, 1987). This lesson carries into office practice.

The second thrust is to integrate more fine arts and literary exposure into assessment classes. Through this integration we think more openly and fluidly, and know more clearly that like practitioners of other disciplines, we discover and create realities in our efforts to express them. The third thrust is to teach students to integrate qualitative/phenomenological research into their assessment work, just as we do with our psychotherapy work. For example, as I watch Mr. Mitchell impatiently flipping and forcing blocks during the WAIS-R, I think of Donna Coufal's dissertation (in progress) on being impatient. I realize that Mr. Mitchell likely has narrowed his intentions, which are all the more intense as some treasured image of himself has come to be at stake as time runs out. We later relate this structure to what a recent performance review said about his being abrupt with slower employees.

Practicing assessment in these ways ourselves will continue to change psychological practice, as others see how feasible and rewarding it is to humanize psychological assessment.

## References

Allport, G. W. (1937). *Personality: A psychological interpretation.* New York: Holt.
Allport, G. W. (1961). *Pattern and growth in personality.* New York: Holt, Rinehart & Winston.
Arcaya, J. (1973). The multiple realities inherent in probation counseling. *Federal Probation, 37,* 58-63.
Coufal, D. (in progress). Being impatient: An existential- phenomenological study. Doctoral dissertation in progress, Duquesne University, Pittsburgh.
Craddick, R. (1972). Sharing oneself in the assessment procedure. *Professional Psychology, 6,* 279-282.
Dailey, C. A. (1971). *Assessment of lives: Personal assessment in a bureaucratic system.* San Francisco: Jossey-Bass.
Dana, R. H. (1982). *A human science model for personality assessment with projective techniques.* Springfield, IL: Thomas.
Dana, R. H. & Leech, S. (1974). Existential assessment. *Journal of Personality Assessment, 38,* 428-435.
Erdberg, P. (1979). A systematic approach to providing feedback from the MMPI. In C. Newmark (Ed.), *MMPI: Clinical and research trends.* New York: Praeger.

Fischer, C. T. (1970). The testee as co-evaluator. *Journal of Counseling Psychology, 17*, 70-76.
Fischer, C. T. (1972). Paradigm changes which allow sharing of results. *Professional Psychology, 3*, 364-369.
Fischer, C. T. (1985). *Individualizing psychological assessment*. Monterey: Brooks-Cole.
Fischer, C. T. (1987). Empowering clients by deconstructing psychological reports. *Practice: The Journal of Politics, Economics, Psychology, Sociology, and Culture, 5*,134-139.
Fischer, C. T. & Brodsky, S. L. (Eds.). (1978). *Client participation in human services: The Prometheus Principle*. New Brunswick, N.J.: Transaction.
Harrower, M. (1956). Projective counseling: A psychotherapeutic technique. *American Journal of Psychotherapy, 20*, 74-86.
Juster, N. (1961). *The phantom tollbooth*. New York: Scholastic Book Services.
Kelly, G. (1955). *The psychology of personal constructs* (Vols. 1 & 2). New York: Norton.
Klopfer, B., Ainsworth, M. D., Klopfer, W. G., & Holt, R. R.(1954). *Developments in the Rorschach technique. I: Theory and technique*. Yonkers-on-Hudson, N. Y.: World Book Co.
Lerner, P.M. (1991). *Psychoanalytic theory and the Rorschach*. Hillsdale, N. J.: The Analytic Press.
Murray, H. A. (1938). *Explorations in personality*. New York: Oxford University Press.
Richmond, J. (1967). Reporting diagnostic results to patients and their families. *Journal of Projective Techniques and Personality Assessment, 31*, 62-70.
Riscalla, L. M. (1972). Is secrecy in the client's best interest? *Journal of Rehabilitation, 38*, 1 9-20.
Rosenwald, G. C. (1963). Psychodiagnositcs and its discontents. *Psychiatry, 26*, 222-240.
Rosenwald, G. C. (1965a). Physicalism and psychodiagnostics. *The Psychiatric Quarterly, 39*, 1-16.
Rosenwald, G. C. (1965b). Training in psychodiagnostics. Preconference papers. *Conference on the professional preparation of clincal psychologists*. Washington, D. C.: American Psychological Association.
Rosenwald, R. G. (1968). Personality description from the viewpoint of adaptation. *Psychiatry, 31*, 16-31.
Strauss, E. L. (1967). The Rorschach as an encounter. *The Psychiatric Quarterly Supplement, 41*, 255-261.
Towbin, A. P. (1964). Psychological testing from end to means. *Journal of Projective Techniques and Personality Assessment, 28*, 86-91.
Vane, J. R. Getting information from school and clinical psychologists. *Professional Psychology, 3*, 205-208.

# 16

# Humanistic Contributions to the Field of Psychotherapy: Appreciating the Human and Liberating the Therapist

*Anthony Barton*

### The Idea of Humanism: Appreciation and Comprehension

Humanism is a style of thought or an attitude which makes the *human* central, important, valuable, crucial, pivotal, wonderful, powerful — even miraculous. In doing so, humanism comprehends the full bodily, social, symbolic, cultural, value laden, choosing and meaning creating nature of the human being. Although a particular psychologist may give special emphasis to feeling, to symbolism, or to free agency, the humanistic way of approaching any feature is to see it as arising out of the whole. Humanistic psychology tends to grasp the human in the large and comprehensive gestalts, including dimensions of action and value. When a humanist emphasizes unconscious factors, such features will characteristically be integrated, at least implicitly, with the cultural and social life which participate in constituting the unconscious life. Humanists strive deliberately to see motivational, bodily, personal, social, and historical moments of human life in their mutual intertwining.

### Mechanism and Reductionism

Psychology as a field has been strongly influenced by the ideas of materialism and mechanism, which have reduced the enormous complexity and richness of the *human* to something elemental, manageable and controllable. Psychological practitioners have sometimes pursued the ideal of quantification, management, and control of elements. Instead of seeking to comprehend the human-as-a-whole in preparation for full-scale liberation, theoretical psychology has developed a series of reducing metaphors for the human being: as machine, as purely behaviorally conditioned, as driven animal, as aggressive beast, as cognitive network, as information processing computer, as neural networks, etc. These images all tend to strip away from the idea of the *human* precisely those features which humanism affirms: the creative, free, symbolic, metaphorical, aesthetic, tragic, meaning and value bearing, spirited life of humanity. In these reduced views, there is also no space for gods, creators, divine spirits nor angels.

## Psychotherapy: Where Humanism Meets Mechanism

*The Client*

Psychotherapy is a striking situation for the encounter between humanistic and mechanistic views, because those who present themselves for therapy often appear as driven, unfree, mechanistically caught in repetition; as brain washed victims of unfortunate ideas; as conditioned victims of forces beyond their control. They present situations in which their powers appear reduced. They report being compelled, anxiously driven, bedeviled by powerful moods, and replaying old, self destructive habits endlessly. "I know I shouldn't do (or feel or think like) that doctor, but I can't help it."

Hence, views that strip the human being of power, dignity, and creativity often match the helpless, despairing stories that patients tell their therapists. The mechanistically oriented therapist responds in rapport to such a story by saying, "That's right, you can't help it — you have been badly conditioned, brain washed, or unconsciously driven." Of course the second part of the message given by such a therapist is that there is real hope because "We can recondition you, rewash your brain, or analyze your unconscious!" The ones who do the conditioning or analysis assert a certain freedom and power, whereas those who are conditioned or analyzed are seen as unfree and powerless.

*The Therapist*

To the extent that clients are conceived as reduced, mechanized, determined, and powerless, therapists also undergo a reduction in humanity. They act as mere functionaries, adjuncts to the machines they are adjusting: conditioners, feeble interpreters of essentially anonymous impersonal dynamics, or objective witnesses to the conflicted energies over there. And in this reduced status, therapists also lose their possibilities of full speaking and acting; impassioned, aesthetic, poetic, inspiring, spell binding, creative, free speaking and acting are out of place, improper, and can not occur in this bound, impoverished realm (Bugental, 1965).

*Implicit Humanism, Movement Towards Humanism in Psychotherapy*
It should be said that good therapists using reductive theories may in practice allow, acknowledge and promote the full humanness, including the freedom and power of the client, though this may done informally and without theoretical or even systematic practical support. Such trends go hand in hand with the many humanistic modifications of orthodox, reductionistic theory, such as Schafer's use of "action language" in psychoanalytic theory and Bandura's proposal of reciprocal determinism in learning theory. Psychotherapeutic practice and theory are more humanistic today than they were at mid-twentieth century. Psychotherapy is one area of psychology in which practitioners have benefited from extended face-to-face encounters with persons in their full concreteness and complexity, which is a condition par excellence for a recognition of humanness by the open-minded. This growing humanism is also partly due to a cross-fertilization with systematically humanistic psychology, which is well known in the field of psychotherapy. However, the distinctive contribution of humanistic psychology proper is its development of the explicit recognition and fostering of the unique capacities and wholeness of human existence, which still remain at best largely implicit in and ahead of other approaches.

### Rogers' Contribution: An Accepting, Feeling-Filled Humanism

Carl Rogers' appreciative response to his client's helplessness and feeling of diminishment is quite direct, impassioned, and committed as he evokes a more ample, free world. First, he understands clients on their terms, emphasizes their feelings and regards them as valuable beings. He proposes that the therapeutic cure is a matter of attitude. When the therapist attends carefully to the meanings that the client expresses and positively values the client, and when the client experiences this understanding and being valued, then therapy will occur and the client's life will transform itself. "You really feel —" said accurately and with acceptance are therapeutic (Rogers, 1951). This evocation of meaning, when done as a congruent expression of the therapist's real valuing and respecting of the client, is a strikingly emancipatory.

In Rogers' overarching comprehension, this attitude works because clients were taught to doubt their experience and, in disregarding themselves, to loose touch with the very source of their capacity for growth. They have taken in attitudes which deprecate and despise their humanity, seeing themselves as frail, weak, mistaken, stupid, and wrong. Having taken in these idealizing conditions of worthlessness and worthiness, they find themselves deficient and unworthy. Therefore, they distrust their own experience, discounting it as irrelevant, and despise themselves. They inwardly try to shape themselves into what they *should* be or *think* they are, rather than attending to and rejoicing in their experiential processes, which provide the most comprehensive and truest frame of reference for living. Hence, the therapist's valuing of clients' experience and selves directly impacts clients: they learn to attend to their feelings and to value themselves-in-process.

The technique part of Rogers' contribution is rather simple: reflect faithfully the words & feelings of the client (communicate understanding) and do so respectfully, caringly, and warmly (communicate unconditional positive regard). The mastery of the client-centered technique and attitude requires commitment, diligence, and practice. And it remains a strongly transformative approach — especially when done wholeheartedly and well. In fact, Rogers insists that it must be done wholeheartedly (congruently) in order to be most beneficial. In Rogers' career, he came to place increasing importance upon the therapist's being genuinely present (transparent) as a distinct person to the person of the other, experiencing the client as a real, free, valid world-making person.

Hence, Rogerian technique and attitude liberates therapists to become full, resonating affective, thinking, imagining, listening, and speaking presences. They come to inhabit fully their clients' worlds: language, gesture, meaning, imagining, perception, understanding, and sociality with a special emphasis on feeling. And in entering into those worlds and mirroring them understandingly, all the clients' regions enter the therapeutic situation. The therapist is not limited to this or that region, but takes in and responds to as much of the client's world as possible. The aesthetic, spiritual, religious, impassioned commitments, and cherished values of clients are available for response by therapists. Therapists enter and respond to all the meanings of the client (with an emphasis on feeling as the incarnating and integrating core of meaning). Therapists make themselves deliberately present to the full resonant multiplicity of the client's person-hood.

Skepticism about what Rogers taught and practiced sometimes directly expresses an implicit anti-humanism. The skeptic finds it hard to believe that simple, careful, disciplined, attentive understanding, and the positive valuing implicit in such a caring attentiveness, can be transformative for clients. The skeptic finds it hard to believe that the capacity for betterment resides within the personhood, the multifaceted and ever changing experiential processes of the client. In fact, attaining a sense of the symbolic as a power to transform is necessary for appreciating the possibilities of such profound therapeutic changes. For when the power of spells and counter-spells is understood, the symbolic power of human beings as co-creating each other is appreciated, and the human order is valued and expanded.

Carl Rogers had an exquisite sense of a corrosive spell or curse that is often visited on people as they grow up and live in the world. He understood that negating spell as an anti-humanism concretized. The curse visited on them is: you are only worthy when you match my needs or fit my purposes (said by parents, teachers, and other authorities to young and vulnerable others); you should fulfill my values and purposes; you are not worth understanding; you are in various ways bad and worthless; you must conform to the expectations and wishes of the others; you are only worth what you produce and perform; and your own feelings and thoughts don't count. This curse against their feeling-filled, growthfully directed humanity, when visited on the vulnerable young, leads to timidity, inhibition, conformity or angry anti-social action, as well as a variety of other social and personal pathologies (Rogers, 1961).

Rogers' counter-spell expresses an incarnated humanism which says: you are worthy in yourself, you can discover and fulfill your values and your purposes, you are worth my attentive understanding, you are fundamentally and in many specific ways good and valuable, you can be guided by the deepest feelings and values of your very own self, and your thoughts and feelings count and are greatly important. This vision asserts that the client's feelings, wishes, intentions, and values are to direct the process of therapy and of life; the therapist in this sense is non-directive, except insofar as he directs clients respectfully to attend to themselves.

In proposing to therapists that a feeling-focused understanding, respectful positive regard, and congruent self-expression are basic transformative powers of psychotherapy, Rogers was essentially correct. If clients or patients treated within a variety of therapeutic orientations are asked what they found helpful, a majority refer to factors like acceptance, attentive listening, understanding, genuineness, and respectful, warm, good treatment as crucial to their transformative experience of therapy.

That Rogers emphasizes the feeling-self, calls it good, and sees its positive contribution is characteristic of the affirming views of humanistic psychology. Rogers finds this centered-feeling-self to be a rich flow of energy and evaluations, a guide to the genuine, a source of full contact with reality, and an empathic desire for connection and linkage with others. This is Rogers' vision of what Heidegger speaks of as a fundamental structure of being human, *Befindlikeit*: the mooded and feeling filled finding of one's self already in the world (Heidegger, 1927/1962). This grounded, feelingful being, already thrown in the world, already in touch with situations and with others, richly registers, responds, and resonates with the personal and social world (Gendlin, 1962). Most radically, Rogers sees feelings as highly responsive to reality — including the distorting reality of social suppression and condemnation. The client's feelings make sense and reveal the world as perceived, meant, and lived. Hence, feelings are not mere irrationality, drive, machine like reactions, or conditioned — but rather are an exquisitely rational presence and response to the world.

### Frankl's Contribution: Freedom to Give Meaning

Carl Rogers responds to the helpless, driven, conditioned, endlessly repeating client with understanding and with a vision of a centered, personal, feeling self. However, Viktor Frankl appeals to the patient's freedom to take up an attitude, to give meaning, to transform life through a chosen standpoint, and to take responsibility. Once again, determinism and mechanism come into collision with a humanistic view. The despairing obsessive compulsive clients who wash their hands until they are a raw and bloody witness to the unconsciously driven character of human life. The machine like repetition of their behaviors, the clock like regularity of their rituals, cries out for an understanding through analyzing drives, mistaken ideas, conditionings, or forces.

Frankl admits and allows, as Rogers did, for the conditioned or determined within his viewpoint. The parents punitive stringency with their child, their purity training, their emphasis on perfection conditioned the child to be in terrible doubt about achieving perfect performances. And now this emotional tyranny, taken up by the sensitized adult whose thinking and acting tends to circle, leads to the extraordinary irrational symptom of incessant hand washing. However, there is more to patients, even in those extremely corrosive cases in which the person has built a whole life around these compulsive rituals. Patients can and do take up various standpoints toward their condition (conditioning) and a new freely taken up attitude changes the meanings and often relieves the symptoms as well.

For instance, patients can take up a spirit of accepting the compulsion instead of fighting it. They can decide to spend an extra hour doing their compulsive hand and bathroom washing. By freely putting in an extra hour, in the case of the insomniac who decides to stay awake, the patient takes up an attitude of freedom. This is curative because the compulsion stays in place by a willful fight against it. This fighting creates a battleground which intensifies the compulsion. In the everyday natural attitude the compulsion is something to contend with, to force oneself to stop doing. Paradoxically, it is that attitude which creates a force versus counterforce and holds the compulsion tensely in place (Frankl, 1955).

The paradoxical directive to do the symptom on purpose rather than fighting it exemplifies Frankl's comprehensive idea of persons as free to form meanings and responsible for choices: the human being is always able to shift attitudes. In addition, patients can learn to question the 100% goal of absolute purity and cleanliness, and to play with various other possibilities, such as leaving their bathroom rituals incomplete, and even dirtying both hands deliberately just before exiting the bathroom. In asking patients to consider the philosophical idea of one hundred percentedness (perfection) as unrealistic, as well as inviting them to play with alternative behavioral and attitudinal possibilities, the therapist brings the patient into the specifically human realm of freedom where meanings can be responsibly chosen.

Viktor Frankl posits his patient as existentially free to choose a standpoint, an attitude, a position, and to act responsibly from that position. Frankl comprehends his patient as able to choose values, meanings, purposes, ideals, goals, and behaviors in accord with spiritual meanings. Frankl spiritually endured and survived the experience of a concentration camp, which gives a special and convincing poignancy to his emphasis on the chosen attitude, the existential freedom to take a stance, the realization of responsibility as a basic feature of being human (Frankl, 1964).

Frankl's therapeutic method and attitude is rather simple in principle. He seeks to find just how patients can grasp their freedom and use it to transform their lives. He looks for that place, space, standpoint, or attitude which can become a place of free realization of meaning.

The particular techniques of paradoxical instructions, de-reflection, and gentle self mockery which Frankl taught his clients are of course valuable as part of the repertoire of therapists. However, his most enduring contribution is the concrete appreciation of the human freedom to create meaning. His method, Logotherapy, is primarily a comprehending perspective, an attitude, a question on the part of the therapist: where is my client free to move, to take up an attitude freely, to make a new meaning? It presupposes that the freedom to make meanings belongs to the human world essentially, and that all human beings have regions in which they can take up freedom and make meaning. The creative ingenuity of the therapist finds and mines those regions of freedom to help patients.

All therapists appeal to the freedom of their clients, implicitly or explicitly, for it is the ground for inviting the client to change and transform. Frankl has explicitly concretized that sense of free responsibility in his techniques and attitude. As this precise sense of free ability is often what the patient has lost, it can be very helpful to have the therapist sharply attuned to that realm of freedom. Helping patients to shift perspective, to structure meaning, to find freedom, and to generate humor transforms their existence.

The idea of Logotherapy also introduces freedom to the therapist's action and speech as well. In Rogerian therapy, therapists are encouraged to be transparent, but the central emphasis is not on their own vision and world. In contrast, Frankl opens up the field for the therapist to explicitly enact and express values other than the patient's. Precisely for the expansion of the patient's freedom, the therapist is free to give advice and instructions, to make jokes, to propose freedom making interpretations, and to stand explicitly for freedom and responsibility. Therapists do not limit themselves to being appreciative co-resonators with clients' worlds, but enact another range of activity and expression within a discipline of enlarging the patient's free responsiveness.

### Perls: Liberating the Therapist to Act Fully Human

For Rogers the realm of feeling-flow as central to the person was focused and accepted: positive valuing regard and contact with feelings facilitated growth. For Frankl the realm of freedom and responsibility was central: searching out the place where patients could free themselves and become responsible was his special way of restoring wholeness. And for both Rogers and Frankl, respectively feeling and freedom were pivot points of comprehension around which the whole complex social, symbolic, meaning creating life of human beings could be focused.

For Fritz Perls, the flow of here-and-now awareness was focused, differentiated, and owned — contacting that flow of experience and taking ownership of it was the core to cure. As is characteristic of humanistic psychotherapy, Perls also comprehended both awareness and personal agency central to his approach (Perls, Hefferline, & Goodman, 1951).

Rogers responds to his client with "You really feel —— ," and he does so with acceptance and care. After showing some understanding, Frankl responds to his client with "You can freely, spiritedly, humorously choose, and in this choosing is your dignity as a free person." Fritz Perls uses a much more widely and wildly eclectic technical virtuosity and is not so easily simplified at the level of what he might do or say.

In fact, an enduring part of Fritz Perls' contribution to the field of psychotherapy was in liberating therapists from the artificial limits which the history of objectivism, mechanism, materialism, and conventional professionalism had taught. Even many existential and humanistic psychotherapists had learned models of interaction which belong to a western scientific spirit of objectivism. For instance, many therapists continue to live out remnants of passive receptivity (poker faced objectivity) which Freud originally recommended as a way to keep the psychic (surgical) field uncontaminated. In saying "um hmm" a lot, or constantly inviting the client to "say more about that," or even in sitting quietly and passively receptive while the client does ninety percent or more of the talking, therapists model themselves implicitly on the medical, surgical, or objective scientist model. They act like scientific data gatherers rather than inspired co-participants in an unfolding drama — they are shaped more by the image of the proper professional than the inspired healer.

Fritz Perls comprehended the project of therapeutic transformation actively and experimentally. Starting with certain basic ideas about awareness, consciousness, attentiveness, and the body, he immediately moved these ideas into vigorous practice. For instance, he started the famous gestalt awareness experiments: "Here and now I am aware of ——!" He encouraged patients to heighten their immediate awareness, borrowing from transformative meditative methods, but added particularly astute parts to the experiment: "Here and now I am aware of ——, in order to —." The "in order to" invited patients to take up the purposive, goal oriented, intentional side of their awareness and to heighten their sense of the choosing involved in awareness. Then he added more to the experiment: "Here and now I am aware of —-, in order to —— and in order not to ——-." The avoidant features, as intentional and purposive, are highlighted in this part of the experiment. Then he added more and more to this experiment: "Here and now I choose to be aware of ——, in order to —— and in order not to ——-" and "Here and now I choose to be aware of —-, in order to —-, and in order not to be aware of ——-." (Pollster & Pollster, 1973).

His spirit of adventure led him both to borrow and invent a variety of methods for experimentally varying experiences. Perls would invite symptomatic parts of the client's body to talk, by calling for their personification. He would ask clients to engage in dialogue between their critical selves (top-dog) and their beaten up criticized selves (under-dog) — each part speaking from a particular chair. He would have clients speak as if they were parts of their own dreams, taking up the role of the house, the tree, the dog, or whatever elements the dream contained.

If clients got stuck, he might ask them to show in detail how they got stuck: how they kept their awareness riveted and on what they were stuck on. Next he might invite clients to stop that, stand up, breathe, and do something else. Or he might get the client to be the part which demanded staying stuck: "shout at yourself, tell yourself to stay paralyzed, tell yourself what a dope you are, how you will never get over this fear — make the worst possible picture of yourself as helpless, anxious, hopeless."

There was pattern and method in his eclectic multi-methods. He could always and often would take the path of detailed analysis of the way the person maintained their difficulty — heightening their awareness and adding all sorts of details to their awareness:

> When you feel self conscious, your awareness narrows down, you cut your breathing off, you hold your shoulders hunched, and what else do you do? What do you say to yourself? Imagine? What don't you notice? What do you ignore? What do your shoulders say about this?

He would invite the person into an enhanced awareness of the problem and of other features of here-and-now reality. The questions usually dealt with present features and the how or what, rather than the why of interactions (Perls, 1969).

He would encourage and insist that the person take ownership of the pattern — of their shoulders, breathing, selective perceptual attentiveness, intentions, etc.: "Whose hand is it that picks up the drink and who says inwardly 'God, I need a drink?'" And he would invite the person to think out and try out new patterns and ways, all the way from breathing differently, to speaking differently inside, to imagining differently, to screaming instead of being quiet. The extraordinary idea of an experimenting therapist who knows that problems are exquisitely structured and maintained, who encourages a client to try new things out as experiments, was at the center of his approach. One of the practices he would encourage clients to do, borrowed from Frankl, was to enact their problems on purpose (practice the symptom or problem in awareness). His techniques implied two active agents in charge of themselves, therapist and client. The therapist's task was to empower clients to take charge of their own awareness and experience. The therapist was to model courage, willingness to experiment, an appreciation of the strength and power of clients: to envisage clients as free and active constructors, feelers, and owners of their own world (Fagen & Shepherd, 1970).

Gestalt therapy techniques empower and enliven clients and therapists to expand openness, to break through the conventionally professional, somewhat passive ideas of what being a therapist and client entails. Both the structural comprehension of how pathologies maintain themselves in present intricate detail, and the boldly experimental approach to helping clients break through these sad, repetitive structures, are permanent contributions of this approach to the field of psychotherapy.

## Satir: Valuing Self in Community and Therapist Liberation

Virginia Satir, like Fritz Perls, was another important innovator at the level of technique. She developed a particularly inspiring, spell binding approach to transformative work, the structures of which were studied by Bandler (Bandler & Satir, 1976), and other structural modelers (Andreas, 1991). Her appreciative humanism stands out in her emphasis on self worth: that each person is worthy and deserving of respect, a piece of the divine, and called to be their own good selves. Even in relation to the most destructive and negative forms of behavior, her characteristic question is: "What good intentions is this behavior trying to fulfill for one's self or for others?" She praises and affirms her clients for their ingenious solutions to their problems, even when those solutions create difficulties. All family members are seen as fundamentally well intended, though at times marred by their own background or ignorance.

She systematically encourages her clients to comprehend themselves and others within a whole framework of life development (as learners who began as children and are still learning), as members of families who learned what to do, think, feel, and how to behave. She strongly emphasizes each person's freedom to select from their history those parts which fit and to discard those parts that don't fit any longer (Satir, 1988).

Satir's genius was in therapeutic action and transformative strategies. She emphasized the importance of self worth and therefore understood the importance of an attitude of respect and reverence for the client. However, in addition, she developed a whole set of stories, teachings, role plays, and activities to foster self worth, some of which were intricately wedded to systematic remakings of personal history. Clients are invited to sculpt a group in characteristic poses belonging to their family of origin and are later directed into role playing, thus re-imaging and redoing a whole new sense of mother, father, and self, while also appreciating mother, father, and self as the children they had been. Satir, like Perls, would not hesitate to stop an old repetitive pattern with a quick — "Oh, that belongs to the past; let's get you up to date! what's happening now? Look again at what you see now?" This active, bodily, enacting co-participation in the unfolding of the therapy is an important part of her transformative method (Satir & Baldwin, 1983).

Satir's systematic and skillful use of a positive reframing, which assumes the underlying good intentions of behavior, enacts that understanding as a presupposition. She often communicates that reframing by embedding it with commands in skillful questions and comments. She uses presuppositions designed for freedom, choice, and enhanced feelings of value. She may say to a client who has just expressed a negative judgment about her husband:

> Oh that's the old feeling you used to have (presupposed as belonging to past), but now you are *getting ready* for another feeling (an instruction to get ready for a different feeling) — *will you like that?* (an instruction to like the new feeling). It's like getting rid of old worn out clothes — they were suitable for that time — but now its time for new ones, eh? (a metaphor of pleasant change). So now — are you ready yet? (implies you are ready now!)— Look at him now and take his hand and notice your feeling (Now you will have a different feeling) (Andreas, 1991).

Satir's contribution, which humanistic therapists can appropriate, includes a disciplined non-blaming together with a positive affirming of the good desires and intentions of her clients. She enacts these systematically, over and over, explicitly and implicitly.

> You had good reasons? That part of you wanted to protect you? Understandably you felt angry at being hurt? Naturally you

wanted what your brother had? You are worth while and the only question is what has kept you from celebrating your own goodness. However, her second contribution was in her linguistic and gestural skillfulness in helping her clients reshape their narratives, their histories. This contribution was made explicit by the work of the structural modelers, who have teased our Satir's transformative skills in considerable detail (Andreas, 1991).

Satir's genius is shown by her use of embedded commands and presuppositions, her instituting breaks between emotional states, her active use of touch as an accepting social connector and feeling enhancer, her systematic expanding of time and space in the unfolding narrative (which she would enlarge to include multiple generations, cultural and economic backgrounds, etc.), her helping clients imagine and enter actively into the feelings and thoughts of others, her placing unfortunate events in the past and good happenings in the present and future (temporal shifting), her making individual contact with each member of the family by getting on their level, etc. In all these, she enlarged the scope of therapist's and client's activities, which may be so limited in the usual training of professional therapists. She kept her heart and mind on the therapeutic question: how to transform, help, and heal. Therefore, she developed a general humanistic orientation together with a large set of freely transformative skills from which therapists will continue to learn.

## Erickson: More Skills for Liberating Humanistic Therapists

Milton Erickson took up an active influencing and directing of patients. His hypnotic approach with its emphasis on unconscious processes appears at first glance to make him a manipulative handler of patients, an idea often anathema to humanistically oriented psychotherapists. In fact, Erickson took up, in his own way, most of the major themes of humanistic psychology. He appreciated the individuality of the client quite explicitly: "No one is quite like you, just like your fingerprint is one of a kind, so are you just one of a kind." And he carried this appreciation very far, suggesting that the therapist had to learn to read each client like a unique alphabet or language. Like Rogers, he presupposed that clients had the resources within themselves to resolve their issues and only needed the therapist's efforts to access these abilities. And much of his skillful rhetoric involves respectfully treating patients as developing their own cures and solutions, rather than having solutions given them from the therapist's standard repertoire (Erickson, 1967).

It is primarily in the enlargement of interventions, in the expansion of rhetorical and influential forms, that Milton Erickson contributes most to the field of psychotherapy. Within a vivid comprehension of the multi-symbolic levels and richness of the human person as an integration of conscious and unconscious, embodied mind and minded body, as profoundly conditioned and profoundly symbolic, he developed skillful ways of creating fluid transformative modes of interactions with his clients.

Existential-phenomenological and humanistic thought has theoretically appreciated and discursively celebrated the freedom and creativity of the human person, without always having the rhetorical and skillful know-how to make that effective for psychotherapists. Orations and preachments about freedom, dignity, creativity, individuality, and the value of the human person do not yet penetrate far enough into the work of psychotherapy, even though they provide an attitudinal ground for therapists to respectfully value each of their clients (Bugental, 1965).

Milton Erickson, in a special way, celebrated the varieties of consciousness which each person was, and taught a new theory and practice of hypnosis to therapists. This form of hypnosis emphasizes the clients' freedom to access and develop their own resources and invites clients to consider all they know and have available, consciously and unconsciously, from past and present, from imagination and feeling, from past learnings and future possibilities (Erickson & Rossi, 1981).

Bringing his client into a trance, Erickson might then say:

> Get in touch with all your inner resources *now* — and appreciate *yourself, D., so much and all those parts* of you that are cooperating in starting to find *good solutions* to these previously vexing problems — *looking back* now at what used to bother you — and *enjoying* the relief at how different it *looks* and *feels* already *now* as you see it from this *different* vantage point — for when you were in the middle of things it often seemed very hard to imagine yet a way out from the troubles — but *now* seeing them as *behind* you already makes them clear and easier to solve. (Erickson, 1986)

The typically humanist vision of a resourceful, free, imaginative, creative, integrative, symbolic, perspectivally gifted, temporally flexible person is directly visible and audible in the evocative rhetorical invitation given to the client. Thus Erickson evocatively co-creates a valued and flexible client. What is less immediately and obviously visible is the way in which basic human existential themes are skillfully evoked and articulated in the patterns of influential rhetoric practiced by Erickson.

For instance, Erickson plays symbolically with human temporality in his work, helping his clients to come to appreciate their past as a dynamic resource (a rich repository of learnings and valuable experiences), their present as their rich flowing from the past toward the future, and their future as inviting, propelling, and motivating them forward. In the brief example above, the therapist's use of past tense as the place of the "vexing problem," and the assertion of "now" as the place for "getting in touch with inner resources," "starting to find good solutions," and "seeing things from a different perspective" all tend to help clients organize their own multi-perspectival, resourceful powers toward resolving difficulties (Bandler & Grinder, 1975).

The accessing of specific resources (a happy time, a courageous time, a time of endurance and survival) from the long ago past and carrying them forth into the present and future, like the skill of riding a bicycle or reading letters, is another Ericksonian rhetorical form ("early learning set"). Again and again, Erickson metaphorically, transformatively evokes and co-constitutes the client as richly symbolic, gifted, resourceful, imaginative, and creative.

> Your unconscious mind knows a lot about these things — and can bring together just what you need now — a sense of competence and joy — pleasure in your own ability to read, write, think — just as you had pleasure in standing up and seeing the world from that wonderful upright position the very first time you stood up — and how different things looked and there was so much more you could do then.

### Summary of Contributions

Rogers, Frankl, Perls, Satir, and Erickson give three major contributions to the field of psychotherapy. The first is that they, as humanistic psychotherapists, perennially celebrate, assert, and evoke the full gifted presence of human beings in opposition to reductive biologism, behaviorism, cognitivism, psychoanalycism, or any other reducing prismatic visions. They all proclaim an attitude of reverent celebration and appreciation as the foundational place and space from which therapy practice ought to come. They assert this appreciative presence as creating a field of interaction within which human possibilities can optimally flourish.

Reductionism, the tendency to metaphorize the human being merely as behavior, neurological process, computer, cognitive pattern, or unconscious drives is not harmless. On the contrary, it has powerful effects in alienating human beings from their roots in the symbolic, spirited, cultural, rhetorical, and imaginative traditions of humanity. Those who imagine they are machines often act the part. A full view which celebrates the gifted, spirited, creative, free, meaning giving aspects of the human being also invites fulfillment within that inspired space of existence.

Humanistic psychotherapy has insisted on a holistic comprehension of the human person and of human interaction. In this sense it moves descriptively toward a rich comprehensiveness even while emphasizing one or another feature. For instance, though Rogers emphasized feelings, his idea of feeling is a comprehensive one in which feeling is organismic, relational, cultural, and as founding mood—not feeling as comprehended as a mere subjective element of human life. Each humanistic psychotherapist, while emphasizing different features, refers to the whole of human life directly or by implication. To carry this comprehensive work further requires an even more systematic descriptive approach to the field of psychotherapy, in which each emphasis, including those not traditionally associated with humanism, can be integrated as perspectival variations on the themes or standard modes of transforming life (see Barton, 1974).

Finally, humanistic psychotherapy has also opened up specific transformative techniques, modes of rhetoric which liberate the therapist for more effective action. The vision of the passively listening, data gathering, manipulating or very occasionally interpreting therapist is replaced in these humanistic therapies with a much more participative co-creator of narrative, action, and meaning: the positive reframing of intentions and meanings; the reaching into the client's narrative space for the realm of freedom where the client can take on new attitudes, behaviors, and thoughts; the movement into dramatic enactments in role playing or family sculpting; encouraging large visions of family and social life in order to contextualize the client's issues; the development of complex linguistic patterns which use temporal tenses, presuppositions, embedded commands, and evocative metaphorical language in order to encourage searches for resources and talents.

There is a growing linguistic and expressive craft to the practice of psychotherapy in which novice therapists can model themselves after therapeutic masters. Thus the freeing activity is directed not only at clients, but also at all those therapists who wish to master the linguistic, metaphorical, and narrative skills of humane liberation and enhancement as practiced by these humanistic therapeutic geniuses.

## References

Andreas, S. (1991). *Virginia Satir: The patterns of her magic*. Palo Alto, CA: Science & Behavior Books.

Bandler, R. & Grinder, J. (1975). *Patterns of the hypnotic techniques of Milton H. Erickson, M.D.* (Vols. 1 and 2). Cupertino, CA: Meta Publications.

Bandler, R. & Grinder, J. (1982). *Reframing: Neurolinguistic programming and the transformation of meaning*. Moab, UT: Real People Press.

Bandler, R. & Satir, V. (1976). *Changing with families*. Palo Alto, CA: Science & Behavior Books.

Barton, A. (1974). *Three worlds of therapy: Freud, Jung, & Rogers*. Palo Alto, CA: Mayfield Press.

Binswanger, L. (1968). *Being-in-the-world*. New York: Harper Torch Books.

Bugental, J. F. T. (1965). *The search for authenticity: An existential-analytic approach to psychotherapy*. New York: Holt, Rinehart & Winston.

Erickson, M. H. (1981). *Advanced techniques of hypnosis and therapy: Selected papers of Milton H. Erickson* (J. Haley, ed.). New York: Grune & Stratton.

Erickson, M. H. & Rossi, E. L. (1981). *Experiencing hypnosis: Therapeutic approaches to altered states*. New York: Irvington Publishers.

Erickson, M. H. (1986). *The collected papers of Milton H. Erickson on hypnosis* (Vols. 1-4) (E. L. Rossi, ed.). New York: Irvington Publishers.

Fagen, J. & Shepherd, I.(Eds). (1970). *Gestalt therapy now*. Palo Alto, CA: Science & Behavior Books.

Frankl, V. E. (1955). *The doctor and the soul: From psychotherapy to logotherapy*. New York: Knopf.

Frankl, V. E. (1964). *Man's search for meaning: An introduction to logotherapy*. New York: Washington Square Press.

Gendlin, E. (1962). *Experiencing and the creation of meaning*. New York: Free Press.

Heidegger, M. (1962). *Being and time*. New York: Harper & Row. (Original work published 1927)

Perls, F. S. (1947). *Ego, Hunger and aggression*. London: Allen & Unwin.

Perls, F., Hefferline, R. & Goodman, P. (1951). *Gestalt therapy: Excitement and growth in the human personality*. New York: Julian Press.

Perls, F. (1969). *Gestalt therapy verbatim*. Moab, UT: Real People Press.

Perls, F. S. (1982). *In & out of the garbage pail*. Moab, UT: Real People.

Pollster, E. & Pollster, M. (1973). *Gestalt therapy integrated*. New York: Bruner Mazel.

Rogers, C. R. (1951). *Client centered therapy: Its current practice, implications, and theory*. Boston: Houghton Mifflin.

Rogers, C. R. (1961). *On becoming a person: A therapists view of psychotherapy*. Boston: Houghton Mifflin.

Satir, V. (1964). *Conjoint family therapy*. Palo Alto, CA: Science & Behavior.

Satir, V. (1972). *Peoplemaking*. Palo Alto, CA: Science & Behavior Books.

Satir, V. & Baldwin, M. *Satir step by step: A guide to creating change in families*. Palo Alto, CA: Science & Behavior Books.

Satir, V. (1988). *The new peoplemaking*. Mountain View, CA: Science & Behavior Books.

# 17

# Secular Humanism and Rational-Emotive Therapy

*Albert Ellis*

In his article, "Humanistic Psychology," in Raymond Corsini's *Encyclopedia of Psychology*, M. Brewster Smith (1984) points out that secular humanism is "a neglected version of humanistic psychology," and shows that where Pascal and Kierkegaard defined the religious version of existentialism, Shakespeare, Montaigne, Nietzsche, Sartre, and other thinkers "proposed a mundane, Godless humanism, also existentialist in its concern with the responsibility entitled by human self-consciousness" (Smith, 1984, p. 158). Smith also contrasts the somewhat irreconcilable perspective of *causal* and *interpretive* understanding in psychological science and argues that "for the distinctly human world, interpretation and causal explanation must somehow be joined...Indeed, the only satisfactory *science* of human experience and action must be one in which the hermeneutic interpretation plays a central part conjoined with causal explanation" (p. 158).

Quite a problem! Secular humanism, which is in many ways opposite to the religious, mystical, and spiritual humanism that seems to have largely prevailed in the Association for Humanistic Psychology (AHP), and even in the Division of Humanistic psychology of APA during the last decade, tries to be quite existential, social, phenomenological, and even post-modernistic in many respects. But it also does its best to be rigorously (not rigidly) empirical, naturalistic, relativistic, and scientific (Clark, 1992; Kurtz, 1973, 1985; Stein, 1985). On the other hand, transpersonal psychology, the dominant theme in recent AHP publications, often claims to be scientific (because it uses *some* of the methods of science) but actually is often dogmatic and absolutist (Ellis, 1972, 1986; Ellis & Yeager, 1989; Kurtz, 1986). I could go on at great length showing what I think are the evils of transpersonal and mystical humanism — including that they are actually antihumanistic — but I have already done this elsewhere (Ellis & Schoenfeld, 1990; Ellis & Yeager, 1989), so let me focus on what secular humanism is and how it specifically applies to humanistic psychology.

Secular humanists see men and women as unique individuals who almost always choose to live in a social group. They are individuals in their own personal right but also are — and had better be — social creatures who try to live together peacefully, fairly, and democratically. Even their discrete "personality," as Sampson (1989) has noted, is *also* a social product. Secular humanists fully acknowledge people to be human — that is, *very* limited and fallible — and in no way are they either superhuman (*more than* human) nor subhuman (*less than* human). They all seem to have good and bad *behaviors* and *traits*; but, as Korzybski (1933) pointed out, they *are* not what they *do*. Men and women are an ongoing, ever-changing, constructing and reconstructing *process*. Although their acts and deeds are measurable or ratable (once they set up goals and purposes, which as humans they invariably seem to do), *they, themselves*, their *essence*, their *being* are too complex and changeable to be given any global rating or report card. We consequently have no accurate or meaningful way of deifying or damning *them*. *They* are not "good" or "bad"; they merely exist. If they *choose* to continue to exist and to enjoy their existence, then again some of their *acts* are "good" because they aid these goals and some of their *behaviors* are "bad" (because they sabotage these goals). People's goals and purposes cannot be assessed scientifically or "objectively" — because, as individuals, they can choose from a wide variety of goals, none of which (except by arbitrary definition) can be assessed as unconditionally "good" or "bad." But once they pick a certain goal (e.g., succeeding at work, love, or psychotherapy) it can often be "scientifically" or empirically determined whether (1) they actually achieve it, and (2) they achieve the results they wanted by achieving it.

Secular humanists, in other words, favor certain values, such as human life and well-being, but don't claim that they are absolutely "good" or "bad." But if they are viewed as "good," it can be "scientifically" shown that they can or cannot be achieved and whether their achievement actually brings about the desired results. The meanings or purposes people subscribe to are largely *chosen* (or adopted from others).

But whether their actions to reach these goals (which are also largely chosen) actually *will* lead to their achievement can be "scientifically" determined by looking for a cause-effect relationship.

Secular humanists acknowledge that humans have the *human* ability to imagine, fantasize, and strongly believe in all kinds of superhuman entities and powers — such as gods, angels, spirits, and fairies; and that, in fact, to creating "meaning" and "explanations" for anything they do not fully understand, they impatiently and cavalierly invent such entities and forces. But, along with Karl Popper (1985), they contend that unless these spirits and forces are in some way empirically falsifiable an infinite number of them are available to any imaginative person, and most of these fantasized creations are contradictory to other supernatural fantasies. The existence of any and all of them is never impossible but is highly improbable. *Belief* in such spirits may of course help some people to overcome some of their emotional problems (such as anxiety) or behavioral problems (such as addiction to alcohol). But devout belief in improbable gods and spirits often creates its own difficulties, such as dependency, dogma, bigotry, pollyannaism, wars with non-believers, etc.

Secular humanists are, almost by definition, relativists, skeptics, and nondogmatists (Clark, 1992). Though many of them, such as Ayer (1936), used to be logical positivists, they now mostly realize that logical positivism in some respects is itself not falsifiable, so they have given it up (Bartley, 1984; Popper, 1985). Although they do not tend to be radical or devout deconstructionists, they do tend to favor the more moderate kind of postmodernism espoused by Levin (1991). As Levin notes, this kind of postmodernism has problematized modernism's near-sacred "assumptions about certainty in knowledge, faith in absolute systems, totalities, and unities." And, he notes, "postmodernism recognizes ambiguities, indeterminacies, undertones and overtones, complexities, uncertainties, tensions, interactions, exchanges, equivocations" (pp. 251-252). This kind of thinking is favored by secular humanism.

What is called "humanistic psychotherapy" today tends to consist of (1) existential encounters between therapists and their clients (Frankl, 1959; May, 1969; Rogers, 1961; Yalom, 1990); (2) experiential and body-oriented exercises (Perls, 1969); and (3) transpersonal therapy (Grof, 1984; Tart, 1975; Walsh & Vaughn, 1980). The first two of these methods have often proven useful and even the third one has shown, at times, that it helps some people, though I still think that on the whole it does much more harm than good (Ellis & Yeager, 1989).

The one form of therapy that has been most neglected by many "humanist therapists" is cognitive-behavioral therapy, perhaps because its main proponents have largely been secular humanists. Thus, Alfred Adler (1927, 1929) was a pioneering cognitive therapist; and so was George Kelly (1955) and both of them were secular humanists. I started to do rational-emotive therapy (RET), the first of the popular cognitive-behavior therapies, in 1955 (when I had read Adler but not Kelly) and I followed a secular humanist model which I largely derived from several philosophers, including Epicurus, John Dewey, George Santayova, Bertrand Russell, and Alfred Korzybski (Ellis, 1957, 1962, 1985, 1988).

Today's cognitive-behavior therapy was originally derived from RET but also went its own way and followed to some extent the computer-oriented aspects of the cognitive revolution in psychology. Consequently, it sometimes became sensationalist, mechanistic, and rationalist, instead of existentialist and philosophic, as RET has always tried to be. Thus, some of the cognitive-behavioral therapies — such as those of Beck (1976), Maultsby (1984) and Meichenbaum (1977) used empirical disputing of irrational beliefs and employed the replacing of them with positive affirmations, as originally proposed by Coue (1923). But they included little of the philosophical flavor of RET.

RET, as noted above, is quite humanistic, but abjures spiritual, religious, and mystical overtones and implications. Its secular humanistic origins lead to some of the following theories and practices.

*Constructivism*

Like Kelly's theory of personal constructs, and in some ways moreso, RET is highly constructivist. It holds that although humans largely learn their goals, standards, and values from their family and their culture, they construct — yes, create — most of their emotional disturbances. For, unlike rats and guinea pigs, they take their strong desires and preferences, and they *raise and propel* them into Jehovian, absolutist *musts, shoulds, and demands*. Thus, when people *want and prefer* to succeed at school, work, or love, they frequently *insist and command*, "At all times and under all conditions I *must*, I *have to* succeed!" Because their self-constructed *musts* are often unrealistic and often impossible to achieve, they thereby do not (as psychoanalysis and behavior therapy claim) *get* disturbed or *acquire* disturbances. More importantly, says RET, they *make* themselves upset — consciously and unconsciously *construct* their musts and the emotional and behavioral disturbances that stem from these imperatives (Ellis, 1973, 1988, 1991a, 1991b; Ellis & Dryden, 1990).

*Phenomenalism*

RET, with Epictetus and several other ancient philosophers, says that it is not things and events that upset us but our *view* of these Activating Events (A's). Unfortunate A's *influence* us; but our B's (Beliefs) about these A's largely bring about disturbed C's (Consequences), such as anxiety and depression. Therefore, to undisturb ourselves, we can proceed to D — to actively and forcefully Dispute our self-defeating, musturbatory B's. The ABCD Theory of emotional disturbance and how to change it is unusually phenomenalistic.

The ABC's of RET also stress the *meanings* and *interpretations* people give to events and to results rather than the events and results *in themselves*. Thus, being thwarted at point A may mean a "horrible hassle" to one person and mean an "adventurous challenge" to another. Also, feeling anxious at point C may be viewed as "awful" and "terrible" by one individual, who thereby creates her own great anxiety *about* anxiety and makes herself doubly or triply disturbed. But another person may view this same kind of anxiety as "damned inconvenient" and may make real efforts to understand and to cope with it. RET tries to help people look at the *meanings and interpretations* they give to events and results and, especially, to their own possibilities of creating *new* meanings and interpretations. It focuses not merely on people's gruesome past and present but on their possibilities for the future (Ellis, 1991a, 1991b).

*Existential Choice*

Unlike most other therapies, RET holds that people, even though they may not be aware of this, largely *choose* their dysfunctional core philosophies and life styles. Consciously and unconsciously, they mainly *train themselves* to feel panicked, depressed, self-hating, and enraged, rather than *get conditioned* to feel these ways. They are biologically and socially predisposed to needlessly upset themselves, usually from childhood onward, to create dysfunctional thoughts, feelings, and behaviors; and they hardly have complete free will. But they still have a significant degree of choice; and they therefore can almost always *choose* to think, feel, and behave in less disturbed and more fulfilling ways.

*Self-fulfillment and Long Range Hedonism*

RET theorizes that people will not enjoy or fulfill themselves very much when they make themselves distinctly disturbed, so it first helps them to significantly reduce their disturbances. But it favors hedonism and fulfillment and tries to help people become less disturbed *and* more enjoying. However, because immediate gratification — like drinking and boozing — may easily lead to harmful results, RET often favors long range rather than short range hedonism.

## Unconditional Self-acceptance

Like person centered therapy (Rogers, 1961), RET accepts people unconditionally, *whether or not* they perform well or are likeable. But it also actively *teaches* them how to unconditionally accept themselves (and others). It shows them they can *choose* to fully accept themselves, no matter what they do, just *because* they choose to do so — because they are human. It also shows them the more elegant philosophical solution: to refuse to rate their *self*, their *totality* at all, but *only* to rate what they do and don't do (Ellis, 1973, 1985, 1988; Ellis & Dryden, 1990, 1991).

## Flexibility and Alternative Seeking

While helping people to give up their dogmatic, rigid shoulds and musts, RET also shows them how to look for other alternative solutions and pleasures. As they work to change their absolutist demands, they also see the wide world for what it is — a place with many possible knowledges and adventures. They learn — and teach themselves — that either/or rules are often unnecessary and that all kinds of both/and and and/also possibilities occur or can be made to occur.

## Profound Philosophical Change

Like the other cognitive-behavior therapies, RET helps people to give up their unrealistic, anti-empirical attributions and inferences — such as, "Because he frowned, I am sure he thinks I acted badly, he hates me, and he knows I am a real loser!" It shows them how to Dispute and challenge these misperceptions and false Beliefs. But it also seeks beyond them to people's absolutist demands by which they often *create* their misperceptions. Such as, "He *absolutely must, and at all times* approve of me. And because he frowned this time — as he *must* not! — that *proves* that I acted badly, that he hates me, and that he knows I am a real loser!" Instead of just getting to people's disparate dysfunctional cognitions, RET tries to help them get to their *basic, core* philosophies from which these spring, and to show them how to actively dispute them until they make a profound philosophic change. As they make this change, they will change their basic patterns of dysfunctional thinking and automatically and tacitly tend to think more rationally in the future.

*Individuality and Sociality*
Though part of the human potential movement since the 1960's, RET tries to avoid its excesses by helping people see that they choose to live in a social group and that they are interdependent with this group. An essential part of people's life is group living; and their economic, ecological, political, and other happiness depends on the well-functioning of their community. While they had better not be *too* self-sacrificing and other-directed they had also better not be too self-indulgent and self-centered. The principle of both/and rather than either/or is important. Active democratic participation in community affairs rather than self-centered isolation will usually help oneself *and* one's social group. RET tries to help each individual in a family, community, or other system understand and healthfully change himself of herself. But it also stresses the importance of improving and changing the system in which all humans interdependently live (Ellis, 1985, 1991a; Ellis & Dryden, 1991).

*Therapeutic Encounter*
RET consists of a therapeutic encounter between the client and the therapist in the course of which the therapist may not personally like or want to befriend all clients but cares very much about helping them overcome their emotional-behavioral problems and lead happier lives. Like their clients, therapists are persons in their own right and are not blank screens, nor purely "objective." They may therefore reveal a good deal of themselves to clients and have human relationships with them, but still take care to be responsible professionals and not get personally involved with their clients. RET practitioners clearly show clients their shortcomings and disturbances, but always try to accept them *as persons*, to give them unconditional acceptance no matter how badly they perform, and to never condemn *them* for their poor *behaviors*. But in addition to giving and modeling what Rogers (1961) calls unconditional positive regard to their clients, RET professionals actively-directively *teach* them how to give it to themselves. For RET holds that most clients *easily and naturally* damn *themselves* as well as their dysfunctional thoughts, feelings, and actions, and that unless they are specifically taught the humanistic *philosophy* of self-acceptance, they are not likely to devise it and work for it entirely on their own. RET, therefore, is collaborative *and* instructive, supportive *and* active-directive. It uses the therapeutic relationship as a vehicle to show clients how to relate to one human, the therapist, and therefore to be able to relate better to others. But it also teaches a large number of cognitive, emotive, and behavioral methods

that clients can use to help themselves function in their intrapersonal, interpersonal, and community relationships.

*Emotional and Behavioral Methods of RET*

Although I once over-optimistically thought that people could logically and rationally be convinced to change their dysfunctional feelings and behaviors, I soon realized that they very often hold on to their musts, misperceptions, and misleading inferences and attributions very *strongly* and they persistently *habituate* themselves to self-defeating emotions and actions. So from the start, I incorporated many *forceful, emotive-evocative* methods (such as my famous shame-attacking exercises) into RET. I also, right from the start, favored in vivo desensitization, implosive deconditioning, and the use of reinforcements and penalties with many of my clients. In addition, RET favors active Disputing by clients of their irrational Beliefs, but also uses a number of other cognitive methods, such as self-help reports, coping self-statements, and bibliotherapy, in its wide-ranging therapeutic armamentarium. So RET is far from being an intellectual or rationalist therapy but is truly rational-*emotive*, also strongly behavioral, and in many ways one of the most integrative of modern therapies.

## Conclusion

Humanism has many aspects, and so does humanistic psychotherapy. A somewhat sadly neglected aspect of humanistic psychology today is secular humanism, which on the one hand espouses many of the values common to other kinds of humanism but on the other hand is opposed to religious, mystical, and spiritual humanism that is so popular today among members of the Association of Humanistic Psychology and the Division of Humanistic Psychology of the American Psychological Association. While not "scientific" in the narrow or logical positivism sense, secular humanism uses many scientific tools to check its (and other group's) hypotheses and accepts nothing on blind, devout faith. It is relativistic, skeptical, and nondogmatic — and in these ways scientific as well as humanistic.

The main mode of therapy that stems from a secular humanist outlook is rational-emotive therapy (RET), which has sparked the creation and growth of most of today's popular cognitive-behavioral therapies. RET tries to combine a tough-minded scientific attitude with a down-to-earth humanistic approach to psychotherapy. To this end, it emphasizes phenomenalism, existential choice, self-fulfillment and long range hedonism, unconditional acceptance, flexibility and alternative-seeking, profound philosophic change, individualism *and* sociality, therapeutic encounter, and the use of a large number of integrated cognitive, emotive, and behavioral methods.

## References

Ayer, A. J. (1936). *Language, truth, and logic.* London: Gollancz.
Bartley, W. W. III. (1984). *The retreat to commitment* (Rev. ed.). Peru, IL: Open Court.
Beck, A. T. (1976). *Cognitive therapy and the emotional disorders.* New York: International Universities Press.
Clark, T. W. (1992). Relativism and the limits of rationality. *Humanist, 52,* 25-32, 42.
Coue, E. (1923). *My method.* New York: Doubleday Press.
Ellis, A. (1957). *How to live with a neurotic: At home and at work.* New York: Crown. Rev. ed., Hollywood, CA: Wilshire Books, 1975.
Ellis, A. (1962). *Reason and emotion in psychotherapy.* Secaucus, NJ: Citadel.
Ellis, A. (1972). What does transpersonal psychology have to offer the art and science of psychotherapy. *Voices, 8* (3), 10-20.
Ellis, A. (1973). *Humanistic psychotherapy: The rational-emotive approach.* New York: McGraw-Hill.
Ellis, A. (1985). *Overcoming resistance: Rational-emotive therapy with difficult clients.* New York: Springer.
Ellis, A. (1988). *How to stubbornly refuse to make yourself miserable about anything — yes, anything!.* Secaucus, NJ: Lyle Stuart.
Ellis, A. (1991a). Achieving self-actualization. In A. Jones & R. Crandall (Eds.), *Handbook of self-actualization.* Corte Madera, CA: Select Press.
Ellis, A. (1991b). The revised ABC's of rational-emotive therapy. In J. Zeig (Ed.), *Evolution of psychotherapy: II.* New York: Brunner/Mazel. Expanded version: *Journal of Rational-Emotive and Cognitive-Behavior Therapy, 9,* 139-172.
Ellis, A., & Dryden, W. (1990). *The essential Albert Ellis.* New York: Springer.
Ellis, A., & Dryden, W. (1991). *A dialogue with Albert Ellis: Against dogma.* Milton Keynes, England: Open University Press.
Ellis, A., & Schoenfeld, E. (1990). Divine intervention and the treatment of chemical dependency. *Journal of Substance Abuse, 2,* 459-468.
Ellis, A., & Yeager, R. (1989). *Why some therapies don't work: The dangers of transpersonal psychology.* Buffalo, NY: Prometheus.
Frankl, V. (1959). *Man's search for meaning.* New York: Pocket Books.
Grof, S. (1984). *Ancient wisdom and modern science.* Stony Brook, NY: State University of New York Press.

Kelly, G. (1955). *The psychology of personal constructs* (2 vols.). New York: Norton.

Korzybski, A. (1933). *Science and sanity*. San Francisco: International Society of General Semantics.

Kurtz, P. (1973). *Humanist manifestos I and II*. Buffalo: Prometheus.

Kurtz, P. (1985). Humanism. In Stein, G. (Ed.), *The dictionary of unbelief* (pp. 328-333). Buffalo: Prometheus.

Kurtz, P. (1986). *The transcendental temptation*. Buffalo, NY: Prometheus.

Levin, D. M. (1991). Psychology as a discursive formation: The postmodern crisis. *The Humanistic Psychologist, 19,* 250-276.

Maultsby, M. C., Jr. (1984). *Rational behavior therapy*. Englewood Cliffs, NJ: Prentice-Hall.

May, R. (1969). *Love and will*. New York: Norton.

Meichenbaum, D. (1977). *Cognitive-behavior modification*. New York: Plenum.

Perls, F. (1969). *Gestalt therapy verbatim*. Lafayette, CA: Real People Press.

Popper, K. R. (1985). *Popper selections* (Ed. by D. Miller). Princeton, NJ: Princeton University Press.

Rogers, C. R. (1961). *On becoming a person*. Boston: Houghton Mifflin.

Sampson, E. E. (1989). The challenge of social change for psychology. *American Psychologist, 44,* 914-921.

Smith, M.B. (1984). Humanistic psychology. In R. J. Corsini (Ed.), *Encyclopedia of Psychology*, Vol. 2 (pp. 155-158).

Stein, G. (Ed.). (1985). *The dictionary of unbelief*. Buffalo, NY: Prometheus.

Tart, C. T. (Ed.). (1975). *Transpersonal psychologies*. New York: Harper Colophon Books.

Walsh, R. N., & Vaughan, F. (1980). *Beyond ago*. Los Angeles: Tarcher.

Yalom, I. (1990). *Existential Psychotherapy*. New York: Basic Books.

# 18

# Andras Angyal, Pioneer in Humanistic Psychotherapy

*E. Mark Stern*

### My Essential Therapist

I was then a college student, home on my first summer vacation and had recently been affected by a severe allergic reaction in my eyes. The tears seemed never to let up. Our family physician, who had recently taken some psychoanalytic training, suggested a possible link to underlying emotions. I was referred to a psychiatrist, who after only a few introductory words asked me to recline on the couch and say whatever came to my mind. The doctor's face was hidden behind an under illuminated lighting fixture. Dr. Max Helfand had the professional persistence which I later learned was characteristic of his erstwhile mentor, Dr. Wilhelm Stekel. I was even later to learn that Stekel, an early break-away figure from Freud's inner circle, regarded neurotics as restless souls hoping to champion their disavowed personal ideals (Stekel, 1943, p. x). Helfand presented the full deck in one sitting: "You must recognize," he insisted, "that you are crying." The immediacy and authority of his words had the power to initiate me into a psychoanalytic context. The effect was to avow my helplessness, and once I surrendered, the tears promptly ceased. I knew then that I would someday become a psychotherapist.

Helfand would be there for me through the summer. The search had begun to find an analyst in my college community. The only doctor who had time availability was still a candidate in a classical Freudian institute. Though we met three times a week, I had no sense of who or what we were about. The enterprise seemed hollow. Classical analysis, for all its careful scrutiny of every word, needs the talents of a practitioner sensitive to the spiritual disposition of the patient. What passed for this process had now left me unfulfilled. My search was to continue.

After speaking with a friend who was in what sounded like a different sort of analysis, I decided to pursue a therapist more sympathetic to the interpersonal school of Harry Stack Sullivan, Karen Horney and Erich Fromm. But it was not yet time to return to New York City. Dealing with my parents had been difficult. I decided my best move was to continue my education in Boston.

I phoned Dr. Clara Thompson, who was then one of the mainstays of the William Alanson White School of Psychoanalysis in New York. Dr. Thompson referred me to a Mrs. Izette de Forest, who she knew practiced in Boston. Between the years 1925-1927 and again in 1929, Mrs. de Forest studied with Sandor Ferenczi both in Budapest and in New York. I was delighted to have been directed to a non-medical practitioner since, beginning with my first encounter with it, I considered psychoanalysis to be a humanistic project - a way of extending understanding, certainly not medical treatment. Although Ferenczi, was a physician, he was an outspoken advocate of non-medical analysis (Grosskurth, 1991).

Izette de Forest, who had also had a decade of association with Erich Fromm, both as student and friend, was most gracious throughout our interview. She said from the outset that she was in the process of retiring, but would be delighted to evaluate my situation and refer me to an appropriate colleague. Like Ferenczi, she had an obvious dedication to what was most personal about therapy. I was later to learn that she was convinced that good therapists work "from an emotional and spiritual capacity to digest and apply in entire beneficence the experiences of life... (through)... what E. M. Forester (called) 'a developed heart'" (deForest, 1954, p. 187). I felt understood about the kind of helper best suited to me: "I have an angel I can refer you to," she said, "I know him well and trust him... He does not rely on a reductionistic. hydraulic model of the mind... You'll know him as Dr. Angyal. In Hungarian, Angyal means angel." Later that day I called the "angel's" office and made an appointment for the following week. I was enthusiastic about my new beginning:

> Like so many others, I (sought) therapy needing to discover the uncommon denominator of friendship... My early life had been a gallimaufry of friendlessness, incessant depression and recurrent parental divorces. In the aftermath I alternately blossomed

and sank. Beyond the extremes, however, arriving at the right place and in the honorable home was the only quest I could morally consider. (Stern, 1989, pp. 187-8)

Andras Angyal was to become my essential psychotherapist. As essential therapist, he helped me attain a qualitative appreciation of my own autobiography. We were destined to share space twice each week for a bit more than two and a half years beginning in 1949. His patients were free to determine how they would negotiate their working presence. He mentioned that some sat while others reclined. He'd worked with one man who would stride back and forth the length of the office. Given the choice, I decided on continuing the use of the couch. Out of respect for the necessary polarity I set between us, Dr. Angyal sat somewhat out of view. I guessed that his decorum might have possibly been different with others. Certainly I was not about to add to my discomfort by keeping him in sight. My most recent attempt at being in analysis was characterized by my nonstop talk. For a time, this uncontrolled pattern continued with Angyal:

> One patient in the course of several sessions never permitted the therapist to get a word in edgewise. This man had worked with therapists who apparently let him monopolize the sessions; he had been helped very little. After the trial period the therapist agreed to work with the patient on the conditions that he was not to associate in the sessions (as this apparently served to disguise his problems), and would agree at any time by a given signal so that the therapist could comment. Tears came to the patient's eyes as he said, "I don't know how you knew it, because I didn't know it myself, but I think I have been hoping all my life to find someone to understand me enough to say 'shut up.'" (Angyal, 1965, p.216-217).

Though that patient might not have been me, I was, for all intentions, still uncommitted to the therapeutic relationship. I was instead, trying to please, and would steer the conversation to aesthetics and spirituality, topics I "knew" were close to him.

"Prodigies" have an uncanny ability to disarm, but Angyal remained faithful to the process, understanding all along that my defenses superseded any premature presence.

He acknowledged that, for the moment I would probably hear little or nothing capable of challenging the stalemate. "One can't change," he said, "if the options are murky," Choice could only be exercised when alternatives were more available. Alternatives would be made known when my design became secure enough to tolerate rearrangement. For the time being it was enough to hear that even collapse has meaning.

Doubts plagued me. The most insignificant opposition resulted in fear and humiliation. Yet our relationship became the necessary new alliance. Angyal was sensitive to the hurts of the past. Early memories and impressions were always cast in a new key. He saw them as opportunities for change. For him, neurosis was not so much a reaction to trauma as it was the relentless panic and anguish embedded in the search for safety.

Dr. Angyal valued the growing ability to regroup experience. "Nothing can give way," he insisted, "not even the suffering, until new options are seen as viable." The present task, he insisted, was to learn to reverence all of the elements of my existence, even the ones which seemed "craziest" in order to allow them to exfoliate into new workable patterns. Angyal believed that the past, no matter how unfortunate, was nevertheless a storehouse of personal and transpersonal value. It was never the future, but the past which was to be transformed. It was presented to me as a matter of a shifting perspective. If I could re-view from another vantage point, what may have once seemed outlandish and unproductive could take on other highlights. As a child, I was often criticized for being too involved in religion, too interested in being observant. Dr. Angyal took this criticism and helped me see how my religious preoccupation had a most positive role to play in my present existence. Even though much of it was obsessive and dreamlike, it was an important hallmark of my "art." When so redefined, the past transcended its purported negative consequences. This new regard for the past has remained the kernel of my working principle as a practicing analyst:

> This approach to therapy and to existence... become(s) apparent as soon as one looks at the world not as something to be reckoned with, an object of mastery, but rather as something to be appreciated a context in which all experience has imminent value. In this frame of reference, the past is more than a fetter. As Andras Angyal has it "causation works back and forth, and the present can change the past as the past is *now*." A therapist who sees experience as something to be appreciated tends to stress mastery less and reverence more. (Stern, 1966, p. 280)

### Angyal's Foundations

Angyal acknowledged his debt to the "organismic" theories of Haldane and Woodger; the Gestalt psychologists Wertheimer, Kohler,

Koffka and Kurt Goldstein; the psychobiology of the then celebrated American psychiatrist Adolph Meyer; the personalistic approach of William Stern; and, perhaps more than the others, to the holism of Jan Smuts, once Prime Minister of the then Union of South Africa.

Beyond these building blocks, there yet remains a story that unfolded during the course of my therapy. Dr. Angyal had been commenting on unexpected congruent happenings:

> In the course of my applying to graduate school, he (Angyal) tells me how he decided to take temporary leave from his medical studies in favor of an immediate Ph.D. in psychology. It seems that he was on a train returning to medical school after his summer vacation. Across from him sat a man who soon proved to be a nuisance. Fighting boredom and annoyance, the young Andras began to fill the man's ears with fanciful psychological theories. He did this to ward off the man's incessant banter. Nevertheless, by the time Angyal arrived at his destination, it dawned on him that he had unleashed seminal ideas that would change his whole life and became the cornerstones for his ultimate work in psychology and psychiatry (Stern, 1981, p.9).

*Foundations for a Science of Personality* (1941) was based on Angyal's University of Vienna doctoral thesis. The bulk of its ideas were introduced in 1937 at the Henry Phipps Psychiatric Clinic of the Johns Hopkins University following his arrival in the United States. Soon after he was asked to join the staff of the Worcester State Hospital, finally becoming head of its psychiatric research unit.

Throughout his years of research and practice, Angyal remained concerned that psychiatry would never attain status as an authentic inquiry into abnormal clinical states if it failed to contribute to a basic understanding of normal functioning. The focus of the healthy paradigm he offered centered on expansiveness and purpose. "The self," he contended is "a finite distance on an infinite line (since)... within the person each process of structure is part of a larger one (Angyal, 1965, pp. 298-299). What remained fundamental was the tenet that "to be part and to become a part means the maintenance of a balance between finitude and one's place in the whole of creation" (Stern, 1985, p.2). Recovery is the process of concretizing the experience of this balance. It is the occasion for re-identification with what Angyal termed the "humility system" (Angyal, 1965, p. 260). Here the person grasps his or her essential awe and helplessness even while being in the process of making positive shifts in relating to others. These shifts may further entrap confusion since they contain trends toward both the homonomous, i.e., an orientation involving increased participation, and the autonomous, i.e., self-governance. Re-identification is, however, holistic since both autonomy and homonomy can together become the expansive means of relating.

Angyal veered away from classical psychoanalytic notions which stressed the primacy of instincts. Growth, according to Angyal, draws on renewed symbol-structures stemming from the multidimensional phenomena present in the patient's creative unconscious (Deri, 1984). The unconscious is, by definition, unavailable to consciousness, except through symbolization. This symbolization is organized through will and attitude and thus remains malleable. Meaning and value play critical roles in recovery since they are the necessary refinements of will and attitude. It is was this recognition of personal autonomy that anticipated the humanistic directions of ego and self psychologies (Zevin, 1981).

Andras Angyal's therapeutic approach conformed to his theoretical foundations. He remained skeptical of analytic approaches which pinpointed trauma in infancy and childhood as the mainstays of neuroses. According to him, neurotic orientations tend to resist all attempts at destablizing them so that the mere search for early psychic shocks has the potential of becoming an obsessive task in its own right. Though he acknowledged early beginnings of neurotic orientations, he nevertheless insisted that any accounting for symptomology based exclusively on any one epoch of life avoids an authentic understanding of the ubiquitous quality of a neurosis.

Angyal's therapeutic format was transformative and reconstructive. As a therapist, he remained consummately respectful, if not reverential, of the emergence of all experience. Experiences on all levels were seen foundational to recovery. His therapeutic principles provided a constant amplification of the personal perspective. Therapeutic confrontations were managed sensitively and skillfully. He recommended abiding with the patient's experience since it represents all that he or she has.

Angyal steadfastly maintained that holistic insights were the necessary mainstays of "changes in attitude(s) of wide scope" (Angyal, 1965, p.265). Much in the spirit of St. Augustine's motto that sins themselves need to baptized. he claimed that neurotic behavior is bound to prevail until its healthy substructure is fully experienced. In making his case, he described the plight of a man who had been experiencing a strong aversion to birthmarks as far back as he could recall. His abhorrence of these "dirty blemishes" made it virtually impossible for him to not "get the dirt on" anyone who dared show concern or care for him. An earlier "incomplete" analysis explained his abhorrence by citing the probable shock of having been confronted by the "blackness" of his mother's nipples while still being nursed. While this "genetic" material might well have been historically accurate, it merely scaled the surface without providing the patient with a way of dealing with the larger cluster of negative attitudes which had accrued over the years and which appeared to block the emergence of his more productive critical faculties (Angyal, 1965, p.206).

Neurosis, for Angyal was never simply a blend of morbid aberrations, be they obsessive or hysteric. More precisely, each neurosis is its own life style, consistent with its own unique pains and pleasures. Nevertheless, each neurotic style, complete in itself, represents a therapeutic challenge. Angyal proclaimed the necessity of neurotics needing to learn to embrace the authentic guilt which invariably arises during the course of treatment. Such guilt speaks directly to the need to go beyond "the betrayal and falsification of {self}" (Angyal, 1965, p.191).

Angyal observed significant links between the contrasting neurotic worlds of obsessiveness and hysteria. Both are personifications of noncommitted patterns. Obsessives are preoccupied with the search for safety at any price. Their struggle for self-worth is set against a backdrop of imagined derisions. Correspondingly, the hysteric sees the world as dangerous and ungiving and seeks to remediation with inappropriate instant gratification.

Obsessives become paralyzed by the ambiguities of the demands of good and evil in their lives. Owing to its ubiquitous and painful state of uncertainty, obsessive confusion obscures any underlying trust. Since they usually see others as hostile and blaming, obsessives are never clear about people's motives. Their fundamental doubts appear to arise out of the double messages they received as children and continue to permeate as the years move ahead. Obsessives remain ever watchful, fearful of retreating into crippling "weakness." They discourage any meaningful dialogue with those who offer love and support. Hysterics, on the other hand, having convinced themselves of their phantasmagoric emptiness, ward off the world's friendlessness with their own brand of bizarreness. Health and neurosis paradoxically blend as mirror reversals forming something of a pervasive harmony in the contradiction (Stern, 1980a, p. 2). Angyal's bipolar model views each person as having parallel healthy and neurotic potentialities. Each remains a latent presence in the other. This uneasy contrast forms the basis of "a poetic process... ratify[ing the] entire composition" (Stern, 1980b, p. 80). Each personality is ripe with the potential of becoming transformed on an almost daily basis. Even where the daily struggle for health endures, a person may at any moment give way to neurotic trends. Angyal was early to recognize the Alcoholics Anonymous program as the desirable model for psychological recovery. Alcoholics are never "recovered" but always "recovering." Accordingly, the maintenance of psychological health in Angyal's bipolar system becomes a day-to-day task. He suspected that self-annihilating motifs are bound to persist in the absence of some recognition of alternatives. And while relapses back into a neurosis are to be expected, love and the tasks involved in learning to be of meaning to others aid the reinforcement of new reconstructions. Angyal's bipolar arguments conclude that whatever constitutes personhood may be productively or counter-productively rearranged. This "ambiguous Gestalt... suggests a Janus-faced organization of both healthy and neurotic features... with every conceivable characteristic represented in each organization" (Frick, 1984, p. 227). Angyal was quick to reassure his patients that within the transformation of the neurotic, no experience is ever lost since every condition of life represents the font of personal value.

Angyal was convinced that any viable option to neurosis had to correspond to the patient's personal readiness and ultimate resourcefulness. "If (the patient) shows stamina in standing up for his neurosis, he will show stamina later in standing up for his health" (Angyal, 1965, p.224). I recall his speaking of the stepped-up need for a dynamic reconstruction of attitude following any serious negotiation to change. The single-minded demolition of a neurotic pattern must be initiated by the patient's despair. This bottoming-out happens when all neurotic resources prove repugnant. "While the patient is completely caught up in his neurotic existence," he wrote, "he has neither the possibility nor the wholehearted desire to find his way out" (Angyal, 1965, p. 227). After the neurotic stance is weakened, whatever insights were available for that weakening, become the building blocks for a creative emotional reconstruction. Each insight furthers the ability to stand outside of the entangling confusion. Yet as stated earlier, health is not an outside position, but rather is within the body of the neurosis. Neurosis is always the distortion of health. Health is achieved as the patient reckons with "the realization that in a wrong way he has been fighting for the right purpose" (Angyal, 1965, p. 229). The unbridled appeal of health abates shame and provides the necessary courage to move ahead.

Steady recovery requires consistent diligence set against the background of neurotic deterministic closure. Taking due cognizance of the power of this Gestalt dynamic, it would follow that closure narrows options and obtrudes flexibility. Systems need to remain open in order to be present to a new attitudinal and behavioral repertoire. For the recovering neurotic, as for the recovering addict, new options are a daily choice.

Momentary flares, no matter how cathartic, rarely lead to lasting changes. More than likely, bona fide insights are the products of long-term hard-won assemblages of awareness. Authentic insights echo throughout one's life, constantly enriching the individual Leitmotif. Such insights become axioms for meaningful conduct since they create the ground for authentic participation in a relevant social nexus. Induced into a re-relationship with others, the person slowly begins to appreciate the uniquenesses and importance of autonomous personhood. Autonomy is the foothold for full engagement in superindividual relationships, extending from personal kinship to participation in the community. Angyal saw superindividual involvement as the spearhead for any transpersonal encounter with God and the cosmos.

Angyal's holism never segmentalized any one human function. He considered each to be representative of an enlarged and enlarging ensemble. Given the appropriate setting, all elements in this seeming heterogeneity, become capable of radical rearrangement:

> Setting can be defined as the construction of a system. The parts have multiple functional possibilities, but after being arranged in a given system, they function in one definite way, namely, in accordance with the system principle. The other functional possibilities of the parts are excluded; they become activated only when the parts are rearranged in other systems and work in accordance with the new system principle... Setting and shifting may thus be regarded as the key mechanism of an organized activity. (Angyal, 1965, p. 54)

### Transformation

> The person as far as he is known to us is not complete. As part of a whole he must be larger than we know him, so our knowledge begins with an openness, a door to a larger context... By becoming a part of increasingly larger wholes, the person gains a larger territory in which he can feel at home. (Angyal, 1965, p. 299).

Angyal's belief in the potential of the human will made him much admired by Abraham Maslow. They became friends in the mid to late 1940's. Angyal found in Maslow's depiction of peak experiences an elaboration of the outer limits of belonging and participation. Both men recognized latent capacities for experiencing awarenesses of self beyond the usually encrusted boundaries. Through epiphanies or peak moments, the self is preserved, even as it is donated to a superindividual possibilities. For Angyal, these epiphanies or peak experiences were fortunate clues to radical personality reconstruction.

Angyal's notion of superindividuality is reminiscent of the mystical doctrine of the Flemish John Ruysbroeck who visualized a discreet unity within the self as it moves into something transpersonal before finally vaulting into its unique union with the supernatural (Merton, 1961). It was, for Angyal, the experience of greater and more discrete superindividual units which related person to person, person to community and finally, person to the cosmos. This superindividuality never diverts from the unique struggle to reconstruct and express autonomy and participation in what Angyal refers to as the trend toward homonomy or recognizable unity of all experience. What makes Angyal's thesis fundamental to humanistic and transpersonal psychology is that it focuses on homonomy, not as some curious mystical state, but bound within the *terra incognito* of the individual's life.

Maslow, intrigued by his friend's holistic paradigm, helped sponsor the Angyal seminar at Brandies University. Similar seminars were given at Harvard, notes from which served as the background for his posthumous text *Neurosis and Treatment: A Holistic Theory* (Angyal, 1965).

## Unity

Health, like personality and aesthetics, is best understood as a holistic construct. In Angyal's sense, each aspect of the whole invokes definite rules which result in a startling reinterpretation of the field. New truths emerge which, in turn, are based on the unique operating principle of these relationships.

Each segment re-presents the whole. To view any one personal episode, no matter how serendipitous, as just another add-on is to miss the richness of the whole. The essence of the whole is to be found wherever disparate parts adhere as a system, not because of their qualities, but more as a result of their various "positional values" (Angyal, 1941, p.257). This locus or unity assumes a central role in the therapeutic relationship. Its animating principle alive in Wordsworth's words has caught sight of that immortal sea of a unity which "rolls through all things." Relationships experienced in any one biography all forth an exemplification of the whole. "This need," according to Angyal, "is not a luxury or a superstructure, but a part of man's very nature" (Angyal, 1941, p. 198). A unitary life history, differentiated into successive developmental stages, each with its own contrasting relationships, includes all of the characteristics of the whole. Dynamic unity coheres as all traces of the person become highlighted against the backdrop of all other traces. Even chance, in Angyal's code, is determined by the structure of the consummated whole. Relationship of past to present is thus transformable, resulting in the potential for "an increased metaphysical anchoring" (Angyal, 1941, p.356).

As with the individual, so too do all life forces cohere to the dynamic interplay of "organismic autonomy and environmental heteronomy" (Angyal, 1941, p. 379). Each person is the expression of intrasomatic and extrasomatic occurrences. What are termed quality relationships in all of life and non-life involve a unified interaction of the full spectrum of ethical and aesthetic attitudes (Stern, 1991). Angyal's ethics and aesthetics were always congruent with their trends toward the superindividual, communicating inherent messages only fortuitous as opportunities arise.

For Dr. Angyal, every person and every object has a meaningful expressive function as a constituent body of the whole. My personal therapy with Andras Angyal opened up relational passageways amid painful stresses and pressures. The effect was a widening and ripening of my vision. Most important was my realization of Dr. Angyal's correlation between personal growth and the amplification of the aesthetic:

> The perception of opening horizons, of widening meanings, makes the aesthetic experience a striking expression of the homonomous orientation. The person's separation from the world is overcome together with the separateness of objects, and wider patterns emerge. (Angyal, 1965, p.28)

This was Angyal's message: The whole is ideally at one with its parts. He stressed this intactness throughout his professional life. For him the system ideally and effortlessly emerges as the expression of a well-integrated experience of the autonomous and homonomous. What results becomes the unfixed dynamic of self-surrender and personal mastery.

## Summing It Up

Angyal synopsized his holistic view of the vivacity of the life course in recording made in the summer of 1949, and later recommended by Abraham Maslow for publication in the *Journal of Humanistic Psychology*. As he linked the simplicity of the aesthetic to the ethical experience, Angyal once again underscored that for him "no existence is separate from the others" (Angyal, 1962, p.124). For him, sublime unity was to be found in the appreciation of the ordinary. Here is how he summed it up. It was during a momentary contemplation of a tree on the way home. The tree, he observed, was

> like a bridge between the earth and the sun... And even when it is dead it has strength, it has grain, it has fiber; it still has the energy it had absorbed and transformed... And when... fire burns out (its) heat, after having warmed us, is dissipated again in the world and what has been taken from the earth is there in a few handfuls of ash, the cycle is completed. It is the end of one cycle and the beginning of another. (Angyal, 1962, p. 125)

## References

Angyal, A. (1941) *Foundations for a science of personality*. New York: The Commonwealth Fund.

Angyal, A (1951) The convergence of psychotherapy and religion. *Journal of Pastoral Care, 4*, 4-14.

Angyal, A. (1962) Aesthetic experience. *Journal of Humanistic Psychology, 2* (2), 123-125.

Angyal, A (1965) *Neurosis and treatment: A holistic theory* (E. Haufmann & R. M. Jones, Eds.) New York:John Wiley & Sons.

de Forest, I. (1954) *The leaven of love: A development of the psychoanalytic theory and technique of Sandor Ferenczi*. New York: Harper & Brothers.

Deri, S. (1984) *Symbolization and creativity*. New York: International Universities Press.

Frick, W. (1984) Angyal's theory of the ambiguous gestalt: Its implications for psychotherapy. *Psychotherapy, 21*, 226-231.

Grosskurth, P (1991) *The secret ring: Freud's inner circle and the politics of psychoanalysis*. Reading, MA: Addison-Wesley.

Merton, T. (1961) *The new man*. New York: The Noonday Press.

Stekel, W. *The interpretation of dreams: New developments and technique*. (E. Paul & C. Paul, Trans.) New York: Liveright.

Stern, E. M. (1966) Reverence for experience. *The Journal of Existentialism, 6*, 279-287.

Stern, E. M. (1980 A) Interface with Asya: Experiences in the poetics of one psychotherapy. *Voices: The art and science of psychotherapy, 15* (4), 2-5.

Stern, E. M. (1980 B) Comment on W.B. Frick A therapist encounters the ambiguous gestalt. *Voices: The art and science of psychotherapy, 15* (4), 80-81.

Stern, E. M. (1981) Out of chaos: beginnings. In E. M. Stern (Ed.) *The other side of the couch: What therapists believe* (pp. 5-14). New York: The Pilgrim Press.

Stern, E. M. (1989) At last my friend. *Voices: The art and science of psychotherapy, 25* (1/2), 177-181.

Stern, E. M. (1991) Foundations for a soul psychology. In K. Gibson, D. Lathrop & E. M. Stern (Eds.) *Carl Jung and soul psychology* (pp. 2-7). New York: Harrington Park Press.

Zevin, R. N. (1981) An alternative to psychoanalytic metapsychology: The contribution of Andras Angyal. *Dissertation Abstracts International, 42* (6-B) 2559.

# 19

# Education and the Humanistic Challenge

*Anne C. Richards and Arthur W. Combs*

**Education and the Humanistic Challenge**

Soon after the twentieth century was underway, a humanistic orientation in education and psychology developed simultaneously among teachers (especially in pre-school and elementary school) and psychologists (especially in counseling and clinical work). Practitioners in each of these fields began to question traditional ways of approaching their responsibilities and to explore more humane, meaningful, and effective ways of working with their students and their clients.

In the 1920's, 1930's and 1940's, the Progressive Education movement in education grew out of the philosophy of John Dewey. Dewey (1916, 1938) sought to clarify the innate nature of the desire to learn in human beings, the ways in which human learning is a social act, and the importance of involving students in learning experiences that fostered rather than arrested or distorted their capacity for subsequent growth. He encouraged teachers to relate what they taught to the interests of the learner, to downplay their authority role as teachers, to involve students in the learning process through hands-on activities, and to make the classroom setting more user friendly. Progressive educators seeking to implement these ideas began to experiment with new ways of teaching (Bestor, 1985, p. 41).

These efforts met resistance in many quarters. Some blamed the movement for redefining "the aims of education itself," for undermining "the great traditions of liberal education" (Bestor, 1985, p. 47). Progressive education aroused hostility and fear that teachers were watering down the traditional curriculum and coddling students. Without support from other social sciences, and in the face of so much antagonism, Dewey's philosophy provided too tenuous a base for sustaining the movement, and it faded away with America's entrance into World War II.

In the course of this war the armed forces called upon psychologists for aid in selection and placement of draftees on entrance, counseling of men and women while in service, and facilitation of the re-entry of military personnel into the peace-time economy. These demands greatly increased the numbers of psychologists engaged in close relationship with persons and their human problems. Existing perspectives offered by psychoanalytic and behavioristic psychologists seemed less than helpful in understanding the complex realities of people's personal lives. As a consequence, many psychologists began to search for more adequate conceptualizations. This led to the emergence of a "third force" in psychology and to a more appropriate framework within which to understand matters of concern to both therapists and educators.

Among others, this new psychology gave emphasis to three fundamental principles particularly significant for therapeutic and educational purposes. Humanistic psychology:
1. took "the universe of naive experience in which each individual lives, the everyday situation of self and surroundings which each person takes to be reality" (Snygg & Combs, 1949, p. 15) as its point of departure for better understanding persons (self and others);
2. proposed new concepts of healthy psychological development and functioning (predicated on an innate striving toward actualization, maintenance and enhancement of the self);
3. identified the dynamics of human relationships which contributed to synergic psychological climates conducive to learning and growth in human beings.

## Human Experience as a Point of Departure

*Foundations in Humanistic Psychology*

Turning away from a preoccupation with environmental factors impacting on human behavior or from efforts to account for behavior in terms of unconscious forces, humanistic psychologists sought to discern reality as perceived by individuals, the nature of the here and now world in which individuals lived and acted or behaved (Rogers, 1951, p. 486). They were particularly interested in aspects of experience that make us human and distinct from other species, that is, thoughts, beliefs, emotions, feelings, values, opinions, attitudes, interests, wishes, desires and self-awareness (Shaffer, 1978).

*The Relationship Between Experience and Behavior.*

Carl Rogers (1939) and Kurt Lewin (1935) were among the earliest to articulate concepts suggesting a relationship between experience and behavior. Snygg (1941) and later Snygg and Combs (1949) proposed a theoretical perspective, known as Perceptual Psychology, which took as a basic premise that all behavior, without exception, was a function of (determined by) the subjective world of experience of the behaving individual (Snygg & Combs, 1949, pp. 12-15). Semanticists (Hayakawa, 1939; Johnson, 1946) pointed out that words and symbols could represent reality in reliable or distorted fashion — as a map might represent a given territory. Similarly, Adelbert Ames' work (see Ames, 1955; Ittelson & Ames, 1968) offered dramatic demonstrations of the ways in which this relationship also applied to perception and reality, that (1) reality-as-perceived is best understood not as what exists, but as what one *believes* exists and that (2) what is perceived is what we have learned to perceive as a result of our past opportunities or experience. These demonstrations stimulated the thinking of persons seeking to develop more meaningful understandings of the relationship between experience and behavior (Cantril, 1957; Ittelson & Cantril, 1954; Snygg, 1941).

*The Significance of the Self*

Among the experiences of persons are experiences of self — a sense of personhood, of identity, a sense of being in the world (Lecky, 1945; Raimy, 1943). Humanistic psychologists began to explore the significance of such conceptions, the ways in which concepts of self are learned in the course of a person's interaction with other human beings, and the factors which enable them to change these concepts. Frankl (1959), Horney (1942, 1950), Moustakas (1956), Rogers (1951), Snygg and Combs (1949) and many others contributed to our understandings in this area. Today, conceptions of the self and its dynamics have become a major topic in the psychological literature.

*Experience in the Context of Humanistic Education*

Educational critics drew attention to the high drop-out rates in our schools, to the dehumanizing forces operating in them, and to the ways in which "students were becoming increasingly alienated from learning and from almost anything else related to school" (Postman & Weingartner, 1973, p. 8). George Leonard (1963), a journalist and later president of the Association for Humanistic Psychology, maintained that too many students were "mainly learning... to despise school and all intellectual activity" (p. 48). "Instead of 'getting tough' and making the learning process as unpleasant as possible," he recommended that "educators... join in the search for improved methods of teaching and learning that will make their schools more effective, more pleasant, and more *human*" (p. 48). Later, he wrote *Education and Ecstasy* (Leonard, 1968, 1987) as a way of suggesting what schools might look like if one took this approach.

Humanistic psychology's emphasis on experience enabled educators to understand motivation and learning in new ways. For many years the predominant concept of motivation in America's schools has been a question of what teachers do to get students to respond the way teachers want them to. This is an objective view of motivation, an outgrowth of behavioristic thinking. From the humanistic view, motivation is an internal matter of human need, goals, desires, hopes, aspirations, fears. Operating in terms of this view, innovative teachers, especially in alternative schools, have sought to be more empathic, to understand their students and to adapt methodologies and curricula to student needs.

When learning was understood simply as a change in behavior — as something students *did* in the educational setting — the teacher's job was one of reinforcing desired behavior by manipulating circumstances or conditions in the classroom setting. Teaching was a matter of doing something *to* students rather than with them, of bringing student behavior under the control of the teacher. Few seemed to appreciate the irony of such an autocratic approach in an educational system given the responsibility to prepare the nation's youth to function in a democratic society.

Understood from a humanistic viewpoint, learning is not a purely rational or intellectual endeavor. It is not simply a matter of student performance on tests or in the classroom. Instead, it is grounded in the complex capacities of human perception and awareness (Ornstein, 1972). It is a lifelong natural process of discovering the personal meaning of ideas or information. It is an experiential activity dependent on experiential dynamics in the learner. As a consequence, it is critically affected by such factors as the learner's concept of self, feelings about the subject matter and/or the teacher, perception of challenge or threat, sense of identification or belonging, etc. Regrettably, many present-day attempts to address the problems of drop-outs, vandalism and violence in our nation's schools ignore such basic considerations, fail to meet students' needs, and, consequently, do little to improve matters or engage students in learning.

Educators concentrating on the impact of the self concept in teaching and learning offered a plethora of teaching strategies, activities and insights which might promote the development of positive views of self and enhance learning and achievement (Canfield & Wells, 1976; Purkey, 1978). Others sought to make learning opportunities more meaningful and relevant by integrating "affective" dimensions such as emotions, feelings, interests and values with traditional content approaches in the development of school curricula (Brown, 1971; Jones, 1968; Tyrrell, McCarty & Johns, 1977; Weinstein & Fantini, 1970). Still others explored the power of imagery for facilitating learning processes in a variety of subject areas (Ornstein, 1972; Roberts, 1975).

Humanistic psychologists thought more attention should be given to topics too-long-neglected by or omitted from the profession, among them "higher values" such as responsibility, justice, beauty, dignity, freedom, truth, courage, goodness, etc. (Goble, 1970, pp. 45-46; Shaffer, 1978, pp. 1-2). Raths, Harmin and Simon (1966) called attention to the importance of helping students clarify and explore their values, and offered teachers practical strategies for promoting "values clarification" in the classroom. Many voices in contemporary society now clamor for educational experiences focusing on values, character development and ethics (e.g., Coles & Bullard, 1992; Hunt, 1991). Unhappily, some seek to indoctrinate instead of to provide students with opportunities to develop greater wisdom, character and integrity.

As experience became the point of departure for understanding behavior, new light was also shed on the problem of teaching effectiveness. Focusing on what teachers *did*, or how they behaved, research on teaching had been "unable to establish any specific knowledge, method or behavior clearly and reliably associated with either good teaching or bad" (Combs, 1982, p. vii). Examining teaching humanistically, the quality of teaching appears to be primarily a function of the belief system or the experiential world of the teacher, providing the basis for a teacher's behavior moment to moment in the classroom setting.

This has been documented by a series of studies on good and poor practitioners, the results of which indicate that good teachers can be clearly discriminated from poor ones in the nature of their belief systems about self, others, behavior and its causes, the nature of learning, the social climate most conducive to learning, the goals and purposes of education, etc. (See Combs, 1986, for a review of these studies.) For example, good teachers characteristically seek to understand the internal life of those with whom they interact — their feelings, attitudes, values and ways of understanding their world. They "typically see people in positive ways": as able and resourceful and motivated toward meaningful goals. Their purposes in relation to "themselves, their students and society in general tend to be... socially constructive and personally fulfilling" (Combs, 1991, pp. 127-128).

## Healthy Psychological Development and Functioning

*Foundations in Humanistic Psychology*

Some of the earliest writings on healthy development (Allport, 1955; Angyal, 1941; Buhler, 1959; Jersild, 1942; Jourard, 1958; Lecky, 1945; Maslow, 1954; May, 1953; Moustakas, 1956; Murphy, 1958; Snygg & Combs, 1949; Rogers, 1951) suggested that human beings were, by their very nature, oriented toward growth, engaged from conception to death in a process of becoming more fully human or more fully functioning. They also possessed the capacity to realize this through personal effort and as a consequence of quality relationships with significant others (Maslow, 1962, p. 36). Pathology and maladjustment certainly occurred, but these were increasingly understood as efforts at self defense in the face of serious threats to a person's experienced self (Snygg & Combs, 1949; Rogers, 1939; Maslow, 1954).

Based on clinical observations of what constituted genuine progress in therapy as well as on personal and intellectual reflection, humanistic psychologists developed descriptions or images of human beings at their best. Some of these descriptions emphasized behavioral expressions of health and well-being, indicating what optimally healthy persons might *do* in given situations [i.e., behave spontaneously or "naturally" (Maslow, 1954, p. 208), behave more authentically (Bugental, 1965; Moustakas, 1968), or be more self-disclosing to others (Jourard, 1964)].

Other descriptions presented characteristic ways in which healthy individuals experienced themselves and others. For example, healthy persons were characterized by greater openness to experience or acceptance (Rogers, 1961, pp. 115-118), an ability to acknowledge whatever they experienced, allow it entrance to their consideration, and relate it in some way to the existing concepts they held of themselves and the world around them. They felt a sense of connection, kinship or identification with their fellow humans, despite overt differences in age, race, sex, socio-economic status, country of origin, or the like.

The fully-functioning, adequate, self-actualizing or healthy individuals described by humanistic psychologists were seen as ideal citizens for a self-governing democratic society. They were independent thinkers, people of wisdom and integrity, people who saw the world more in terms of challenges than threats, people who were flexible and not rigid, who could perceive broadly rather than narrowly, and who had achieved a sufficient level of life satisfaction as to have the time and energy to devote to the problems of their fellow human beings.

*Healthy Personality as the Goal of Humanistic Education*
Understandings of the nature of healthy persons and their capacities offered new challenges to educators to broaden the goals and purpose of their mission from the transmission of basic knowledge and skills to the question of what constitutes "the fullest possible flowering of human potentiality" (ASCD, 1962, p. 2). Responding to this challenge, the Association for Supervision and Curriculum Development (1962) published a yearbook entitled *Perceiving, Behaving, Becoming: A New Focus for Education*. The book began with four papers on the healthy personality contributed by humanistic psychologists Carl Rogers, Abraham Maslow, Earl Kelley and Arthur Combs. These papers were studied by a commission of educators drawn from all parts of the country and all levels of education. The rest of the book is devoted to the commission's explorations of the far-reaching implications of such concepts for educational thought and practice. The book had an enormous impact. It sold more copies than any educational yearbook in history, and continues to be in demand now, nearly thirty years later. Numerous others have since offered humanistically-oriented ideas about how to foster healthy growth (Simpson with Gray, 1976).

## Synergic Human Relationships

*Foundations in Humanistic Psychology*
Persons do not develop in a vacuum or as isolated entities. The course of human development is linked to and dependent on relationships with other persons. From the earliest days of the Third Force viewpoint, the nature and quality of person to person relationships have been of particular concern to humanistically-oriented theorists and practitioners. Numerous authors and researchers focused on the dynamics in human relationships which both foster and inhibit psychological growth, or the development of human potential and creativity in individuals and groups.

Carl Rogers (1939, 1951) was among the first psychologists to call attention to the significance of the "helping" relationship in promoting positive change in human experience and behavior. Various studies and reports have since confirmed that it isn't knowledge, schools of psychology/psychotherapy, or methods that distinguish effective practitioners from non-effective ones. Instead, it's the quality of the helping relationship that makes the critical difference (Combs, 1986; Russell, 1981).

Maslow found meaning in Ruth Benedict's distinction between high and low synergy societies and sought to promote high synergy social relationships in which people "cooperated together for mutual advantage" (Goble, 1970, p. 108) instead of working at cross purposes with one another or operating as if their interests and those of others were "necessarily mutually exclusive and antagonistic" (Goble, 1970, p. 110). For "without development of unity, mutuality, valuing of self and other on some level, the struggle to know oneself and to know other persons does not move forward" (Moustakas, 1972, p. 102).

Whatever their position in society or line of work, Jourard (1974) described healthy persons as moving in directions that were "life-giving" to them "and not destructive to other people. . . " (p. v). Jourard (1975) underscored the importance of genuine dialogue and proposed a "psychology of invitation" for facilitating growth in self and others (Jourard, 1968, p. 53). Farson (1974, pp. 30-31) and Maslow (Lowry, 1979) pointed out that calamities or conditions of frustration or adversity might lead to maturity and growth, but whether they did so or not was a function of the meanings people derived from such circumstances, whether they were perceived as challenges rather than threats.

Gordon (1955) explored forces that might "threaten democracy from within" (p. 6), and sought to clarify the means by which group leadership might help a "group actualize and utilize its... creative potential" (p. 93) and minimize conditions which inhibited communication and discouraged those within them from making their resources (ideas, facts, capacities) available to the group. For some years prior to his death, Rogers (1977) discussed and utilized humanistic group dynamics for the resolution of local, national and international conflicts.

Additional insights came from experimental "sensitivity-training groups, initially known as T-groups" (Shaffer, 1978, p. 4). "Developed by the National Training Laboratories in Bethel, Maine . . . as a means of helping administrators and business executives become more sensitive to the interpersonal aspects of their jobs and organizations," they enabled people to learn more about themselves and about group dynamics (Shaffer, 1978, pp. 4-5).

*Quality Human Relationships in Humanistic Education*

Inspired in the main by the work of Carl Rogers (1939, 1951, 1957, 1969, 1983), many educators have explored the kinds of relationships that might be conducive to optimal growth and learning for all involved in the educational endeavor (e.g., Aspy, 1972; Combs & Avila, 1985; Fairfield, 1977; Jersild, 1955). Rogers' (1951, 1957) postulation of the importance of empathy, congruence and unconditional positive regard in human relationships has deeply influenced the thinking of many teachers, counselors and supervisors in educational settings. Indeed, he is still probably the best known psychologist in the educational establishment.

The focus upon relationships in humanistic psychology has slowly but steadily found its way into educational theory and practice. Its presence can be observed in curricula emphasizing implications of political, scientific or environmental events on people and societies. It can be seen also in greater concern for subjective experience in place of exclusive attention to objective facts and detail. Concern for human relationships may also be observed in the movement from preoccupation with lectures, demonstrations and rote memory to dialogue, group discussion, cooperative exploration, inquiry learning, and the like.

Since much of education is carried on in groups, the literature and research on group dynamics and leadership has been helpful to educational professionals at all levels, offering insights, strategies and techniques for enhancing personal and interpersonal functioning and for avoiding approaches known to be detrimental to learning and performance (Benne & Muntyan, 1951; Eiben & Milliren, 1976; Glasser, 1969; Gordon, 1974; Hunter, 1972; Otto, 1970; Schmuck & Schmuck, 1979).

Applied to personnel questions humanistic thinking is increasingly found in analyses of the professional roles of teachers, administrators, counselors and supervisors — shifting from models emphasizing management and control to facilitation and guidance (e.g., Dreikurs & Cassel, 1972; Ginott, 1972; Gordon, 1974, 1988; Moustakas, 1966).

### Attacks on Humanistic Education

Many of the criticisms of humanistic education have been based on misunderstandings. The term "humanistic education" is often misunderstood by the general public (Goud, 1982; Welch, Medeiros & Tate, 1981). Some equate it with the 18th century philosophy of humanism which held that human beings ought not rely solely upon God to cope with their problems. Rather, they needed to use available knowledge to solve their problems. Fundamentalists interpreted it as a denial of God's will and strenuously objected to its applications in the public schools. They failed to understand the emphasis humanistic psychology gives to the significance of human experience — including the experiences persons might label as religious or spiritual in nature (Goud, 1982).

Popularized versions of humanistic perspectives tend to present a distorted picture what healthy growth, over-emphasizing personal autonomy and an orientation which might be characterized as self-centered (e.g., Adler with Wingert, Wright, Houston, Manly & Cohen, 1992; Lasch, 1979; Marin, 1975; Yankelovich, 1981). Such representations focus on particular aspects of humanistic writings to the exclusion of others and fail to acknowledge the significance of quality human interrelationships for optimal self-development, healthy growth, and a synergic society. Not all of the criticisms were so unfounded or misplaced. Some were justified. For example, ways in which humanistic educators missed opportunities for helping students develop their human potentials more optimally were addressed in Hart (1970). On occasion the balance tipped too far in the affective direction, and educators lost sight of the broader mission of preparing whole persons to function effectively in a democratic and advanced technological society (Misiak & Sexton, 1973; Moustakas, 1972).

As initial, exploratory formulations of humanistically-oriented approaches to education reached a wider audience, were implemented and subsequently evaluated, revisions and/or clarifications of earlier statements emerged. In response to confusion and criticisms raised about *Summerhill* (Neill, 1960), for example, Neill (1966) wrote a follow-up book entitled *Freedom — Not License!* Language used to communicate Rogerian perspectives shifted from "non-directive" to "student-centered" to "person-centered." The latter term makes it clearest that the resources, capabilities and wisdom of *all* participants involved in the educational enterprise must be taken into account for humanistic education to occur. Humanistically-oriented teachers are not surrendering their authority or undermining their influence as educators, but are moving from a role as director/manager to a role as helper/facilitator. For years, experiential "reports of students and teachers seemed to indicate that more significant learning took place in" humanistically-oriented classrooms (Rogers, 1983, p. 2), but supportive research was limited or lacking (Houts & Serber, 1972; Rogers, 1983; Simpson with Gray, 1976,

p. 66). Aspy and Roebuck (1976), Rogers (1983) and others subsequently made helpful contributions with research studies demonstrating that humanistic practices did indeed produce more positive outcomes.

Authors brought together by Weller (1977) pointed out the value of foundational conceptualizations as well as limitations, lacks and excesses associated with the humanistic movement in education. Welch, Richards and Richards (1974) sought to provide practical, philosophical and theoretical support for those seeking a humanistic and person-centered approach to accountability. But, as Allender (1982, p. 99) pointed out, "there is no coordinated way to stop the occasional misuse of developing programs... the dangers of anti-intellectualism, techniques orientation, manipulation, freedom without responsibility, and preoccupation with self in the absence of sensitivity to others."

Efforts to humanize education have been most salutary when they have become an integral part of the learning experience, and less successful when they have been reduced to gimmicks or games peripheral to the substantive curriculum. They have been most successful when they have honored a sense of persons functioning as whole human beings who have capacities for feeling, performance, creativity and intellectual understanding (Caine & Caine, 1991).

## Prospects for the Future of Humanistic Education

Humanistic psychology has been of great value to humanistic education in providing scientific or theoretical corroboration for ideas derived from practice and observation, suggesting new ways to tackle long-standing problems, and providing new assumptions for the design and introduction of much-needed innovation. Some of the more significant areas in which humanistic psychology has influenced education may be found in the following:

1. Growth of school counseling as a necessary service to students and teachers.
2. Increased understanding of the importance of student self concepts upon learning and growth and consequent inclusion of positive self concepts among the goals of education.
3. Recognition of the limitations of lecture/recitation as primary means of teaching and growing appreciation of the teacher's role as facilitator/helper rather than director/manager.
4. Increased recognition of the need for empathic approaches to students and teaching demonstrated by the search for caring

faculties and inclusion of students in all aspects of decision-making processes.
5. Attempts to make schools more pleasant, inviting places for consumers and to develop warmer, more personal relationships among teachers and students.
6. Acknowledgment of the uniqueness and diversity of human beings, providing greater support for individualized instruction and multicultural education.

Yet individuals and groups monitoring the condition of education in this country have emphasized ways in which this foundational aspect of our form of government has been failing or could more effectively fulfill its mission in our society [e.g., Alexander, 1991; Carnegie Task Force on Teaching as a Profession, 1986; Holmes Group, 1986; National Commission on Excellence in Education [NCOEE] 1983; Study Group on the Conditions of Excellence in American Education (1984)]. We have arrived at a place in our history where a national commission describes us as "A Nation at Risk" (NCOEE, 1983), a text examining the preparation of public school teachers is entitled *Ed School Follies. The Miseducation of American Teachers* (Kramer, 1991).

DeCarvahlo (1991) suggests that education in the U.S. may continue to deteriorate if it fails "to introduce a more humanistic dimension to teaching and learning" (p. 101). In the main, our present schools are the products of objective-behaviorist thinking no longer adequate for today's students or for society's pressing demands (Miller, 1990; Combs, 1991). The problems and "crises of our contemporary society... all call for an understanding by human beings of each other at a considerably higher level than ever before" (Bakan, 1965, p. 190). Humanistic psychology has done its part in providing these understandings and humanistic educators have done their part in articulating the implications of these understandings for educational purposes, processes and practices. The humanistic movement in education "is the product of and is supported by... massive data from the biological and the social sciences" (Combs, 1988, p. 103). Its contributions are here to stay.

Yet the tide has not turned. The educational establishment is extraordinarily resistant to change and to the incorporation of new ideas in psychological thought. This may in part be attributable to the distribution of power in relationships such as those between and among teachers, academic and other research and development personnel, district administrators, and the communities in which they work (Simpson with Gray, 1976, pp. 66-67).

Recent findings of neuroscientists about the functioning of the human brain [the implications of which for education are spelled out so capably by Caine & Caine (1991)] provide strong support for the perspectives which humanistic psychologists and humanistic educators have discovered and promoted over the past several decades. Such findings make it clear that "focusing on feelings without regard to performance, creativity, and intellectual understanding is inefficient and as cumbersome from the point of view of the brain as ignoring the emotional impact of the learning experience" (Caine & Caine, 1991, pp. 127-128). Presenting these findings as having implications for "brain-based education," as Caine and Caine (1991) do, may enable educators and the general public to by-pass resistance associated with the term "humanistic" while moving us, slowly but surely, in the directions advocated by the literature in humanistic psychology and education.

Bakan (1965) offers further insights into the slow pace of change. As he explains, breakthroughs in the thinking of physical scientists (as regarding heat, electricity, etc.) impact on society in the form of processes, equipment and devices which most of us can utilize without understanding what the scientist knows. Physical scientists are thus able to turn their knowledge into use without teaching us what they know. The situation is different in the social sciences where "the value of understanding of human functioning *does not inhere in its application in the usual sense, but in its possession*" (Bakan, 1965, p. 191).

When problems in education are seen as things we can tinker with outside ourselves, as methods, techniques, which can be operationally defined in behavioral-objective format, we may believe we are following in the footsteps of the pioneers in the sciences. Changes in education resting on a humanistic base, however, are dependent upon changes in people's understandings, belief systems and worlds of experience, as well as changes in the nature and quality of their relationships with significant others. These sorts of changes come slowly, as a consequence of people discovering the personal meaning of the ideas discussed in this article; as a consequence of changes in the hearts, minds, relationships, and experiences of those involved in the educational enterprise. They cannot come about through some sort of "quick fix" which brings about change easily and with little effort (Leonard, 1991). The path to long-lasting and meaningful change, the path Leonard (1991) calls the path of "mastery," is a much longer one, but therein lies the key to success and long-term fulfillment. Therein also lies the challenge we face as humanistic psychologists and humanistic educators.

## References

Adler, J., with Wingert, P., Wright, L., Houston, P., Manly, H., & Cohen, A. D. (1992, February 17). Hey, I'm terrific! *Newsweek*, 46-51.

Alexander, L. (1991). *America 2000. An education strategy*. Washington, DC: U.S. Department of Education.

Allender, J. S. (1982). Affective education. In H.E. Mitzel (Ed.), *Encyclopedia of educational research* (5th ed.) (pp. 94-103). New York: Free Press.

Allport, G. W. (1955). *Becoming*. New Haven: Yale University Press.

Ames, A. (1955). *An interpretative manual: The nature of our perceptions, prehensions and behavior*. Princeton: Princeton University Press.

Angyal, A. (1941). *Foundations for a science of personality*. New York: Commonwealth Fund.

Aspy, D. N. (1972). *Toward a technology for humanizing education*. Champaign, IL: Research Press.

Aspy, D. N., & Roebuck, F. N. (1976). *A lever long enough*. Dallas, TX: The National Consortium for Humanizing Education.

Association for Supervision and Curriculum Development. [ASCD]. (1962). *Perceiving, behaving, becoming. A new focus for education*. Washington, DC: ASCD.

Bakan, D. (1965). The mystery-mastery complex in contemporary psychology. *The American Psychologist, 20*, 186-191.

Benne, K. D., & Muntyan, B. (1951). *Human relations in curriculum change*. New York: Dryden Press.

Bestor, A. (1985). *Educational wastelands* (2nd ed.). Urbana, IL: University of Illinois Press. (Original work published 1953).

Brown, G. I. (1971). *Human teaching for human learning*. New York: Viking.

Bugental, J. F. T. (1965). *The search for authenticity. An existential-analytic approach to psychotherapy*. New York: Holt, Rinehart and Winston.

Buhler, C. (1959). Theoretical observations about life's basic tendencies. *American Journal of Psychotherapy, 13*, 561-581.

Caine, R. N., & Caine, G. (1991). *Making connections. Teaching and the human brain*. Alexandria, VA: Association for Supervision and Curriculum Development.

Canfield, J., & Wells, H. C. (1976). *100 ways to enhance self concept in the classroom*. Englewood Cliffs, NJ: Prentice-Hall.

Cantril, H. (1957). Perception and interpersonal relations. *American Journal of Psychiatry, 114*, 119-126.

Carnegie Task Force on Teaching as a Profession. (1986). *A nation prepared: Teachers for the 21st century*. New York: Carnegie Forum on Education and the Economy.

Coles, R., & Bullard S. (1992, Spring). Interview. Celebrate values! *Teaching Tolerance, 1* (1), 18-22.

Combs, A. W. (1982). *A personal approach to teaching.* Boston: Allyn and Bacon.
Combs, A. W. (1986). What makes a good helper? A person-centered approach. *Person-Centered Review, 1,* 51-61.
Combs, A. W. (1988). Is there a future for humanistic or person-centered education? *Person-Centered Review, 3,* 96-103.
Combs, A. W. (1991). *The schools we need.* Lanham, MD: University Press of America.
Combs, A. W., & Avila, D. L. (1985). *Helping relationships.* Boston: Allyn and Bacon.
DeCarvahlo, R.J. (1991). The humanistic paradigm in education. *The Humanistic Psychologist, 19,* 88-104.
Dewey, J. (1916). *Democracy and education.* New York: Macmillan.
Dewey, J. (1938). *Experience and education.* New York: Collier.
Dreikurs, R., & Cassel, P. (1972). *Discipline without tears* (rev. ed.). New York: Hawthorn.
Eiben, R., & Milliren, A. (1976). *Educational change: A humanistic approach.* La Jolla, CA: University Associates.
Fairfield, R. P. (1977). *Person-centered graduate education.* Buffalo: Prometheus Books.
Farson, R. (1974). *Birthrights.* New York: Macmillan.
Frankl, V. E. (1959). *Man's search for meaning. An introduction to logotherapy.* Boston: Beacon Press.
Gibb, J. R., and Gibb, L. M. (1957). Humanistic elements in group growth. In J. F. T. Bugental (Ed.), *Challenges of humanistic psychology* (pp. 160-170). New York: McGraw Hill.
Ginott, H. G. (1972). *Teacher and child.* New York: Macmillan.
Glasser, W. (1969). *Schools without failure.* New York: Harper & Row.
Goble, F. G. (1970). *The third force. The psychology of Abraham Maslow.* New York: Grossman.
Gordon, T. (1955). *Group-centered leadership.* Boston: Houghon Mifflin.
Gordon, T. (1974). *Teacher effectiveness training.* New York: Wyden.
Gordon, T. (1988). The case against disciplining children at home or in school. *Person-Centered Review, 3,* 59-85.
Goud, N. (1982). Type I and type II humanists. *The Journal of Humanistic Education and Development, 20,* 9-17.
Hart, H. H. (Ed.). (1970). *Summerhill: For & against.* New York: Hart.
Hayakawa, S. I. (1939). *Language in thought and action.* New York: Harcourt Brace and World.
Holmes Group. (1986). *Tomorrow's teachers: A report of the Holmes group.* East Lansing, MI: Holmes Group.
Horney, K. (1942). *Self-Analysis.* New York: Norton & Co.
Horney, K. (1950). *Neurosis and human growth.* New York: Norton.

Houts, P. S., & Serber, M. (Eds.). (1972). *After the turn on, what? Learning perspectives on humanistic groups.* Champaign, IL: Research Press.

Hunt, M. (1991). *The compassionate beast.* New York: Doubleday.

Hunter, E. (1972). *Encounters in the classroom.* New York: Holt, Rinehart and Winston.

Ittelson, W. H., & Ames, A., Jr. (1968). *The Ames demonstrations in perception.* Darien, CT: Hafner.

Ittelson, W. H., & Cantril, H. (1954). *Perception: A transactional approach.* New York: Random House.

Jersild, A. T. (1942). *In search of self.* New York: Teachers College Press.

Jersild, A.T. (1955). *When teachers face themselves.* New York: Teachers College Press.

Johnson, W. (1946). *People in quandaries. The semantics of personal adjustment.* New York: Harper.

Jones, R. M. (1968). *Fantasy and feeling in education.* New York: New York University Press.

Jourard, S.M. (1958). *Personal adjustment: An approach through the study of healthy personality.* New York: Macmillan.

Jourard, S. M. (1964). *The transparent self.* Princeton, NJ: Van Nostrand.

Jourard, S. M. (1968). *Disclosing man to himself.* Princeton, NJ: Van Nostrand.

Jourard, S. M. (1974). *Healthy personality: An approach from the viewpoint of humanistic psychology.* New York: Macmillan.

Jourard, S. M. (1975). Marriage is for life. *Journal of Marriage and Family Counseling, 1,* 199-208.

Kramer, R. (1991). *Ed school follies. The miseducation of America's teachers.* New York: Free Press.

Lasch, C. (1979). *The culture of narcissism.* New York: Norton.

Lecky, P. (1945). *Self consistency. A theory of personality.* New York: Island Press. (Edited and interpreted by F.C. Thorne and reprinted in Hamden, CT: Shoestring, 1961)

Leonard, G. B. (1963, June 4). Are we cheating twenty million students? *Look, 27* (11), pp. 36-40, 42, 45, 48.

Leonard. G. B. (1968). *Education and ecstasy.* New York: Delacorte Press.

Leonard, G. B. (1987). *Education and ecstasy: And the great school reform hoax* (rev.ed.). Berkeley, CA: North Atlantic.

Leonard, G. B. (1991). *Mastery. The keys to success and long-term fulfillment.* New York: Dutton.

Lewin, K. (1935). *A dynamic theory of personality.* New York: McGraw Hill.

Lowry, R. J. [in cooperation with Bertha G. Maslow]. (1979). *The journals of A. H. Maslow* (vol. 1). Monterey, CA: Brooks/Cole.

Marin, P. (1975, October). The new narcissism. The trouble with the human potential movement. *Harper's, 251,* 45-50, 55-56.

Maslow, A. H. (1954). *Motivation and personality*. New York: Harper.
Maslow, A. H. (1962). Some basic propositions of a growth and self-actualization psychology. In Association for Supervision and Curriculum Development [ASCD]. *Perceiving, behaving, becoming* (pp. 34-49). Washington, DC: ASCD.
Maslow, A. H. (1968). Some educational implications of the humanistic psychologies. *Harvard Educational Review, 38*, 685-696.
May, R. (1953). *Man's search for himself*. New York: W.W. Norton.
Miller, R. (1990). Beyond reductionism: the emerging holistic paradigm in education. *The Humanistic Psychologist, 18*, 314-323.
Misiak, H., & Sexton, V. S. (1973). *Phenomenological, existential and humanistic psychologies. A historical survey*. New York: Grune & Stratton.
Moustakas, C. (Ed.). (1956). *The self. Explorations in personal growth*. New York: Harper & Row.
Moustakas, C. (1966). *The authentic teacher*. Cambridge, MA: Howard A. Doyle. (Revision of *The teacher and the child*, 1956).
Moustakas, C. (1968). *Individuality and encounter*. Cambridge, MA: Howard A. Doyle.
Moustakas, C. (1972). *Loneliness and love*. New York: Prentice-Hall.
Murphy, G. (1958). *Human potentialities*. New York: Basic Books.
National Commission on Excellence in Education [NCOEE]. (1983). *A nation at risk*. Washington, DC: Government Printing Office.
Neill, A. S. (1960). *Summerhill*. New York: Hart.
Neill, A. S. (1966). *Freedom — Not license!* New York: Hart.
Ornstein, R. E. (1972). *The psychology of consciousness*. New York: Viking.
Otto, H. A. (1970). *Group methods to actualize human potential*. Beverly Hills: Holistic.
Postman, N., & Weingartner, C. (1973). *The school book*. New York: Delacorte.
Purkey, W. W. (1978). *Inviting school success. A self-concept approach to teaching and learning*. Belmont, CA: Wadsworth.
Raimy, V. C. (1943). *The self concept as a factor in counseling and personality organization*. Unpublished doctoral dissertation, Ohio State, Columbus.
Raths, L. E., Harmin, M., & Simon, S. B. (1966). *Values and teaching*. Columbus: Merrill.
Roberts, T. B. (Ed.). (1975). *Four psychologies applied to education*. Cambridge, MA: Schenkman.
Rogers, C. R. (1939). *The clinical treatment of the problem child*. Boston: Houghton Mifflin.
Rogers, C. R. (1951). *Client-centered therapy*. Boston: Houghton Mifflin.
Rogers, C. R. (1957). The necessary and sufficient conditions of therapeutic personality change. *Journal of Consulting Psychology, 21*, 95-103.
Rogers, C. R. (1961). *On becoming a person*. Boston: Houghton Mifflin.

Rogers, C. R. (1969). *Freedom to learn. A view of what education might become.* Columbus, OH: Charles E. Merrill.
Rogers, C. R. (1977). *On personal power.* New York: Delacorte.
Rogers, C. R. (1983). *Freedom to learn for the 1980's.* Columbus: Charles E. Merrill.
Russell, R. (1981). *Report on effective psychotherapy: Legislative testimony.* New York: R.R. Latin Associates.
Samples, B., & Wohlford, B. (1973). *Opening. A primer for self actualization.* Menlo Park, CA: Addison-Wesley.
Schmuck, R. A., & Schmuck, P. A. (1979). *Group processes in the classroom* (3rd. ed.). Dubuque, IA: William C. Brown.
Shaffer, J. B. P. (1978). *Humanistic psychology.* Englewood Cliffs, NJ: Prentice-Hall.
Simpson, E. L., with Gray, M. A. (1976). *Humanistic education: An interpretation.* Cambridge, MA: Ballinger.
Snygg, D. (1941). The need for a phenomenological system of psychology. *Psychological Review, 48,* 404-424.
Snygg, D., & Combs, A. W. (1949). *Individual behavior.* New York: Harper & Brothers.
Study Group on the Conditions of Excellence in American Higher Education. (1984). *Involvement in learning. Realizing the potential of American higher education.* Washington, DC: U.S. Department of Education, National Institute of Education.
Tyrrell, R., McCarty, H., & Johns, F. (1977). *Growing pains in the classroom: A guide for teachers of early adolescents.* Reston, VA: Reston Publishers.
Weinstein, G., & Fantini, M. D. (Eds.). (1970). *Toward humanistic education: A curriculum of affect.* New York: Praeger.
Welch, I. D., Medeiros, D. C., & Tate, G. (1981). Education, religion and the new right. *Educational Leadership, 39,* 203-208.
Welch, I. D., Richards, F., & Richards, A. C. (1974). *Educational accountability: A humanistic perspective.* Ft. Collins, CO: Shields.
Weller, R. H. (Ed.). (1977). *Humanistic education. Visions and realities.* Berkeley, CA: McCutchan.
Yankelovich, D. (1981). *New rules. Searching for self-fulfillment in a world turned upside down.* New York: Random House.

# 20

# The Humanistic Core of Industrial/Organizational Psychology

*Fred Massarik*

The various sub-fields of psychology necessarily are, and always have been, influenced by cross-currents of intellectual and emotive pressure. Prior conceptual, even passionate confrontations between humanistic psychologists and Behaviorism, Positivism, and Psychoanalysis are well known. Further, of special significance in recent years, and of particular importance in this time of rapid technological change and socio-political transformation, is the encounter between humanistic and technocratic values. Yet, clear-cut definitions of such terms as "humanistic" or "technocratic" tend to be elusive, and one may argue with fair merit that there are upon the land identifiable Technocratic Humanists and Humanistic Technocrats. However, while polarities assuredly have their pit-falls, they still may prove helpful in highlighting key differences and central issues in psychology as the profession faces another hundred years and a new century.

In this context, this paper suggests that the sub-field of Industrial Organizational (I/O) Psychology broadly defined, including for present purposes Organizational Behavior (OB), has been importantly influenced by humanistic values. My belief is that the professional practice of psychology, when genuinely living up to its true aim of serving people, is at core humanistic, even when the training, research, and theories of the practitioners is not explicitly so. This influence of humanistic perspective is not across-the-board and, at any rate, is not to be taken for granted in the development of the field's future direction.

Let us begin with a consistently-acknowledged mile post, the recognized starting point of the "Human Relations in Industry" movement: the *Western Electric Studies* (see for example *Management and the Worker* (Roethlisberger & Dickson, 1943), descriptively sub-titled "An Account of a Research Program Conducted by the Western Electric Company, Hawthorne Works, Chicago").

Both basic reports and follow-up literature relating to this series of investigations, that had their inception circa 1927, are vast (Mayo, 1933; Roethlisberger, 1968; 1949). It is important to note that these proliferating and impactful inquiries were spawned in a corporate setting with a distinctly humanistic "going-in position"; the company's Industrial Relations Branch, as host and participant, based its activities on a set of principles known tongue-in-cheek as the "Ten Commandments" (Roethlisberger and Dickson, 1943, pp. 7-9) headed as follows:

I. To pay all employees adequately for services rendered;
II. To maintain reasonable hours of work and safe working conditions;
III. To provide continuous employment consistent with business conditions;
IV. To place employees in the kind of work best suited to their abilities;
V. To help each individual to progress in the Company's services;
VI. To aid employees in the time of need;
VII. To encourage thrift;
VIII. To cooperate in social, athletic and other recreational activities;
IX. To accord to each employee the right to discuss freely with executives any matters concerning his or her welfare or the company's interest;
X. To carry on the daily work in a spirit of friendliness.

Considered as a whole, humanistic values are implicit throughout this set of policies; it is not difficult to link some of them to such lower-level D-(deficiency) needs in Abraham Maslow's (1954) hierarchy as the physiological, safety, belonging, love, and self esteem, (i.e. I, II, III, VI, VII), while others (i.e. IV, V, VIII, IX, X) relate variously to higher-level B-(being) needs, encouraging development of and leaving the road open to personal growth and possible self-actualization, much prior to the coining of these now recited 'humanistic' terms.

Of course, all this happened long before the formulation of Humanistic Psychology as a discernible *contemporary* field; indeed humanistic values have their philosophic roots with the ancients. But the extent to which the Western Electric Studies were conceived and carried out in a context of humanistic value affirmation, points to the humanistic core in the evolution of I/O Psychology, and more directly of OB, at its modern inception.

Much of what was to follow in the I/O and OB field explicitly developed and dialogued with the emerging humanistic thought. The studies of morale, employee relations, on-the-job counseling, interviewing and in the analysis of internal organization structure, can be understood in the light of the mosaic of humanistic considerations that gave rise to the Western Electric Studies.

Beyond these beginnings, which date back to the late Twenties, and in decades thereafter focused on 'human factors in management' (Hoslett, 1946), the UCLA Human Relations Research Group, with a deliberately humanistic focus, began its work in the early Fifties (Tannenbaum, Weschler and Massarik, 1961). While aware of the Harvard/Western Electric effort, it was essentially nourished by diverse intellectual roots. These included, from the outset, the writings of Kurt Lewin, (Lewin, 1935; 1948; Leeper, 1943; Marrow, 1969) and initially an intellectual discipline associated with the University of Chicago approach to industrial relations. Further, this group's efforts involved collegial association with such humanistic 'founders' as Carl R. Rogers and Abraham H. Maslow. Its current work proceeds in a context of Human Systems Development (Tannenbaum, Margulies and Massarik, 1985), integrating various viewpoints in systems theory, clinical, phenomenological and social psychology (with its earlier 'HRRG' label no longer in use).

With selective focus, more needs to be said about the role of Kurt Lewin. While Lewin's name is not normally recited in the roster of humanistic founders, his impact on humanistic elements in I/O psychology is of continuing importance. His field-theoretic conceptions have influenced studies of behavior change in organizations, from individual to large system. His empirical work on groups, including seminal experiments with group atmospheres (Lewin, Lippitt and White, 1939) has widely affected humanistic viewpoints on decision-making, team building and small-group training. As a related conceptualization, influenced by Lewin, Douglas McGregor's *Theory X* and *Theory Y*, contrasting control-centered/non-trusting and participative/trusting management styles is well-known, far beyond academic boundaries (McGregor, 1960). Also noteworthy in this context is Rensis Likert's work on *New Patterns of Management* (Likert, 1961).

Gestalt pioneers, contemporary with and antedating Lewin, have likewise left their mark. Some of I/O psychology in its specific form and much of OB variously makes use of concepts affirming the integrity of Wholes (including whole *Systems*) and cautions against the dangers of examining (or trying to change) individuals or organizations on a piece-meal basis. The interrelatedness of parts (viz. sub-systems), and the need to understand such parts, however bounded, within context of the encompassing Whole, is well recognized. Early contributors such as Wolfgang Kohler (1929, 1969) and his contemporaries (Koffka, 1935; Wertheimer, 1950) have grounds for posthumous satisfaction as regards their contributions to humanistic aspects of I/O psychology of the 1990's.

In a very direct way, Abraham H. Maslow occupies a special place in the present framework. One aspect of his work is widely-known, indeed ubiquitous, in the OB literature: the motivation hierarchy (Maslow, 1954). Maslow did not initially intend any specific application to industrial or organizational subject matter in this connection, but such application turned out to be widespread. Maslow's theoretic position holds that human needs are generally (though not rigidly) hierarchic in their priorities and demands for satisfaction, ranging along a hypothetical 'ladder' or 'pyramid' somewhat in the order: physiological / safety / belonging or love / self-esteem / to self-actualization.

Maslow's ideas relating to these formulations date back to the late Thirties and Forties, prior to the establishment of the disciplines considered here. His interest was in a *general* theory of personality which, as matters developed, found particular resonance in the field of Organizational Behavior, including efforts in research follow-up (Huizinga, 1970).

A second aspect of Maslow's impact is of later origin and focused more directly on the subject matter of industry and organization. It is, however, less widely recognized than the first. In the summer of 1962, Maslow visited Southern California. He spent the time in a kind of open role as observer and as a learner at what would now be called a high-tech company, Non-Linear Systems, Del Mar, CA. He also linked variously with the then-current version of the UCLA Human Relations Research Group referred to earlier. From these activities resulted a mimeographed publication initially entitled *Summer Notes on Social Psychology of Industry and Management*, and later published as *Eupsychian Management* (1965).

As Warren G. Bennis (1985; 1989), still another important contributor to humanistic thought in the field, notes in a Foreword to this volume (Maslow, 1965): "(Maslow) bypasses conventional academic jargon...(and) approaches his material... with a powerful innocence that is both threatening and receptive to widely held beliefs." In this spirit, Maslow ranges across a vast panoply of topics including the attitude of self-actualizing people to duty, work (and) mission; management principles at different levels in the motivation hierarchy; self-esteem in the work situation; management as a psychological experiment; creativeness, the entrepreneur, existential psychology, profits, low grumbles, high grumbles and metagrumbles; and many others. To interpret all this, it is useful to understand the term *Eupsychian*: this might be written alternatively as *U-psychian*, in the sense of Utopian... addressing a kind of idealized psychological and management world.

Carl R. Rogers' influence on the humanistic in I/O psychology as well has been far-reaching. Particularly his approaches to client-centered therapy, e.g. see *Counseling and Psychotherapy* (1942), have affected directly, or have been infused indirectly into numerous styles of interviewing in industry and organizations, for the most eclectic purposes: employee counseling, selection and placement, exit interviews, assessment for promotion or reassignment, and the like. And his views of "the person" and associated concepts relating to people's capacity for growth, have left their mark on human resources/personnel policies, professional training and organizational development (Rogers, 1961; Evans, 1975; Kirschenbaum & Henderson, 1989).

A further word on groups. We have previously noted Lewin's central role in this connection. Through a series of transformations, NTL — the National Training Laboratories (erstwhile addition "for Group Development") grew from Lewin's original impetus. NTL's approach links substantially (though arguably with some exceptions) to humanistic values and continues currently in a considerable variety of small-group training formats, many of these serving managers, in profit and not-for-profit settings (Bradford, 1974; Benne et.al., 1975; Hirsch, 1987). In *Eupsychian Management*, Maslow reports on his experiences with unstructured (UCLA) training groups at Arrowhead, CA., and Rogers entered the small-group training field in the Sixties and early Seventies, with the "encounter group" approach, in 1970. At UCLA, with an explicit emphasis on humanistic values and associated facilitation styles, the University Extension Ojai Leadership and Organization Development Laboratories offer an average of 20-25 groups annually, for middle and upper level managers and others. This program has had a continuous 'run' of more than forty years (Weschler & Reisel, 1960).

In the application of I/O psychology and human resources, again without explicit label, some humanistic 'ways of doing things' are finding increasing acceptance. An example is "outplacement". This procedure involves 'best effort' by an employer (typically with outside help) to place an employee who had been separated from the organization, often in process of 'downsizing' or for other non-derogatory reasons, on a new job. Here we find evidence of shared responsibility by employer and (ex-)employee to aspire a professionally and personally growthful state of affairs for the employee, on a choiceful basis, with at least nominal and often deeper commitment and mutual trust to 'make it happen.'

Another set of procedures, with a long history and varied results, drawing on implicit or explicit humanistic considerations, relates to 'participation in decision-making' and to aspects of 'democracy' (however defined) in organization as a subject of experiment and experience in a plethora of settings (Massarik, 1983).

More topics over the many years, their sources and contributors, might be examined (e.g. Argyris, 1953, 1957; Schein & Bennis, 1965). A thorough consideration of the humanistic core of industrial/organizational psychology should occupy a long essay or small monograph. Here I've made a brief effort only to identify a few highlights, focusing on the field's contemporary beginnings and major visible humanistic contributors, with a tilt toward the organizational behavior aspects of the inevitable disciplinary melange. Disciplinary boundaries necessarily remain fuzzy, and so they probably should remain.

Time boundaries, too, are an issue. In Freud's journal *Imago* (1924) there are references to the direct application of psycho-analytic principles to 'business and commerce,' with nuances that might well be regarded as humanistic. And I/O psychology has precursors surely going back at least to the turn of the past century.

What *is* of importance, as I see it, is building on an evolving humanistic core toward on-going future-oriented development of an industrial/organizational psychology that, more than ever, responds to, seeks to understand and cares about the *whole* human being, not paying attention simply to isolated, even technics-perfect fragments. It is always the *whole* person who comes to work and who goes home, not a test score, not an optimum posture at the computer screen, not even a specified desired procedure in the latest Total Quality enhancement program. The full range of human experience matters, and yes, this *is* a value judgment. More needs to be done, by psychologists and others, to avoid becoming overly technocratic, recovering in stead the truly and fundamentally human in the widening scope of a changing industrial and organizational psychology.

## References

Argyris, C. (1953). *Personality fundamentals for administrators*. New Haven, CT: Labor and Management Center, Yale.

Argyris, C. (1957). *Personality and organization*. New York: Harper.

Benne, K. D.; Bradford, L.P.; Gibb, J. R. Lippitt, R. O. (eds) (1975). *The laboratory method of changing and learning*. Palo Alto, CA: Science and Behavior Books.

Bennis, W., Nanus, B. (1985). *Leaders - the strategies for taking charge*. New York: Harper & Row.

Bennis, W. (1989). *On becoming a leader*. Reading, MA: Addison-Wesley.

Bradford, L. P. (1974). *National Training Laboratories - its history: 1947-1970*. Bethel, MN: Leland P. Bradford.

DeCarvalho, R. J. (1991). *The founders of humanistic psychology*. New York: Praeger.

Evans, R. I. (1975). *Carl Rogers - the man and his ideas*. New York: Dutton.

Giese, F. (1924). "Psychoanalytische Psychotechnik" (Psychoanalytic Psychotechnology), in *IMAGO*, x. 93-132.

Hirsch, J. I. (1987). *The history of the National Training Laboratories 1947-1986*. New York: Peter Lang.

Hoslett, S. D. (ed.), (1947). *Human factors in management*. New York: Harper.

Huizinga, G. (1970). *Maslow's need hierarchy in the work situation*. Groningen, Netherlands: Wolters - Noordhoff.

Kirschenbaum, H. G. Henderson, V. L. (eds). (1989). *The Carl Rogers reader*. Boston: Houghton Mifflin.

Koffka, K. (1935). *Principles of Gestalt psychology*. New York: Harcourt, Brace.

Kohler, W. (1929). *Gestalt psychology*. New York: Horace Liveright.

Kohler, W. (1969). *The task of Gestalt psychology*. Princeton, NJ: Princeton University Press.

Leeper, R. W. (1943). *Lewin's topological and vector psychology*. Eugene: University of Oregon.

Lewin, K., Lippitt, R., & White, R. K. (1939). Patterns of aggressive behavior in experimentally created "social climates." *Journal of Social Psychology*, X, 271-299.

Lewin, K. (1948). *Resolving social conflict*. New York: Harper.

Likert, R. (1961). *New patterns of management*. New York: McGraw-Hill.

Marrow, A. J. (1969). *The practical theorist — The life and work of Kurt Lewin*. New York: Basic Books.

Maslow, A. H. (1954). *Motivaiton and personality*. New York: Harper & Row.
Maslow, A. H. (1965). *Eupsychian management*. Homewood, IL: Irwin/Dorsey.
Massarik, F. (1983). *Participative management*. New York: Pergamon Press.
Mayo, E. (1933). *The human problems of an industrial civilization*. New York: Macmillan.
McGregor, D. (1960). *The human side of enterprise*. New York: McGraw-Hill.
Roethlisberger, F. J. & Dickson, W. J. (1943). *Management and the worker*. Cambridge: Harvard University Press.
Roethlisberger, F. J. (1949). *Management and morale*. Cambridge: Harvard University Press.
Roethlisberger, F. J. (1968). *Man-in-organization*. Cambridge: Belknap Press of Harvard University Press.
Rogers, C. R. (1942). *Counseling and psychotherapy*. Boston: Houghton-Mifflin.
Rogers, C. R. (1961). *On becoming a person*. Boston: Houghton-Mifflin.
Rogers, C. R. (1970). *Carl Rogers on encounter groups*. New York: Harper & Row.
Schein, E. H. & Bennis, W. G. (Eds.). (1965). *Personal and organizational change through group methods: The laboratory approach*. New York: Wiley.
Tannenbaum, R., Margulies, N., & Massarik, F. (1985). *Human systems development*. San Francisco: Jossey-Bass.
Tannenbaum, R., Weschler, I. R., & Massarik, F. (1961). *Leadership and organization*. New York: McGraw-Hill.
Wertheimer, M. (1950). Gestalt therapy. In W. Ellis (Ed.), *A source book of Gestalt psychology*. New York: Humanities Press.
Weschler, I. R. & Reisel, J. (1960). *Inside a sensitivity training group*. Los Angeles: Institute of Industrial Relations, UCLA.
Wexley, K. N. & Yuki, G. A. (Eds.). (1975). *Organizational behavior and industrial psychology*. New York: Oxford University Press.

# 21

# Humanistic Psychological Centers for Scholarship and Personal Growth

### Humanistic Psychology Archive
*David Russell*

In 1986, the sponsorship of the University of California at Santa Barbara and the Association for Humanistic Psychology gave birth to the Humanistic Psychology Archive. Housed in the Special Collections Department of UCSB, the purpose of this international archive is to acquire, organize, preserve, and make available to researchers primary sources, especially the papers and libraries of those who pioneered the development of humanistic psychology. The archive is inclusive, containing materials on the philosophical and psychological antecedents of humanistic psychology, and from individuals in private practice, centers, and academic institutions. The range of materials also extends to the artistic, literary, historical, and social aspects of humanistic psychology.

The archive is housed in the Special Collections Department of the UCSB Library, which provides spacious reading room, several seminar rooms, and smaller offices equipped with audiovisual equipment, microfilm readers, and a photocopy stand. Although the holdings are non-circulating, the department is accessible through interlibrary loan and can handle restricted materials from other lending institutions. Photocopying services are also available for researchers within the Department.

The archive contains over 3000 linear feet of books and manuscript materials from leading institutions and figures in the field. The Association for Humanistic Psychology Collection is the largest, containing 123 research boxes of manuscript materials related to administration, annual meetings, correspondence, regional council meetings, field activities, publicity, and other records from AHP chapter and regional offices, as well as one of the largest audio tape collections on Humanistic Psychology. Recorded at annual meetings of AHP, the tape collection includes presentations by such individuals as Rollo May, Fred Massarik, Stanley Grof, M. B. Smith, Stanley Krippner, Jacqueline Doyle, James Bugental, Carl Rogers, Virginia Satir, Michael Murphy, and Don Johnson.

The archive also has accumulated substantial collections of works by, and has received major commitments from such important individuals as Walter Anderson, James F.T. Bugental, George Brown, Joseph Campbell, Stanley Keleman, Rollo May, Clark Moustakas, Michael Murphy, Carl Rogers, Virginia Satir, Charlotte Selver, Bob Tennenbaum, and John Vasconcellos. The archive also has significant holdings of important organizations, such as the *California Task Force to Promote Self-Esteem, Personal and Social Responsibility, Center for the Studies of the Person, Esalen, the Journal of Humanistic Psychology, the Journal of Transpersonal Psychology, AHP Perspective, UCSB Graduate Program in Confluent Education*, and the *Western Training Lab.*

The Oral History Project represents the first step in a continuing program to generate primary materials. In addition to the usual text, bibliography, and name index, each of these bound volumes includes a photograph of the subject, a history of the interview process, and a three page introduction written by a person selected by the subject. The final interview, which looks to the future, is videotaped. The Oral History Office also received tape collections of Walter Anderson, including interviews with Dick Price, and the recorded proceedings of the 1962 Sonoma State College Conference on Existential Psychology and Psychotherapy, featuring Rogers, Maslow, and May in the same workshop.

The HPA, which welcomes donations of materials relevant to the field, including personal or institutional papers, correspondence, manuscripts, memoranda, minutes of meetings, as well as audio and video tapes, provides a central repository that is secure and available to researchers. It offers the opportunity to preserve a detailed account of the past for future generations of scholars in this field of thought.

## Simon Silverman Phenomenology Center

*Richard Rojcewicz*

The goal of Duquesne University's Simon Silverman Phenomenology Center is to build and make available to scholars the most comprehensive possible collection of literature in Phenomenology and to actively promote original phenomenological work to be added to the corpus acquisitions.

The Silverman Center, established in 1980, was largely the brainchild of Amedeo Giorgi, at that time a professor of psychology at Duquesne and a foremost exponent of phenomenological psychology. The name of the Center honors the late president of Humanities Press, who was the Center's main benefactor.

The Silverman Center is located in the library of Duquesne University and the materials of the Center are housed in a handsome room in the special collections area. The Center conceives of Phenomenology in a broad sense, not limited to any one discipline. Yet by phenomenology is meant specifically movement founded by the German philosopher Edmund Husserl (1859-1938). The holdings of the center are equally comprehensive in phenomenological philosophy and psychology, reflecting that long-standing orientation of the philosophy and psychology departments of Duquesne University.

The collections of the Center include:

A) Published material. The Silverman Center attempts to obtain every book published in any language on the topic of phenomenology. The holdings at present include nearly every book dealing with phenomenology published within the last twenty-five years and a great deal of the older literature as well. An active effort is made to acquire even the most obscure works.

In addition to the volumes that fit directly within the domain of phenomenology, the Center has also built up a comprehensive collection of works by and about two of the precursors of Phenomenology, Kierkegaard and Nietzsche. Furthermore, the Center has acquired an extensive collection in Gestalt psychology, including copies of the unpublished papers of Max Wertheimer.

B) Periodical literature. The Center subscribes to and has obtained full back-lists of 22 journals: *Philosophy and Phenomenological Research, Journal of Existentialism, Research in Phenomenology, Journal of Phenomenological Psychology, Phenomenology and Pedagogy, Journal of the British Society for Phenomenology, Man and World, Philosophy Today, Husserl Studies, Heidegger Studies, Human Studies, Review of Existential Psychology and Psychiatry, Etudes Phenomenologiques, Tijdschrift voor Filosofie, Humanitas, The Humanistic Psychologist, Methods, Phenomenological Inquiry, Reflections: Essays in Phenomenology, Daseinsanalyse, The Human Context, and Phanomenologische Forschungen.* In addition, the Center has an indexed collection of approximately 3,000 off-prints, most donated by the authors.

C) Alcoves. The Center actively seeks and provides special space for the personal libraries and papers of distinguished phenomenologists, retired or deceased, who wish to bequeath their collections. These libraries are kept intact and treated as archival treasures. The Center has established the Alcoves of Erwin Straus, Aron Gurwitsch, and Stephan Strasser. The Jan Bouman and the Charles Maes collections have been established.

D) Special collections.

1) The Husserl Archives. The Silverman Center is an officially recognized branch of the Husserl Archives of the Catholic University of Leuven, Belgium. The Center is one of only five such branches in the world, places where the directors of the Husserl Archives have deposited copies of the unpublished papers of the founder of the phenomenological movement, to make them more easily accessible. These branch includes the entirety of the transcribed papers of Husserl, i.e., the fraction (approximately 30,000 pages) of Husserl's posthumous work that has been transcribed into longhand German from Husserl's Gabelsberger stenography.

2) Heidegger lecture transcripts. The Center possesses copies of the "Moser transcripts" of the lectures of Heidegger at Marburg in the 1920's.

3) Unpublished papers of Buytendijk. The *Pensees Repensees*, the posthumous papers of F.J.J. Buytendijk of the Utrecht School of phenomenological psychology, are available at the Center. These are handwritten manuscripts in the Dutch language.

4) Lacan. The Silverman Center has obtained unpublished English translations of the entirety of four of Lacan's seminars (unpublished in French as well and available only in typescript): Seminar III (Psychoses), V (The unconscious), VI (Desire), VIII (Transference), and the essay on Family Complexes.

The Silverman Center was never meant to be merely a "dead" repository of books and materials. The Center desires to promote the advancement of phenomenology by sponsoring original scholarship. The first of these "live" functions was the annual Symposium. These conferences take place during the first week of March each year and bring together four scholars for two days to present papers and debate a specific issue. The conferences alternate between a more philosophical topic and a more psychological one. The eleventh annual symposium will be held in 1993, on the topic of the phenomenological approach to feminism. The Silverman Center has also begun a project of publication, beginning with the proceedings of the annual symposia. These proceedings are all available for sale, as is a book of essays by and about Stephan Strasser, "Clefts in the World."

The Center occasionally brings visiting lecturers to the Duquesne campus and hopes eventually to be able to support visiting scholars using the resources of the Center. The staff of the Silverman Center is more than willing to cooperate with scholars seeking travel grants from scholarly foundations. The Center welcomes donations of books, offprints, dissertations, or larger collections, and encourages inquiries concerning its research materials and programs.

### Center for Studies of the Person
*William Stillwell*

The Center for Studies of the Person (CSP) was born in a weekend simulation. The 1968 staff of a California behavioral sciences organization experimentally grouped themselves into two units. A first group primarily wished to follow socially constructive research directions, and the other was composed of those people more concerned with the direct application of their knowledge to ongoing circumstances.

This second group found the simulation so enlivening that it formed into independent CPS. They were those two dozen educators, psychologists, consultants, and religious leaders most involved learning in and leading the group encounter work that Carl Rogers was initiating at the time. They determined to create a professional community aimed at actualizing human potential. They wished to live in the freedom, exploration, and support mode all had experienced in their encounter group work.

Members were particularly eager to work in an organization that expressed few constraints on their individual professional and personal efforts. CSP became a "psychological community". Members approached each other from personal motivation rather than organizational role. This opposition between self and organization has continued to keep felt community (or lack of it) at the center of our mutuality. Projects undertaken by individuals or groups under the banner of CSP were honed and approved by all members in a "person centered" process of face-to-face encounter. The not-for-profit organization was managed democratically and funded by membership dues and generosity, a few grants, and considerable market success. A number of highly respected members dropped their other organizational affiliations.

In retrospect, some of the excitement I experienced as an early member of CSP appears naive. We had our eyes on what Carl Rogers had termed "the person of the future;" we were forming the "organization of the future." In those early years, the international social environment buoyed our excitement. "Revolution" was a term easily bandied about. We followed Carl Rogers as "quiet revolutionaries." The demand was high for our kind of services in facilitating the humanistic revolution in other folks.

And the power of these ideas in nowhere near spent. Several hundred former members sustain their versions of the work in new situations. Some original founders continue their CSP membership today, and new members, visiting scholars, students, and clients continue to reinforce our convictions and create new applications. The teachings and methods of Carl Rogers and his colleagues flow significantly in the experiences and discoveries of people exploring self-awareness and deep interpersonal relationships.

Today the CSP community is less intensely a part of the everyday life of its members, and a tiny bit more organizational constraint has emerged concerning members' projects. Waves and waves of new thought and experience — feminist, deconstructionist, professionalization, movements of men, multiculturalities, spiritualities, and peace-seekings among them — have crashed through our cultural beachheads during this past quarter century. Each of these has impacted the conversations held and services offered at CSP. I find us now less on the cutting edge of any wave and still deeply radical in our approaches to personal and organizational life.

In the last twenty five years, a wide variety of ideas and experiences have been given birth and brought to fruition at CSP. Some have been published as articles, books, and videos. Perhaps more important are the wildly thoughtful, innovative application projects. CSP experimental groups for the most part have been started on financial shoestrings, but they have involved and impacted thousands of client participants for the rest of their lives. Most of these projects are no longer offered — if vivacity cannot be sustained, an effort is allowed to pass away — surely a new life will bloom again.

Unique projects extending the Person Centered Approaches continue: The La Jolla Program emphasizes personal encounter and group leadership training; Living Now and the Carl Rogers Peace Project aid citizens in pursuing their own social action; The Carl Rogers Institute for

Psychotherapy and Training provides training and internships in multicultural settings.

Except for the library of Carl Rogers and his colleague's work, CSP does not function as a major institution. Some members and their friends find this disappointing. Each member gains his or her economic support outside CSP. Yet CSP persists even at the expense of its institutional self, so that individuals might here find their personal power, and not be misled in their searchings to cling to the power of any organization.

Rogers helped found CSP during the later years of his life. His work then was taking a wider and more philosophical perspective. He lived a personal, uniquely powerful way in facilitating one's self-knowledge, creativity, leadership, and citizenship. He attracted people on their own search for a supportive way, people who preferred to work in collegial groups at common approaches.

Some of what he could do has been abstracted and reintegrated by others. Mostly we have learned from him that we could inspire our own unique experience in life. CSP members are followers less, perhaps, of Rogers' specific practices, than followers each of his or her own way. They trust their organic experiences in their social relationships. They endeavor so that others may develop and enhance similar abilities.

## Esalen Institute and the Growth of the Growth Movement

### Walter Truett Anderson

The Esalen Institute and the other "growth centers" that appeared on the American (and European) scene during the 1960's and 1970's were closely linked to the humanistic psychology movement that emerged at about the same time — closely linked, but the two were not precisely the same and the relationship between them was not always harmonious.

Both the closeness and the difficulties were evident in the relationship between Abraham Maslow, who probably did more than any other single person to organize humanistic psychology into a recognizeable movement, and Esalen. Maslow wandered into Big Sur Hot Springs one night in 1962, looking for a place to stop over for the night, and found that the little California coastal resort was in the process of transforming itself into the Esalen Institute, a seminar center for the study of new trends in psychology and religion. The people there had read Maslow's books and welcomed him warmly. He soon became one of Esalen's many friends and champions; he led seminars there and praised it enthusiastically to his professional colleagues.

Maslow had some peak experiences at Esalen, but he also had some difficult ones — most notably the celebrated weekend of the "language of being" conference, when he assembled a group of psychologists and thinkers to address some lofty questions concerning self-actualization, and the meeting degenerated into a ludicrous confrontation between Maslow and Fritz Perls, the capricious founder of gestalt therapy. Maslow lectured Esalen about maintaining its intellectual responsibility, and Fritz called him a sugar-coated fascist.

Esalen in the 1960's was a place where a lot of things happened. At one time or another, most of the major figures involved in the humanistic psychology movement — such as Maslow, Rollo May, Carl Rogers, and James Bugental — led seminars at Esalen. So did other thinkers from various fields: Arnold Toynbee, Paul Tillich, Gregory Bateson, Alan Watts, Paul Tillich. When Esalen was first getting started, in the early 1960's, its programs were mostly weekend gatherings — beginning on a Friday evening after dinner, continuing through Sunday lunch — and the format was fairly staid: the seminar leader talked, and the guests, seated in chairs arranged lecture-hall style in the dining room, sat and listened. Sometimes, to vary the program, there were poetry readings or small concerts of classical music.

This was what Esalen's co-founders, Michael Murphy and Richard Price, called its "Apollonian period." The rapid move into the Dionysian period coincided with a shift to "experiential" programs that included some kind of "activity," such as a demonstration of gestalt therapy or an encounter group, and with the appearance of psychedelic drugs — which were officially forbidden at Esalen but were very much a part of what went on there. The arts were still part of the program, but the flavor was increasingly more counter-culture than culture. For several years, Joan Baez held a folk music festival that brought in major figures from the folk and rock scene — even, on one occasion, a couple of Beatles.

As Esalen changed, imitators proliferated. Soon there were growth centers all over the U. S. and Europe. None of them had geographic sites quite as attractive as the spectacularly beautiful coastal shelf that held Esalen, but some were located in or near major cities — such as Chicago, Los Angeles, New York City and Washington, D.C. — and many of their programs were well-attended. Collectively, the growth centers became a sort of Chataqua circuit for human potential program leaders. Some of the star performers on this circuit were psychologists, but many — such as Bernie Gunther, a masseur and yoga teacher who had developed a repertoire of "sensory awareness" exercises — were not. Like Esalen, the larger growth centers developed residential programs and trained encounter group leaders.

These developments caused some friction between humanistic psychology and other schools of therapy, since many conventional therapists felt threatened by the increasing popularity of nonlicensed practitioners associated with humanistic psychology and the human potential movement. The growth of the growth centers also caused some friction within the humanistic psychology movement, since some of the humanistic psychologists were closely associated with the growth centers and others were increasingly apprehensive about the possible dangers of excessively exuberant group activities led by practitioners with little or no formal training.

After the rather rowdy 1968 convention of the Association for Humanistic Psychology, some members — including Rollo May, one of the movement's founders — threatened to resign from the association in protest against what they saw as increasing anti-intellectualism and immaturity, and which they tended to identify with the influence of the growth centers. At the next AHP meeting, in Silver Spring Maryland, president Floyd Matson organized a "gathering of the growth centers" for the specific purpose of placing them at some distance from the mainstream of the convention — a move that Esalen co-founder Michael Murphy strongly resented.

I would not say that these various conflicts were ever really resolved, any more than the other social conflicts that opened up in the 1960's were really resolved. Times moved on, things changed. Many of the people who had been participants in growth center programs became followers of est or found other activities. Eventually most (if not all) of the Esalen clones went out of business; the institutions surviving today that most resemble the growth centers are in the business of New Age spirituality, shamanism, and ecological consciousness.

The growth centers were sometimes described as "launching pads" for new ideas and techniques, and the term is a good one. Many of the things they launched went elsewhere. You cannot find an encounter group at Esalen today — they more or less outlawed the word there some years ago — but "marriage encounter" weekends sponsored by churches are a thriving part of life in middle America. You do not find much public excitement about the "touchy-feely" exercises popularized by Bernie Gunther and others, but my wife Maurica — who attended and led workshops with me at Esalen and other growth centers in the 1960's and 1970's, and who now works in addiction-recovery programs in hospitals

— tells me that many of those same exercises are now commonly (and quite effectively) used with groups of nervous addicts who never heard of humanistic psychology and know nothing about the excitements and conflicts of a quarter-century ago.

Esalen today is still lovely — in fact, after a few decades of building and landscaping, far more impressive than it was in the 1960's. Although it is no longer the place where you would go in search of cutting-edge ideas or practices, it is a thriving organization. Many of its clients come from outside the US, particularly Europe, and they come not only to participate in programs but with a sense of visiting a sort of historical shrine.

# 22

# The Presence of Humanistic Psychologists in the Academy

*Scott D. Churchill*

## The Presence of Humanistic Psychologists in the Academy

Prior to its formal inception in the late 1950's, humanistic psychology had a presence in the academy as far back as the turn of the century in the spirit of the work of William James and G. Stanley Hall. A similar orientation would later be found in the holistic approach to personality theory adopted by university-based research psychologists such as Gordon Allport (1937) and Henry Murray (1938), as well as Kurt Goldstein (1939, 1940) who had immigrated from Europe. Soon thereafter, Carl Rogers (1942) and Abraham Maslow (1943) began publishing their foundational statements of humanistic theory and practice, even though they did not formally describe themselves as "humanistic" at this time. These and other American psychologists sharing an orientation toward non-reductionistic research and theory-building found themselves drawn to an already existing philosophical literature of European origin as a way of both grounding their critique of existing theories and inspiring their own development of a personalistic, "existential" psychology (May, 1960). By joining together under one name, the "humanistic psychology" movement served as a way of designating and thereby offering a kind of legitimacy to those who had found a sheltering place for their work.

## Humanistic Psychology's Changing Role within the Academy

### An Alternative to "Traditional" Psychology

The "third force" appears at first to have represented only an *alternative* to the dominant behaviorist and psychoanalytic traditions.

Psychologists associated with the movement were united by a common opinion: namely, that the traditionally defined "scientific" schools of psychology had lost sight of their human (i.e., emancipatory) interests and human (i.e., empathic) methods of addressing those interests, with regard to both research and therapy. Humanistic psychology was being perceived, from both inside and outside of the movement, as a kind of separate entity within the academy as a whole. The work of humanistic psychologists has often been dismissed by those in the ranks of experimental psychology as "soft" research because of its failure to provide operational definitions, an absence of quantification in its results, and its lack of interest in the technological goals of prediction and control. It was also sometimes disdained for its association with the Sixties counterculture, which resulted in its being branded as a "protest movement" (M. B. Smith, 1982; Giorgi, 1987). By its very nature as a counter-movement serving to offset the dominating paradigm within a discipline in its pre-paradigmatic stage of development (Kuhn, 1962), humanistic psychology has been kept safely at bay by mainstream psychologists and has not received recognition for having the value and credibility that its adherents have believed it to possess.

*A Complement Within an Eclectic Family of Approaches*

With the advent of the cognitive revolution, a new tradition of psychologists began to supplant the behaviorists' dominance within the academy; at the same time, psychologists started referring to their orientations in ways that allowed for differing paradigms to be merged into complementary associations, such as "cognitive-behaviorism," "social cognitive theory," and so on. Uncommitted to any one specific paradigm within academic psychology, some researchers and especially clinicians were apt to describe their approaches in these hybrid terms, and thus an eclectic climate was established in which humanistic psychologists could begin to settle into a more complementary role within the American scene. As such, albeit still a minority with respect to its number of advocates within the academy as a whole, the humanistic movement could be perceived as providing a balance (and not merely a protest) within the status quo in psychology.

*An Integrative and Complete Psychology*

From its very inception in the writings of Allport (1937), Murray (1938), Goldstein, (1940), Maslow (1943), May (1951, 1960), Van Kaam (1966), and others, humanistic psychologists within the academy have offered an integrative vision that could potentially provide a theoretical context for a synthesis of the fragmented field of psychological research into a unified theory of the human person. For instance, Maslow's (1943) outline of a "hierarchy of needs" allowed for conventionally defined "drives" and "instincts" to find their place within an organized motivational structure — not simply alongside, but structurally integrated with the more distinctively human "growth" motives revealed by Maslow's own research. Likewise, Rogers (1951) presented a theoretical conception of motivation wherein "physiological tensions" are not viewed as simple causes, but as perceived needs interpreted with reference to the individual's overarching orientation toward self-enhancement. He argued that it is the perceived meaning of one's bodily excitations, and not the excitation itself, that moves one toward action: "Behavior is basically the goal-directed attempt of the organism to satisfy its needs as experienced, in the field as perceived" (Rogers, 1951, p. 491). A similar integration of traditional theories of anxiety within a broader existential framework can be found in texts such as May's (1951).

Psychologists in the academy have also provided a conceptual framework for integrating not just subfields of research, but the field as a whole. Van Kaam's *Existential Foundations of Psychology* (1966) remains unsurpassed for its comprehensiveness in scope in addressing the question of the foundations of *all* psychology. Far from being simply a text on the foundations of an existential psychology, this text provides an existential context for situating virtually *all* of the diverse field of academic psychology. Van Kaam suggests that there is something both "differential" and "comprehensive" in the primordial structure of existence itself that makes possible the division of psychology into branches focusing upon specific content areas as well as more comprehensive understandings of the person. Thus, the "differential psychologies" (that is, areas such as perception, cognition, learning, and so on) are understood to exist in the academy as a kind of institutional expression of the individual's differential psychological capacities; and, just as the individual's differentiated perceptual apparatus is integrated by a central nervous system, so also the academy of psychology can integrate its differential research findings by means of a "comprehensive psychology" derived from the tradition of "understanding" (Dilthey, 1894/1977; Jaspers, 1913/1963) and "existential psychology" (May, 1960). Unfortunately, introductory psychology textbooks have not taken notice of Van Kaam's visionary work, notwithstanding the continual call (heard at APA Convention symposia in recent years) for a genuinely integrative (i.e., not merely eclectic) approach in the teaching of psychology.

More recently, with the ranks of existential, holistic, phenomenological, transpersonal, and human-science psychologists joining together within the APA under the ever broadening rubric of "Humanistic Psychology," the movement as a whole has begun to take on an even more research-oriented and integrative role, and has been strengthened by this consolidation. This has been in part the result of an entry into the APA's Division 32 of academic psychologists dissatisfied with the prevailing anti-intellectual qualities of humanistic psychology (during the Sixties and early Seventies). Publications over the past two decades by Barton (1974), C. T. Fischer (1985), W. F. Fischer (1970), Friedman (1984), Giorgi (1970, 1971), Knowles (1986), MacLeod (1975), Pollio (1982), Pribram (1981, 1986), Royce (1970), Strasser (1974), von Eckartsberg (1978, 1981), Wertz, (1982) and others have helped to fortify the movement by helping to provide it with the philosophical basis, intellectual rigor, and research orientation it has needed. As such, we can say that the work of humanistic psychologists in the academy today is helping to contextualize and thereby to integrate the research findings of academic psychology as a whole.

Humanistic psychologists have been drawing upon and assimilating, firmly situating themselves within the existing scientific and philosophical academies. In contrast, one finds traditional psychologists to be more monolithically oriented, unwilling or unable to incorporate the legitimate insights revealed in different lines of research. The late B. F. Skinner, for example, certainly recognized as "a" if not "the" leading voice in American psychology, adamantly refused to acknowledge humanistic psychology, psychotherapy, or even cognitive psychology as being anything but a diversion at best, or a pitfall at worst, on the "steep and thorny way to a science of behavior" (Skinner, 1975, 1987, 1990). Neuroscientists like Roger Sperry (1969, 1970, 1986, 1987), although addressing the subtler philosophical issues at stake in developing a theory of the mind, have proceeded in a way that has remained aloof to the parallel and even antecedent developments in phenomenological research that have addressed issues such as the integrative functioning of the human nervous system and the nature of the relationship between "body" and "mind" (Buytendijk, 1965/1974; Merleau-Ponty, 1942/1963; Straus, 1956/1963).

In general what is lacking in the field today is a successful effort to develop a metapsychology that could place into perspective the various content areas of psychology and thereby situate the relative contributions of differing research paradigms. At best we have the solution offered by psychology textbooks: an eclecticism that in essence says that the whole of psychology is the sum of its parts. It is perhaps the continued disinterest and ignorance on the part of mainstream psychologists with regard to the nature and the potential contributions of humanistic psychology that has prevented the former from entering into an integrative dialogue with the humanistic tradition. (One notable exception would be Willard Day's [1969, 1975] confrontation of behaviorism with phenomenology.) In part, this unyielding response from psychologists in the mainstream has led some within the humanistic movement to believe that, for the time being, there can only be a plurality of paradigms within a constellation of "psychological studies" (M. B. Smith, 1982). Giorgi and others in the "human-science" tradition, however, continue to hold to a belief in "the possibility of psychology as a coherent science" (Giorgi, 1987, p. 15). Echoing van Kaam (who in 1966 said that existential psychology was only a temporary movement and that as soon as psychology had assimilated the existential notion of perspectivity, there would be no further need for such a movement because psychology would then *be* existential), Giorgi has stated that if humanistic psychology were given its chance to influence the theory-building enterprise of American psychology with "a workable but theoretically solid vision of human science," then the expression "humanistic psychology" would "become redundant and we will have only psychology" (1987, p. 19).

## Introductory Textbooks and Scholarly Publications

Given the potentially integrative role that humanistic psychologists might play in the academy, it is disappointing that our influence continues to be rather marginal, as evidenced by the way in which the movement has been represented in introductory psychology textbooks (which generally aim to provide a comprehensive, balanced, and unbiased introduction to the field as a whole). Recent surveys of these texts (Churchill, 1988; Henley & Faulkner, 1989) have shown that very little space (typically only a few pages) is allotted to the contributions of humanistic psychologists — and this is generally limited to the influence of Maslow on personality theory and to that of Rogers in the field of psychotherapy. It is as though there were nothing worthy of mention in the last thirty years with regard to the research and theory-building efforts of humanistic psychologists.

Although the movement has long ceased being merely a protest movement and is generating published research in a variety of bulletins and journals, the problem may be that textbook writers and publishers are simply not used to seeing humanistic psychology taken seriously in textbooks, and thus do not assume the responsibility of representing the movement more faithfully. Or, it may be that only the polemical humanistic literature, and not the research articles confined mostly to "in-house" journals (e.g., *Journal of Humanistic Psychology, Review of Existential Psychology and Psychiatry, Journal of Phenomenological Psychology, The Humanistic Psychologist, Methods: A Journal for Human Science, Journal of Transpersonal Psychology*), have found their way to the desks of textbook writers. Writers of textbooks almost unanimously continue to misrepresent humanistic psychologists as though the latter were all stuck in a time warp back in the Sixties, feeling good about themselves and espousing values of "peace, love, and happiness." Even if this were true of *some* who currently call themselves humanistic psychologists, it is far from being an accurate reflection of the majority within the academy. In this sense, to the extent that the "presence" of humanistic psychologists in the academy is defined in terms of its representation in journals and texts, the movement would appear to be in trouble: If humanistic psychologists are touting ideas and values that are hardly given mention in the educational texts of our discipline, then to those who read and write those texts, humanistic psychologists professing their rich understanding of the human psyche must appear out of touch with what psychology "really" is.

## People and Programs

Notwithstanding the political importance of documentation and the practical use of texts for pedagogical purposes, textbooks and publications are in one sense merely tracks left behind on the path of thinking and research; the existential presence of psychologists in the academy is to be found (to paraphrase Marx) in the activity of psychologists in pursuit of their ends — that is, in the concrete praxis of individuals and institutions.

*Formal Programs*

Literature summarizing graduate programs in humanistic psychology includes the *Directory of Graduate Programs in Humanistic-Transpersonal Psychology in North America* (Arons, 1988) as well as reports in *The Humanistic Psychologist* about specific graduate programs (Aanstoos, 1989; Daniels & Siroky, 1986; Ellis, 1989; Frager, 1987; Henley & Meguiar, 1988; Judy & Schmitt, 1989; Kostere, 1987; Kunz, 1986; Milner, 1986; Romanyshyn, 1985; Smith, 1985; Voigt, 1985;

Walker, 1987). On the basis of that literature, I have found the following programs at colleges, universities, and institutes leading to masters and doctoral degrees.

*Masters programs.* There are 14 terminal M.A. programs, including Antioch University, Atlantic University, Avalon Institute, Boulder College, Center for Humanistic Studies, Institute for Culture and Creation Spirituality, JFK University Graduate School of Professional Psychology, Lesley College, Mankato State University, Naropa Institute, Salve Regina College, Seattle University, Sonoma State University, and West Georgia College. Of these, all except for Antioch University and Goddard College (which are interdisciplinary "off-campus" programs for adult learners) and Seattle University (which has an existential-phenomenological orientation) emphasize "holistic" and "transpersonal" studies in their program descriptions.

*Doctoral programs.* Of the 15 programs offering various combinations of M.A., Ph.D., Psy.D. and Ed.D. degrees, none are APA approved; and only eight offer regular courses of study in the classroom. Of these, two (Northern Illinois University and Temple University) are humanistically oriented programs in educational psychology leading to the Ed.D. degree; five (California Institute of Integral Studies, Institute of Transpersonal Psychology, Pacifica Graduate Institute, Rosebridge Graduate School of Integrative Psychology, and the University for Humanistic Studies) are private nontraditional academic institutes offering M.A. and Ph.D. degrees in transpersonal, holistic, or archetypal studies. This leaves only two functioning doctoral programs that offer a formal course of classroom instruction leading to both M.A. and Ph.D. degrees in a traditional university setting: Duquesne University's graduate program in existential-phenomenological psychology and the University of Quebec at Montreal's program in Humanistic-Psychoanalytic psychology. The remaining six programs offering doctoral degrees are non-residential programs offered by private institutes and nontraditional "colleges" and "universities." These include the Fielding Institute, Institute of Transpersonal Psychology, International College, Saybrook Institute, Sierra University (formerly the University Without Walls), and Union Graduate School.

*Individuals*

A 1991 follow-up study of Ph.D. graduates from the Department of Psychology at Duquesne University shows approximately 50 graduates teaching full- and part-time at 34 institutions of higher education across the United States. Only four of these institutions are included in the lists above, which means that there are at least 30 colleges and universities without formal programs in humanistic or phenomenological psychology that nonetheless have phenomenolgically-oriented individuals on their faculty. However, not one of these phenomenologically educated academicians has been able to assume a position in an APA accredited Ph.D. program in psychology. The same can be assumed to be true for graduates of humanistic/transpersonal doctoral programs who are not currently teaching at the institutions listed above: they are dispersed throughout the academy in such a way that does not make it easy to assess the full presence of humanistic psychology within the current academic scene. Then there are those individuals whose education might not have been from humanistic graduate programs but who are major contributors to the advancement of humanistic psychology (broadly defined) in America: people like Joseph de Rivera at Clark University, Robert Elliot at the University of Toledo, Franz Epting at the University of Florida, George Howard and William Tageson at Notre Dame, Ernest Keen at Bucknell, Al Mahrer at University of Ottawa, Fred Massarik at UCLA, Don Polkinghorne at the University of Southern California, Howard Pollio at University of Tennessee (Knoxville), Karl Pribram at Stanford, Joseph Rychlak holding the Maude C. Clarke Chair of Humanistic Psychology at Loyola University of Chicago, Brewster Smith at the University of California (Santa Cruz), Mark Stern at Iona College, and Richard Zaner at Vanderbilt, just to name a few. The total number of such individuals working alone at their respective institutions is unknown at this time and would be difficult to assess, considering that not everyone teaching humanistic psychology is on the membership list of APA's Division 32.

## Closing Remarks

In light of the above consideration of contexts within which humanistic psychologists have positioned themselves in the academy, I will close with some observations and suggestions.

1. The vast majority of graduate schools listed above under the heading of "formal programs" are institute-type programs that seem oriented more toward the self-actualization of the student (who is often an adult learner and is not very likely to begin an academic career upon graduation), and to the training of clinicians, than to research and theory building. Thus, many of the critical assessments of humanistic psychology made earlier by Rogers (1965), Misiak & Sexton (1973), and Giorgi

(1987) still stand: (a) countercultural features (better described here as interests in consciousness-raising and self-enhancement) still predominate in humanistic programs; (b) there continues to be a strong orientation toward therapeutic training, which results in less emphasis being placed on research and publishing; and (c) notwithstanding the consolidation of several camps (i.e., holistic, transpersonal, existential-phenomenological, human science, and archetypal orientations) within the APA's Division of Humanistic Psychology, there still remains a sense of obscurity with regard to the presence of humanistic psychology in academic textbooks: the writers of these texts do not have a clear image of what constitutes the variegated field of humanistic psychology today, apart from statements made by Maslow and Rogers almost a half century ago. In other words, we are still being confined to positions that are far too limited and even misleading.

2. It is gratifying to see that graduates of humanistic doctoral programs are teaching throughout the academy at a wide range of institutions. Although this positioning does bear pedagogical as well as political implications, we must remember that it is publication that enables teachers to transcend their immediate contexts and fortify their credibility by expanding the range of their audience. Within any particular institution, one's work does have its effect upon individual students, to be sure; but, like ripples sent out by pebbles tossed into a small pond, there is only a contained effect — one that is certainly not enough to ensure humanistic psychology's place in the future history of psychology.

Thus, if humanistic psychology is to prevail in the academy, we will need to address ourselves to the following issues: First, if we cannot unify ourselves under a less eclectic, more comprehensive perspective than already exists within humanistic psychology, then we should at least try to clarify the roles played by all of the major camps within Division 32, as well as the relationships between these camps. Second, we must avoid further redundancy in our publications, which sometimes continue to critique the traditional metapsychology while offering little more than programmatic statements of what direction needs to be taken in future research. Instead, the emphasis should be on solid research that can add to the database drawn upon by textbook authors, and to placement of such research in journals of wider circulation. Third, we must bring humanistic psychology "out of the closet" in course syllabi and catalogue descriptions. This may be politically difficult in some teaching environments where the inclusion of humanistic material might be considered a subversive act; but it is important that humanistic insights — as well as correctives to older, more simplistic views — be given proper recognition within the academy. Fourth, it is imperative that educators do more to inspire students to pursue careers in teaching and research. Notwithstanding the important contributions made by humanistic psychologists in the various fields of professional application, the field as a whole critically depends upon the continuing growth of a research base for further application, as well as for eventual theoretical integration.

Finally, I think it important that we take very seriously our potential role in furthering the efforts of the foundational humanistic theoreticians, by working toward the development of an intellectual framework capable of integrating the field of psychology as a whole. We are, indeed, part of what Polanyi (1966) called a "society of explorers"; and, while it may seem that the current society of psychologists has splintered off into differentiated groups, we must not forget the vision we have inherited from people like Maslow, May, Rogers, and Van Kaam: our own self-enhancement depends much on how we participate in the integrative goals of the broader society of academicians within which we ultimately find our place. What is important, ultimately, is not simply for humanistic psychology to be set up alongside other psychologies, but for all the current schools to be eventually incorporated into a more embracing enterprise of psychology as a unified discipline. In the meantime, even if the academy continues to be slow to respond to the vision offered by humanistic psychology, just maintaining some presence within the academy, if only as an alternative, will hopefully serve as a benefit to psychology in the long run.

## References

Aanstoos, C. M. (1989). The graduate program at West Georgia College. *The Humanistic Psychologist, 17, 1*, 77-85.

Allport, G. W. (1937). *Personality: A psychological interpretation*. New York: Henry Holt.

Arons, M. (Ed.). (1988). *Directory: Graduate programs in humanistic-transpersonal psychology in North America* (3rd ed.). Carrollton, GA: West Georgia College Psychology Department.

Barton, A. (1974). *Three worlds of therapy: An existential-phenomenological study of the therapies of Freud, Jung, and Rogers*. Palo Alto, CA: National Press Books.

Boss, M. (1979). *Existential foundations of medicine and psychology* (S. Conway & A. Cleaves, Trans.). New York: Jason Aronson.

Buytendijk, F. J. J. (1974). *Prolegomena to an anthropological physiology*. Pittsburgh: Duquesne University Press. (Original work published 1965)

Churchill, S. D. (1988). Humanistic psychology and introductory textbooks. *The Humanistic Psychologist, 16*, 2, 341-357.

Churchill, S. D. & von Eckartsberg, R. (1991). Emerging methods and paradigms in a changing epistemology. *Methods: A Journal for Human Science*, 43-64.

Colaizzi, P. F. (1973). *Reflection and research in psychology*. Dubuque, Iowa: Kendall/Hunt.

Daniels, V. & Siroky, F. R. (1986). Humanistic psychology at Sonoma State University. *The Humanistic Psychologist, 14*, 113-117.

Day, W. F. (1969). Radical behaviorism in reconciliation with phenomenology. *Journal of the Experimental Analysis of Behavior, 12*, 315-328.

Day, W. F. (1975). Contemporary behaviorism and the concept of intention. In W. J. Arnold (Ed.), *Nebraska symposium on motivation 1975* (pp. 65-131), Lincoln: University of Nebraska Press.

Dilthey, W. (1977) Ideas concerning a descriptive and analytic psychology (1894). In W. Dilthey, *Descriptive psychology and historical understanding* (pp. 21-120), The Hague: Nijhoff. (Original work published 1924)

Ellis, N. (1989). The Boulder Graduate School. *The Humanistic Psychologist, 17*, 2, 182-185.

Fischer, C. T. (1985). *Individualizing psychological assessment*. Monterey, CA: Brooks/Cole.

Fischer, W. F. (1970). *Theories of anxiety*. New York: Harper & Row.

Frager, R. (1987). Psychology, geo-justice, and creation spirituality (The Institute for Culture and Creation Spirituality). *The Humanistic Psychologist, 15*, 219-221.

Friedman, M. (1984). *Contemporary psychology: Revealing and obscuring the human*. Pittsburgh: Duquesne University Press.

Giorgi, A. (1970). *Psychology as a human science: A phenomenologically based approach*. New York: Harper & Row.

Giorgi, A. (1971). Phenomenology and experimental psychology (I & II). In A. Giorgi, W. F. Fischer, & R. von Eckartsberg (Eds.), *Duquesne studies in phenomenological psychology* (Vol. I, pp. 6-29), Pittsburgh: Duquesne University Press.

Giorgi, A. (1987). The crisis of humanistic psychology. *The Humanistic Psychologist, 15*, 5-20.

Goldstein, K. (1939). *The organism: A holistic approach to biology derived from pathological data in man*. New York: American Book.

Goldstein, K. (1940). *Human nature in the light of psychopathology*. Cambridge: Harvard University Press.

Heidegger, M. (1962). *Being and time* (J. MacQuarrie & E. Robinson, Trans.). New York: Harper & Row. (Original work published 1927)

Henley, T. B. & Faulkner, K. A. (1989). An addendum to Churchill's review of introductory texts. *The Humanistic Psychologist, 17*, 329-330.

Henley, T. B. & Meguiar, T. M. (1988). Phenomenology at the University of Tennessee. *The Humanistic Psychologist, 16*, 358-360.

Husserl, E. (1982). *Ideas pertaining to a pure phenomenology and a phenomenological philosophy. First Book: General introduction to a pure phenomenology* (F. Kersten, Trans.). Boston: Nijhoff. (Original work published 1913)

Jaspers, K. (1963). *General psychopathology* (J. Hoenig & M. W. Hamilton, Trans.). Chicago: University of Chicago Press. (Original work published 1913)

Judy, D. H. & Scmitt, R. (1989). The Institute of Transpersonal Psychology. *The Humanistic Psychologist, 17*, 294-297.

Knowles, R. T. (1986). *Human development and human possibility: Erikson in the light of Heidegger*. Lanham, MD: University Press of America.

Knowles, R. T., Lydon, J. A., & Peiritsch, J. D. (1991). *Follow-Up study of Ph.D. graduates*. Pittsburgh: Duquesne University Department of Psychology.

Kostere, K. M. (1987). A brief account of the Center for Humanistic Studies. *The Humanistic Psychologist, 15*, 56-58.

Kuhn, T. S. (1962). *The structures of scientific revolutions*. Chicago: University of Chicago Press.

Kunz, G. (1986). The graduate program at Seattle University. *The Humanistic Psychologist, 14*, 194-198.

Laing, R. D. (1960). *The divided self: An existential study in sanity and madness*. London: Tavistock Publications.

MacLeod, R. B. (1975). *The persistent problems of psychology*. Pittsburgh: Duquesne University Press.

Maslow, A. H. (1943). A theory of human motivation. *Psychological Review, 50*, 370-396.

Maslow, A. H. (1968). *Toward a psychology of being* (2nd. ed.). New York: Van Nostrand Reinhold.

Maslow, A. H. (1970). *Motivation and personality* (2nd. ed.). New York: Harper & Row.

May, R. (1951). *The meaning of anxiety*. New York: Ronald Press.

May, R. (Ed.). (1960). *Existential psychology*. New York: Random House.

Merleau-Ponty, M. (1962). *Phenomenology of perception* (C. Smith, Trans.). London: Routledge & Kegan Paul. (Original work published 1945)

Merleau-Ponty, M. (1963). *The structure of behavior* (A. L. Fisher, Trans.). Boston: Beacon Press. (Original work published 1942)

Milner, T. (1986). Humanistic Psychology: Saybrook Institute Graduate School and Research Center. *The Humanistic Psychologist, 14*, 38-41.

Misiak, H. & Sexton, V. S. (1973). *Phenomenological, existential, and humanistic psychologies: A historical survey*. New York: Grune & Stratton.

Moustakas, C. E. (Ed.). (1956). *The self: Explorations in personal growth.* New York: Harper & Row.

Moustakas, C. E. (1986). Origins of humanistic psychology. *The Humanistic Psychologist, 14,* 122-123.

Murray, H. A. (1938). *Explorations in personality.* New York: Oxford University Press.

Polanyi, M. (1966). *The tacit dimension.* Garden City, N.Y.: Doubleday.

Pollio, H. R. (1982). *Behavior and existence: An introduction to empirical humanistic psychology.* Monterey: Brooks/Cole.

Pribram, K. H. (1981). Behaviorism, phenomenology, and holism in psychology: A scientific analysis. In R. S. Valle & R. von Eckartsberg (Eds.), *The metaphors of consciousness* (pp. 141-151), New York: Plenum Press.

Pribram, K. H. (1986). The cognitive revolution and mind/brain issues. *American Psychologist, 41,* 507-520.

Rogers, C. R. (1942). *Counseling and psychotherapy.* Boston: Houghton Mifflin.

Rogers, C. (1951). *Client-Centered therapy: Its current practice, implications, and theory.* Boston: Houghton Mifflin.

Rogers, C. R. (1965). Some questions and challenges facing a humanistic psychology. *Journal of Humanistic Psychology, 5,* 1-5.

Romanyshyn, R. D. (1985). The graduate program at the University of Dallas. *The Humanistic Psychologist, 13* (1), 23-27.

Royce, J. R. (Ed.). (1970). *Toward unification in psychology.* Toronto: University of Toronto Press.

Sartre, J.-P. (1956). *Being and nothingness* (H. Barnes, Trans.). New York: Philosophical Library. (Original work published 1943)

Skinner, B. F. (1975). The steep and thorny way to a science of behavior. *American Psychologist, 30,* 42-49.

Skinner, B. F. (1987). Whatever happened to psychology as the science of behavior? *American Psychologist, 42,* 780-786.

Skinner, B. F. (1990). Can psychology be a science of mind? *American Psychologist, 45,* 1206-1210.

Smith, D. L. (1983). The history of the graduate program via existential-phenomenological psychology at Duquesne University. In A. Giorgi, A. Barton, & C. Maes (Eds.), *Duquesne studies in phenomenological psychology* (Vol. IV, pp. 259-300), Pittsburgh: Duquesne University Press.

Smith, D. L. (1985). The graduate program at Duquesne University. *The Humanistic Psychologist, 13* (2), 28-32.

Smith, M. B. (1982). Psychology and humanism. *Journal of Humanistic Psychology, 25,* 7-24.

Snygg, D. & Combs, A. W. (1949). *Individual behavior: A new frame of reference for psychology.* New York: Harper.

Sperry, R. W. (1969). A modified concept of consciousness. *Psychological Review, 76*, 532-536.
Sperry, R. W. (1970). An objective approach to subjective experience: Further explanation of a hypothesis. *Psychological Review, 77*, 585-590.
Sperry, R. W. (1986). Discussion: Macro- versus micro-determinism. *Philosophy of Science, 53*, 265-270.
Sperry, R. W. (1987). Structure and significance of the consciousness revolution. *The Journal of Mind and Behavior, 8*, 37-66.
Strasser, S. (1974). *Phenomenology and the human sciences: A contribution to a new scientific ideal*. Pittsburgh: Duquesne University Press.
Straus, E. (1963). *The primary world of the senses: A vindication of sensory experience* (2nd Ed., J. Needleman, Trans.). New York: Macmillan. (Original work published 1956)
Tageson, C. W. (1982). *Humanistic psychology: A synthesis*. Homewood, Ill.: The Dorsey Press.
Valle, R. S. & Harari, C. (1985). Current developments in transpersonal psychology. *The Humanistic Psychologist, 13* (1), 11-15.
van den Berg, J. H. (1972). *A different existence: Principles of phenomenological psychopathology*. Pittsburgh: Duquesne University Press.
van Kaam, A. (1966). *Existential foundations of psychology*. Pittsburgh: Duquesne University Press.
Voigt, W. (1985). Bridging east and west in graduate education (California Institute of Integral Studies). *The Humanistic Psychologist, 13* (3), 27-31.
von Eckartsberg, R. (1978). Person perception revisited. In R. S. Valle & M. King (Eds.), *Existential-Phenomenological alternatives for psychology* (pp. 182-202), New York: Oxford University Press.
von Eckartsberg, R. (1981). Maps of the mind: The cartography of consciousness. In R. S. Valle & R. von Eckartsberg (Eds.), *The metaphors of consciousness* (pp. 21-93), New York: Plenum.
Walker, R. (1987). Contemplative psychotherapy at the Naropa Institute. *The Humanistic Psychologist, 15*, 98-104.
Wertz, F.J. (1982). The findings and value of a descriptive approach to everyday perceptual process. *Journal of Phenomenological Psychology, 13*, 169-195.

# 23

# Whither Humanistic Psychology?

*Amedeo Giorgi*

What is the role of humanistic psychology for contemporary psychology and for the psychology of the future? To clarify its future role, it is critical to know whether or not the unique contribution that humanistic psychology can make, has already been made. In other words, are our greatest achievements behind us? Have we become an historical footnote, whose final chapter is being written even as we stand here worrying about our fate? Are the contributions that we wanted to make to psychology as manifestly present as we would like? Or, perhaps, has our message been co-opted by mainstream psychology in diluted form, and have we become another spent force devoured by that omnivorous, proliferating institutional sprawl known as "the science and profession of psychology"? Has the adjective "humanistic" become redundant? Let's scan the record.

## The Humanistic Psychology Movement: Contributions and Limits

Almost thirty years ago, humanistic psychology emerged on the national scene as a protest movement against the state of the art conceptualizations and practices of psychology. At the time — the late 1950's and early 1960's — psychology in academia was dominated by a "methodological behaviorism" that emphasized experimental conditions, a quantitative perspective and the study of peripheral factors, Clinical psychology was dominated either by an unimaginative Freudianism that focused on "homo natura" (Needleman, 1963) or a testing approach also limited to grasping certain external particulars. The protest made by persons such as May, Rogers, and Maslow was that psychology was missing the heart of the matter. The human being, the human person, the very core of psychology that made everything else viable was not being addressed. The methods adopted by the field were constraining it. Indeed, the protesters claimed that psychology was method-centered and not topic-centered. A shift of emphasis was called for: psychology, in its conceptualizations and practices, had to become adequate for the whole person.

Thus the protest movement known as "humanistic psychology" was born. The human person was to become the focus of psychological studies. But even as the protest began to sweep the country along with the liberalizing attitude of the 1960's, voices of caution were expressed, but rarely heard. Rogers (1964) warned us early on that if humanistic psychology turned out to be only a protest movement, its effect would be only temporary. My impression is that humanistic psychology has not made the transition from protest movement to positive research program very well, and we are at a critical point in the history of humanistic psychology — the time when the generation of the founders is terminating — and unless those of us still trying to carry the torch respond creatively to the contemporary dilemma, the movement may cease altogether.

In an earlier paper (Giorgi, 1987) I described the crisis of humanistic psychology as one in which its theorizing did not match its promises. I had argued that humanistic psychology offered three promises to the community of psychologists: the human potential promise, the promise of a better image of the human person, and the promise of better and more relevant research. I stated that the movement met the human potential promise most adequately, but in doing so its impact was primarily on the culture at large rather than on the academic community. I also argued that it helped put pressure on psychologists to clarify the implicit philosophical anthropology of their systems. Thus, the extrapolation from pigeons or rats to humans was no longer so taken for granted and those using mechanical models became a little more defensive. However, the humanistic psychologists did not link their concept of "human" to the strong humanistic traditions of antiquity or of the Renaissance. Their conception was spontaneous, individualistic and pragmatic rather than theoretical, social or historical. Finally, I argued that when it came to its research program, humanistic psychology failed almost completely. That's because it tried to fit the new-found emphasis on the human person into the framework of the natural scientific approach. It didn't fully realize that the complexity and uniqueness of the person also required a different interpretation of science.

I have reviewed what I perceive to be the crisis of humanistic psychology because I believe that the crisis is still with us, as indeed it is with the entire field of psychology. The point is that after one generation of effort, humanistic psychology's protest against mainstream's definition of the field of psychology has failed. Indeed, humanistic psychology is now caught up in the crisis rather than being a solution to it. The reason for this, I have argued, is that a framework as radical as its aspirations was not chosen by humanistic psychology. It strove to reintroduce the concrete human person into psychology, but it left the context of science with which it approached human beings untouched and unclarified — just as mainstream psychology insists upon subsuming the human person under the framework of the natural sciences. I might add that I am speaking primarily of theoretical-academic psychology rather than the therapeutic context, where more exceptions prevail, even though the same mentality dominates. Remember, it was Carl Rogers (1985) himself who defined the failure of humanistic psychology in terms of its lack of penetration of the academic establishment.

Now, I have always criticized this state of affairs by a direct attack upon the logic of the natural sciences vis-a-vis its application to human phenomena (eg. Giorgi, 1970). This time I shall try to do it indirectly, by attempting to clarify the meaning of human as humanistic psychology might want to use it and by that means, perhaps, get some indication of the direction humanistic psychology might want to move. The deeper question I am probing is: has humanistic psychology clarified the meaning of human in a sufficiently radical way? Has this radical conception of being human been allowed to influence the framework with which humanistic psychology studies its phenomena? Perhaps if the meaning of being human could really be seen in its depths, at least the inadequacy of the natural scientific paradigm could be made even more manifest, and the motivation for developing an alternative framework would be more apparent.

### Being Human And Humanisms

This leads us squarely to the issue of the meaning of being human and of an appropriate philosophy or philosophical anthropology for humaness — a complex issue if there ever was one. Certainly, I shall not clarify this issue within the context of a single article when 2,000 years of human effort have not satisfactorily clarified it. Moreover, this has been a theme of numerous articles within the pages of the *Journal of Humanistic Psychology* (eg. Smith, 1982; Moustakas, 1985; Smith,

1986; Mahrer, 1989; O'Hara, 1989; Smith, 1990). I shall refer to some of these articles shortly, but first I want to indicate my strategy regarding this issue. If one cannot determine once and for all what the essence of being human is or if one cannot articulate a humanistic philosophy with which all interested parties agree, what is left to be done? My strategy is to pick a significant dimension of being human, even if it does not exhaustively define humanness, and then to demonstrate that that dimension cannot be appropriated within the framework that supports the contemporary practices of psychological science. For this purpose I shall use the act of transcendence as depicted by several twentieth century philosophers.

The issue, it should be recalled, is the tension between the idea of science held by psychologists and the characteristics of humanness manifested by human beings in the everyday world. Basically, traditional psychology has kept to the framework and criteria of natural science and it has modified human phenomena or else studied only those aspects of human phenomena that lent themselves to the paradigm, and my claim is that what is capable of being so studied does not include the essential aspects of humanness. Most frequently, humans are understood as entities with measurable characteristics, and the relationship between the characteristics as measured and the essential characteristics of being human is merely contingent or accidental. So, if it can be shown that an essential dimension of being human escapes the framework of the psychological natural scientific approach, the argument for a different framework, a human scientific one, will be logically evident.

It is perhaps not fully appreciated the extent to which naturalism pervades the culture of science. Naturalism refers to that philosophy that asserts that one need not appeal to factors beyond the reality of nature, or the sciences of nature, in order to explain human phenomena. While naturalism is logically independent of them, it is frequently defined in combination with physicalism or materialism. The predominance of philosophical naturalism is, in part, a consequence of the success of the sciences of nature, a success that has catapulted its perspective into such a dominating world-view that almost all other perspectives are on the defensive. Pragmatically, who can argue against success? Everyday, it seems, science and its handmaiden, technology, are unlocking more and more secrets of nature. Thus, it is only "natural" that the same attitude is brought to bear upon human beings. The result of this extrapolation is naturalistic, or secular, humanism. Klemke (1981, p. viii) has summarized this kind of humanism in the following terms:

Most humanists (of this type) subscribe to all or most of the following specific tenets. (1) The natural world is the totality of that which exists. (2) Humans are evolutionary by-products of the workings of Nature. (3) Human consciousness is dependent upon bodily functioning; hence men and women are not immortal. (4) A human being can mature and solve problems through reason and the scientific method. (5) All values are grounded within the natural universe. (6) The highest goal for moral striving is the happiness and enhancement of human life here on earth. (7) The best social orders are those which allow for and contribute to the freedom and welfare of human beings as individuals.

I think that most of us will recognize the above set of assumptions as quite harmonious with the framework of natural sciences within which mainstream psychology operates. This should not be a surprise, however, since most mainstream psychologists frankly admit that humans are understood as complex specimens of nature, fully in continuity with nature, and not even the fact of human consciousness, with all the difficulties it introduces for psychological theory, motivates a change of perspective. That this is not an anachronistic view can be easily demonstrated. In a recent theoretical debate about everyday memory, Banaji and Crowder (1991, p. 79) write:

> Part of the disenchantment with the experimental method in psychology may stem from an erroneous conception of the discipline of psychological science. This conception, not peculiar to everyday memory researchers, emerges from the notion that humans (as the unit of analysis of most psychological research) are infinitely more complex, mysterious, variable in behavior, and resistant to understanding than other entities in the universe. The supposedly greater complexity of human behavior necessitates leaving controlled environments that apparently suffice in the studying of less complex phenomenon (sic.) such as light, time, gravity and entropy!... The notion that human behavior is vastly more complex than chemical reactions can only emerge from a lack of acquaintance with other sciences.

Thus, the argument presented by Banaji and Crowder is that certain phenomena of nature are equally as complex as human phenomena and so no change in methodology is called for. Obviously, the writers misconstrue the key point. Of course, there is a type of reductionism that reduces complex phenomena to simple ones, but that is not the theoretical point here. The issue about the meaning of being human revolves around qualitative differences. Do human phenomena intrinsically lend themselves to the same approach, concepts, and methods as the natural sciences when human subjectivities that can bestow meanings in situations in the world are inevitably being expressed? My point is that phenomena involving acts of transcendence (to take one example) introduce a qualitative difference such that a different sense of method must be introduced to capture human phenomena essentially.

Now there are also humanistic psychologists who share the same assumptions, and Smith (1982; 1986) has even lamented that there are too few such within the ranks of humanistic psychology. Of course, if this version of humanism is taken in its strictest sense, as the tenets listed by Klemke indicate, then the philosophical anthropology of humanistic psychology is no different from that of mainstream psychology and all of its protests are in vain. However, Smith's (1986) version of secular humanism allows for the possibility of transcendence. For example, Smith (1986) writes:

> From the standpoint of a secular humanism, what does it mean to be human? This is surely the oldest, most central question known to human self-consciousness, and the core of any serious attempt to answer it must be that we are the sort of creatures who can frame such a question about ourselves... We know that wherever and whenever we find them, human beings seek meaning and create it, individually and collectively. To be human is to be engaged in a life infused with meaning... Mead argued persuasively that reflective selfhood is "functional," in that the implicated ability to "take the role of the other" is essential for our participation in the coordinated activities of organized social life. So it surely is. But consider the costs: Human self-consciousness breaks the unity of human beings and Nature and, when forethought and afterthought are added as gifts of language, the human existential predicament emerges in full force... Insofar as selfhood can flourish only in a context of committed human ties within a tradition of shared meanings that anchor individual lives in goals and projects beyond their own immediate interest ("transcendence" in a sense that I firmly believe people require), the individualistic "solution" does not really work. (pp. 12-21)

When Smith speaks of humans as self-questioning beings, as beings that seek meanings, as creatures that have the ability to take the role of the other, of self-consciousness as a phenomenon that breaks the unity of humans and nature and affirms a sense of transcendence, he is preserving and articulating descriptive characteristics of being human that one finds in other walks of life (eg. literature, law, art and even science itself) and as part of the matrix of human culture wherever historical records are found. Surely psychologists can differ about the interpretation of such characteristics, but that some type of reference to such descriptions or their analogs belong as part of the fundamental sense of being human is what I claim humanistic psychology should be defending. If humanistic psychology has a raison d'etre, it is to resist the reduction of humanness to Nature, not only philosophically and theoretically, but also in its practices, even its scientific practices. My critique then, of humanistic psychology, is that it has not systematically thematized some common acceptable sense of humanness, even though the problem is intrinsically difficult, and more importantly, humanistic psychology has not let that articulated sense of being human inform its scientific practice in a theoretically radical way. Again, the practices of therapy within humanistic psychology are more likely to respect what is essentially human, because the culture of psychotherapy is less influenced by the natural scientific model (although the medical model has had the same type of influence as the natural sciences did in research practices) and because the nature of the pathologies or life problems discussed tend to protect the client.

Thus, it can be seen that there are types of secular humanism that can affirm the unicity of being human. As Moustakas (1985) pointed out, it is the meanings associated with the various types of humanisms that matter, not their labels. On the other side, certain recent movements, such as social constructionism, deconstructionism, certain types of postmodernism affirm human subjectivity, but then leave it so powerless that, in the end, there is really nothing to affirm. The contextual efforts are so potent that the human subject is not so much de-centered as rendered centerless.

This perspective actually has a fairly long history. It has been observed that human self-centeredness has received one blow after another as a result of the work of Copernicus, Darwin, Marx and Freud. Copernicus displaced the human's dwelling place from the center of the universe; Darwin showed that humans evolved "naturally," as a product of biological evolution; Marx stressed how social forces, especially economics, determined us and Freud completed the Darwinian picture by showing that even individually sexual and aggressive instincts largely determined our behavior. The human person has gotten smaller and smaller, but contemporary interpretations have even taken that little bit away. The "forces" that once belonged to nature have been extended to society and culture, so that while a strict naturalism does not exist, its spirit does. Does it make much difference whether humans are determined by physical nature or culture, if the subjective perspective is totally effaced? Here's Jonathan Culler (1991, pp.77-78) on how deconstructionists approach their topic!

> However, once the subject is in place, once he is firmly established at the center of the analytical domain, the whole enterprise of the human sciences becomes one of deconstructing the subject, of explaining meanings in terms of systems of convention which escape the subject's conscious grasp. The speaker of a language is not consciously aware of its phonological and grammatical systems, in whose terms his judgments and perceptions will be explained. Nor is the subject necessarily aware of its own psychic economy or of the elaborate system of social norms which govern behavior. The subject is broken down into its constituents which turn out to be interpersonal systems of convention. It is dissolved as its functions are attributed to a variety of systems which operate through it. As Foucault writes, the researcher of psychoanalysis, of linguistics, of anthropology, have "decentered" the subject in relation to the laws of its desire, the forms of its language, the rules of its actions, or the play of its mythical and imaginative discourse.... The distinction between the subject and the world is a variable one that depends on the configurations of knowledge at a given time and (contemporary) disciplines... have chipped away at what previously belonged to the subject until it has lost its place as center or source of meaning. As it is deconstructed, broken down into component systems which are all trans-subjective, the self or subject comes to appear more and more as a construct: the result of systems of convention.

Thus, the determinism begun by naturalism was picked up by social-cultural forces, but in the same manner as though it were nature. In this view, lack of awareness is more determinative of our meanings and identity than awareness is, and the removal of subjectivity a more important achievement than acknowledging it. This interpretation is significant when one considers that the emphasis on the social-cultural context could have also been the occasion to expand subjectivity as Goldmann (1973/1977) did when he introduced the term "transindividual subject."

Is there, then, no recourse for the human subject, except to be displaced and buffeted about by all these forces? Would this be the meaning of the human subject that humanistic psychology would want to endorse — a diminished and almost wholly determined subject?

It in no way eliminates the truths contained in the deconstructionistic perspective to affirm a role for consciousness. While no person starts from absolute zero, — the truth of the deconstructionist perspective —

it's also true that some centering functions remain for the subject. Indeed, one could argue that there is a type of decentering that happens on the side of consciousness as well. The possibilities offered to human subjectivity through imagination are also a type of decentering. Persons can be where they are not by imagining possibilities for themselves that could have seemed unattainable.

Again, if the human potential movement was overly optimistic in this regard, it doesn't mean that there is no truth to the fact that decentering can also imply something positive — not just a reduction to nature or a reference to unconscious determination. It can imply that one can place oneself in a possible situation that can be actualized through effort. Apparently, one of the most disastrous effects of positivism on psychology has been the devaluation of imagination to the benefit of facts. Psychologists tend not to employ their imagination well, and even when they inevitably must, and do, they tend not to give it credit (an exception is Murray, 1987).

Again, humans in other fields of endeavor are not so reluctant to speak about the creative use of imaginative possibilities. To take two brief examples, if one turns to literature, Kundera (1986, p.83) writes that, "The novel is a meditation on existence as seen through the medium of imaginary characters." And certainly, anyone who has read sufficiently can witness that he or she has been moved by the type of truth portrayed in the unfolding drama of such imaginary characters. And on the side of "hard" sciences, we get expressions such as the following by Martin Gardner (1988, p. 18) commenting on Hawking's book on time, "It is hopeless to explain the new model in any detail here because it makes use of a special kind of time called 'imaginary time' which plays a role in calculating the most probable paths of particles," and "The two spots are regions where disorder is total, the arrow of real time vanishes, and quantum events fluctuate aimlessly and forever in imaginary time." There is no hesitation to both use and credit the imagination here, either. My first point is that humans in other roles, whether as artists or natural scientists, constantly use and appeal to the imagination, whereas psychologists seem more bound to facts. My second point is that the use of imagination is a type of decentering that would argue for the uniqueness of humans rather than a devaluation that would account for actions in terms of extra-conscious factors. Obviously, such factors exist, and may account for some actions, but what seems not to be spoken to are the moments when such extraconscious factors are taken up and owned, or modified, or even imaginatively extended by the centering functions of eccentric subjectivities. To the extent to which imagination allows one to be present to situations other than the given factual ones humans are engaged in, to that extent an act of transcendence is already manifested, and it, too, would have to be accounted for in a complete psychology.

## Some Contemporary Philosophical Views on Being Human

The point of this section is to indicate that intrinsic to the elaboration of the meaning of being human on the part of some twentieth century philosophers, the idea of humans as being capable of transcendence is indubitable. If this is true, is it possible for humanistic psychology to simply accept or adapt the methods and procedures of the natural sciences?

Unfortunately, despite their emphasis on humanness and personhood, many humanistic psychologists also failed to appreciate that a different meaning of science was necessary to approach the qualitative differences that human phenomena present to a researcher's consciousness. When empirical studies do appear in the *Journal of Humanistic Psychology*, the methods employed are no different than those found in mainstream journals. Thus, Prasinos and Tittler (1984) used scales and self-ratings to study existential styles of love and Ebersole and Quiring (1991) developed a rating system for measuring meaning in life in depth. My complaint here is that the methods employed cannot really capture the phenomena toward which they are directed in an essentially human way. And if the goal of such studies is only to measure such phenomena, then they reflect a technological attitude toward human phenomena which is highly criticizable from a humanistic perspective. Briefly, then, here are the views of some key twentieth century philosophers.

### *Buber*

Maurice Friedman is the foremost interpreter of Martin Buber in our time so I will use him as a spokesman for Buber. Friedman (1988, p. 124) writes: "I approach the 'self in context' in terms of Martin Buber's ontology of the 'between' according to which persons find their reality ever again through meeting one another in dialogue... when two individuals 'happen' to each other, there is an essential remainder that reaches out beyond the special sphere of each — the 'sphere of the between'." The themes we've been discussing are implied in Friedman's quotation. Human subjectivity is decentered in the sense that a self is not wholly defined by relation to itself. A relationship to the other is equally essential. In addition, Friedman (1988, p. 126) says: "Genuine dialogue is two-sided, beyond the control of the will." This means that in order to be fully present to another person, I must transcend myself. I reach out beyond my own facticity. Friedman cautions throughout his writings that Buber's I—Thou relation cannot be reduced to psychological categories such as "interpersonal relations" or the "social self" and so on. Being human essentially implies the "between" and a confirmation by another person that transcends the self in order for a human being to be fully a human being. This discourse takes place on an ontological level that psychology must somehow respect and take into account. Since we've mentioned ontology, let's move on to Heidegger.

*Heidegger*

In his Letter on Humanism, Heidegger, in response to a question by Jean Beaufret, pondered over the problem of a renewed meaning for the term "humanism." In his lengthy response, Heidegger displaces the center of gravity of being human from "human" to Being. That is, for Heidegger, humans can only be understood in terms of their relationship to Being. Heidegger (1947/1977, p. 200) writes: "For this is humanism: meditating and caring, that man be human and not inhuman, "inhuman," that is, outside his essence. But in what does the humanity of man consist? It lies in his essence." But what is man's essence? Here Heidegger explains how every humanism, understood "in general as a concern that man become free for his humanity and find his worth in it" (Heidegger 1947/1977, p. 201), "is either grounded in a metaphysics or is itself made to be the ground of one. Every determination of the essence of man that already presupposes an interpretation of being without asking about the truth of Being... is metaphysical" (Heidegger, 1947/1977, p. 202). Heidegger then shows that metaphysics, which deals with beings, has to be overcome so that Being can become the theme of analysis. From the viewpoint of Being, a human can be understood as ek-sistence (standing-out), and hence, for Heidegger (1947/1977, p. 213), "the point is that in the determination of the humanity of man as ek-sistence what is essential is not man but Being."

In brief, Heidegger's answer to the renewal of the term "human" almost sounds like an anti-humanism: he stresses Being rather than human. However, Heidegger (1947/1977, p. 210) responds to the accusation by saying, "the sole implication is that the highest determinations of the essence of man in humanism still do not realize the proper dignity of man... Humanism (in this sense) is opposed because it does not set the humanitas of man high enough." As Biemel (1973/1976, p. 130) phrases it:

> The entire "Letter on 'Humanism'" revolves round the ek-sistence of man, that is to say, round the attempt to understand man not as one living being among others but as the being who is distinguished by his relationship with Being. Heidegger's aim is to throw open for us the only realm in which a determination of the essential nature of man is possible. In this manner, man now is in fact invested with a dignity which surpasses every form of humanism, in so far as the latter puts man in the center.

Thus, humans must transcend themselves toward Being and return, so to speak, in order to achieve their essential dignity.

*Husserl*

As many scholars know, it is because Husserl's phenomenology argues for the necessity of a transcendental attitude that many of his disciples turned away from him. It seemed as though, with this request, Husserl was asking the impossible — indeed, the inhuman! Yet Husserl (1913/1983) affirmed both that the assumption of the transcendental attitude was achievable and the "givens" that presented themselves through the assumption of the transcendental attitude, describable. The resistance to the attainment of a transcendental attitude was based upon the fact that it signified the assumption of a metapersonal attitude toward the objects of consciousness. That is, the level of consciousness called transcendental implies that one's biographical historicity, and other facticities, with respect to the given objects are rendered nonfunctional so that a more generalized intuiting or "seeing" can take place. Of course, if one remains within a psychological attitude, or even a naively realistic one, it would be impossible to reach such an achievement. However, if one can effectively enter into the phenomenological reduction, and if one can exercise the imaginative possibilities offered by consciousness, then it seems to me to be an achievable task. Is it so different, after all, from assuming the perspective of the other, or of the oppressed, or imagining life on another planet? The point here is that the very possibility of assuming a transcendental attitude demonstrates a nonreducible human potentiality.

*Merleau-Ponty*

The last philosopher I shall briefly consider is Merleau-Ponty. Merleau-Ponty defines humanness precisely in terms of the act of transcendence. Humanness is understood not in terms of a specific content or characteristic, but precisely in terms of the ability of a person, on his or her own initiative, to overturn any given received structure. Merleau-Ponty (1942/1963, p. 175) writes: "What defines man is not the capacity to create a second nature — economic, social or cultural — beyond biological nature; it is rather the capacity of going beyond created structures in order to create others." Consequently, humanness should not be defined by a specific content — such as a social, political, religious or economic order — but the sheer fact that another order is always possible. Humans are not trapped within the context of a specific fixity. One could say that it is the relationship to possibilities that matter, and the power to bring possibilities into being.

### Implications of the Above Philosophical Definition of Being Human for Humanistic Psychology

What have I been doing by covering the thought of these relatively abstruse philosophers and what is the relevance of their thinking for humanistic psychology and its direction? I have tried to show both, that in psychology our understanding of being human has been biased in the direction of nature rather than transcendence and that richer, more faithful understandings of being human are readily available in philosophical sources. As long as the dimensions of humanity are related to physical descriptions, quantifying expressions, physiological or neural terms, computer models, or even social-cultural determinants, a radical break with nature is not established. Moreover, what determines the selection of these themes is the natural scientific paradigm. That is why I have argued in this paper that one should first turn to some clarified understanding of being human, with depth and richness, and then turn to the articulation of a scientific framework that would not reduce the clarified dimension of being human. To be clear, the claim is not that these determinants have no value. It's just that limiting rigorous psychological analyses, in the name of science, to only those dimensions that a natural scientific framework will allow, misses the most important essential characteristics of being human.

If, on the other hand, one allows the dimension of transcendence that is implied or directly spoken to in the philosophers mentioned above to be taken up in psychological analyses, then it is clear that different means of practicing rigorous psychological analyses will have to be discovered or created. I speak of rigor, not rigidity, and the concept is broader than the way it is defined by the natural sciences. One would be confronted with one of the "epistemological ruptures" that Bachelard (1972) speaks about.

I have obviously been using the act of transcendence in a symbolic way. That is, not all of the philosophers spoke directly of transcendence, but it was implied in their key concepts. In general, to transcend means to go beyond or to rise above. With respect to the natural sciences, it means that human experience, behavior or action cannot be accounted for in terms of all the determinants that act on it. Every human situation has a certain gap or leakage which prevents the situation from being closed deterministically, and the gap is human subjectivity which has the power to transform situations through meaning bestowal or interpretation. Thus Buber speaks of how a free act of confirmation is essential for the emergence of genuine selfhood, and this can only come from the free, undetermined act of another; when Heidegger says that a genuine humanness requires that the self develop its "nearness to Being," this act of relation to Being cannot be forced; when Husserl speaks of a transcendental attitude, he means that humans can freely adopt a metapersonal, metabiographical attitude and participate in a structure of consciousness that cannot be determined by social or psychological factors; finally, when Merleau-Ponty speaks of those acts whereby persons transcend their background or their social class, he is also implying an undetermined initiative on the part of subjectivity. There are always "forces" influencing these acts, but to call them acts of transcendence means precisely that they are not fully determined by the influencing forces.

Now, what if humanistic psychology took these acts of transcendence seriously. First of all, it would help articulate even better the image of personhood that humanistic psychology wants to uphold. Secondly it should motivate humanistic psychologists to such alternative methods. If human action cannot be wholly determined by situational conditions and factors and a reference to the human subject's meaning bestowals becomes necessary, then at least an analysis of the expressed meanings that persons live in situations can help make them intelligible. Thus, it seems to me that humanistic psychology should adopt a scientific framework that concentrates on a rigorous analysis of expressed meanings. Theoretical discussions concerning the relationship between acts of transcendence and psychological dynamics and their implications for the image of the person plus the development of methodologies for the analysis of meaning should keep humanistic psychology busy well into the next century.

### Endnote

I want to mention a point that could not be developed within the publication constraints of this paper. To my knowledge, the only group of psychologists who have stressed what might be called the "transcendent" possibilities of being human are the transpersonal psychologists. (Humanistic psychologists, in general, are a mixed group: some do, some don't). However, there are several difficulties with the literature of the transpersonal psychologists. When reading it, there seems to be: (1) unclarity about just what the meaning of transpersonal psychology is; (2) an emphasis on the transpersonal dimension of being human to the exclusion of all else; (3) a confusion about whether transcendence is a psychological experience or a metapsychological experience; and (4) an emphasis on the religious sphere, especially Eastern religions, or else esoteric phenomena, the "more-than-human" type of experience. While this latter point is legitimate if one wants to focus specifically on religion, or else extraordinary experiences, it helps little when dealing with the relationship between psychology and ontology. None of the four philosophers referred to in this article have made either appeal. Consequently, an attempt to relate the philosophical sense of "act of transcendence" to the themes expressed by transpersonal psychologists is a complex affair and it will have to await another work.

### References

Bachelard, G. (1972). *La fonction de l'esprit scientifique. Contribution a une psychanalyse de la connaissance objective* (11th ed.) Paris: PUF.

Banaji, M. R. & Crowder, R. G. (1991). Some everyday thoughts on ecologically valid methods. *American Psychologist, 46*, 78-79.

Biemel, W. (1973/1976). *Martin Heidegger: An illustrated study* (Trans. by J. L. Mehta). New York: Harcourt Bruce Jovanovich.

Culler, J. D., Ebersole, P. & Quiring, G. (1991). Meaning of life depth: *The Journal of Humanistic Psychology, 31*, 113-123.

Friedman, M. (1988). Dialogue, confirmation, and the image of the human. *Journal of Humanistic Psychology, 28*, 123-135.

Gardner, M. (1988). [review of S. Hawking's *A brief history of time. New York Review of Books, 35*, Nov. 10, pp. 17-20.

Giorgi, A. (1970). *Psychology as a human science.* New York: Harper & Row.

Giorgi, A. (1987). The crisis of humanistic psychology. *The Humanistic Psychologist, 15*, 5-20.

Goldmann, L. (1977). *Lukacs and Heidegger.* (W. Q. Boelhower, Trans.) London, Routledge & Kegan Paul. (Original work published 1973)

Heidegger, M. (1977). Letter on humanism. (D. F. Krell & J. G. Gray, Trans.). In D. F. Krell (Ed.), *Martin Heidegger: Basic writings* (pp. 193-242). New York: Harper & Row. (Original work published 1947)

Husserl, E. (1983). *Ideas pertaining to a pure phenomenology and to a phenomenological philosophy I.* (F. Kersten, Trans.). The Hague: Nijhoff. (Original work published 1913)

Klemke, E. D. (1981). An introduction. In J. A. C. S. Auer, & J. Hartt (Eds.), *Humanism vs. theism.* Iowa State University Press, VII-IX.

Kundera, M. (1986). *The art of the novel.* New York: Grove Press.

Mahrer, A. R. (1989). The case for fundamentally different existential-humanistic psychologies. *Journal of Humanistic Psychology, 29,* 249-262.

Merleau-Ponty, M. (1942/1963). *The structure of behavior* (A. Fisher, Trans.). Boston, Beacon Press.

Moustakas, C. (1985). Humanistic or humanism? *Journal of Humanistic Psychology, 25,* 5-12.

Murray, E. L. (Ed.) (1987). *Imagination and phenomenological psychology.* Pittsburgh: Duquesne University Press.

Needleman, J. (1963). Systematic explanation and the science of psychoanalysis. In J. Needleman (Ed.) *Being-In-The-World: Selected papers of Ludwig Binswanger.* New York: Basic Books.

O'Hara, M. (1989). When I use the term Humanistic Psychology... *Journal of Humanistic Psychology. 29,* 263-273.

Prasinos, S., & Tittler, B. I. (1984). The existential context of love-styles: An empirical study. *Journal of Humanistic Psychology, 24,* 95-112.

Rogers, C. (1964). Some questions and challenges facing a humanistic psychology. *Journal of Humanistic Psychology, 5,* 1-5.

Rogers, C. (1985). Toward a more human science of the person. *Journal of Humanistic Psychology, 25,* 7-24.

Smith, M. B. (1982). Psychology and humanism. *Journal of Humanistic Psychology, 22,* 44-55.

Smith, M. B. (1986). Toward a secular humanistic psychology. *Journal of Humanistic Psychology, 26,* 7-26.

Smith, M. B. (1990). Humanistic psychology. *Journal of Humanistic Psychology, 30,* 6-21.

# 24

# Relational Humanism: A Psychology for a Pluralistic World

*Maureen O'Hara*

At last count there were over four hundred different therapies competing for the therapist's training dollars and the client's health insurance benefits. Whether major established schools or "treatments of the month," all claim their approaches are valid and are "true" in some objective way. On the basis of such claims, whole professions of helpers have evolved with elaborate legitimizing structures and procedures. Increasingly patients/clients are taking their therapist the task (and to court) for failure to provide some abstract and absolute standard of care, basing their claims on scientific assumptions about the nature of psychological knowledge.

At the same time, though, members of marginal groups, like women and people of different racial and ethnic groups, are busily deconstructing the whole edifice, advancing postmodernist arguments that the most firmly established theories and practices — whether medical model or humanistic — are based on modernist world-views reflecting the habits of mind, realities and values of the people who are inventing them. These post-structural critics believe all totalizing discourses — in ordinary words, grand theories of everything — are suspect, that even in the physical and biological sciences, knower and known are fundamentally inseparable, and that advanced technological society has created a psychology in its own image. And if that isn't confusing enough, a lively conversation exists within humanistic psychology, feminism, transpersonal psychology, critical theory, and some areas of analytical psychology, that suggests that the image of psychological "health" enshrined within the mental health community is actually deeply sick, and the treatments based upon it make people worse, not better.

Whether we are aware of it or not, we have all become postmodernists. When we include studies from social-learning theory, cognitive science, neurological studies, perception, depth psychology, sociology, anthropology and any number of critical studies, we come to the conclusion that the inner psychological world of human beings, our consciousness or subjectivity, is a creative product. The "I" each of us knows is produced through dialogical engagements with the world into which one is born and lives. Inner physical sensations and perceptions of external events are interpreted, symbols, narratives and conceptual schemas generated, against which new experiences are referred. This produces, with varying degrees of permanence or fluidity, our subjective inner symbolic map for the self-in-the-world. If this constructivist view is correct then we should expect different socio-cultural landscapes to produce different kinds of inner selves. And they do.

## Selves in Cultural Contexts

In Western cultures, especially in the United States, people seem to experience themselves with a clear, lived sense of the "I," which they refer to as "myself," and which is the same "I" throughout life, a self that is clearly distinguishable from other selves. Radical transformations or discontinuities are expected to be accompanied by anxiety, often intense. Not to know clearly who one "is," to lose one's sense of coherence and continuity is felt as a loss of self. In Western culture, this kind of disintegration and disorder has become equated with mental illness or even madness. Freedom and respect for the integrity of that self by others is also highly prized. This ideal of an autonomous, clearly bounded, self-assertive, self-responsible individual, who acts consistently and coherently is the definition — the *sine qua non* — of psychological health for both males and females. Recently this view of self, which is the self firmly ensconced at the center of humanistic psychology, has been shown to be culturally and contextually exclusive. In other cultures overseas, among individuals from non-dominant and immigrant groups within our own culture, and under varying relational circumstances even within the same group, ideals of "personhood" might not necessarily imply such a strong sense of a distinct, individuated and stable self. We now know that far from representing some absolute "ideal human nature" many cultures go to considerable lengths to discourage such psychological patterns for adults. The ideal person is not one with a strong sense of personal identity, expressiveness and creativity, but is someone who participates within their own social contexts. This "sociocentric" self is almost identical to the "relational" self of feminist psychology, and the "process" self I have described elsewhere.

The "I" at the center of our world-view, our system of laws and social conventions, the educational system of our psychology is based on a Western, egocentric view of the person. Within the humanistic psychological community, the egocentric version of self has been so central to self-actualization theory that the frequent observation that females and non-dominant males or ethnic groups often fall outside this description, did not, until recently, result in any real modification of this picture. Rather it resulted in discrepancies being attributed to failures within the "deviants" themselves, who were deemed less developed, and less psychologically healthy. In the time-honored tradition of blaming the victim, this conclusion was then used to justify traditional patterns of economic and political discrimination, and ultimately abuse. It also lead to psychologists interested in the psychology of women and other marginal groups departing the humanistic psychology community in droves, greatly diminishing our intellectual vitality.

## Postcards from the Edge

In recent years the egocentric bias in psychology has been subjected to increasing criticism - especially from those seen as "other" to this cultural norm and as marginal to the definitional centers of society. Realizing how much of the research upon which maps of the human psyche were drawn reflected the theoretical schemas of the minds of privileged elites, or if empirical, were based upon studies of white male college students, feminists, people of color and people from other non-dominant groups have begun to accumulate other views of the psyche drawn by phenomenological investigation of and by diverse peoples.

The feminist work is well developed and seems to show that women live their lives in their connections and relationships, evaluate their well-being in contextual, concrete terms and appear to develop their sense of self in concrete, relational terms. Studies of women seem to suggest that psychological well-being is not an individualistic affair, as women concern themselves not only with how they themselves are doing, but also how their relationships are doing and how those they belong to, love and care for, are doing too. Self concept — whom a woman believes herself to be — is multi-determined, moment by moment, and over time, by the different relational contexts in which she operates.

The postmodern discussion now underway — whether by feminists, non-european ethnic groups or other "others" — marks a return to the center of discussions in psychology of the experiencing Subject. Gaining ground throughout human studies is the recognition that human beings do not all live in the same perceptual universe, do not all have the same kinds of selves, do not all care about, value or believe the same things. At the level of individual psychology, respect for individual subjectivity, although long championed within humanistic psychology by people like Carl Rogers, Abraham Maslow, Clark Moustakas, Eugene Gendlin, Rollo May, has nevertheless assumed a largely homogeneous (European, masculine, elite, modernist) cultural context. Now it is time to extend our theory to embrace the multi-hued, multi-voiced, multi-contexted worlds we actually inhabit and to recognize that any decontextualized abstraction that attempts to separate persons from their life-worlds is bound to seriously distort and mis-understand human experience.

We must now take responsibility for the ways in which our theories and observations are themselves formative acts serving to construct realities as much as to describe or define them. When abstractions are based in and reflect the particular interests and world views of the dominating elites, such discourses have the power to, and historically have lead to patterns of social and interpersonal abuse. It may also be the case that the desire for and popularity of abstract theory are themselves both effect and cause of a great deal of the psychological pain we see around us.

I would like to propose that if humanistic psychology is to seize the opportunity for intellectual leadership now offered it by virtue of the epistemological fragmentation occurring within mainstream psychology, it is time to develop nothing short of a new, postmodern psychology. In particular we must take up the task left unfinished by our founding giants and advance a psychology reflective of and which can contribute to the pluralistic worlds we all now inhabit. Such a new humanistic psychology will need a contextual, relational, flexible vision that combines features of both the abstract-egocentric views of individual Subjectivity with which we are all familiar, with the less familiar contextual-sociocentric views which try to understand psychological life within specific concrete relational contexts. We must also bring to our work what we have learned from social theory, anthropology, religious and cultural studies, political theory, feminism and ethnic studies, toward a greater understanding of the interplay between individual Subjectivity and broader cultural forces.

In these postmodern times it is no longer feasible for psychologists of any stripe — but particularly humanistic psychologists who have always granted epistemic validity to individual experience — to consider questions of psychological development, functioning and psychotherapeutic treatment of anyone, without considering the specific, concrete situations and contexts in which they participate, the basic world-view at the center of both the client's and therapist's psychological landscapes, and how these all interact within the therapeutic context. Once we accept that where the question of what constitutes the fully human life concerned there are no absolute answers, we — clients and therapists — become existentially free, and actually obliged, to make our own choices about who we shall be and how we shall live and what we will let matter to us.

## Beware the Back-lash

This much freedom is a job for grown-ups. Life with no externally-given moral compass or ready-made sources of meaning can be terrifying, overwhelming, and bewildering. Responses to such freedom are varied and often troubling. In the next decades humanists who affirm the primacy of human experience must expect to become the targets of intensified attacks. Attempts to discredit our work will come from within mainstream psychology, from those who have made investments in the scientific modernist traditions in psychology, as well as from "true believers" — left and right — who see in the postmodern discourse nothing but anarchy, superficiality and narcissistic inflation.

Humanistic emphasis on the pursuit of one's own authenticity and self-fulfillment has become a popular target for criticism in recent years. It has been condemned from conservatives as leading to selfishness, moral relativism, and the breakdown of traditional values, condemned from the radical left as hopelessly individualistic, and politically naive, and condemned by orthodox psychiatry as romantic, shallow and irresponsible. Common to all these criticism is an underlying misanthropy and suspicion that too much freedom and self-development is a dangerous thing. Such criticisms mis-frame the problem and take the symptom for the illness. The critics are correct when they say that Americans feel disconnected and alienated. They are also correct that the search for self-fulfillment can easily become an excuse for endless pursuit of self-gratification. Demands for freedom have increasingly come to mean freedom from commitments and responsibility rather than freedom to be one's own self. And they are right to point to disintegration of our environment and communities, and responsibility rather than freedom to be one's own self. And they are right to condemn the victimization of the vulnerable, as a social ill on a catastrophic scale. But they are wrong when they identify the humanistic search for self-fulfillment as the culprit; they are wrong when they suggest that the health of a community must always be pitted against the freedom of the individual; and they are dangerously wrong when they suggest that we have gone too far down the road to freedom and it is time to roll back our freedoms "for our own good."

An increasingly significant voice within and without psychology points in another direction. People from the margins, those historically silenced by the dominating world views that has deemed them "object," are discovering the vastly expanded sense of empowerment, creativity and joy that comes when one first begins to recognize truth within one's own experience. Humanistic psychologies have been the route for many to reclaim their subjective voice. In humanistic therapy, workshops, classrooms, and organizations people have learned to base their actions and life-choices on their own particular authentic experience. And they have discovered that it is only by making such choices for oneself that one becomes a fully emancipated member of society.

Humanistic psychology has a long standing love affair with individual human beings, seeing us not as children to be taught, patients to be cured or as victims to be protected but as unique centers of consciousness, responsibility, intentionally and choice.

The problem, as I see it, is not that humanism has gone awry because of too much emphasis on the search for fulfillment of the individual self, but rather that we have misunderstood the nature of that search and in some ways have made it impossible to succeed. So that instead of our searches for self-actualization leading to more meaningful lives as intended they actually end up making us feel less connected, less whole and more alienated. Because the self at the center of humanistic psychology has been framed in a modernist ego-centric world view, it misconstrues the nature of the selves to be realized, and in doing so fails to recognize that genuine individuality can only flower within those social contexts in which such individuality is protected, nurtured and developed.

Through a fabric of cultural forces, from religion to psychiatry, from Marxism to marketing, we in the West have lost touch with, and so have betrayed the very sources of our humanness and have been persuaded to accept a shrunken version of ourselves. And we have also been persuaded, and been very ready to be persuaded, to bolster this shrunken self-concept with externally derived compensations and fortifications.

Bigotry, sexism, racism, turning people including ourselves into categories — such as "Adult Children of Alcoholics" "the homeless", AIDS victims, "senior citizens," "white males," liberals and conservatives, and so on — are all ways of bolstering our puny stripped-down modern selves.

### The Personal and the Political

When we started out, humanistic psychology was largely populated by compassionate idealists who had embraced the notion that the personal was political. Many of us took that to mean that if I perfect myself in some mysterious way, that would perfect society, making the egocentric error of drawing the boundaries of self too close to our own skin. If we did enough inner work, if we found a good enough therapist, if we withdrew to our mountain-top and into our private choices, cut ourselves off from oppressive forces "out there," many believed we could radically transcend the human condition. But while we were turned inward our communities were falling into the hands of the greedy, the glib, the slick, the cynical and the fanatical. And because we are all woven from the fabric of our shared world, bit by bit the poverty, fear, despair, violence, bigotry, and pollution that is the daily experience of millions of people — who are, after all, our co-creators — creeps into our consciousness and into our selves.

It is obviously important for all of us to develop greater awareness of our inner landscapes and to undertake the kinds of practices that for millennia have opened our consciousness, but relational selves cannot withdraw permanently into a private search for self and hope to keep on growing. It doesn't work. Eventually we must reconnect. We must make a commitment to each other, to our communities and to the earth we share. Relational selves sink or swim together.

A commitment to the emancipation of a human self, understood as a relational self, far from leading to hopeless relativism, nihilism, political correctness, self-indulgence, inevitable isolation and atomistic disconnection — as our critics maintain — will lead to the development of one's own unique particular self. But such development can only succeed if we make a shift towards responsibility, caring, accountability and community. Once we come to view our selves as creatively woven from experiences within the world around us, then that world takes on a whole new significance. No longer seen as hostile impediment to true self-fulfillment or even as "a worldly distraction" but as the very source of who we are and of who we might possibly become, it is not longer feasible to separate the work of self realization from the work of the realization of the potential of the communities we inhabit. A fully humanistic psychology must see environment interests, community interests and personal interests as the same thing.

I am convinced that our pluralistic world is waiting for a fully humanistic psychology, that is, one based in a new relational humanism that understands selves as contextual and relational, that will acknowledge individual subjectivity in all its glorious diversity, that will establish and value relational norms of mutuality, civility, responsibility and accountability.

# 25

# Celebrations and Problems of Humanistic Psychology

*Eugene T. Gendlin*

This paper celebrates the history and victories of Humanistic Psychology, and it also considers the tasks ahead, especially the problem that Humanistic Psychology may not be reproducing itself into the next generation.

I remember the day in the 1950's, when Abe Maslow had just presented his paper on Peak Experiences. As a young student, I came up afterwards to talk to him. I expressed my enthusiasm and admiration for what he had said. He responded by saying: "Isn't it a shame that this paper will never be published?" Surprised, I asked why not. He said "It can't be published. Nothing like it can be published." He explained that things like this did not fit the prejudices of all the journals and the whole field.

Here we celebrate how wrong his prediction was. The paper (1957) is now a classic, reprinted countless times. But whether we have changed the underlying conditions that so discouraged him, remains to be seen.

Humanistic Psychology began in a separate room and meeting-time just before the APA convention each year. In those years there were just enough such psychologists to fill one medium-sized room. The group eventually grew to put on its own convention, sometimes larger than the APA's — but still before APA and separate from it. Why always still separate? It is part of the problem I want to discuss. Humanistic Psychology and its experiential outlook are still very much separated from the rest of the field of psychology and psychotherapy.

I pressed into Maslow's hand a paper of my own about something similar: times in therapy when there is suddenly a clearer perception. The world seems poignant and sharply etched; it is as if the windows had just been washed — one sees the same things as before, but what a difference! I wrote that "at such times experience is vastly better than all the meanings in one's perceptual set." It seemed to me (and it still does) that what really matters is not the content, and not the forms and definitions, but the *manner and quality* of the ongoing experiencing. I got to know Abe Maslow later on, but others writing in this volume knew him better. Humanistic Psychology had many sources. I can add something about two of them: Carl Rogers, and Encounter Groups.

## Carl Rogers

I was trained by Carl Rogers and his group (John Shlien, Jack Butler, Don Grummond and others). Then I worked closely with him for eleven years. As I said in the obituary (1988) I wrote for him:

> Rogers thought that optimal health was the absence of blockage, the seamless functioning of every aspect of experience in relation to every other. During the fifties he wrote a paper on "The Fully Functioning Person." It was accepted for publication but then the editor insisted on adding a paragraph of his own in front, explaining his disagreement. Rogers withdrew the article. This and other experiences led me to begin a new journal, *Psychotherapy: Theory, Research and Practice* in 1963. I published Rogers' paper in our first issue.

Rogers went against almost everything that seemed known in the field of therapy. He changed the role of the therapist. They were not to impose their interpretations. (Anyone can think of two or more interpretations of most any human thing.) No longer did "well" therapists look down on "sick" patients. The patient was no longer to be a passive object of "treatment." Rogers changed the very name of "patient" to "client." He eliminated the medical model and took the new term from the field of law. The lawyer is an expert and advocate but not a decision-maker concerning the client's life. Clients were invited to go deeply into their own experience. The therapist was to listen and share every nuance of the patient's experience. I will say more about how different it is to understand and accompany someone in this way. Rogers eliminated the couch. So unusual was this, that one textbook of those years devoted one its few pictures to a photograph of two people sitting across a desk from each other. It was a picture of Client-Centered

Therapy! He eliminated diagnosis, the patient's history, note-taking, clinical distance, and all the old frost-bitten attitudes. A graduate from his program was a new kind of psychologist. Rogers made a completely fresh start. It took immense courage.

Early on I didn't know the field very well. I didn't know how entirely different Rogers' starting point was, and what a long-lasting barrier to communication this difference is in our field. I want to emphasize how drastically Rogers' basic assumptions differed from the usual assumptions. Most theories in our field assume that all reason and all values come to human beings from the outside, from society and culture. Animals have quite complex interactions with each other, but this is said to be due to (little understood) "instincts." Since human beings are supposed to lack those, all meanings and values must be imposed on us from outside. These are still the underlying assumptions that are built into most theoretical concepts.

Rogers assumed instead that a human being's organismic experience is an *internal* source of life-direction, of making sense, and of values.

It made for endless misunderstandings of Rogers: He emphasized listening, but why listen to confused clients? Didn't they come to therapy because there is something wrong with them? Rogers said that the value-direction develops from inside, but other therapists thought they could not proceed without deciding on some goal in advance.

I agreed with Rogers' assumptions, but I was a philosophy student. I had to articulate *how* and *why* those assumptions are right. I could not be satisfied with the mere assertion of a *self-actualization "principle."* I wanted to *show* it. Isn't every living organism "adaptive," and doesn't that mean that it holds itself together and maintains its living? If it did not, it would tend to disintegrate, I argued then, and now.

Or, take the *positive social tendencies* that Rogers saw in everyone. Those could sound like mere optimism. But a human being isn't possible except in interaction with others. If its living arises from inside, and its living is interaction, then of course it has "social" tendencies for interaction originating from inside. That is a very different sense of "social" than that all values and ways of living have to be imposed "by society" on the individual.

## The Need for New Concepts

But to articulate our assumptions so that others can grasp them requires changing what we mean by all the main words. For example, if there is *organismic* knowing and internal evaluating, then the word "body" cannot any longer mean just a machine; it must mean something inherently interactional that projects its actions from inside. If the body is reconceived as inherently interaction, as consisting of ongoing living interaction, when such a body senses itself, of course it contains (it *is*) a lot of information about its situation. Our experiential knowing is not a mysterious reception of something from outside. We know the world not mainly through the five external senses, but much more basically through the body's self-sensing, because the body *is* interaction with its environment.

To redefine the words, to turn words from being obstacles to being bridges so that the new understanding from one area can enter and change other areas — that is precisely the function of theory. The *practice* of most therapists has changed greatly in our direction. The Humanistic movement has also been one factor in levening the whole society so that today it is immensely more open to direct experience than it was in those days. But Humanistic Psychology has not succeeded in communicating its theoretical and philosophical basics to the rest of psychology and to other intellectuals in the social sciences and other disciplines that promulgate the basic assumptions of the society. After fifty years the old assumptions are still built into most theoretical concepts in the social sciences. (1987)

The lack of theoretical and philosophical communication might be due to the fact that it takes a long time and many people to develop and communicate an entirely new vocabulary. There has been insufficient appreciation of the size of this task, and not enough attention and training for theory among us. Certainly it is a different kind of theory we need, one that brings and uses live experience along with the concepts (Gendlin, 1961, 1963, & 1992) In such a theory the concepts should not even make sense unless they also generate the relevant experiences in the reader.

It lies in the nature of the Humanistic approach that it depends first on experience, and only then on thinking further — from the experiences. Since experiential knowing comes first, we can live and work with that alone, so that theory can seem unnecessary. Is that why not so many Humanistic psychologists have gone on to develop theory? Perhaps that is one reason I have felt rather lonely in my theoretical work, whereas I have gotten a great deal of attention on focusing and the practice of therapy.

What Rogers discovered could be observed by anyone, he said, if one simply tried out responding to people with the reflective listening that he taught. He asked people to adopt his method only as an "operational hypothesis," as he phrased it. You didn't need to agree with him; you didn't need to believe these assumptions. You needed only to try out responding to someone by listening and saying back the crux of what that person intended to communicate. If you did just only this, you would soon find all the rest for yourself. That is so. If you only listen, if you impose nothing, then what people open before you is very intricate and very beautiful. It is also always new, unique, an intricate mesh of their livings and meanings. These are not on the surface. They lie always a few steps further in from the more tritely formed feelings and meanings that the person has mostly thought and felt. When this intricacy and these deeper meanings open, they are new and fresh not only the therapist, but also to the person.

A person says something; one responds by saying back its crux. The person hears it said back. It isn't quite what the person intended. The person corrects it. The therapist accepts the correction (of course, since it is the client's meaning that is to be grasped here). The client hears it. Yes, now that is mostly right, but there is still a little wrinkle that wasn't heard. That too is said, heard, and said back. Then the client says the next thing, and again it is said back and the saying-back is corrected, until the client feels heard. There may be another message and another, but quite soon that flow ends. Now it seems there is no more to say. A silence comes.

What the client had there, waiting to be said, *has now been said.* Where that had lain, stuck, waiting, trying to be said, there is now a space. Of course there is more to say; the problem is not solved. One feels the unresolved discomfort, but there are no ready words, no items from the problem ready and waiting. The client feels (knows, has, is,) the inner silent edge of more.

From silently attending to that edge, the next thing to say will arise. It is into this space that the next thing rises — something from deeper, something that the person never heard or felt before. As step after step comes from the depths, one discovers one's own intricacy, one's own errors and one's own good sense. Without this process it is obvious that people remain mostly unknown to themselves — and certainly to us. "Are you angry to cover up the fear? Or are you afraid of the anger because it seems so big? Or how is it?" Without going inside to that edge, without actually finding it so or so, or more intricate yet, how can we possibly find out? Once we have seen this process of steps from the edge, how could we possibly want to impose some set of simplistic generality-concepts and judgments on a person instead?

When one of my early clients, a Lesbian woman, terminated after two years of very successful therapy, she kissed me on the cheek and said something about how unusual it was to find someone who could understand and not misconstrue a Lesbian person. At the time that did not seem special to me because I did not think of it in terms of prejudices toward a specific group. Rogers' training had made it obvious to me that I knew very little about *any* other person's sexuality and life-meanings, unless they explored it from inside. To do therapy I have to let *any* next person teach me their intricate mesh, their world, their step-by-step revelation of how it is. That seemed just obvious to me (and it still does).

Someone trained by Rogers needed no special insight or ideology to listen and try to follow a gay person, or a member of any other special group, because it was obvious that *every* individual must teach the therapist. And no person's inner life can be known, not even by the people themselves, without entering into those little steps that come from the depth, from that edge where at first one doesn't know how to go on. It seems so obvious, that it has taken me many years to recognize how missing this insight still is in most of our field.

Reflective listening was promulgated as an easily-learned technique, and as a complete method of therapy, all one needs. A deep therapy process does indeed arise just from active listening, when genuine. But it isn't a complete method alone.

More than half the clients did not know where in themselves they could find organismic knowing and internal evaluating. Fred Zimring and I collected what we called "dimensions of experiencing" (Gendlin and Zimring, 1955), which became Rogers' "Process Scale" and later the "Experiencing Scale" (Psychiatric Institute, University of Wisconsin). These scales led to the finding that the successful clients were able to contact experiencing directly already at the start of therapy, while those with failure outcomes never achieved it. Since therapy did not show clients how to contact organismic experiencing in themselves, I developed what we now call "Focusing:" a systematic teachable way to help people discover this in themselves (Gendlin, 1981).

Most therapists quite rightly use not only listening and focusing, but also every other helpful kind of response. (Whatever else one does, one should quickly listen again right afterwards.) It is not as an exclusive method that I feature it here. Rather, it is a door to the Humanistic basics — not as beliefs to have in advance — but as direct happenings which we can *then* think further about. Let us think a little further about those happenings now.

By saying-back one keeps a person company with each step, and with the silences between so that next steps can come. It is not up to the therapist to decide whether the client's feelings and perceptions are valid. Rather, their validity rests on the inner discovery that each little step that comes is meaningful. With such steps something stirs and comes alive in the client, more and more. After a string of such steps early in therapy, one client, inwardly moved, felt the tears coming as she said: "Oh.... I *do* make sense."

There is also a gradually discovered honesty and sincerity that comes there. The worst experiences feel richer and better than blocking and fearful pretense. One can breathe and feel continuous inside. Truth comes to be valued very directly, strange as that assertion might seem in general. The client says: "That *is* how it is — whew, (breath, relief) — that feels true; it's straight; it's clean."

Inside every human body is an "I" who looks at you from behind the eyes. That "I" struggles with all the stuff of life, struggles to find something of value, and it wants to expand into caring for others. If we have any other project, other than to serve that "I" in there, what could such an other project be? To sell the person a car? To get them to join some ideological group to which we belong? To shape them to fit some social performance? Sometimes we want those things but not if it is therapy. For therapy I cannot imagine any other project than to see that "I" in there, to respond to that "I", to keep that person company, to follow each of that person's efforts to make/find something positive that is continuous from inside. And indeed, if that inner edge and the little steps are pursued, what is continuous from inside always turns out to be deeply positive, even if it begins as a shoddy project.

We need to show our colleagues this "I," this edge, the steps from inside, and this inner intricacy. We cannot do it in terms of the current concepts of mechanical bodies and socially constructed persons. But we can re-conceive the basic concepts of nature and living bodies. I did some of this (Gendlin, 1962, 1973, 1979, 1991, & 1992). We can use a new kind of concept to think about truer and wider observations of the human person.

## Encounter Groups

The Encounter Group Movement went beyond therapy and did much to bring all this into the fabric of society. I observed some of the history of this movement.

Experiments in group process were pioneered for many years in at the National Training Laboratories (NTL) at Bethel, Maine, and at Tavistock in England. Certain seeming "laws" of group process had been discovered there. Some of those still held when we conducted groups with our new assumptions and attitudes; others did not. With our new approach a very different and quite explosive group process arose.

In Wisconsin between 1959 and 1962, I and some others went to various towns in the State, and offered something odd, and at that time quite undefined: a group whose membership was quite open and which continued for many hours or days. The excitement generated by it was sometimes reported in the newspapers. We had created/discovered the Encounter Group. Later I found that many others had been doing the same sort of thing at about the same time all over the country.

The Encounter Movement and all that led to it undoubtedly changed our society. Today one hears ordinary people talk of interior experience and inter-personal relations in ways that only psychologists and clients near the end of therapy ever talked of before. Multitudes of people came to be in touch with feelings, who had never known what that was like. It has made many other changes possible.

## The Need for New Institutions

After some years we all noticed that such groups had no real way to continue: It is now well known that each new group goes through an explosive discovery of inward richness. People find that their inward experience is not at all only what the common categories and shared phrases say. It is vastly more, very much their own from inside, and it opens a new world of human complexity. After that, one wants and needs to live differently. But now what?

The Encounter Group Movement slowed and died around our failure to build social institutional patterns in which one could continue to live in and with this new world of inner human complexity. People would come to each subsequent group hoping to continue the intensity of the previous time. They needed to live some more at the level of intensity they developed in another group the previous weekend. Instead, with new people one had to begin afresh. People came again and again seeking some sort of continuation, a new life, now that this inner break-through had occurred. But each group would start again at the beginning. Some people — those new to the process — would have the usual break-through. But those who had often had this already could only pretend to be doing it now. After many such efforts they were frustrated.

The Encounter Group Movement fed on ever new people, but it developed no continuation, no patterns of meeting or association that could become part of the social fabric.

In those years I was (and still am) full of half-shaped ideas for new social institutions in which one could live with and after this now well-known break-through to one's inner intricacy. How could institutions change so as to give room to intricate personal experience, even give it an essential role in our routines? Marriage and women's patterns *have* changed in this way, but business, schools, and hospitals have not. Business wants your experiential openness for creativity, but only within the limits of hierarchical control. Doctors treat your leg and ignore the fact that you are attached to it. This year there is a two million dollar project in one hospital to find out if healing proceeds better when patients have the right to make themselves a cup of coffee! Innovations arise, but they are soon suppressed. Experimental wings in mental hospitals last about a year. Innovative schools such as the universities without walls find that their graduates are rejected by the licensing boards. I will have more to say about licensing. Let me first mention our own institutional innovations.

In 1967 we developed CHANGES, a group that has continued now for some twenty five years and has numerous ranches. People engage in any helpful psychological process we know, or any that someone present can teach us. Ongoing training in these processes enables them to be engaged in successfully by anyone that comes. While other networks practice only one skill, we welcome them all.

Changes also rests on two organizational discoveries we made early on, concerning the destructive kind of group process.

It is vital that the business meeting happen in a different room and at a different time than our main content which are the personal processes. With this separation a small motivated group very smoothly does all the business of the organization. Others are welcome to join the business meetings but do not usually do so unless they have something special to take up. In this way the kind of group process that has torn up most experientially open organizations does not arise.

The other innovation is that in our main personal meeting there is *only support*. We do not engage in the mutually hurtful kind of group process in which people dump raw emotions on each other. In another room two people in conflict may get a neutral person to listen slowly first to one person and then the other. Some conflicts stay unresolved but the group-space is always safe. There is always someone who undertakes to listen carefully and reflectively to anyone who is not being heard by the group. We listen to individuals one at a time.

Very recently we have again become interested in group process, but we are learning how many preconditions must be in place before a positive group process can happen.

Later on we developed PARTNERSHIP (two people splitting time in half, taking turns being client and listener). During Changes meetings this happened all the time, but now we are arranging a more or less regular partner for everyone, quite apart from any meetings. Partners divide two hours or whatever time they have. In one's own time one does whatever one feels might be helpful. To make this possible, one teaches any skill one knows to the partner. Listening, focusing, and other psychological processes are usual, but one might want to show one's partner photographs or talk about any topic. No one tells us how to use our own time.

These two social-institutional pattern have gone far enough and lasted long enough to be hopeful today. Both were built around listening and focusing, but they have always included every other helpful method and way of working that any one of the participants can bring in (Gendlin, 1981 and 1987). The Focusing Institute in Chicago has more information on both.

The lack of new social patterns clouds the future of Humanistic Psychology today. Along with its lack of theory to communicate with the wider intellectual community, the lack of embodiment in the social institutions is a second strand of the problem we face.

## The Lack of Humanistic Training Settings

If by "Humanistic" we mean third-camp therapists (neither psychoanalytic nor behaviorist) then we are now 80 or 90 percent of all psychotherapists in the country. Of course there are many narrower definitions, but we had a lot to do with the size of the third camp, and that is surely something to celebrate on our anniversary.

On the other hand, younger graduates now tend to be more rigid. Third-camp attitudes are not what clinical programs teach. There are very few humanistically oriented training and internship settings. Humanistic psychologists seem not to have wanted to organize and build. We need to know and help expand those training settings that do exist, and to set up many more where we can.

Currently, most clinical students who are humanistically inclined must endure training programs that are inimical to their basic commitments. They live as underground persons. Many do not last until graduation. The more humanly sensitive their attitudes, the less are they likely to last. They have no problem mastering all the irrelevant material. They can also learn much from the psychoanalytic and behavioral approaches. The problem consists in the attitudes inherent in most training programs. Usually it is dangerous to show one's feelings (one can be thrown out for being "unstable"). Clinical distance is required. Human beings are treated as subjects upon whom the student is required to impose alien patterns. Few can pretend to be doing this well. The sort of student who would become a Humanistic psychologist, if admitted at all, now frequently drops out.

## We Are Not Reproducing Ourselves

Training is the main way for a group of professionals to reproduce their type into the next generation. Since so much official training is designed by others with an inimical outlook, it is doubtful whether Humanistic Psychology can continue into future generations. The relative lack of official training programs is the third strand of the problem to which I am pointing.

## Innovation and Diversity in Therapy is Being Made Illegal

There is now also a new trend which drastically changes the conditions for practicing that obtained until now. I mean the licensing of psychotherapists. Already in many states, new laws prohibit new discoveries and new attitudes in clinical training. Psychology, social work, counseling, and family practice are being legally required to rigidify their training and limit it to the old contents and the old attitudes that are embodied in those contents. I experience it most painfully when I participate in discussing and redesigning clinical programs. Years ago we argued about what would best train a therapist. Today the discussion begins with the requirements for licensing, and they are the main concern at every turn. If our program does not look orthodox, our graduates won't be allowed to practice.

The State licensing board requires a long list of traditional psychology-contents, and does not specify how much of each it wants. Could three courses cover all those topics, or will they want to see a course in each? That would leave no open slots at all. We sit down to design a new program, but we find that we can design only two or three electives. Almost the whole program must consist of the old (largely irrelevant) content of orthodox psychology. The whole therapy literature must be covered in one survey course. Anything more, and certainly any innovative training increases the risk that our graduates won't be legally permitted to practice.

I served on the Licensing Board of my State for some years, and fought hard for specificity. How many courses for this old irrelevant stuff? Five? Seven? Nine? But such a board likes its undefined power to approve or disapprove programs. Since the number of years they can be on the Board is also unlimited, they become identified with its power.

They do sincerely attempt to be neutral as to orientation. If Humanistic Psychology could formulate itself, then — in principle — its requirements could be included. In principle, but not actually, because: What would our course-requirements be? We would want to include a philosophical capacity to question established concepts and to formulate new ones. We would include discussions of therapy attitudes and issues, as well as literature, poetry, and other creations of sensitive people. We would lead students to practice and come to know therapeutic processes inside themselves, and to become more sensitive people. Many clients are already more sensitive and well-suffered than their therapists. It is absurd that the law will require therapists to be boorish about the human spirit, personally defended, hidden, unknown to themselves, legally forced to treat people entirely in terms of mechanistic attitudes and diagnostic vocabularies (which, moreover don't stand up to simple research). But the courses we would want would not be recognized as psychology by my Board.

But something even more important is being outlawed, something we cannot yet even see and may never see. It is what innovative psychologists of any kind *would* discover and formulate in future years (which my Board *would then* perhaps respect and accept), which will never emerge and will never be formulated, because the field of psychotherapy will have become uniform, and will march off as a *humanly uneducated* profession, as so many other specialized fields have already become. Then new approaches cannot be promulgated. We won't get the chance to formulate a more specific humanistic vocabulary relevant to our practice.

Of course there should be sanctions against unethical practices, and that *is* a proper sphere for law. We need simple laws against unethical practices, not a straightjacket for everyone. And even if everyone must be licensed, one need not mix educational requirements into ethical sanctions. The frequency of unethical practice is the same at the Ph.D. and M.A. levels. It is not a reason to give control of the whole of our education over to a government body.

Behind this licensing is the irresistible force of money. Insurance payments are now essential to most of our clients. Psychiatry is fighting to get a slice of every reimbursement. Psychologists want to be strong and look strong in this battle with psychiatrists. Those concerned with this battle have little time to think about our need for innovative service and education. If we could get them to think about it, these needs would not be hard to reconcile. We can at least demand a limit on *the number of courses* of which the law determines the content. That would leave the rest of a program free.

In a democracy it seems hardly right to determine everyone's education by the judgment of six or seven government appointees. Indeed it is probably unconstitutional. Court challenges are coming. But courts feel that they must leave education to the professionals in each field. So long as licensing laws are uniformly the wish of the APA, and so long as the APA is nearly only official voice in the field, court challenges to licensing must fail. We can hope to stop the trend only if we can organize a group within APA to defend educational diversity and innovation, and to show that professionals are not of one mind on this. Then the court would overturn these laws.

The trend is not only toward licensing but far worse: toward outlawing unlicensed practitioners altogether. That is what the APA vociferously advocates in every state. Such a law which makes even unpaid clinical practices illegal without the license did already pass both state houses in Illinois. It was stopped only by our Governor's veto.

In the future, people like Rogers and Maslow will not be able to train psychologists in a new way, because the law will prohibit such graduates from practicing. That is a great change in our field. If it is not reversed, the continuation of Humanistic Psychology is doubtful.

We need to appreciate how much we have achieved, and that at the moment we are still in a good position to safeguard the future.

### References

Gendlin, E. T. and Zimring, F. (1955). The qualities or dimensions of experiencing, and their change. *Counseling Center Discussion Papers*. Chicago: University of Chicago Library.

Gendlin, E. T. (1962). *Experiencing and the creation of meaning*. New york: The Free Press, Macmillan.

Gendlin, E. T. (1973). Experiential phenomenology. In M. Natanson (Ed.), *Phenomenology and the social sciences*. Evanston: Northwestern University Press.

Gendlin, E. T. (1979). *A process model*. Unpublished manuscript.

Gendlin, E. T. (1981). *Focusing*. New York: Bantam Books.

Gendlin, E. T. (1987). A Philosophical critique of the concept of narcissism. In D. M. Levin, (Ed.), *Pathologies of the modern self*. New York: N.Y.U. Press.

Gendlin, E. T. (1988). Obituary for Carl Rogers, *American Psychologist, 43* (2).

Gendlin, E. T. (1987). Partnerships. *Focusing Folio* (Vol. No. 6, 2).

Gendlin, E. T. (1990). On emotion in therapy. *Focusing Folio* (Vol. 9, 1). Also in: Safran, J. D. and Greenberg, L. S., (Eds.), (1991). *Emotions, Psychotherapy, and Change*. New York: Guilford.

Gendlin, E. T. (1992). Thinking beyond patterns: Body, language, and situations. In B. denOuden & M. Moen (Eds.), *The presence of feeling in thought*. New York: Peter Lang.

Maslow, A. H. (1957). Cognition of being in the peak experience. *Counseling Center Discussion Papers*. Chicago: University of Chicago Library. (Rogers "published" the paper for our group.)

Rogers, C. R. (1958). A tentative scale for the measurement of process in psychotherapy. In E. Rubinstein & M. Parloff (Eds.), *Research in Psychotherapy*. American Psychological Association, Washington, DC.

Rogers, C. R. (1963). The concept of the fully functioning person. *Psychotherapy: Theory, Research and Practice, 1* (1).

# Representations of the "Third Force" in History of Psychology Textbooks

Frederick J. Wertz

How is the "Third Force" — phenomenological, existential, and humanistic — approach to psychology represented in contemporary text books on the history of psychology? This report is based on a sample of twenty four textbooks, including six in two editions. The complexity of the subject and the variability among the texts are most striking. In order to make the findings relatively manageable, I will discuss the form and length of the presentation, the content — both breadth and depth — of the coverage, changes in the most recently revised editions, the "accuracy" of the information, and the evaluations offered. Finally, I will spell out some implications of this study for historians of psychology and for humanistic psychologists.

## The Form and Length of Presentation

Most of the text books published since the late 1970's contain coverage of the "Third Force" movement in psychology. Many include whole chapters, entitled "Humanistic Psychology" (e.g., Lundin, 1985; Stagner, 1988; Kendler, 1987), "Third Force Psychology" (e.g., Hergenhahn, 1986 & 1992; Brennan, 1982 & 1991), "Humanism, Phenomenology and Existentialism" (Hillner, 1984), and "Existential Psychology" (Lundin, 1985). These ranged from twenty-two to forty-two pages each (forty-two in Hillner, thirty-nine in Kendler, thirty-one in Hergenhahn, thirty in Stagner, twenty-seven in Lundin, and twenty-two in Brennan).

Equally common was the inclusion of a section or sections ranging from two to eleven pages in chapters such as Hilgard's (1987) "Personality and the Self," "Clinical Psychology," and "Psychology as a Science" (eleven pages total), Marx and Hillix's (1979) "Varieties of Personality Theory" (nine pages), Schultz and Schultz'(1987) "More Recent Developments beyond the Schools of Thought" (eight pages), Leahey's (1987) "Years of Turmoil — 1956-68" (five pages), Wertheimer's (1987) "The Postschools Era" (four pages), Murphy and Kovach's (1972) "History in the Making" (three pages), Murray's (1983) "Eclectic Psychology — 1940-80" (two and a half pages), and Watson's (1978) "Recent Psychology in the United States" (two pages).

Finally, though it was common in the 1960's to make no mention whatsoever of the movement or any of its adherents (e.g., Esper, 1964), this rarely occurs since the late 1970's. Benjamin's (1988) and Fancher's (1979, 1990) omission arises from the scope of their texts; they do not include any treatment of approaches which emerged in the last three decades, including the cognitive movement. Hothersall's (1984, 1990) reasons for omission are not obvious from any explicit statement or from his focus and approach. However, hints may be gleaned from his last chapter on whether psychology is "a true science." The author seems troubled by detractors who claim psychology is "soft" or a "pseudoscience" with its research "ignored or ridiculed as a waste of money." He notes that the Nobel Prize winners associated with psychology have been physiologists (Hubel and Wiesel), a neurosurgeon (Sperry), and an information processing scientist (Simon), that the research is less rigorous than the "older" sciences, and that the number of established laws is small. But he argues that "careful" consideration will show "progress" and calls upon the advances in technology and size of the profession to substantiate the field's merit. It might be that humanistic psychology does not live up to the author's criteria for and sense of science, which is an implicit principle of selection for inclusion, or perhaps an emphasis on humanistic detractors would introduce more equivocation than could be resolved by the type or semblance of progress to which the author clings. In a rough but reliable way, the length of the presentation corresponds to the author's overall estimation of the movement's importance.

## The Content of Coverage

*Historical Antecedents*

Hergenhahn and Leahey trace the orientation back to the early Greeks, particularly the Hellenistic cynics and skeptics. Kendler links the notion that man is the measure of all things as well as the call to freedom, spontaneity, natural goodness, and anti-dogmatism to the humanism of the Italian Renaissance. Kendler also traces the idea that human beings require a method of study fundamentally different from inanimate things, the notion of *human science*, to Vico's insistence on and privileging of empathic methodology in history. In Hergenhahn's view, both modern humanism and existentialism arose from Romanticism, with its emphasis on the natural goodness of humans and the enslaving character of society. Brennan, Kendler, Hilgard and Watson and Evans refer to Dilthey's distinction of *Naturwissenschaft* from *Geisteswissenschaft* in establishing the proper methodology for human sciences, *verstehende-psychologie*. Hilgard and Watson and Evans trace *Geisteswissenschaft* as well as the idiographic/nomothetic distinction to Windelband (1849-1915). Hillner, Hergenhahn, Brennan, Hilgard, and Kendler stress the central importance of the phenomenology of Husserl and Heidegger as well as, with Wertheimer, the existentialism of Kierkegaard, Nietzsche, Heidegger, and Sartre. Merleau-Ponty, Tillich, and Buber are occasionally mentioned and discussed. The most commonly mentioned psychologists are Adler and Allport, with Horney following close behind. Also stressed in some texts is the Gestalt school (e.g., Kohler and Koffka). Occasionally mentioned are Stumpf, Kulpe, Jung, James, Binswanger, Boss, David Katz, van Kaam, Frankl, Buhler, MacLeod, May, Child, Snygg & Combs, Goldstein, Fromm, Erikson, and William Stern.

One cannot help but be struck by the richness of this diverse group of forerunners, which seems to form a strong and yet elusive unity given its ambiguity and contradictions. It is difficult to make out any general rhyme or reason concerning which text cites which precursors. However, those who present the premoderns in connection with humanistic psychology tend to be favorable to the movement, and those who do not delve into the modern philosophical influences tend to be the most unfavorable (a notable exception, discussed below, being Leahey).

*Social Context*
The Schultzes and Leahey alone mention the Zeitgeist surrounding the movement, and both paint a vivid picture of a socially troubled time in the United States, with the status quo seeming about to fall apart, face to face with the counter-cultural stance of youth and intellectuals (social critics outside of psychology, e.g., the Putney's attack on the adjustment morality). Many began to oppose the perceived mechanization,

materialism, dehumanization, alienation, deindividualization, regimentation, rigidification, bureaucratization, powerlessness, and phoniness of humankind in the 1960's. The Schultzes go so far as to say that this Zeitgeist is what turned mere historical antecedents into a movement, and Leahey sees both the rise and fall of the movement as parallel to that of the youth counter-culture (e.g., the hippies and yippies).

It is interesting to note that both authors who emphasize this Zeitgeist tend to downplay the impact of the movement on psychology and to offer the darkest picture of the movement's present status and future outlook.

*Institutionalization*

There is not much stress placed on institutionalization, perhaps in keeping with its sparsity. Only Stagner notes that Maslow wrote a letter to Fromm, Rogers, Allport, and Horney in 1954 suggesting that there be a formal organization of a new approach to psychology. The Schultzes include the respective founding dates of the American Association of Humanistic Psychology (1962), the *Journal of Humanistic Psychology* (1961), and the Division of Humanistic Psychology (1971). Brennan notes the publication of translations of european existential-phenomenologists, the initial sponsoring of the *Review of Existential Psychology and Psychiatry*, and the founding of the *Journal of Phenomenological Psychology* in the early 1970's at Duquesne University. Schultz brings out the observation that most of the adherents of the movement are practicing psychologists rather than academicians.

*Characterizations of the Movement*

Since it would be impossible to describe in detail the depiction of the movement in each text, I will forgo anything like an inventory. Instead, I will present the representations along a quasi-continuum of completeness and integration.

*The grossly incomplete text.* Murray's text book was far below the level of the others, and not merely by virtue of the shortness of the presentation, for it could have taken a more central perspective in an even briefer statement. The impression given, reminiscent of some introductory psychology text books, is that humanistic psychology is a therapeutic movement which arose from a disenchantment with psychoanalysis. Its task is said to be the encouragement of a new set of positive outlooks for the individual, enhancing the person's self-regard and happiness. The movement sounds more like a common sense approach to therapy than a science. More is suggested only by the mention of such unelaborated catchwords as becoming, authenticity, anti-determinism, self-experience, actualization, and holistic. That Maslow studied healthy people is mentioned. Rogers is seen as a "forerunner" of a "plethora" of psychotherapeutic methods which have challenged psychoanalysis, the only example offered being Albert Ellis, who is said to make patients' false beliefs more rational.

*Significant figures and principles in "humanistic" psychology.* The next level entails a limited but entirely respectable, sometimes even excellent exposition of the supposed key figures in humanistic psychology, always including and often limited to Rogers and Maslow. Representatives of this characterization are Schultz & Schultz and Leahey. More characteristic than the limitation to Rogers and Maslow is an emphasis on the substantive content of humanistic therapy and theory with little or no attention to philosophical underpinnings, theory of science, research methodology, or the perplexing diversity of works in the "Third Force" movement. Only allusions to these are made. For example, in the area of research methodology, the Schultzes mention Maslow's small sample size and Rogers' "phenomenological" aim, but the implications of these remain unaddressed. Critiques of the other approaches (e.g., theories of humans based on animal research) and general principles of the humanistic movement (e.g., freedom, holism) are given. Little if any conflict among representatives and virtually no exposition of phenomenology or existentialism emerge in what appears to be more a closed book than an open and evolving movement.

Another similar characterization includes greater diversity but without profound unity. A number of different figures in the "movement" may be discussed without much sense of overview or integration. For instance, Stagner only contrasts the long standing debate between the "tough-minded" and "tender-minded" before discussing five different representatives of the latter camp who have attempted greater impact by their association with the movement. He chooses Maslow, Rogers, Allport, May, and Murphy. Stagner even notes the common insistence on scientific status, indeed an expanded conception of science aimed at doing justice to human subject matter, but he gives no more detailed exposition of this issue.

*An uneasy integration of the "Third Force."* Most of the texts attempted, not without difficulty, to differentiate and closely relate together the diverse movements of phenomenology, existentialism, and humanism, and a number of different representatives of what in these texts is usually called the Third Force (in order to distinguish different strands, e.g., humanistic and existential), in which both diversity and unity are found.

The meaning and method of "science" in these texts is consistently taken as problematic, and much detail is devoted to philosophical assumptions and methodological distinctions. Murphy and Kovach expose the need for "new models and new ground rules for drawing the lines of unity within itself and within the totality of the sciences" (1972, p. 475). In the opening sentence of his chapter, Hillner says that this movement highlights the question of the "resolvability" of human phenomena by science. Hergenhahn too calls attention to the problematic nature of "science" in the study of humans and stresses the question of whether scientific methods are adequate. Hilgard views the Third Force as an alternative conception of psychology which proposes the holistic study of significance and values as a compliment to abstract nomothetic theory. Brennan emphasizes the distinctiveness of the "human science model" as an *approach* (Giorgi, 1970) and Kendler traces this distinction from Vico to Brentano, Dilthey and Husserl. The latter stresses the distinction of different forms of knowledge (e.g., deductive versus interpretive, theoretical versus practical) and the different forms of validity and criteria for truth peculiar to each. Topics like *Geisteswissenschaft*, intentionality, bracketing of preconceptions, and the phenomenological reduction are elaborated.

Contributions of those less well-known and "mainstream" than Rogers and Maslow are often included, for example the "rigorous humanism" of Rychlak (in Hillner), Kelly's personal construct theory (in Hillner and Hergenhahn), Polkinghorne's work on human science methodology (in Kendler), Giorgi and the phenomenological psychology of the Duquesne group (in Hillner, Hilgard & Brennan), and transpersonal psychology's attempt to approach spirituality through mysticism and Eastern religions (Murphy & Kovach; Hilgard). Specific theories, methodological approaches, and therapeutic contributions are placed in the context of foundational scientific issues. Authors often make efforts to see the differences among diverse representatives of the movement and grapple with the question of whether a particular psychologist ought to be included as a member of the movement, sometimes arriving at different or ambivalent conclusions (e.g., about Allport and Kelly).

## Comparison of Most Recent with Earlier Editions

Marx and Hillix (1979) included a section describing phenomenology, existentialism, and humanism as well as the theories of Maslow and

Rogers in the third edition's chapter on "Personality" psychology. In the forth edition, this entire chapter was removed because users complained that it too often overlapped with more extensive materials in courses on personality (Marx & Cronan-Hillix, 1987).

Watson (1978) included the sections "Humanistic Influences," "Existential Theory," and "Phenomenological Methods" in his chapter on "recent developments in psychology." Evans, who reworked the text after Watson's death, replaced these with synopses on Allport, Rogers, and Maslow in a section on personality theory and a mention of the attack on mechanization by May, Rogers, Perls, Frankl, and Kelly in the section on clinical psychology (Watson & Evans, 1991). In the new edition, all references to van Kaam, Child, MacLeod, David Katz, Combs, Snygg, and Speigelberg are removed, though there is a general statement that all areas of psychology have been influenced by phenomenology. In contrast to the previous edition, the new one closes with a substantial treatment of cognitive psychology.

Brennan's (1991) third edition format is essentially the same as the second, but coverage is expanded. Both volumes emphasize the opposition of the "human science" and "natural science" approaches, but the recent edition goes so far as to call the natural science foundation of psychology, based upon Wundt's supposed metapsychology, "a false beginning" in light of recent recognitions of Wundt's voluntaristic and folk psychology. May is newly covered in the second edition. There is expanded treatment of the existential-phenomenological psychology at Duquesne University as well as, in particular, of Giorgi (whose first name is now spelled correctly!).

While Hergenhahn considered the Third Force "very popular and growing" in 1986, he noted that the movement "began to wane in the 1980's and continues to do so," apparently on the basis of a drop in Division 32 membership from 955 to 726. Nevertheless, Hergenhahn still considers the movement "highly influential" and his treatment in the second, 1990 edition is considerably enhanced and expanded by seven pages. In particular, the philosophical foundations — e.g., Kierkegaard, Nietzsche, and Husserl, the antecedents, and phenomenological methodologies are more fully presented and related to contemporary humanistic psychology. He now notes that the movement makes no apologies for its emphasis upon subjectivity and characterizes it as a call for a new mode of science, "human science" which, rather than approaching the subject matter as do natural sciences, takes human awareness, choice, valuing, emotion, and uniqueness into account throughout (p. 500). A section in the previous edition concerning the acceptance of the humanistic image of the person in experimental social learning theory (e.g., Mischel) has now been removed, suggesting an increased purity of the movement's treatment. Finally, in a section on artificial intelligence in the last chapter, Hergenhahn sympathetically presents the phenomenological critique by the philosopher Searle at considerable length.

It appears that coverage has diminished when the movement has been identified with a particular content area in psychology and when the foundations of psychological science are viewed as securely established by another approach. Coverage increases when the movement is seen as contributing to important foundational disciplinary debates with implications for a wide variety of psychological subject matter.

## The Accuracy of Representation

For the most part, what was covered received as accurate a treatment as other approaches in the history of psychology (which is admittedly sometimes poor). Probably the most global exception was Murray, who is more guilty of omission and slant than of downright inaccuracy, though given the brevity of Murray's presentation, it is certainly misleading not to mention any theory. On a more specific plane, despite his general carefulness, Hillner placed memory, perception, cognition, and learning exclusively in the domain of experimental psychology's subject matter in a diagram and discussion of overlaps with humanistic psychology's, overlooking the work done in these areas (e.g., by Maslow, Kelly and various phenomenological psychologists). Other specific errors arose in the area of the phenomenological orientation. For instance, Hillner called Husserl's method "deductive." Brennan, after characterizing existential-phenomenological psychology as an application of philosophical principles to the clinical setting, gave the name of Merleau-Ponty as one of two representative psychologists who derived ways "to treat the individual" from philosophy. Marx and Hillix considered Sartre "pessimistic," holding the beliefs that there is no meaning in human existence, that people are absurd, and that the world is absurd! These errors occurred in the more sketchy discussions.

It must be admitted that there is nothing very glaring to complain about. However, the few inaccuracies found, especially along with the variations in breadth and depth of coverage, do suggest that the treatment of the philosophical and methodological areas is the most frequently inadequate.

## The Evaluation of the Movement's Impact and Worth

One group of texts evaluated the movement as wholly negative, another as mostly negative, with some limited past contribution but little future prospect, and another as a problematic alternative with difficult but very important possibilities.

*Totally negative*

Those authors who evaluated the movement most negatively seem to have had their sensibilities offended. Stagner complains of the movement's sappy sentimentality and naivete as instanced in Maslow's idealization of the child, Rogers' apparent unfamiliarity with sadism, and Schaffer's call to experience the world freshly in the manner of a prelanguage child, to which he replies, "Scientific psychology will not be benefitted by a regression to childish cognition" (1988, p. 338). Stagner finds more promise in computers for the purpose of representing the subtleties of affective-cognitive space (in three dimensions!) and in the methodological innovations of Rokeach. Although he sees the basic controversy in psychology to be the conflict between the tough- and tender-minded in his final chapter, the omission of any reference to the Third Force there implies that it does not figure in the problem or solution.

Leahey's sensibilities are more erudite. While by no means ultimately rejecting the positions of humanistic psychology, he believes its intellectual impact was dwarfed and rendered unnecessary by the likes of Chomsky's critique of behavioralism and the attack on logical positivism by philosophers of science (e.g., Kuhn and Toulman). In Leahey's view, humanistic psychologists offer at best a faint-hearted echo of Aristotle's *scala naturae* and the call to feeling and intuition by the anti-science romantics. He asserts that in ignoring the incompatibility of their emphasis on human purpose with science's commitment to determinism and natural law, "Humanistic psychology is a sort of fraud trading on the good name of science to push ideas entirely at variance with modern science" (1987, p. 435). While Dilthey offered Leahey good reasons for a different kind of science, humanistic psychologists could barely articulate a protest against scientism. Leahey's critique becomes even more scathing in the domain of values and society, drawing a precise parallel between the basic inadequacies of humanistic psychology and the hippie movement. "As humanistic psychology failed to displace behavioralism, so the hippie movement failed to overthrow the straight society... All that remains of the humanistic revolt is (the yuppies') "feel good about yourself." In both the psychology and youth movements,

Leahey finds glaring contradiction and a conservativism at heart in the demand that everyone conform to their particular brand of "non-conformity." "They did not really question the value of adaptation or social control; they just wanted to change the standards to which people had to adapt" (p. 436).

Wertheimer likens humanistic psychology to psychoanalysis in its being popular but marginal to academic psychology. Humanistic psychology pales in the face of the major achievement of twentieth century psychology, namely the establishment that everything can and must be studied scientifically, i.e., in the laboratory with "reliance on impersonal scientists with their precise measurements, their cold numbers, and their electronic computers" (Wertheimer, 1987, p.156). Whereas there was room for the "mystical humanist" in 1900, science is now irrevocably opposed to literary and philosophical, "armchair" traditions, rendering die-hard humanists tangential and irrelevant, at best raising questions which only science of the above description can answer.

*Mixed, mostly negative*

Murray puts in a nutshell the most common overall evaluation when he concedes that humanistic psychology did contribute to clinical practice but observes that psychologists concerned with the explanation of behavior remained relatively untouched.

The Schultzes elaborate the same basic view. They complain of the vagueness of the movement's objectives and its greater unity of protest than of positive contribution. In general, they feel that Rogers' and Maslow's theories have had poor showings of scientific validity and that the research has suffered from problems (e.g., vagueness of concepts) and inadequacies (e.g., small sample size). The human potential movement and Maslow's applications in industry are said to have been of limited value at best and at worst positively harmful. Overall, the conclusion, corroborated by the 1985 AHP meeting, is that the movement never became a school and was a failed experiment, that there has been no recognized theory of science and no impact or perceived importance. The Schultzes offer the possible reasons that: 1) the advocates were largely practitioners rather than academicians and therefore failed to produce research and train a new generation; and 2) the behavioristic and psychoanalytic positions attacked were already abandoned within these schools by the 1960's and 1970's. However, they still recognize the "help" the movement offered in developing therapeutic methods, shifting psychology away from Freud, and reinforcing cognitive psychology's reintroduction of consciousness.

Brennan does not offer much evaluation but also stresses the movement's impact on the clinic and therapy. Although admitting an influence in American psychology, he does not believe the movement is a serious alternative to the prevailing dominance of Behaviorism, primarily due to the fragmentation of the movement. It is interesting to note that in Brennan's final chapter, his view of psychology at large runs parallel to the above, i.e., that it is fragmented, riddled with theoretical and methodological disagreements and controversies, and most clearly successful in the applied, professional domains. Marx and Hillix claim that the potentially great height to which history will carry Rogers depends on the fate of the Third Force movement as a whole.

*A problematic but worthwhile alternative*

Hilgard views the Third Force approach as having impact on the practice of psychology, e.g., in the clinic, but remaining either ignored or reinterpreted in the area of lab research. He points to the importance of phenomenological knowledge but relates its small influence on academic psychology to its lack of systematic relation to other knowledge. Hilgard concludes that although humanistic and transpersonal trends made academic psychology aware of important topics (e.g., self perception, locus of control, self disclosure, ecological psychology, and values issues), their influence at the center has not been great inasmuch as it only spurred the study of new problems in traditional ways. Finally, he complains that despite its name and its interest in topics from the humanities (e.g., religion, art, music, literature), humanistic psychology has not resolved the problem of the inadequacy of nomothetic methods in approaching these topics; the relation of psychology to the humanities remains one of its dilemmas as a science. Hilgard still sees the contributions of the Third Force as important in a rightfully pluralistic psychology.

Hillner (perhaps unfairly) downgrades both Rogers and Maslow for underestimating the role of the environment and failing to provide theoretical conceptualization of the interrelation of self and environment. He also recognizes the lack of impact on undergraduate and graduate psychology (with the exception of Duquesne University), but concedes the great respect accorded to Rogers' and that the movement is still evolving. Rychlak is applauded for going beyond idealistic preaching and ritualistic criticism to a thoroughly reasoned, conceptually oriented, methodologically sound system. In the final picture of psychology,

Hillner places the Third Force alongside neobehaviorism, latter-day depth psychology, and dialectical psychology (Riegel), implying the continuing place of the movement, which still holds positive potential.

Hergenhahn goes so far as to "in fairness" defend Third Force Psychology from common criticisms. For instance, he asserts that the movement has not ignored the worth of other psychologists, as it has been accused of doing, and that it is not so much abandoning the concept and methods of science as redefining them in accordance with the intrinsic characteristics of its subject matter which is legitimate if not necessary. He then emphasizes what he sees as the chief contribution of expanding both psychology's subject matter and methods. It is interesting to note that Hergenhahn holds the general belief that the basic concepts of human being have recurred through history, the modern "scientific" era being distinguished more by its technology than its insights. Concerning the status of psychology as a science, Hergenhahn cites approvingly the doubts periodically expressed, e.g., by James, Heidbredder, and Koch.

Kendler explicitly assumes a meta-evaluative position, stressing that the evaluation of the movement will be positive or negative depending upon whether the evaluator is oriented within human science or natural science traditions. He then suggests "history" as an independent standard. While many contributions of the movement are not historically credited solely to the movement (e.g., Kohut independently came to stress empathy in psychoanalysis, rendering Rogers less distinctive), the Third Force is credited with shifting attention to significant, ignored problems of human life such as the search for meaning, love, and death. However, the greater problem is the controversy over *how* these phenomena are to be studied, for the mere introduction of new subject matter does not a revolution make. Therefore the critical historical question shifts to methodology, and in particular the relative merit and relationship of human science and natural science approaches. So far, Kendler argues, these two approaches have lacked unity and psychology has lacked absolute criteria for choice between them. The two major obstacles to unity are: 1) the complexity of human phenomena; and 2) the unsettled debate about the nature of psychology itself. At this point in history, a "choice of life-style" determines the approach to which one adheres. "Human science" remains a important as a fundamental historical alternative.

The evaluation of the movement becomes more positive inasmuch as the movement is seen as: 1) an authentic recovery of early Greek, Renaissance, and Romantic thought; 2) a heterogeneous group including, beyond Rogers and Maslow, existential and phenomenological psychologists; 3) rooted in a sophisticated alternative philosophy and theory of science; 4) offering a rigorous, original methodology aimed at the distinctive characteristics of human subject matter.

## Conclusions

*For Historians*

Certainly, the history of the victors is free to sound the death knell, as roughly half of our sampling did. However, this is by no means even a unanimous conclusion, let alone a foregone one. Moreover, it is one based on a significantly incomplete treatment of the movement, the complexity of which has eluded such an historian. To the extent to which phenomenological, existential, humanistic, and transpersonal trends within the movement are recognized, traced from their ancient roots through the modern era, and grasped in their philosophical, metascientific, and methodological implications, a univocal dismissal of the significance of the movement was not found.

For a comprehensive treatment of the movement, the frequent emphasis on the humanistic faction and the specific postulations of Rogers and Maslow in theory and therapy must be at least supplemented if not rendered secondary by more difficult scholarship. It is a credit to our historians of psychology that such scholarship is readily available, and if the present sample is indicative, becoming more and more the norm. However, the movement's rich history, complexity, and virtual integration, which can be seen from reading a number of these texts, is not easily visible in most taken singly, which is unfortunate for students and for the field of psychology.

*For Third Force Psychologists*

It would be erroneous to rest the limitations in completeness on the shoulders of historians alone. Third Force psychologists have themselves not been careful enough in addressing the diversity of the movement and particularly its historical precedents, philosophical foundations, and methodological implications, all of which still present questions and problems. Third Force psychologists would be well advised to take a good share of the responsibility for the shortcomings in these historical reflections of their work. The clear conclusion from them is that the movement is now in a state of crisis, at worst fading from view and at best a very difficult and problematic alternative awaiting the future for a secure place on solid ground. The tasks involved in establishing that place, all of which have been begun but not completed, are implicit in the shortcomings and criticisms present in these history texts.

Despite their value and significance, contributions in the clinical domain are insufficient to support the movement and must be at least strongly supplemented by work in other areas. A treatment of all content areas of psychology is necessary, and this in turn calls for radical reflections on what constitutes psychological subject matter proper as well as specific research aimed at the complete spectrum, including a critical dialogue confronting mainstream psychology with original findings on common topics. A rigorous methodology must be articulated in conjunction with carefully conceived philosophical foundations, both contrasted with inadequate ones. The question of the meaning of science with reference to human subject matter must have a loud and clear answer. The question of unity in the movement, of what work is to be included in the movement, must be addressed on the basis of the propadeutic reflections indicated above. The movement must thereby become more self-critical. This naturally leads into the question of the movement's relationship to other approaches to psychology and the question of the unity and diversity of psychology at large. Humanistic psychology must certainly assume a leadership role in a more satisfying dialogue with the humanities and arts. The issue of values and the relationship of psychology to society, particularly the issue of power, must be addressed. Last but not least is the task of institutionalization and the training of future psychologists.

Needless to say, all this is far from being achieved and is likely to seem a formidable task to even the most ambitious Third Force psychologists. It might be some consolation to realize that these tasks are by no means pressing upon the Third Force alone; as several historians have recognized, the crisis of this movement, its marginal status notwithstanding, is the central crisis of psychology itself (with the exception of the problem of institutionalization). Mainstream psychology is limited in scope, frought with methodological dilemmas, unclear about philosophical commitments, fragmented and ambiguously boundaried, more successful in practice than in theory, not foundationally self-critical, unsatisfying in its relationship with the humanities, and profoundly challenged by ethical and societal problems. A second and more satisfying consolation may be found in the seminal work already done in each of these areas by Third Force psychologists (Wertz, 1992). A continuing humanistic response to these global disciplinary problems can bring the movement beyond being merely another school, for it would provide a sound basis for the entire enterprise of psychological science.

## References

Benjamin, L. T. (1988). *The history of psychology: original sources and contemporary research*. New York: McGraw Hill.

Brennan, J. F. (1982) *History and systems of psychology* (2nd. ed.). Englewood Cliffs, NJ: Prentice Hall.

Brennan, J. F. (1991). *History and systems of psychology* (3rd ed.). Englewood Cliffs, NJ: Prentice Hall.

Esper, E. A. (1964). *A history of psychology*. Philadelphia: Saunders.

Fancher, R. E. (1979). *Pioneers in psychology*. New York: Norton.

Fancher, R. E. (1990). *Pioneers in psychology* (2nd ed.). New York: Norton.

Hergenhahn, B. R. (1986). *An introduction to the history of psychology*. Belmont, CA: Wadsworth.

Hergenhahn, B. R. (1992). *An introduction to the history of psychology* (2nd ed.). Belmont, CA: Wadsworth.

Hilgard, E. R. (1987). *Psychology in America: A historical survey*. San Diego: Harcourt Brace Jovanovich.

Hillner, K. P. (1984). *History and systems of modern psychology: A conceptual approach*. New York: Gardner Press.

Hothersall, D. (1984). *History of psychology*. New York: Random House.

Hothersall, D. (1990). *History of psychology* (2nd ed.). New York: Random House.

Kendler, H. H. (1987). *Historical foundations of modern psychology*. Philadelphia: Temple University Press.

Leahey, T. H. (1987). *History of psychology* (2nd ed.). Englewood Cliffs, NJ: Prentice Hall.

Lundin, R. W. (1985). *Theories and systems of psychology* (3rd ed.). Lexington, MA: Heath.

Marx, M. H. & Hillix, W. A. (1979). *Systems and theories in psychology* (3rd ed.). New York: McGraw Hill.

Marx, M. H. & Cronan-Hillix, W. A. (1979). *Systems and theories in psychology* (4th ed.). New York: McGraw Hill.

Murphy, G. & Kovach, J. K. (1972). *Historical introduction to modern psychology* (3rd ed.). New York: Harcourt Brace Jovanovich.

Murray, D. J. (1983). *A history of western psychology*. Englewood Cliffs, NJ: Prentice Hall.

Shultz, D. P. & Shultz, S. E. (1987). *History of modern psychology* (4th ed.). New York: Harcourt Brace Jovanovich.

Stagner, R. (1988). *A history of psychological theories*. New York: McMillan.

Watson, R.I. (1978). *The great psychologists*. New York: Lippincott.

Watson, R. I. & Evans, R. B. (1991). *The great psychologists: a history of psychological thought*. New York: Harper Collins.

Wertheimer, M. (1987). *A brief history of psychology* (3rd ed.). Fort Worth, TX: Holt, Rinehart, & Winston.

Wertz, F.J. (1992). The role of the Third Force in the history of psychology. Invited Address at the 100th Convention of the American Psychological Association, Washington, D.C., August.

# About the Authors

***Christopher M. Aanstoos*** received his Ph.D. from Duquesne University, and is currently Professor of Psychology at West Georgia College. He is the editor of the journal *The Humanistic Psychologist* and has edited three books: *Exploring the Lived World, The World of the Infant,* and *Studies in Humanistic Psychology.* Address: Chris Aanstoos, Psychology Department, West Georgia College, Carrollton, GA 30118.

***Walter Truett Anderson***, Ph.D., author of numerous books including *Open Secrets*; *The Upstart Spring: Esalen and the American Awakening*; and *Reality Isn't What It Used To Be,* is a fellow of the Meridian Institute and an associate editor of Pacific News Service. Address: Walter Anderson, 1112 Curtis Street, Albany, CA 94706.

***Mike Arons*** completed his doctoral dissertation on creativity under Paul Ricoeur at the Sorbonne in 1965. He helped pioneer humanistic psychology programs at the University of Prince Edward Island and at West Georgia College, where he has spent the past twenty-five years as Chair. Address: Mike Arons, Psychology Department, West Georgia College, Carrollton, GA 30118.

***Anthony Barton***, after getting his Ph.D. from the University of Chicago, became one of the founders, in the 1960's, of a doctoral program in existential-phenomenological clinical psychology at Duquesne University, where he is currently Professor of Psychology. He has published *Three Worlds of Therapy: Freud, Jung, Rogers.* Address: Anthony Barton, Department of Psychology, Duquesne University, Pittsburgh, PA 15282.

***James F. T. Bugental***, Ph.D. is the author of *The Search for Authenticity, The Search for Existential Identity, Psychotherapy* and Process, *The Art of the Psychotherapist* and *Intimate Journeys: Stories from Life-Changing Therapy*, and he edited *Challenges of Humanistic Psychology*. Currently Distinguished Adjunct Professor, California School of Professional Psychology (Alameda); Emeritus Professor, Saybrook Institute; Emeritus clinical faculty, Stanford Medical School. Address: Dr. James Bugental, 24 Elegant Tern Road, Novato, CA 94949.

*Edward Bruce Bynum*, Ph.D. is a clinical psychologist and currently is Director of the Behavioral Medicine Clinic at the University of Massachusetts Health Services in Amherst, Massachusetts. He is the author of *The Family Unconscious*, *Families and the Interpretation of Dreams* and *Transcending Psychoneurotic Distortions*. Addrress: Edward Bruce Bynum, University Health Center, University of Massachusetts, Amherst MA 01003.

*Scott D. Churchill* received his Ph.D. from Duquesne University. Currently he is Associate Professor of Psychology at the University of Dallas. He is the editor of *Methods: A Journal for Human Science* and associate editor of *Theoretical and Philosophical Psychology*. Address: Scott Churchill, Psychology Department, University of Dallas, 1845 East Northgate Drive, Irving, Texas 75062.

*Arthur Combs*,, Ph.D. is currently in private practice. Early work with Donald Snygg included *Individual Behavior* and *Perceptual Psychology*. Later work includes *A Personal Approach to Teaching*, *The Schools We Need* and, with Avila, *Helping Relationships*. His university affiliations have been with Syracuse, University of Florida, and as Distinguished Professor at the University of Northern Colorado. Address: Arthur Combs, 1975 28th Ave., Unit 19, Greeley, CO 80631.

*Larry Davidson* received his Ph.D. in Psychology from Duquesne University, and postdoctoral training in Clinical & Community Psychology in the Department of Psychiatry of the Yale University School of Medicine. Currently on the faculty at Yale, he is Secretary of the Society for Phenomenology and Psychiatry. Address: Larry Davidson, Yale University School of Medicine, 34 Park Street, New Haven, CT 06519.

## About the Authors

**Roy J. deCarvalho** has a Ph.D. in the History of Science from the University of Wisconsin-Madison and is Associate Professor of History at the University of North Texas. He is author of *The Founders of Humanistic Psychology* and *The Growth of Hypothesis in Psychology*. He is a member of the editorial board of *The Journal of Humanistic Psychology*. Address: Roy J. deCarvalho, Department of History, University of North Texas, Denton, TX 76203.

**Jacqueline Larcombe Doyle**, Ph.D. is President Emerita of the Association for Humanistic Psychology, and a licensed psychologist and a marriage and family counselor. She is on the Board of Editors of the *Journal of Humanistic Psychology*, a director of the Saybrook Institute Graduate School and Research Center, and a member of the advisory board of the Rollo May Center for Humanistic Studies. Address: Jacqueline Doyle, 21 Alcatraz Ave., Belvedere, CA 94920.

**Albert Ellis**, Ph.D. is President of the Institute for Rational-Emotive Therapy in New York. He is the author of over fifty books on psychotherapy and sex, love, and marital relationships, including *Reason and Emotion in Psychotherapy, Sex Without Guilt, A New Guide to Rational Living,* and *The Practice of Rational-Emotive Therapy*. Address: Albert Ellis, Institute for Rational-Emotive Therapy, 45 East 65th Street, New York, NY 10021.

**Franz R. Epting** received his Ph.D. from Ohio State University. Currently he is Professor of Psychology at the University of Florida and he holds an adjunct appointment in the University Counseling Center. Professor Epting has published four books: *Personal Construct Counseling and Psychotherapy, Personal Meanings of Death, Anticipating Personal Construct Psychology, Personal Construct Psychology: Clinical and Personal Assessment*. Address: Franz Epting, Department of Psychology, University of Florida, Gainesville, FL 32611.

**Esalen Institute**. Address Correspondence to Esalen Institute, Big Sur, CA 93920 [(408) 667-3000)].

# About the Authors

*Constance T. Fischer*, Ph.D. joined the Duquesne University Psychology Department faculty in 1966. There she developed a human-science approach to psychological assessment. She has authored seventy publications, on client access to records and decision-making, human-science psychology, and psychological assessment, including the book *Individualizing Psychological Assessment*. Address: Constance Fischer, Psychology Department, Duquesne University, Pittsburgh, PA 15282.

*Eugene Gendlin*, Ph.D. is Professor of Psychology at the University of Chicago. He also teaches and conducts workshops at the Focussing Institute in Chicago. He founded the journal *Psychotherapy*, which he edited for thirteen years. He is the author of *Experiencing and the Creation of Meaning, Focussing,* and *Let Your Body Interpret Your Dreams*. Address: Eugene Gendlin, Department of Psychology, University of Chicago, 5848 South University Avenue, Chicago, IL 60637.

*Amedeo Giorgi*, Ph.D. is Professor of Psychology at the University of Quebec at Montreal and at Saybrook Institute in San Francisco, CA. He is the editor of the *Journal of Phenomenological Psychology*, and author of *Psychology as a Human Science*. Address: Amedeo Giorgi, University of Quebec at Montreal, Department of Psychology, Case Postale 8888, Succursale A, Montreal, Quebec, Canada H3C 3P8.

*Carmi Harari*, Ph.D. is founding director of Humanistic Psychology Center of New York, and of Interactions: Psychological Services for the Whole Family. He has taught at Columbia University, New York University, and the University of New Rochelle. Address: Carmi Harari, Interactions, 10 Wyndham Lane, New York, NY 10956-4527

*George Howard*, Ph.D. is Professor of Psychology at the University of Notre Dame, where he has served as Director of Graduate Studies and Department Chair. His books include *Dare We Develop a Human Science, A Tale of Two Stories, Adaptive Counseling and Therapy,* and *Basic Research Methods in the Social Sciences*. Address: George S. Howard, Department of Psychology, University of Notre Dame, Notre Dame, IN 46556.

**Stanley Krippner** holds a Ph.D. from Northwestern University in educational psychology. He is the former director of the Child Study Center at Kent State University, and the Dream Laboratory at Maimonides Medical Center. He is currently Professor of Psychology at Saybrook Institute, and Distinguished Professor of of Psychology at the California Institute of Integral Studies. He is the editor of *Advances in Parapsychological Research; Personal Mythology: Psychological Perspectives*; and *Dreamtime and Dreamwork* and the co-author of *Personal Mythology* and *Spiritual Dimensions of Healing*. Address: Stanley Krippner, Saybrook Institute, 1550 Sutter Street, San Francisco, CA 94109.

**Larry M. Leitner** received his Ph.D. from the University of Nebraska. He is Professor of Psychology and Associate Chair of the Department of Psychology at Miami University. Dr. Leitner has co-edited two books: *Personal Construct Psychology: Personality and Psychotherapy* and *Critical Issues in Personal Construct Psychotherapy*. Address: Larry Leitner, Department of Psychology, Miami University, Oxford, OH 45056.

**Fred Massarik**, Ph.D. is a professor in the Graduate School of Management at the University of California, Los Angeles. He is Past President of the Division of Humanistic Psychology (APA), and is the author of *Participative Management* and the co-author of *Human Systems Development*. Address: Fred Massarik, 6245 Scenic Avenue, Los Angeles, CA 90068.

**Rollo May**, after graduating from Oberlin College, went to Vienna to study wtih Alfred Adler for two years. Dr. May was important in the development of the profession of psychological counseling through such books as *The Art of Counseling*. He has also authored *The Meaning of Anxiety, Existence, Psychology and the Human Dilemma, Man's Search for Himself, The Discovery of Being, Love and Will, Power and Innocence, My Quest for Beauty,* and *The Cry for Myth*. He has received seventeen honorary degrees, and two Christopher Awards. Address: Rollo May, 98 Sugarloaf, Tiburon, CA 94940.

*Clark Moustakas*, Ph.D. is President of the Center for Humanistic Studies and a core faculty member of The Union Institute. He is also Co-Chair of the Consortium for Diversified Psychology Programs. He has authored *The Teacher and the Child; Loneliness; The Authentic Teacher; Creativity and Conformity; Individuality and Encounter; Personal Growth; Loneliness and Love; Teaching as Learning; Finding Yourself, Finding Others; Portraits of Loneliness and Love; The Touch of Loneliness; Creative Life; Turning Points; Rythyms, Rituals and Rleationships; Phenomenology, Science and Psychotherapy;* and *Heuristic Research.* Address: Clark Moustakas, Center for Humanistic Studies, 40 E. Ferry Ave., Detroit, MI, 48202.

*Maureen O'Hara*, Ph.D., is Past President of the Association for Humanistic Psychology, Associate Editor of the *Journal of Humanistic Psychology,* was a long time colleague of Carl Rogers at the Center for Studies of the Person in LaJolla California, has taught women's studies, and is currently a Fellow of the Meridian International Institute, a San Francisco Bay-area think tank on governance and the future. She is in private practice as a Marriage, Family and Child Counselor. Address: Maureen O'Hara, Encinitas Center for Family and Personal Development, Encinitas, CA 92024.

*Donald Polkinghorne*, Ph.D. is Professor of Counseling Psychology at the University of Southern California. He is Author of *Methodology for the Human Sciences* and of *Narrative Knowing and the Human Sciences,* and articles on qualitative research. Address: Donald Polkinghorne, University of Southern California 503G, Los Angeles, CA 90089-0031.

*Anne Richards*, Ed.D. is Professor of Psychology at West Georgia College. Her studies at Brandeis University and the University of Florida sparked her continuing interest in theoretical and applied aspects of humanistic psychology in education. Address: Anne Richards, Psychology Department, West Georgia College, Carrollton, GA 30118.

*Richard Rojcewicz*, Ph.D. has been full time manager of the Silverman Center since its founding in 1980. He is the co-translator of Husserl's *Ideas II*, Heidegger's *Parmenides*, and Heidegger's *Basic Questions of Philosophy*. Address: Richard Rojcewicz, The Simon Silverman Phenomenology Center, Duquesne University, Pittsburgh, PA 15282-0801 [(412) 434-6038].

*Barbara G. Sapienza*, Ph.D. is a clinical psychologist in private practice. She graduated from the Pacific Graduate School. She has worked as an educator with special children in both a school setting and at SFSU, and she served as a psychologist at the Golden Gate Regional Center. Address: Dr. Sapienza, 343 Seventeenth Avenue, San Francisco, California 94121.

*E. Mark Stern*, Ed.D. is Professor at Iona College, and former editor of *Voices: The Art and Science of Psychotherapy*. Address: E. Mark Stern, 215 East 11 St., New York, NY 10003.

*William Stillwell* , Ph.D. has devoted his professional life to learning and being as an organizational consultant, university faculty member, trainer, and group leader. He is a former Director of CSP and is author of *Primal Presence*. Address: William Stillwell, CSP, 1125 Torrey Pines Road, La Jolla, CA 92037 [(619) 459-3861].

*Eugene Taylor*, Ph.D. from Boston University, is an Associate in Psychiatry at Harvard Medical School, Consultant in the History of Psychiatry at the Massachusetts General Hospital, and author of *William James on Exceptional Mental States*. Address: Eugene Taylor, The Harvard Medical Archives, Countway Library of Medicine, 10 Shattuck St. Boston, MA 02115.

*Frederick J. Wertz* received his Ph.D. in Phenomenological Clinical Psychology at Duquesne University in 1982. Currently an Associate Professor of Psychology at Fordham University, he has served as Editor of *Theoretical and Philosophical Psychology*. As well as practicing psychotherapy in New York City, he has co-edited the book *Advances in Qualitative Research in Psychology: Themes and Variations*. Address: Division of Social Sciences, Fordham University, New York, NY 10023.

# Name Index

Aanstoos, C., v, 1, 10, 21, 105, 297
Adams, J., 15
Adams-Webber, J., 138
Adler, J., 215
Adler, A., 236
Agnew, J., 138
Akishige, Y., 182
Alexander, L., 267
Allender, J., 266
Allport, G., 13, 16, 24, 67, 105, 108, 172, 173, 202, 261, 292, 293, 350
Alpert, R., 57, 84, 175
Amerikaner, M., 129
Ames, A., 258
Anderson, W., v, 77, 78, 196, 283, 288
Anderson, M., 290
Andreas, S., 225
Angel, E., 106
Angyal, A., 15, 81, 173, 243ff., 261
Arcaya, J., 204
Argyris, C., 279
Arons, M., v, 18, 22, 45, 53, 56, 76, 77, 80, 82, 84, 86, 112, 297
Asante, M., 188
Asch, S., 51
Aspy, D., 264, 266
Auribindo, 182
Avila, D., 264
Ayer, A., 235
Bachelard, G., 319
Baez, J., 289
Bagley, K., 138
Bakan, D., 21, 110, 118, 268
Baker, G., 204
Balowin, M., 226
Banaji, M., 98, 310
Bandler, R., 225, 229
Bandura, A., 217
Bannister, D., 136, 138, 139
Barker, E., 118
Barrett, W., 107

Barron, F., 51
Bartlett, F., 92
Bartley, W., 235
Barton, A., v, 215, 230, 295
Barzun, J., 16, 173
Bateson, G., 172, 289
Battista, J., 115
Beck, A., 236
Behnke, M., 138
Belenky, M., 120
Bellah, R., 120
Benedict, R., 263
Benjamin, L, 345
Benne, K., 264, 278
Bennis, W., 277, 279
Berger, P., 147
Berlyne, D., 32, 35, 109
Bernal, M., 188
Berry, J., 155
Berson, M. 65
Bester, A., 256
Biemel, W., 317
Bindrim, P., 77
Blank, L., 21
Bleicher, J., 112
Bohr, N., 160
Boles, G., 80
Boss, M., 172
Bouman, J., 285
Bradford, L., 278
Braginsky, B., 110
Braginsky, D., 110
Bramley, J., 139
Brennan, J., 344, 346, 349, 354
Brentano, F., 32, 89
Brett, G., 4
Brodsky, S., 204
Bronowski, J., 45
Brown, N., 82
Brown, G., 260, 283
Brown, L., 152

# Name Index

Browne, M., 121
Bruce, D., 98
Bruner, J., 40
Buber, M., 141, 166, 315
Buckley, W., 115
Bugental, F.T., v, 13, 16, 31, 76, 88, 132, 149, 165, 172, 217, 228, 261, 283, 289
Buhler, C., 15, 16, 17, 54, 81, 172, 173, 261
Bullard, S., 260
Bullock, A., 25, 28, 31, 35
Butler, J., 331
Buytendijk, F., 285, 295
Bynum, E., v
Bynum, B., 186, 190
Caine, R., 266, 268
Caine, G., 266, 268
Campbell, J., 283
Campbell, E., 35, 84, 85
Camus, A., 59
Canferd, J., 260
Cantrill, H., 258
Cassel, P., 264
Chein, I., 93, 110
Child, I., 105, 118, 350
Churchill, S., v, 2, 292, 296
Clark, T., 233, 235
Clinchy, B., 120
Cohen, A., 265
Cohen, S., 15, 24
Coles, R., 260
Combs, A., v, 55, 85, 256, 258, 260, 261, 262, 264, 267, 350
Conway, C., 148
Corbin, J., 121
Corsini, R., 233
Cosgrove, L, 35
Coufal, D., 213
Coulson, W., 122
Cove, E., 236
Coward, H., 118
Craddick, R., 204
Craig, E., 80, 82
Criswell, E., 18, 84, 85
Cronan-Hill, ix, w, 350
Crowder, R., 98, 310
Crown, B., 21
Crutchfield, R., 51

Culler, J., 313, 315, 320
Curtin, T., 148, 150
Dailey, C., 204
Dalai Lama, 182
Dana, R., 204, 211
Daniels, V., 297
Danzinger, K., 110, 114
Darwin, C., 47
Davidson, L., v, 24, 35, 38, 39
Day, W., 296
de Forest, I., 244
de Rivera, J., 299
de Carvalho, R., v, 13, 25, 32, 164, 165, 172, 173, 267
de Hartman, T., 71
Dennett, D., 38
Deri, S., 248
Dewey, J., 31, 55, 116, 236
Di Gangi, M., 148
Dickson, W., 275
Dill-Standiford, T., 135, 140
Dilthey, W., 30, 89, 107, 294, 346
Diop, C., 187, 188
Doyle, J., v, 76, 77, 192, 283
Draucker, C., 39
Dreikurs, R., 264
Dreyfus, H., 10
Dryden, W., 237, 238
Durow, N., 155
Easthope, G., 117
Ebersole, P., 315
Ehrlich, P., 154
Eiben, R., 264
Eliot, T.S., 149
Elkins, D., vi
Ellenberger, H., 106
Elliott, R., 111, 299
Ellis, N., 297
Ellis, A., v, 21, 83, 233, 234, 235, 237, 238
Engel, G., 39
Epting, F., v, 129, 134, 135, 137, 138, 299
Erdberg, P., 204
Erickson, M., 227
Erikson, E., 54
Esper, E., 345
Evans, R., 278, 346, 350
Evans-Wentz, W., 187

## Name Index

Fadiman, J., 84, 174, 182, 185
Fagan, J., 21
Fagen, J., 225
Fairervis, W., 187
Fairfield, R., 264
Fancher, R., 345
Fantini, M., 260
Farley, F., 19
Farson, R., 263
Faulconer, J., 94, 98
Faulkner, K., 2, 296
Ferenzi, S., 244
Ferren, J., 59
Fidler, J., 115
Fields, R., 175
Finch, C., 187, 188
Fischer, C., v, vi, 39, 119, 202, 204, 205, 295
Fischer, W., 295
Fisher, T., 150
Forester, E.M., 244
Fox, T., 69
Frager, R., 175, 182, 297
Francis, B., 193
Frankl, V., 172, 174, 220, 221, 223, 235, 258, 350
Fransella, F., 135, 136, 138
Freud, S., 57, 121, 188, 223
Frick, W., 250
Friedman, M., 35, 37, 106, 295, 315
Fromm, E., 25, 33, 173, 244
Furgeson, K., 185
Gadamer, H., 114, 116
Garbarino, J., 155
Gardner, H., 111
Gardner, M., 314
Geertz, 40
Geller, L., 35
Gelso, C., 120
Gendlin, E., vi, 220, 325, 330, 335, 336, 339
Gergen, M. 114, 117
Getzels, J., 49, 51
Ghislen, B., 57
Gibb, J., 14, 16
Gibbons, D., 19, 20, 22, 82
Ginott, H., 264
Giorgi, A., iv, v, 25, 32, 35-36, 39-40, 89-90, 96, 106-108, 110, 118-119, 172, 179, 284, 293, 295-296, 299, 306-308, 349-350
Glasser, B., 117
Glasser, W., 264
Goble, F., 260, 263
Goldberger, N., 120
Goldman, L., 313
Goldstein, K., 13, 15, 25, 173, 247, 292, 293
Goleman, D., 175
Goodman, P., 55, 223
Gordon, T., 263, 264
Gottsegen, G., 21
Goud, N., 264, 265
Graham, S., 19
Graham, M., 182
Graumann, C., 25, 35
Gray, W., 115
Gray, M., 262, 265, 267
Green, E., 175
Green, A., 175
Greening, T., 15, 23, 24, 76, 78
Grinder, J., 229
Grof, S., 174, 175, 189, 235, 283
Grosskurth, P., 244
Grummond, D., 331
Gudjieff, F., 58
Guilford, J.P., 46, 54
Gunther, B., 289
Gurwitsch, A., 285
Gusdorf, G., 89
Habermas, J., 115
Hagan, T., 39
Hall, G.S., 292
Hanfling, O., 110
Harari, C., v, vi, 17, 19, 20, 21, 76, 80, 82, 185
Harman, W., 179
Harmin, M., 260
Harrower, M., 202
Hart, H., 265
Hartley, D., 4
Hartman, R., 15
Hawkins, E., 182
Hayakawa, S.I., 258
Heber, R., 80
Hefferline, R., 223
Heidegger, M., 30, 34, 70, 100, 116, 220, 316, 319

Held, R., 87
Helfand, M., 243
Hempel, C., 108, 117
Henderson, V., 278
Hendlin, S., 80, 82
Hendon, M., 138
Henley, T., 2, 296, 297
Hergenhahn, B., 33, 344, 349, 350
Hesse, M., 111
Hilgard, E., 172, 345, 346, 354
Hillex, W., 345
Hillman, J., 121
Hillner, K., 344, 349
Hirsch, J., 278
Hobbes, T., 4
Holland, R., 129
Horney, K., 25, 33, 244, 258
Hornung, E., 188
Hoshmand, L., 118, 121
Hothersall, D., 345
Houston, J., 60
Houston, P., 265
Houts, P., 265
Howard, G., v, 118, 146, 148, 149, 150, 155, 299
Huang, A., 82
Hubbard, R., 118
Huizinga, G., 277
Hume, D., 4
Hunter, E., 264
Husserl, E., 5, 10, 30, 38, 101, 115, 116, 118, 284, 317
Huxley, A., 177, 183
Irvin, C., 76
Ittleson, W., 258
Jackson, P., 49
Jackson, G., 187
Jacob, F., 115
James, G., 188
James, W., 31, 57, 105, 116, 156, 171, 183, 192, 292
Jaspers, K., 294
Jayaswal, S., 67
Jencks, C., 3
Jersild, A., 261, 264
Johnson, A., 148
Johnson, D., 283
Johnson, W., 258
Johns, F., 260

Jones, J., 155
Jones, R., 87, 260
Jourard, S., 82, 85, 87, 174, 263
Judy, D., 297
Jung, C., 57, 69, 84, 88, 183, 188, 198
Juster, N., 211
Katz, D., 350
Keeley, S., 121
Keen, E., 299
Kelly, G., 16, 129, 131, 173, 202, 262, 350
Kelman, H., 110
Keleman, S., 283
Kendler, 106, 344, 346
King, R., 188, 190
Kinget, G., 105
Kirschenbaum, H., 278
Klee, J., 18, 21, 25, 32, 58, 80, 84
Klemke, E., 309
Klopfer, B, 202
Knapp,B., 21
Knoles, R., 295
Koch, S., 110
Koffka, K., 25, 247, 276
Kohler, W., 25, 277
Korzybski, A., 234, 236
Kostelmy, K., 155
Kostere, K., 297
Kovach, J., 345, 348
Kramer, R., 267
Kreiger, S., 138
Krippner, S., 23, 76, 79, 185, 190, 192, 283
Kuhn, T., 14, 114, 293
Kundera, M. 314
Kunz, G., 297
Kurtz, P., 233, 234
Kvale, S., 3, 121
Krippner, S., v, 17, 80
LaBerge, S., 190
Laing, R. D., 39
Ladd, G., 95
Lange-Eichbaum, W., 48
Lanier, J., 77
Lanier, S., 77
Lasch, C., 265
Laszlo, E., 115
Lawrence, d. H., 66
Leahey, T., 114, 345, 352

# Name Index

Leary, T., 57, 84, 114, 204
Leckey, P., 258, 261
LeCompte, M., 117
Lee, D., 15, 51, 67
Leech, S., 204
Leeper, R., 276
Leitner, L., v, 129,132, 133, 134, 135, 140, 141
Leonard, G., 258, 268
Lerner, M., 36
Lerner, P., 205
LeShan, L., 21
Leventhal, T., 203
Levin, D., 36, 235
Levine, I., 155
Levinson, D., 72
Levy, J., 20, 77, 86
Lippitt, R., 276
Lewin, K., 55, 77, 258, 276
Likert, R., 276
Lowen, A., 81
Lowrey, R., 263
Lundin, R., 344
MacIntyre, A., 110, 111
MacLeod, R., 295, 350
Madsen, R., 120
Maerlander, A., 150
Maes, C., 285
Mahrer, A., 132, 133, 299, 309
Mair, J., 132, 135, 139, 140, 150
Malinowski, B., 117
Malthus, T., 154
Manaster, A., 21
Mandler, G., 4
Mandler, J., 4
Manly, H., 265
Mann, T., 31
Marcuse, H., 82
Margolis, J., 116
Margulies, N., 276
Marin, P., 265
Marrow, A., 276
Marx, M., 345, 350
Maslow, A., iv, 11, 13, 16, 18, 19, 22, 24, 37, 45, 53, 55, 56, 57, 58, 67, 84, 86, 107, 118, 121, 164, 172, 173, 174, 175, 178, 251, 254, 261, 262, 275, 276, 288, 289, 292, 293, 294, 306, 325, 330, 331

Massarik, F., v, vi, 21, 276, 279, 283, 299
Mathiessen, P., 73
Matson, F., 25, 32, 290
Maultsby, M., 236
May, R., v, 13, 15, 16, 20, 35, 53, 58, 76, 77, 82, 106, 147, 164, 165, 172, 173, 185, 192, 193,198, 235, 261, 283, 290, 293, 306, 325
Mayo, E., 275
McAdams, D., 149, 150
McCarty, H., 260
McDermott, R., 182
McGregor, D., 276
McHugh, P., 34
McKnight, S., 3
Mead, M., 172
Meadow, M.J., 22
Meguiar, T., 297
Meichenbaum, D., 236
Medeiros, D., 264
Melton, G., 155
Meltzer, B., 117
Merleau-Ponty, M., 5, 30, 34, 38, 96, 98, 116, 295, 317
Merton, T., 252
Meyer, A., 247
Michael, D., 196
Miles, M., 112
Milgram, S., 148
Mill, J., 4
Miller, J., 115
Miller, R., 267
Milliren, A., 264
Millroy, W., 117
Milner, T., 297
Mintz, E., 21
Mishler, E., 40
Misiak, H., 32, 108, 109, 265, 299
Mitchell, E., 175
Mooney, R., 67
Montegue, A., 172
Morgan, D., 83
Morrow-Bradley, C., 111
Moustakas, C., v, 15, 62, 119, 173, 258, 261, 263, 264, 265, 283, 308, 312, 325
Mumford, L., 15, 173
Muntyan, B., 264

Murphy, G., 16, 25, 57, 81, 172, 173, 261, 345, 349
Murphy, M., 174, 283, 289
Murray, D., 345
Murray, E., 314
Murray, H., 25, 105, 172, 173, 202, 212, 292, 293
Myers, P., 148, 150
Nazario, Jr., A., 131
Needleman, J., 306
Neill, A., 265
Neimeyer, R., 135, 137, 138
Neisser, U., 87, 111
Nelson, A., 87
Newell, A., 9
Nold, M., 185
O'Hara, M., v, 35, 84, 309, 322
Oppenheimer, J., 161
Ornstein, R., 259, 260
Orwell, G., 152
Otto, H., 264
Patterson, C., 118
Patton, M., 112
Peirce, C., 116
Penn, W., 138
Perls, F., 78, 82, 222, 235, 289, 350
Perry, C., 65
Petras, J., 117
Piaget, J., 111
Pittman, S., 129
Polanyi, M., 84, 86, 301
Polkinghorne, D., v, 40, 105, 108, 109, 112, 113, 114, 115, 116, 117, 118, 120, 121, 122, 146, 149, 299
Pollio, H., 295, 299
Polster, E., 224
Polster, M., 224
Popper, K., 235
Postman, N., 258
Prasinos, S., 315
Preissle, J., 117
Pressley, A., 139
Pribram, K., 295, 299
Price, R., 283, 289
Prichard, S., 138
Prilleltensky, I., 35
Probert, J., 129
Purkey, W., 260
Radley, A., 138

Quiring, G., 315
Raimy, V., 258
Rank, O., 71
Raskin, J., 131
Raths, L., 260
Ravenette, A., 135, 137
Read, J., 98
Reisel, J., 278
Reason, P., 112, 119
Reisman, D., 15, 173
Reynolds, L., 117
Rhine, J.B., 57
Richards, A., vi, 256, 266
Richards, F., vi, 266
Richman, J., 204
Ricoeur, P., 18, 116
Rifken, S., 59
Rigdon, M., 129
Riscalla, L., 204
Roberts, T., 260
Roebuck, F., 266
Roethlisberger, F., 275
Rogers, C., iv, 13, 16, 19, 20, 24, 32, 35, 36, 37, 55, 67, 78, 84, 118, 122, 150, 153, 165, 166, 171, 173, 217, 227, 235, 258, 261, 262, 263, 264, 265, 266, 276, 278, 283, 286, 289, 292, 294, 299, 306, 307, 325, 331, 350, 352
Rojcewicz, R., v, 283
Romanyshyn, R., 297
Rorty, R., 114
Rosen, S., 80, 82, 83
Rosenberg, A., 155
Rosenthal, A. M., 154
Rosenthal, B., 110
Rosenwald, G., 203
Rossi, E., 228
Rowe, D., 135
Rowen, J., 119
Royce, J., 118, 295
Rushdie, S., 73
Russell, B., 236
Russell, D., v
Russell, R., 263
Ruysbroeck, J., 252
Rychlak, J., 118, 132, 134, 135, 147, 299
Salmon, P., 137, 138

# Name Index

Sampson, E., 234
Sanford, N., 110
Santayova, G., 236
Sapienza, B., v, 149
Sarason, S., 111
Saraswati, S., 90
Sarbin, T., 116
Sartre, J., 30, 34
Satir, V., 225, 283
Schein, E., 279
Schmuck, P., 264,
Schmuck, R., 264
Schoenfeld, E., 234
Schultz, A., 115
Schultz, D., 345, 347
Schultz, S., 345, 347
Schutz, W., 77
Schwaller de Lubicz, R., 188
Scmitt, R., 297
Segal, B., 176
Selver, C., 283
Serber, M., 265
Sexton, V., 32, 108, 109, 265, 299
Seyle, H., 198
Shaffer, J., 258, 260, 263, 264
Shaw, J., 9
Shepherd, I., 225
Shlien, J., 331
Shostrom, E., 21, 83
Siatczynski, A., 148
Siderits, M., vi
Simon, H., 9
Simon, S., 260
Simpkin, J., 82
Simpson, E., 262, 265, 267
Siroky, F., 297
Skinner, B. F., 4, 110, 295
Slavney, P., 34
Smillie, D., 67
Smith, D., 297
Smith, E., 187
Smith, H., 175
Smith, M. B., 19, 34, 35, 106, 112, 233, 283, 293, 296, 299, 308, 311
Smutz, J., 247
Snygg, D., 257, 258, 261, 350
Spence, D., 40
Sperry, R., 295
Spiegelberg, H., 33

Spranger, E., 89
Stagner, R., 344, 352
Stein, G., 233
Steiner, R., 182
Stekel, W., 243
Stern, E. M., v, vi, 19, 80, 81, 243, 245, 246, 249, 253, 299
Stern, W., 247
Sternberg, R., 59
Stillwell, W., v, 286
Stocking, G., 117
Strasser, S., 285, 286, 295
Straus, E., 285, 295
Strauss, A., 117, 121
Strauss, E., 38, 204
Strauss, J., 39
Streitfeld, H., 81
Strom, R., 21
Stumpf, C., 33
Sullivan, H.S., 244
Sullivan, W., 120
Suppe, F., 114
Sutich, A., 14, 22, 24, 31, 84, 93, 172, 174, 175
Suzuki, D., 172
Szasz, T., 131
Tageson, C., 146
Tageson, W., 299
Tannenbaum, R., 276
Tappan, G., 18
Tart, C., 174, 175, 235
Tarule, S., 120
Tate, G., 264
Taylor, E., v, 32, 170, 171
Tennessen H., 35
Terman, L., 48
Thomas, H., 18, 77
Thomas, L., 120
Thomas, R., 77
Thompson, C., 244
Tillich, P., 168, 289
Tipton, S., 120
Tittler, B., 315
Torrance, E., 55
Toulmin, S., 3, 110, 152
Towbin, B., 203
Toynbee, A, 289
Trungpa, C., 175
Tyrrell, R., 260

van Deusen, W., 172
van Kaam, A., 172, 293, 294, 350
van Zuuren, F., 117
Vane, J., 204
Vasconcellos, J., 283
Vaughn, F, 175, 189, 195, 235
Vich, M., 14, 15, 22, 171, 174, 185
Vico, G., 30
Voigt, W., 297
von Eckartsberg, R., 295
Walker, R., 298
Walsh, R., 175, 189, 235
Warmoth, A., 84
Washburn, M., 189
Watson, J., 7, 108
Watson, R., 345, 346, 350
Watts, A., 172, 289
Weber, S., 153
Weingartner, C., 258
Weinstein, G., 260
Weizenbaum, J., 10
Weizsaecker, V., 161
Welch, I., 264, 266
Weller, R., 266
Wells, H., 260
Welwood, J., 175
Werner, H., 38

Wertheimer, M., 25, 91, 281, 284, 345, 353
Wertz, F., vi, 7, 8, 10, 21, 23, 39, 88, 119, 121, 192, 295, 344, 357
Weschler, I., 276, 278
Wexley, K., 281
Wilber, k., 175, 189, 196, 201
Wilbur,K., 34, 195
Williams, C., 155
Williams, R., 94, 98
Wilson, C., 55, 86
Wilson, F., 67
Wingert, P., 265
Wittgenstein, L., 114
Woodman, M., 164
Wright, L., 265
Wundt, W., 4, 114, 350
Yankelovich, D., 265
Yalom, I., 132, 141, 235
Yeager, R., 234, 235
Young, J., 155
Youngs, W., 148
Yuki, G., 281
Zaner, R., 120, 299
Zaraleya-Harari, S., 21, 80
Zimring, F., 335
Zinker, J., 53

# Subject Index

Activating Events, 237
Alcohol, 148, 235, 250
Alcoholics Anonymous, 250
Altered states of consciousness, 174
Alternative seeking, 238
Alverno Center, 84
American Association for Humanistic Psychology, 31, 77, 81
American Psychological Association, iv, 46, 58
    Division 29, 21
    Division 32, 13, 19, 22, 176, 233, 248, 295, 299, 300, 330, 347
    Ethics, 93
Anger, 199
Anthropology, 172
Anticipation, 132
Antioch University 298
Anxiety, 235, 237
Assessment, 135
    Humanizing Psychological, 202
    Individualized, 205
    Teaching, 209
Association of Humanistic Education, 82
Association for Humanistic Psychology (AHP), 13, 67, 82, 112, 173, 233, 240, 259, 282, 283, 290
Association for Supervision and Curriculum Development, 262
Atlantic University, 298
Aureon Institute, 81
Avalon Institute, 298
Awareness, 223
Barron-Welsh test, 51
Behaviorism, 13, 14, 91, 134, 171
    Vs. Humanism, 109
    and Secular Humanism 234
    in texts, 354
Being human, 308, 315, 318
Belief, 237

Bender Test, 206, 210
Binge eating, 148
Biopsychosocial model, 39
Birth rate, 154
Boulder College, 298
Boundaries, 279
Bucknell University, 299
Brandies University, 252
California Institute for Asian Studies, 172
California Institute of Integral Studies, 182, 298
California Institute of Transpersonal Psychology, 175
California Task Force to Promote Self-Esteem, 283
Catholic University of Leuven, 285
Causal influence, 147
Causality, 94, 98
Center for Humanistic Studies, 68, 298
Center for the Study of the Person, 283, 286
*Changes*, 338
Clark University, 298
Client-centered therapy, 278, 331
Cognitive psychology, 9, 110, 129
    Behavior, 236, 293
    Science, 59
    Social, 293
Children
    Assessment of, 135
    Personal construct, 137
    Traumatization, 155
Commitment, 110
Common Ground, 82
Communication, 181, 218
Community of self, 139
Complaint, 131
Computers
    Psychology of, 9

Conditioning, 221
Conformity, 51, 148
Consciousness, 56, 112
   Altered States, 174
   Levels of, 132
Constructive alternalism, 130
Constructivism, 114, 236
Contemporary psychology, 6
Contrast reconstructionism, 134
Control, 97
Convenience
   Focus of, 134
   Range of, 134
Council Grove Conference, 80
Counseling
   Projective, 202
Counter-culture movement, 82, 173
Creativity, 45
   Cross-cultural, 51
   Humanistic shift, 53
   Research, 50
   and Transpersonal revolution, 58
Credulous approach, 130
Crime, 155
Cross-cultural studies, 51
Darwinism, 47
Death, 135
   Rate, 154
   Threat Index, 138
   Threat Profile, 138
Decision-making, 279
Depression, 135, 237
Development
   Healthy, 261
   and Humanistic psychology, 261
Diagnostic & Statistical Manual of Mental Disorders (DSM), 205
Dichotomy, 164
Division of Humanistic Psychology (32), iv, 32, 58, 82, 299, 300, 347
   *Newsletter of*, 21
Doctoral dissertations, 112, 298
Duquesne University, 205, 209, 283, 298, 347, 350
Education
   Doctoral programs, 298
   Humanistic challenge, 256ff.
   Master Programs, 298
   Progressive, 256

Ego, 193
Emergentism materialism, 34
Emotions, 199
Empathy, 167
Encounter group, 55, 82, 278, 336
Enlightenment, 29
Environment, 155, 257
Epistomological tradition, 113
Esalen institute, 13, 55, 77, 82, 182, 283, 288
   *Eupsychian*, 278
   *U-psychian*, 278
Exercise, 148
Existential-Humanistic Therapy, 132
Existentialism, 25, 30, 34, 77, 106, 116, 172, 227, 292
Existential Phenomenology, 116, 227
Experience
   and Behavior, 258
   Dimensions of, 335
Experience Scale, 335
Experiential Therapy, 132, 133
Experimental psychology, 57
Feeling-flow, 222
Feminism, 285, 324
Field-theory, 276
Fielding Institute, 298
Firebrand, 62
First Council Grove Conference, 174
Flexibility, 238
Focusing, 335
   -Institute, 339
Foresight, 152
Freedom, 146, 147, 220
*Geisteswissenschaften*, 30, 89, 107, 346
Gestalt therapy, 25, 32, 91, 116, 164, 173, 225, 250, 277, 284
Goddard College, 298
Grounded theory, 117
Groups, 278
   Encounter, 278
   Small, 278
Growth model, 55
Harvard University, 252
Health model, 54
Hedonism, 237
Henry Phipps Psychiatric Clinic, 247
Here-and-now, 223
Heuristic, 69

## Subject Index

History of psychology texts, 344
Holistic health, 181
Homelessness, 155
Human experience, 257
Human factors
   in Management, 276
     Human as human, 95
Human phenomena, 96
Human Potential Movement, 82, 173
"Human Relations in Industry", 275
Human science, 89
   and Assessment, 205
Human as human, 95
   Meaning, 94
   and Phenomena, 102
   Relativization, 96
   in Texts, 346
Human Systems Development, 276
Humaness, 317
Humanism, 25, 106
   Appraisal, 33
   vs. Behaviorism, 109
   Movement, 217
   Relational, 322
   Theory, 121
Humanistic education
   Attacks on, 264
   Future of, 266
   and Healthy personality, 262
   and Publications, 296
   Quality relationships, 264
   Settings, 339
*The Humanistic Psychologist*, iv, 21, 297
Humanistic Psychology
   Academy of, 292
   Alternative, 1
   and American Zeitgeist, 45
   Archive, 23, 282ff.
   Association for, 13
   Characteristics, 25
   Contributions to psychotherapy, 215, 306
   Critiques, 203
   Current trends, 306
   Defined, iv, 235
   Division of, iv
   and Education, 257
   Figures in, 348
   Foundations of, 257
   Future trends, 306
   Future of, 36
   History, 3
   Institute, 16, 18, 173
   Institutionalization of, 13
   Limits of, 306
   Methodology, 117
   Oral history, 76, 81
   Origins, 129, 172, 292
   Personal construct theory, 132
   Perspective, 160
   Philosophical foundations, 24
   Postmodern, 325
   Principles in, 348
   Problems of, 330
   Protest movement, 307
   Research programs, 118
   Research methods, 105ff.
   Scientific, 92
   Service dimension, v
   Themes in personal construct, 130
   Theorists, 147
   Tradition, 25
   Transformations, 56
   Transpersonal, 22
   Values, 146, 152
   Virtues, v
Humanistic Psychology Archive, 23
Humanistic Psychology Institute, 16, 18
Humanistic psychotherapy, 230
Humanistic values, 146
Humility system, 247
Husserl Archives, 285
Hypnosis, 227
Hysterics, 249
"I", 323, 336
Identity, 149
*Imago*, 279
Individuality, 69, 71, 239
Industrial/Organizational psychology (I/O)
   Application of, 279
   Development, 279
   Humanistic core, 274
Information Age, 10
Information processing system, 9
Institute of Transpersonal Psychology, 298
Interdisciplinary communication, 181

International College, 298
International Transpersonal Psychology Association, 175
Interpersonal connection, 135
I.Q. test, 47
Invitational mood, 131
Institute of Noetic Sciences, 175
Iona College, 299
I-Thou, 141, 163, 166
JFK University, 298
Johns Hopkins University, 24
*Journal of Humanistic Psychology*, 14, 24, 172, 174, 283, 308, 315, 347
*Journal of Phenomenological Psychology*, 119
*Journal of Transpersonal Psychology*, 174, 283
Judgement, 122
Laboratory, 97
Lesley College, 298
Life-theme, 150
Linguistics, 119
Logotherapy, 222
Loyola University of Chicago, 299
Machine Age, 7, 10
Mainstream psychology
   Humanistic alternative, 1
Mankato State University, 298
Marxism, 34
Meaning, 141
Measurement, 100
Me-Epoch, 167
Menninger Foundation, 173, 174, 175
Merrill-Palmer Institute, 119
Methodology, 148
Migration, 155
Mind, 135
Naropa Institute, 175, 298
Mystical experience, 57
National Training Labs, 55, 77, 85, 263, 278, 337
Natural setting, 98
Naturalism, 309
Neo-Platonists, 34
Neurosis, 250
New Breakthrough, 17
New Underground, 20
Non-directive approach, 171
Non-Linear Systems, 277

Northern Illinois University, 298
Objective, 161
Obsessives, 249
Oceanic Experience, 57
Old Saybrook Conference, 129
Ontopsychology, 24, 34, 38
Oral History Project, 283
Organizational Behavior (OB), 274, 277
Organizational psychology, 274
Orthopsychology, 24
Outplacement, 279
Overcrowding, 155
Pacifica Graduate Institute, 298
Parapsychology, 57
PARTNERSHIP, 339
Peak experiences, 330
Perceptual psychology, 258
Person psychology, 24, 32, 38, 178, 278, 279
Personal Construct Theory, 129, 236
   Contributions to humanistic psychology, 132
   Humanistic elaboration, 135
   Humanistic themes, 130
Personal growth, 55
Personal and Social Responsibility, 283
Personality, 234
   General theory, 277
   Healthy, 261
Phenomenology, 25, 30, 96, 97, 98, 115, 116, 118, 119, 161, 172, 179, 237, 284, 317
Philosophy of Science and Personality, 132, 134
Population, 153
Population Reference Bureau, 154
Positivism, 107, 110, 111, 114, 235, 314
Pragmatism, 116
Pragnanz, 164
Privacy, 167
Process, 234
Process Scale, 335
Procrastination, 148
Progressive Education, 256
Projective counseling, 202
Protest movement, 109
Psychoanalytic therapy, 121, 171
Psychologists Interested in The Advancement of Psychotherapy (PIAP), 21

## Subject Index

Psychologists Interested in Religious Issues, 22
Psychology as human science
    Differential, 294
    Existential, 294
    Integrated, 294
    Postmodern, 325
    Tensions, 90
Psychometric studies, 203
Psychoneuroimmunology, 181
Psychotherapy, 172
    Humanistic contributions, 215
Psychotherapy: Theory, Research and Practice, 331
Purging, 148
Rational-Emotive Therapy (RET), 233, 236
Reconciling, 149, 163
Recovery, 247, 250
Reductionism, 230
Refections, 167
Refugee, 155
Relational humanism, 322
Relationships
    Foundations, 262
    Synergic human, 262
Religion, 182
Remembering, 149, 162
Research methodology, 105
    Historical, 106
    Intellectual, 106
    New developments, 112
    Qualitative, 178
Resistance, 133
Retardation, 4
Reuniting, 149, 164
Role Construct Repertory Test, 129
ROLE relationships, 131, 140
Rorschach tests, 202, 205
Rosebridge Graduate School of Integrative Psychology, 298
Salve Regina College, 298
Saybrook Institute
    Conference, 173
    Doctoral program, 298
Schizophrenia, 135, 138, 166
Seattle University, 298\Secular humanism, 34
    and Rational-Emotive Therapy, 233
Self-acceptance, 238, 239
Self-actualization, 37, 54, 56, 80, 164, 247, 332
Self in cultural contexts, 323
Self-determination, 146, 147
    Research, 148
Self-direction, 37
Self-enhancement, 301
Self-fulfillment, 237
Self psychology, 24, 139
    in Community, 225
Sensitivity training groups, 173
Shaman, 180
Sierra University, 298
Silver Springs Maryland Conference, 77, 81
Simon Silverman Phenomenology Center, 283
Snacking behavior, 148
Social activism, 146
Sociality, 239
Sonoma State Psychology Program, 77, 173, 283, 298
Stanford University, 299
Stories, 150
Stress, 198
Stuttering, 135, 136
Subjectivity, 132, 161
Superconsciousness, 59
Synergy studies, 262
Systemic organization, 115
T groups, 55
Teleology, 135
Temple University, 298
Tension, 164
Terror, 135, 140
Thematic Apperception Test (TAT), 202
"Ten Commandments", 275
Therapeutic encounter, 239
Theory of therapy, 133
    Client-centered, 278
    Cognitive-behavioral, 236
Therapist, 216
    Liberating the, 222
    Self and, 225
"The they", 70
"Third force" psychology, iv, 20, 24, 56, 77, 257, 262, 292, 344ff.
Traits, 234

Transindividual subject, 313
Transitive diagnosis, 131, 133
Transpersonal psychology, iv, v, 22, 34, 56, 57, 83, 170, 171, 174, 175, 235
   Definition, 193
   Future, 189
   and History of ideas, 187
   Overview, 186
   Research in, 233
   Revolution, 58
   Role in, 192
Unconscious, 248
Understanding, 10, 152, 167
Union Graduate School, 298
Unitarian Religious Education Program, 173
Unity, 252
University of California, Los Angeles (UCLA)
   Education, 299
   Human Relations Research Group, 276, 277
University of California at Santa Barbara (UCSB), 282
   Graduate Program in Confluent Education, 283
   Humanistic Psychology Archive, 282
   Special collections, 282
University of California at Santa Cruz, 299
University of Chicago
   Industrial relations, 276
University Extension Ojai Leadership and Organization Development Laboratories, 278
University of Florida, 298
University for Humanistic Studies, 298
University of Notre Dame, 299
University of Ottawa, 299
University of Quebec at Montreal, 298
University of Southern California, 299
University of Tennessee (Knoxville), 298
University of Toledo, 299
Values, 146
Vanderbilt University, 299
Veterans Administration, 171
Vienna Circle, 108
Vietnam War, 87, 173
Violence, 155
Virtual Reality, 60
West Georgia College, 173, 298
*Western Electric Studies*, 275
Western Training Lab, 283
William Alanson White School of Psychoanalysis, 244
Wholeness, 222, 277, 279
Woman, 324
Worcester State Hospital, 247
World Health Organization, 154
World War II, 25, 171, 199, 257
Zeitgeist, v, 45, 82
   Creative, 46
   in Texts, 346, 347